ASP.NET Core 5 and React
Second Edition

Full-stack web development using .NET 5, React 17, and TypeScript 4

Carl Rippon

BIRMINGHAM—MUMBAI

ASP.NET Core 5 and React — Second Edition

Copyright © 2021 Packt Publishing

All rights reserved. No part of this book may be reproduced, stored in a retrieval system, or transmitted in any form or by any means, without the prior written permission of the publisher, except in the case of brief quotations embedded in critical articles or reviews.

Every effort has been made in the preparation of this book to ensure the accuracy of the information presented. However, the information contained in this book is sold without warranty, either express or implied. Neither the author, nor Packt Publishing or its dealers and distributors, will be held liable for any damages caused or alleged to have been caused directly or indirectly by this book.

Packt Publishing has endeavored to provide trademark information about all of the companies and products mentioned in this book by the appropriate use of capitals. However, Packt Publishing cannot guarantee the accuracy of this information.

Group Product Manager: Ashwin Nair
Publishing Product Manager: Pavan Ramchandani
Acquisition Editor: Nitin Nainani
Senior Editor: Hayden Edwards
Content Development Editor: Aamir Ahmed
Technical Editor: Deepesh Patel
Copy Editor: Safis Editing
Project Coordinator: Kinjal Bari
Proofreader: Safis Editing
Indexer: Manju Arasan
Production Designer: Jyoti Chauhan

First published: December 2019
Second edition: January 2021

Production reference: 1060121

Published by Packt Publishing Ltd.
Livery Place
35 Livery Street
Birmingham
B3 2PB, UK.

ISBN 978-1-80020-616-8

www.packt.com

*I'd like to thank Sarah, Ellie-Jayne, Lily-Rose, and Fudge for all the
encouragement and support they've given me while writing this book.
A special thanks to everyone in the Packt editorial team for their hard work
and great feedback, especially Aamir Ahmed and Mohammed Imaratwale.*

– Carl Rippon

Packt.com

Subscribe to our online digital library for full access to over 7,000 books and videos, as well as industry leading tools to help you plan your personal development and advance your career. For more information, please visit our website.

Why subscribe?

- Spend less time learning and more time coding with practical eBooks and Videos from over 4,000 industry professionals
- Improve your learning with Skill Plans built especially for you
- Get a free eBook or video every month
- Fully searchable for easy access to vital information
- Copy and paste, print, and bookmark content

Did you know that Packt offers eBook versions of every book published, with PDF and ePub files available? You can upgrade to the eBook version at packt.com and as a print book customer, you are entitled to a discount on the eBook copy. Get in touch with us at customercare@packtpub.com for more details.

At www.packt.com, you can also read a collection of free technical articles, sign up for a range of free newsletters, and receive exclusive discounts and offers on Packt books and eBooks.

Contributors

About the author

Carl Rippon has been involved in the software industry for over 20 years, developing a complex line of business applications across various sectors. He has spent the last 9 years building single-page applications using a wide range of JavaScript technologies, including Angular, ReactJS, and TypeScript. Carl has written over 150 blog posts on various technologies.

About the reviewer

Adam Greene is a senior software engineer at Cvent, the market-leading meetings, events, and hospitality technology provider. Adam has close to 20 years' software development experience with Microsoft technologies and has worked for companies of all sizes, from start-ups to multinational corporations, in various leadership capacities. Adam is a full-stack web developer and has developed SaaS applications using ASP.NET, Angular, and React for several years.

Packt is searching for authors like you

If you're interested in becoming an author for Packt, please visit `authors.packtpub.com` and apply today. We have worked with thousands of developers and tech professionals, just like you, to help them share their insight with the global tech community. You can make a general application, apply for a specific hot topic that we are recruiting an author for, or submit your own idea.

Table of Contents

Preface

Section 1: Getting Started

1
Understanding the ASP.NET 5 React Template

Technical requirements	20	Running in development mode	34
SPA architecture	21	Publishing process	38
Understanding the ASP.NET Core backend	22	Understanding the frontend dependencies	41
Creating an ASP.NET Core and React templated app	22	Understanding how the single page is served	43
Understanding the backend entry point	25	Understanding how components fit together	45
Understanding the Startup class	26	Understanding how components access the backend web API	48
Custom middleware	28		
Understanding controllers	31	Summary	53
Understanding the React frontend	33	Questions	53
		Answers	54
Understanding the frontend entry point	33	Further reading	55

2
Creating Decoupled React and ASP.NET 5 Apps

Technical requirements	58	Understanding the benefits of TypeScript	63
Creating a React and TypeScript app	62	Creating the app with CRA	64

Adding linting to React and TypeScript	65	TypeScript	69
		Adding Prettier	70
Configuring Visual Studio Code to lint TypeScript code	65	Resolving errors	72
Configuring linting rules	67	Summary	73
		Questions	73
Adding automatic code formatting to React and		Answers	74
		Further reading	74

Section 2: Building a Frontend with React and TypeScript

3
Getting Started with React and TypeScript

Technical requirements	78	Function props	103
Understanding JSX	78	Implementing component state	106
Understanding and enabling strict mode	81	Using useEffect to execute logic	108
Creating function-based components	83	Using useState to implement component state	110
Creating a Header component	84	Handling events	116
Adding elements to the Header component	86	Handling a button click event	116
Creating a HomePage component	88	Handling an input change event	117
Creating mock data	89	Summary	118
Implementing component props	93	Questions	119
Creating HomePage child components	93	Answers	119
Optional and default props	98	Further reading	120
Children prop	102		

4
Styling React Components with Emotion

Technical requirements	122	Styling the document body	122
Styling components with CSS	122	Styling the App component	123

Styling the Header component	125	Creating a reusable styled component with Emotion	138
Styling components with CSS modules	127	Completing the home page styling	141
Styling components with Emotion	129	Styling the QuestionList component	141
Installing Emotion	129	Styling the Question component	143
Styling the App component	130	Summary	144
Styling the Header component	133	Questions	145
Styling pseudo-classes and nested elements with Emotion	134	Answers	146
		Further reading	147

5
Routing with React Router

Technical requirements	150	Adding the question page route	158
Installing React Router	151	Implementing more of the question page	161
Declaring routes	151	Creating an AnswerList component	166
Creating some blank pages	152	Using query parameters	169
Creating a component containing routes	153	Lazy loading routes	173
Handling routes not found	154	Summary	176
Implementing links	156	Questions	177
Using the Link component	156	Answers	178
Navigating programmatically	157	Further reading	179
Using route parameters	158		

6
Working with Forms

Technical requirements	182	React Hook Form	185
Understanding controlled components	182	Installing React Hook Form	186
Reducing boilerplate code with		Refactoring the Header component to	

use React Hook Form	186	Submitting forms	**201**	
Creating form styled components	188	Implementing form submission in the search form	202	
Implementing the ask form	191	Implementing form submission in the ask form	203	
Implementing the answer form	194	Implementing form submission in the answer form	207	
Implementing validation	**196**			
Implementing validation on the ask form	196	Summary	210	
Implementing validation on the answer form	199	Questions	210	
		Answers	211	
		Further reading	212	

7
Managing State with Redux

Technical requirements	**214**	Creating a reducer	224
Understanding the Redux pattern	**214**	Creating the store	228
Principles	215	**Connecting components to the store**	**229**
Key concepts	215	Adding a store provider	229
Installing Redux	**218**	Connecting the home page	230
Creating the state	**219**	Connecting the question page	234
Creating actions	**220**	Summary	238
Understanding the actions in the store	220	Questions	238
Getting unanswered questions	221	Answers	239
Viewing a question	222	Further reading	239
Searching questions	223		

Section 3: Building an ASP.NET Backend

8
Interacting with the Database with Dapper

Technical requirements	**244**	Creating the database	245
Implementing the database	**245**	Creating database tables	247

Creating stored procedures	248	Writing data using Dapper	265
Understanding what Dapper is and its benefits	250	Adding methods to write data to the repository interface	265
Installing and configuring Dapper	250	Creating a repository method to add a new question	265
Reading data using Dapper	252	Creating a repository method to change a question	266
Creating the repository class	253	Creating a repository method to delete a question	267
Creating a repository method to get questions	256	Creating a repository method to add an answer	268
Creating a repository method to get questions by a search	259	Managing migrations using DbUp	269
Creating a repository method to get unanswered questions	260	Installing DbUp into our project	269
Creating a repository method to get a single question	261	Embedding SQL Scripts in our project	272
		Performing a database migration	274
Creating a repository method to check whether a question exists	263	Summary	277
		Questions	277
Creating a repository method to get an answer	264	Answers	279
		Further reading	279

9
Creating REST API Endpoints

Technical requirements	282	a single question	293
Creating an API controller	282	Creating an action method for posting a question	296
Injecting the data repository into the API controller	284	Creating an action method for updating a question	299
Creating controller action methods	287	Creating an action method for deleting a question	303
Creating an action method for getting questions	287	Creating an action method for posting an answer	304
Extending the GetQuestions action method for searching	290	Adding model validation	306
Creating an action method for getting unanswered questions	292	Adding validation to posting a question	307
Creating an action method for getting		Adding validation to updating a question	309

Adding validation to posting an answer 310

Removing unnecessary request fields 312

Removing unnecessary request fields from posting
a question 313

Removing unnecessary request fields from posting an answer 315

Summary 318
Questions 318
Answers 320
Further reading 320

10
Improving Performance and Scalability

Technical requirements 322
Reducing database round trips 323
Understanding the N+1 problem 323
Using WebSurge to load test our endpoint 326
Using Dapper multi-mapping to resolve the
N+1 problem 329
Using Dapper's multi-results feature 332

Paging data 335
Adding test questions for the load test 336
Load testing the current
implementation 336

Making API controllers asynchronous 341

Testing the current implementation 343
Implementing an asynchronous controller action method 345
Mixing asynchronous and synchronous code 348

Caching data 350
Load testing the current implementation 350
Implementing a data cache 351
Using the data cache in an API controller action method 354

Summary 357
Questions 358
Answers 359
Further reading 361

11
Securing the Backend

Technical requirements 364
Understanding OIDC 365
Setting up Auth0 with our ASP.NET backend 368
Setting up Auth0 368
Configuring our ASP.NET backend to

authenticate with Auth0 371

Protecting endpoints 373
Protecting endpoints with simple authorization 373
Protecting endpoints with a custom authorization policy 376

Using the authenticated user when posting questions and answers	385	Summary	391
		Questions	392
		Answers	393
Adding CORS	388	Further reading	394

12
Interacting with RESTful APIs

Technical requirements	396	processes	421
Using fetch to interact with unauthenticated REST API endpoints	396	Controlling authenticated options	424
		Displaying the relevant options in the header	424
Getting unanswered questions from the REST API	397	Only allowing authenticated users to ask a question	426
Extracting out a generic HTTP http function	400	Only allowing authenticated users to answer a question	429
Getting a question from the REST API	405		
Searching questions with the REST API	407	Using fetch to interact with authenticated REST API endpoints	431
Interacting with Auth0 from the frontend	408		
		Posting a question to the REST API	431
Installing the Auth0 JavaScript client	408	Posting an answer to the REST API	434
Recapping the sign-in and sign-out flows	408	Aborting data fetching	435
Creating the sign-in and sign-out routes	409	Summary	437
		Questions	437
Implementing a central authentication context	410	Answers	438
Implementing the sign-in process	417	Further reading	440
Implementing the sign-out process	418		
Configuring Auth0 settings in our frontend	419		
Testing the sign-in and sign-out			

Section 4: Moving into Production

13
Adding Automated Tests

Technical requirements	444	Testing React components	464
Understanding the different types of automated test	445	Testing the Page component	464
		Testing the Question component	467
Unit tests	445	Testing the HomePage component	469
End-to-end tests	446	Implementing end-to-end tests with Cypress	471
Integration tests	447		
Implementing .NET tests with xUnit	447	Getting started with Cypress	471
		Testing asking a question	475
Getting started with xUnit	448	Summary	480
Testing controller action methods	452	Questions	481
Implementing React tests with Jest	461	Answers	482
		Further reading	483
Getting started with Jest	461		

14
Configuring and Deploying to Azure

Technical requirements	486	Configuring the React frontend for staging and production	505
Getting started with Azure	487		
Signing up to Azure	487	Publishing the React frontend to Azure	507
Understanding the Azure services we are going to use	487		
		Publishing to production	507
Configuring the ASP.NET Core backend for staging and production	490	Publishing to staging	510
		Summary	512
Publishing our ASP.NET Core backend to Azure	492	Questions	513
		Answers	513
Publishing to production	492	Further reading	514
Publishing to staging	502		

15
Implementing CI and CD with Azure DevOps

Technical requirements	516	Implementing CD	531
Getting started with CI and CD	517	Deploying to staging	532
Understanding CI and CD	517	Deploying to production	540
Enabling our tests to run in CI and CD	518	Testing the automated deployment	543
Creating an Azure DevOps project	519	Summary	544
Implementing CI	520	Questions	545
Creating a build pipeline	521	Answers	545
Implementing a build pipeline for our Q&A app	524	Further reading	546

Other Books You May Enjoy

Index

Preface

ASP.NET Core is an open source and cross-platform web application framework built by Microsoft. ASP.NET Core is a great choice for building highly performant backends that interact with SQL Server and are hosted in Azure.

React was built by Facebook in order to improve the scalability of their codebase and was eventually open sourced in 2013. React is now a massively popular library for building component-based frontends and works fantastically well with many backend technologies, including ASP.NET Core.

The book will step you through building a real-world application that leverages both these technologies. You will gradually build the app chapter by chapter to actively learn key topics in these technologies. Each chapter ends with a summary and some questions on the content to reinforce your learning. At the end of the book, you will have a secure, performant, and maintainable **single-page application (SPA)** that is hosted in Azure along with the knowledge to build your next ASP.NET Core and React app.

Who this book is for

If you're a web developer looking to get up to speed with full-stack web application development with .NET Core and React, this book is for you. Although the book does not assume any knowledge of React, a basic understanding of .NET Core will help you to get to grips with the concepts covered.

What this book covers

Section 1: Getting Started

Chapter 1, *Understanding the ASP.NET 5 React Template*, covers the standard SPA template that Visual Studio offers for ASP.NET Core and React apps. It covers the programmatic entry points for both the frontend and backend and how they work together in the Visual Studio solution.

Chapter 2, *Creating Decoupled React and ASP.NET 5 Apps*, steps through how we can create an up-to-date ASP.NET Core and React solution. The chapter includes the use of TypeScript, which is hugely beneficial when creating large and complex frontends.

Section 2: Building a Frontend with React and TypeScript

Chapter 3, *Getting Started with React and TypeScript*, covers the fundamentals of React, such as JSX, props, state, and events. The chapter also covers how to create strongly typed components with TypeScript.

Chapter 4, *Styling React Components with Emotion*, covers different approaches to styling React components. The chapter covers styling using plain CSS and then CSS modules before covering CSS-in-JS.

Chapter 5, *Routing with React Router*, introduces a library that enables apps with multiple pages to be efficiently created. It covers how to declare all the routes in an app and how these map to React components, including routes with parameters. The chapter also covers how to load the components from a route on demand in order to optimize performance.

Chapter 6, *Working with Forms*, covers how to build forms in React. The chapter covers how to build a form in plain React before leveraging a popular third-party library to make the process of building forms more efficient.

Chapter 7, *Managing State with Redux*, steps through how this popular library can help manage state across an app. A strongly typed Redux store is built along with actions and reducers with the help of TypeScript.

Section 3: Building an ASP.NET Backend

Chapter 8, *Interacting with the Database with Dapper*, introduces a library that enables us to interact with SQL Server databases in a performant manner. Both reading and writing to a database are covered, including mapping SQL parameters from a C# class and mapping results to C# classes.

Chapter 9, *Creating REST API Endpoints*, covers how to create a REST API that interacts with a data repository. Along the way, dependency injection, model binding, and model validation are covered.

Chapter 10, *Improving Performance and Scalability*, covers several ways of improving the performance and scalability of the backend, including reducing database round trips, making APIs asynchronous, and data caching. Along the way, several tools are used to measure the impact of improvements.

Chapter 11, *Securing the Backend*, leverages ASP.NET identity along with JSON web tokens in order to add authentication to an ASP.NET Core backend. The chapter also covers the protection of REST API endpoints with the use of standard and custom authorization policies.

Chapter 12, *Interacting with RESTful APIs*, covers how a React frontend can talk to an ASP.NET Core backend using the JavaScript fetch function. The chapter also covers how a React frontend can gain access to protected REST API endpoints with a JSON web token.

Section 4: Moving into Production

Chapter 13, *Adding Automated Tests*, covers how to create unit tests and integration tests on the ASP.NET Core backend using xUnit. The chapter also covers how to create tests on pure JavaScript functions as well as React components using Jest.

Chapter 14, *Configuring and Deploying to Azure*, introduces Azure and then steps through deploying both the backend and frontend to separate Azure app services. The chapter also covers the deployment of a SQL Server database to SQL Azure.

Chapter 15, *Implementing CI and CD with Azure DevOps*, introduces Azure DevOps before stepping through creating a build pipeline that automatically triggers when code is pushed to a source code repository. The chapter then steps through setting up a release pipeline that deploys the artifacts from the build into Azure.

To get the most out of this book

You need to know the basics of C#, including the following:

- An understanding of how to create variables and reference them, including arrays and objects
- An understanding of how to create classes and use them
- An understanding of how to create conditional statements with the `if` and `else` keywords

You need to know the basics of JavaScript, including the following:

- An understanding of how to create variables and reference them, including arrays and objects
- An understanding of how to create functions and call them
- An understanding of how to create conditional statements with the `if` and `else` keywords

You need to know the basics of HTML, including the following:

- An understanding of basic HTML tags, such as `div`, `ul`, `p`, `a`, `h1`, and `h2`, and how to compose them together to create a web page
- An understanding of how to reference a CSS class to style an HTML element

You need an understanding of basic CSS, including the following:

- How to size elements and include margins and padding
- How to position elements
- How to color elements

An understanding of basic SQL would be helpful but is not essential.

You will need the following installed on your computer:

- Google Chrome: This can be installed from `https://www.google.com/chrome/`.
- Visual Studio 2019: This can be download and installed from `https://visualstudio.microsoft.com/vs/`.
- .NET Core 5: This can be downloaded and installed from `https://dotnet.microsoft.com/download/dotnet-core`.
- Visual Studio Code: This can be downloaded and installed from `https://code.visualstudio.com/`.
- Node.js and npm: They can be downloaded and installed from `https://nodejs.org/`. If you already have these installed, make sure that Node.js is at least version 8.2 and that npm is at least version 5.2
- SQL Server Express Edition: This can be downloaded and installed from `https://www.microsoft.com/en-gb/sql-server/sql-server-editions-express`.
- SQL Server Management Studio: This can be downloaded and installed from `https://docs.microsoft.com/en-us/sql/ssms/download-sql-server-management-studio-ssms`.

If you are using the digital version of this book, we advise you to type the code yourself or access the code via the GitHub repository (link available in the next section). Doing so will help you avoid any potential errors related to the copying and pasting of code.

Download the example code files

You can download the example code files for this book from GitHub at `https://github.com/PacktPublishing/ASP.NET-Core-5-and-React-Second-Edition`. In case there's an update to the code, it will be updated on the existing GitHub repository.

We also have other code bundles from our rich catalog of books and videos available at `https://github.com/PacktPublishing/`. Check them out!

Code in Action

Code in Action videos for this book can be viewed at `http://bit.ly/3mB8KuU`.

Conventions used

There are a number of text conventions used throughout this book.

`Code in text`: Indicates code words in text, database table names, folder names, filenames, file extensions, pathnames, dummy URLs, user input, and Twitter handles. Here is an example: "Let's create a file called `.eslintrc.json` in `frontend` with the following code."

A block of code is set as follows:

```
{
  "extends": "react-app"
}
```

When we wish to draw your attention to a particular part of a code block, the relevant lines or items are set in bold:

```
function App() {
  const unused = 'something';
  return (
    ...
  );
};
```

Any command-line input or output is written as follows:

```
> cd frontend
> npm start
```

Bold: Indicates a new term, an important word, or words that you see onscreen. For example, words in menus or dialog boxes appear in the text like this. Here is an example: "Click on **Install** to install the extension and then the **Reload** button to complete the installation."

> Tips or important notes
> Appear like this.

Get in touch

Feedback from our readers is always welcome.

General feedback: If you have questions about any aspect of this book, mention the book title in the subject of your message and email us at customercare@packtpub.com.

Errata: Although we have taken every care to ensure the accuracy of our content, mistakes do happen. If you have found a mistake in this book, we would be grateful if you would report this to us. Please visit www.packtpub.com/support/errata, selecting your book, clicking on the Errata Submission Form link, and entering the details.

Piracy: If you come across any illegal copies of our works in any form on the Internet, we would be grateful if you would provide us with the location address or website name. Please contact us at copyright@packt.com with a link to the material.

If you are interested in becoming an author: If there is a topic that you have expertise in and you are interested in either writing or contributing to a book, please visit authors.packtpub.com.

Reviews

Please leave a review. Once you have read and used this book, why not leave a review on the site that you purchased it from? Potential readers can then see and use your unbiased opinion to make purchase decisions, we at Packt can understand what you think about our products, and our authors can see your feedback on their book. Thank you!

For more information about Packt, please visit packt.com.

Section 1: Getting Started

This section provides a high-level introduction to ASP.NET Core and React and explains how to create projects that enable them to work well together. We will create the project for the app that we'll build throughout this book, which will allow users to submit questions and other users to submit answers to them—a Q&A app.

This section comprises the following chapters:

- *Chapter 1, Understanding the ASP.NET 5 React Template*
- *Chapter 2, Creating Decoupled React and ASP.NET 5 Apps*

1
Understanding the ASP.NET 5 React Template

React was Facebook's answer to helping more people work on the Facebook code base and deliver features quicker. React worked so well for Facebook that they eventually open sourced it (https://github.com/facebook/react). Today, React is a mature library for building component-based frontends (client-side code that runs in the browser); it is extremely popular and has a massive community and ecosystem. At the time of writing, React is downloaded over 8.8 million times per week, which is 2 million more than the same time a year ago.

ASP.NET Core was first released in 2016 and is now a mature open source and cross-platform web application framework. It's an excellent choice for building backends (application code that runs on the server) that interact with databases such as SQL Server. It also works well in cloud platforms such as Microsoft Azure.

In this first chapter, we'll start by learning about the **single-page application** (**SPA**) architecture. Then, we'll create an ASP.NET Core and React app using the standard template in Visual Studio. We will use this to review and understand the critical parts of a React and ASP.NET Core app. Then, we'll learn where the entry points of both the ASP.NET Core and React apps are and how they integrate with each other. We'll also learn how Visual Studio runs both the frontend and backend together in development mode, as well as how it packages them up, ready for production. By the end of this chapter, we'll have gained fundamental knowledge so that we can start building an app that uses both of these awesome technologies, something we'll gradually build upon throughout this book.

In this chapter, we'll cover the following topics:

- SPA architecture
- Understanding the ASP.NET Core backend
- Understanding the React frontend

Let's get started!

Technical requirements

We will need to use the following tools in this chapter:

- **Visual Studio 2019**: This can be downloaded and installed from https://visualstudio.microsoft.com/vs/. Make sure that the following features are selected in the installer:

    a) ASP.NET and web development

    b) Azure development

    c) Node.js development

- **.NET 5.0**: This can be downloaded from https://dotnet.microsoft.com/download/dotnet/5.0.
- **Node.js and npm**: These can be downloaded from https://nodejs.org/.

All the code snippets in this chapter can be found online at https://github.com/PacktPublishing/ASP.NET-Core-5-and-React-Second-Edition.

Check out the following video to see the code in action: https://bit.ly/3riGWib.

SPA architecture

In this section, we will start to understand the **single-page application** (**SPA**) architecture.

A SPA is a web app that loads a single HTML page that is dynamically updated by JavaScript as the user interacts with the app. Imagine a simple sign-up form where a user can enter a name and an email address. When the user fills out and submits the form, a whole page refresh doesn't occur. Instead, some JavaScript in the browser handles the form submission with an HTTP POST request and then updates the page with the result of the request. Refer to the following diagram:

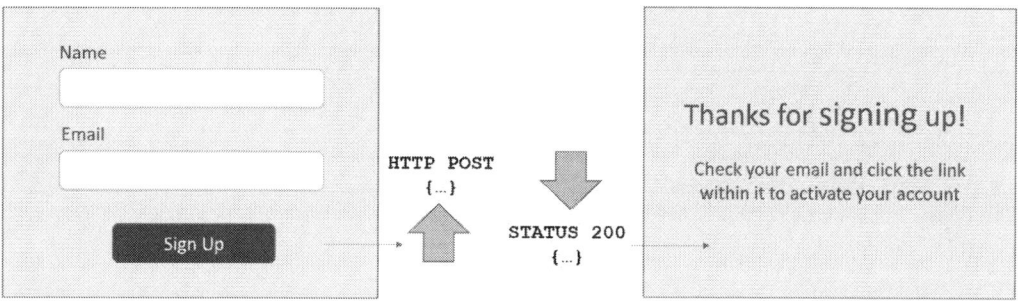

Figure 1.1 – Form in a SPA

So, after the first HTTP request that returns the single HTML page, subsequent HTTP requests are only for data and not HTML markup. All the pages are rendered in the client's browser by JavaScript.

So, how are different pages with different URL paths handled? For example, if I enter https://qanda/questions/32139 in the browser's address bar, how does it go to the correct page in the app? Well, the browser's history API lets us change the browser's URL and handle changes in JavaScript. This process is often referred to as routing and, in *Chapter 5, Routing with React Router*, we'll learn how we can build apps with different pages.

The SPA architecture is what we are going to use throughout this book. We'll use React to render our frontend and use ASP.NET Core for the backend API.

Now that we have a basic understanding of the SPA architecture, we'll take a closer look at a SPA-templated app that Visual Studio can create for us.

Understanding the ASP.NET Core backend

In this section, we are going to start by creating an ASP.NET Core and React app using the standard template in Visual Studio. This template is perfect for us to review and understand basic backend components in an ASP.NET Core SPA.

Once we have scaffolded the app using the Visual Studio template, we will inspect the ASP.NET Core code, starting from its entry point. During our inspection, we will learn how the request/response pipeline is configured and how requests to endpoints are handled.

Creating an ASP.NET Core and React templated app

Let's open Visual Studio and carry out the following steps to create our templated app:

1. In the start-up dialog, choose **Create a new project**:

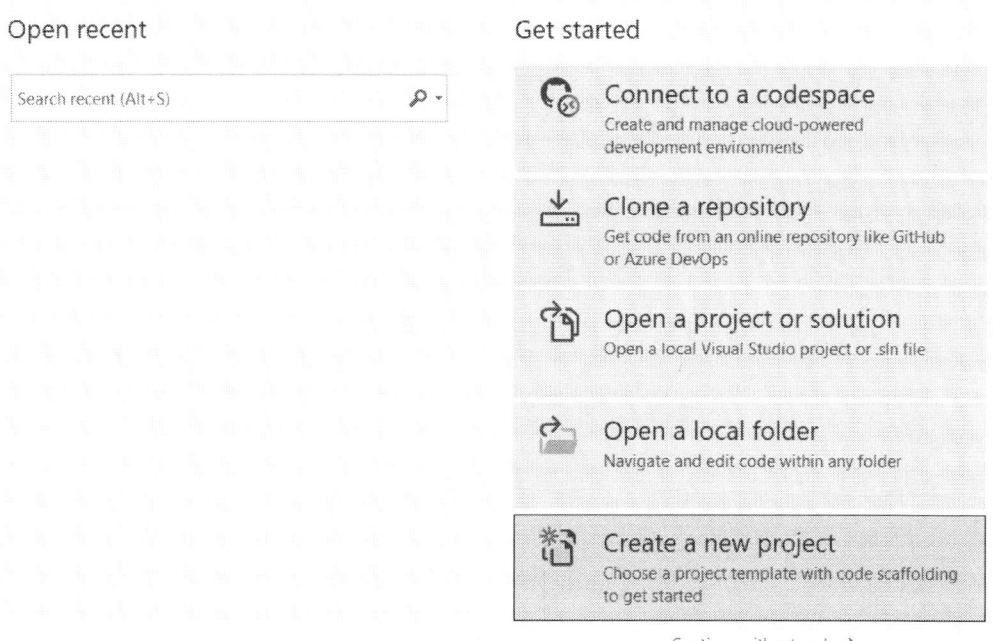

Figure 1.2 – Visual Studio start-up dialog

2. Next, choose **ASP.NET Core Web Application** in the wizard that opens and click the **Next** button:

Understanding the ASP.NET Core backend   23

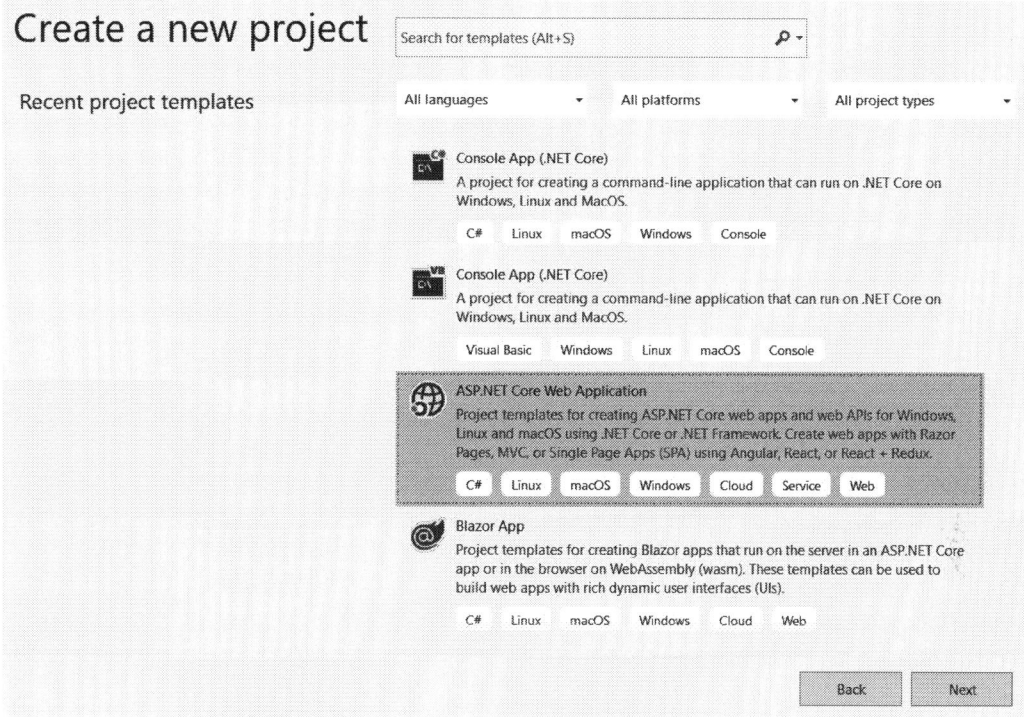

Figure 1.3 – Creating a new web app in Visual Studio

3. Give the project a name of your choice and choose an appropriate location to save the project to. Then, click the **Create** button to create the project:

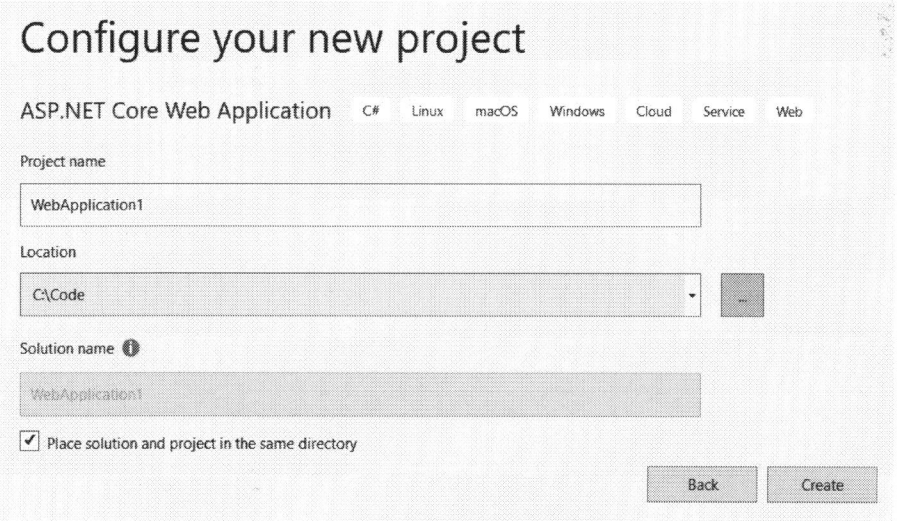

Figure 1.4 – Specifying a project name and location

Another dialog will appear that allows us to specify the version of ASP.NET Core we want to use, as well as the specific type of project we want to create.

4. Select **ASP.NET Core 5.0** as the version and **React.js** in the dialog. Then, click the **Create** button, which will create the project:

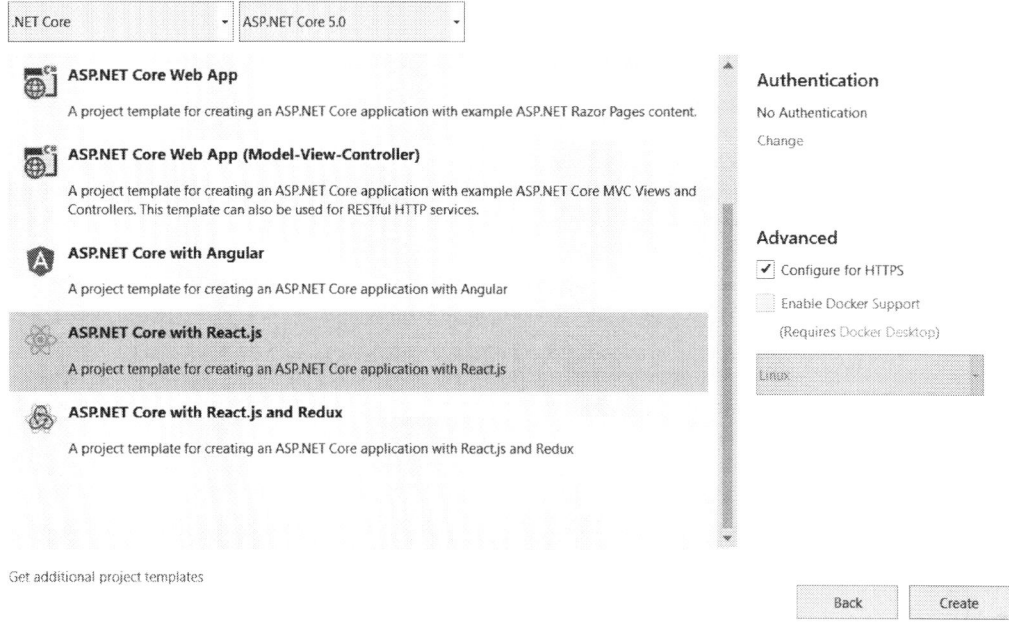

Figure 1.5 – The project template and ASP.NET Core version

> **Important Note**
> If ASP.NET Core 5.0 isn't listed, make sure that the latest version of Visual Studio is installed. This can be done by choosing the **Check for Updates** option from the **Help** menu.

5. Now that the project has been created, press *F5* to run the app. After a minute or so, the app will appear in a browser:

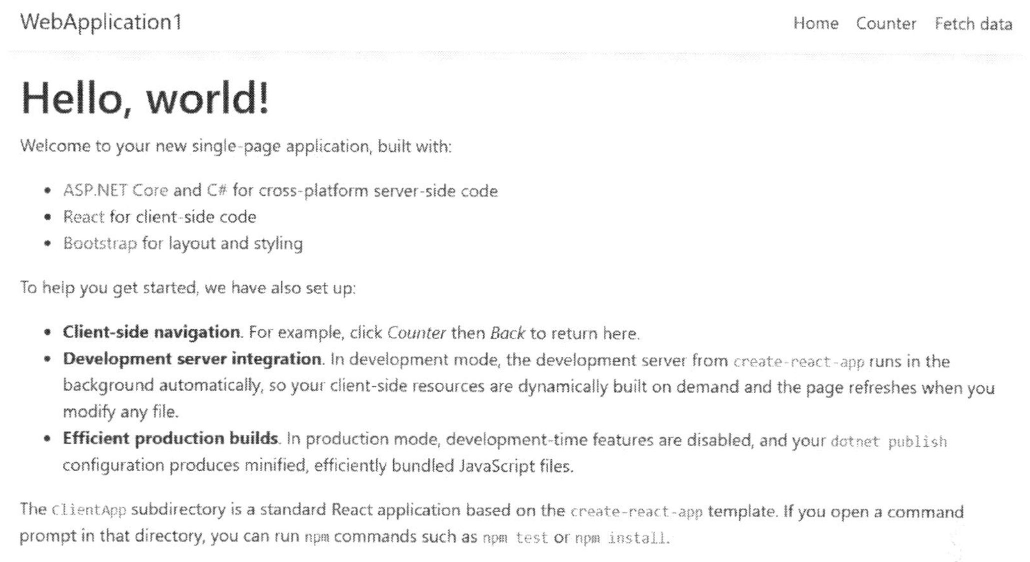

| WebApplication1 | Home   Counter   Fetch data |

Hello, world!

Welcome to your new single-page application, built with:

- ASP.NET Core and C# for cross-platform server-side code
- React for client-side code
- Bootstrap for layout and styling

To help you get started, we have also set up:

- **Client-side navigation**. For example, click *Counter* then *Back* to return here.
- **Development server integration**. In development mode, the development server from create-react-app runs in the background automatically, so your client-side resources are dynamically built on demand and the page refreshes when you modify any file.
- **Efficient production builds**. In production mode, development-time features are disabled, and your dotnet publish configuration produces minified, efficiently bundled JavaScript files.

The ClientApp subdirectory is a standard React application based on the create-react-app template. If you open a command prompt in that directory, you can run npm commands such as npm test or npm install.

Figure 1.6 – The home page of the app

We'll find out later in this chapter why the app took so long to run the first time. For now, we've created the ASP.NET Core React SPA. Now, let's inspect the backend code.

Understanding the backend entry point

An ASP.NET Core app is a console app that creates a web server. The entry point for the app is a method called Main in a class called Program, which can be found in the Program.cs file in the root of the project:

```
public class Program
{
  public static void Main(string[] args)
  {
    CreateHostBuilder(args).Build().Run();
  }

  public static IHostBuilder CreateHostBuilder(string[]
    args) =>
      Host.CreateDefaultBuilder(args)
        .ConfigureWebHostDefaults(webBuilder =>
        {
            webBuilder.UseStartup<Startup>();
        });
}
```

This method creates a web host using `Host.CreateDefaultBuilder`, which configures items such as the following:

- The location of the root of the web content
- Where the settings are for items, such as the database connection string
- The logging level and where the logs are output

We can override the default builder using fluent APIs, which start with `Use`. For example, to adjust the root of the web content, we can add the highlighted line in the following snippet:

```
public static IHostBuilder CreateHostBuilder(string[] args) =>
  Host.CreateDefaultBuilder(args)
    .ConfigureWebHostDefaults(webBuilder =>
    {
      webBuilder.UseContentRoot("some-path");
      webBuilder.UseStartup<Startup>();
    });
```

The last thing that is specified in the builder is the `Startup` class, which we'll look at in the following section.

Understanding the Startup class

The `Startup` class is found in `Startup.cs` and configures the services that the app uses, as well as the request/response pipeline. In this subsection, we will understand the two main methods within this class.

The ConfigureServices method

Services are configured using a method called `ConfigureServices`. This method is used to register items such as the following:

- Our controllers, which will handle requests
- Our authorization policies
- Our CORS policies
- Our own classes, which need to be available in dependency injection

Services are added by calling methods on the `services` parameter and, generally, start with `Add`. Notice the call to the `AddSpaStaticFiles` method in the following code snippet:

```
public void ConfigureServices(IServiceCollection services)
{
  services.AddControllersWithViews();

  services.AddSpaStaticFiles(configuration =>
  {
     configuration.RootPath = "ClientApp/build";
  });
}
```

This is a key part of how the React app is integrated into ASP.NET Core in production since this specifies the location of the React app.

> **Important Note**
> It is important to understand that the ASP.NET Core app runs on the server, with the React app running on the client in the browser. The ASP.NET Core app simply serves the files in the `ClientApp/Build` folder without any interpretation or manipulation.

The `ClientApp/Build` files are only used in production mode, though. Next, we'll find out how the React app is integrated into ASP.NET Core in development mode.

The Configure method

When a request comes into ASP.NET Core, it goes through what is called the **request/response pipeline**, where some middleware code is executed. This pipeline is configured using a method called `Configure`. We will use this method to define exactly which middleware is executed and in what order. Middleware code is invoked by methods that generally start with `Use` in the `app` parameter. So, we would typically specify middleware such as authentication early in the `Configure` method, and in the MVC middleware toward the end. The pipeline that the template created is as follows:

```
public void Configure(IApplicationBuilder app,
IWebHostEnvironment env)
{
   ...
   app.UseStaticFiles();
   app.UseSpaStaticFiles();
   app.UseRouting();
```

```
    app.UseEndpoints( ... );
    app.UseSpa(spa =>
    {
        spa.Options.SourcePath = "ClientApp";

        if (env.IsDevelopment())
        {
            spa.UseReactDevelopmentServer(npmScript:
            "start");
        }
    });
}
```

Notice that a method called `UseSpaStaticFiles` is called in the pipeline, just before the routing and endpoints are set up. This allows the host to serve the React app, as well as the web API.

Also, notice that a `UseSpa` method is called after the endpoint middleware. This is the middleware that will handle requests to the React app, which will simply serve the single page in the React app. It is placed after `UseEndpoints` so that requests to the web API take precedence over requests to the React app.

The `UseSpa` method has a parameter that is actually a function that executes when the app is run for the first time. This function contains a branch of logic that calls `spa.UseReactDevelopmentServer(npmScript: "start")` if you're in development mode. This tells ASP.NET Core to use a development server by running `npm start`. We'll delve into the `npm start` command later in this chapter. So, in development mode, the React app will be run on a development server rather than having ASP.NET Core serve the files from `ClientApp/Build`. We'll learn more about this development server later in this chapter.

Next, we will learn how custom middleware can be added to the ASP.NET Core request/response pipeline.

Custom middleware

We can create our own middleware using a class such as the following one. This middleware logs information about every single request that is handled by the ASP.NET Core app:

```
public class CustomLogger
{
    private readonly RequestDelegate _next;
```

```
    public CustomLogger(RequestDelegate next)
    {
        _next = next ?? throw new
         ArgumentNullException(nameof(next));
    }

    public async Task Invoke(HttpContext httpContext)
    {
        if (httpContext == null) throw new
        ArgumentNullException(nameof(httpContext));

        // TODO - log the request

        await _next(httpContext);

        // TODO - log the response
    }
}
```

This class contains a method called `Invoke`, which is the code that is executed in the request/response pipeline. The next method to call in the pipeline is passed into the class and held in the _next variable, which we need to invoke at the appropriate point in our `Invoke` method. The preceding example is a skeleton class for a custom logger. We would log the request details at the start of the `Invoke` method and log the response details after the _next delegate has been executed, which will be when the rest of the pipeline has been executed.

The following diagram is a visualization of the request/response pipeline and shows how each piece of middleware in the pipeline is invoked:

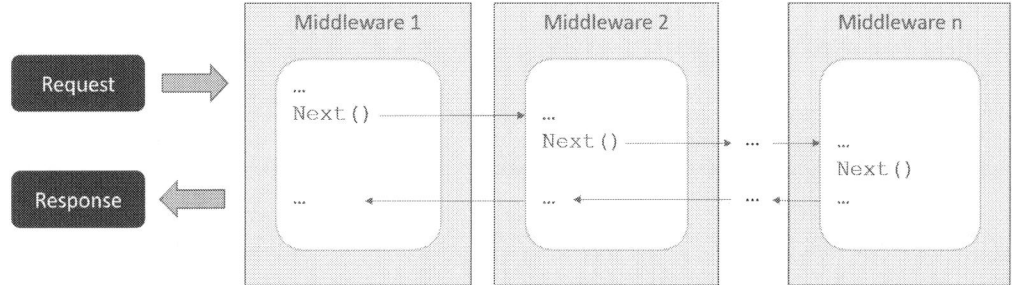

Figure 1.7 – Visualization of the request/response pipeline

We make our middleware available as an extension method on the `IApplicationBuilder` interface in a new source file:

```
public static class MiddlewareExtensions
{
    public static IApplicationBuilder UseCustomLogger(this
    IApplicationBuilder app)
    {
        return app.UseMiddleware<CustomLogger>();
    }
}
```

The `UseMiddleware` method in `IApplicationBuilder` is used to register the middleware class. The middleware will now be available in an instance of `IApplicationBuilder` in a method called `UseCustomLogger`.

So, the middleware can be added to the pipeline in the `Configure` method in the `Startup` class, as follows:

```
public void Configure(IApplicationBuilder app,
IWebHostEnvironment env)
{
    app.UseCustomLogger();

    if (env.IsDevelopment())
    {
        app.UseDeveloperExceptionPage();
    }
    else
    {
        app.UseExceptionHandler("/Error");
        app.UseHsts();
    }

    app.UseHttpsRedirection();
    app.UseStaticFiles();
    app.UseSpaStaticFiles();

    app.UseMvc(...);

    app.UseSpa(...);
}
```

In the previous example, the custom logger is invoked at the start of the pipeline so that the request is logged before it is handled by any other middleware. The response that is logged in our middleware will have been handled by all the other middleware as well.

So, the `Startup` class allows us to configure how all requests are generally handled. How can we specify exactly what happens when requests are made to a specific resource in a web API? Let's find out.

Understanding controllers

Web API resources are implemented using **controllers**. Let's have a look at the controller that the template project created by opening `WeatherForecastController.cs` in the `Controllers` folder. This contains a class called `WeatherForecastController` that inherits from `ControllerBase` with a `Route` annotation:

```
[ApiController]
[Route("[controller]")]
public class WeatherForecastController : ControllerBase
{
    ...
}
```

The annotation specifies the web API resource URL that the controller handles. The `[controller]` object is a placeholder for the controller name, minus the word `Controller`. This controller will handle requests to `weatherforecast`.

The `Get` method in the class is called an **action method**. Action methods handle specific requests to the resource for a specific HTTP method and subpath. We decorate the method with an attribute to specify the HTTP method and subpath the method handles. In our example, we are handling an HTTP `GET` request to the root path (`weatherforecast`) on the resource:

```
[HttpGet]
public IEnumerable<WeatherForecast> Get()
{
    ...
}
```

Let's have a closer look at the web API at runtime by carrying out the following steps:

1. Run the app in Visual Studio by pressing *F5*.
2. When the app has opened in our browser, press *F12* to open the browser developer tools and select the **Network** panel.
3. Select the **Fetch data** option from the top navigation bar. An HTTP `GET` request to `weatherforecast` will be shown:

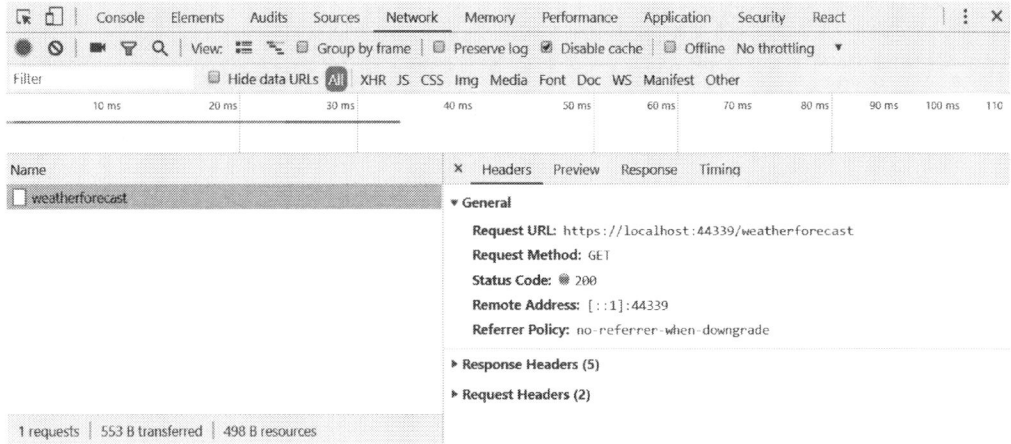

Figure 1.8 – A request to the weatherforecast endpoint in the browser developer tools

4. An HTTP response with a `200` status code is returned with JSON content:

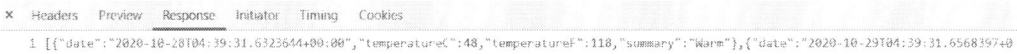

Figure 1.9 – The response body for the weatherforecast endpoint in the browser developer tools

If we look back at the `Get` action method, we are returning an object of the `IEnumerable<WeatherForecast>` type. The MVC middleware automatically converts this object into JSON and puts it in the response body with a `200` status code for us.

So, that was a quick look at the backend that the template scaffolded for us. The request/response pipeline is configured in the `Startup` class and the endpoint handlers are implement using controller classes.

In the next section, we'll walk through the React frontend.

Understanding the React frontend

It's time to turn our attention to the React frontend. In this section, we'll inspect the frontend code, starting with the entry point, which is a single HTML page. We will explore how the frontend is executed in development mode and how it is built in preparation for deployment. We will then learn how the frontend dependencies are managed and also understand why it took over a minute to run the app for the first time. Finally, we will explore how React components fit together and how they access the ASP.NET Core backend.

Understanding the frontend entry point

We have a good clue as to where the entry point is from our examination of the `Startup` class in the ASP.NET Core backend. In the `Configure` method, the SPA middleware is set up with the source path set to `ClientApp`:

```
app.UseSpa(spa =>
{
  spa.Options.SourcePath = "ClientApp";

  if (env.IsDevelopment())
  {
    spa.UseReactDevelopmentServer(npmScript: "start");
  }
});
```

If we look in the `ClientApp` folder, we'll see a file called `package.json`. This is a file that is often used in React apps and contains information about the project, its npm dependencies, and the scripts that can be run to perform tasks.

> **Important Note**
>
> npm is a popular package manager for JavaScript. The dependencies in `package.json` reference the packages in the npm registry.

If we open the `package.json` file, we will see react listed as a dependency:

```
"dependencies": {
  "react": "^16.0.0",
  ...
  "react-scripts": "^3.4.1",
  ...
},
```

A version is specified against each package name. The versions in your `package.json` file may be different to the ones shown in the preceding code snippet. The ^ symbol in front of the version means that the latest minor version can be safely installed, according to semantic versioning.

> **Important Note**
> A semantic version has three parts: `Major.Minor.Patch`. A major version increment happens when an API breaking change is made. A minor version increment happens when backward-compatible features are added. Finally, a patch version happens when backward-compatible bug fixes are added. More information can be found at `https://semver.org`.

So, `react 16.14.0` can be safely installed because this is the latest minor version of React 16 at the time of writing this book.

The `react-scripts` dependency gives us a big clue as to how React was scaffolded. `react-scripts` is a set of scripts from the popular **Create React App** (**CRA**) tool that was built by the developers at Facebook. This tool has done a huge amount of configuration for us, including creating a development server, bundling, linting, and unit testing. We'll learn more about CRA in the next chapter.

The root HTML page for an app scaffolded by CRA is `index.html`, which can be found in the `public` folder in the `ClientApp` folder. It is this page that hosts the React app. The root JavaScript file that is executed for an app scaffolded by CRA is `index.js`, which is in the `ClientApp` folder. We'll examine both the `index.html` and `index.js` files later in this chapter.

Next, we will learn how the React frontend is executed in development mode.

Running in development mode

In the following steps, we'll examine the ASP.NET Core project file to see what happens when the app runs in development mode:

1. We can open the project file by right-clicking on the web application project in **Solution Explorer** and selecting the **Edit Project File** option:

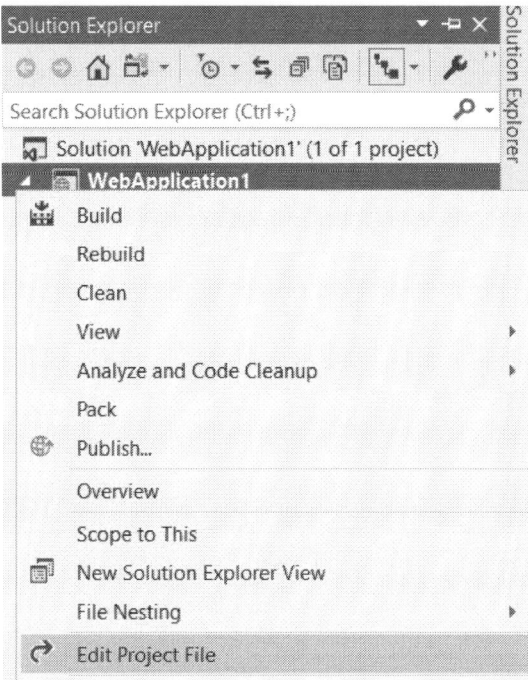

Figure 1.10 – Opening the project file in Visual Studio

This is an XML file that contains information about the Visual Studio project.

2. Let's look at the `Target` element, which has a `Name` attribute of `DebugEnsureNodeEnv`:

```
<Target Name="DebugEnsureNodeEnv" BeforeTargets="Build"
Condition=" '$(Configuration)' == 'Debug' And
!Exists('$(SpaRoot)node_modules') ">
  <!-- Ensure Node.js is installed -->
  <Exec Command="node --version"
    ContinueOnError="true">
    <Output TaskParameter="ExitCode"
      PropertyName="ErrorCode" />
  </Exec>
  <Error Condition="'$(ErrorCode)' != '0'"
    Text="Node.js is required to build and run this
    project. To continue, please install Node.js from
      https://nodejs.org/, and then restart your
      command prompt or IDE."
  />
  <Message Importance="high" Text="Restoring
    dependencies using 'npm'.
```

```
        This may take several minutes..." />
    <Exec WorkingDirectory="$(SpaRoot)" Command="npm
      install" />
</Target>
```

This executes tasks when the `ClientApp/node-modules` folder doesn't exist and the Visual Studio project is run in debug mode, which is the mode that's used when we press *F5*.

3. The first task that is run in the `Target` element is the execution of the following command via an `Exec` task:

```
> node --version
```

This command returns the version of Node that is installed. This may seem like an odd thing to do, but its purpose is to determine whether node is installed. If Node is not installed, the command will error and be caught by the `Error` task, which informs the user that Node needs to the installed and where to install it from.

4. The next task in the `Target` element uses a `Message` command, which outputs `Restoring dependencies using 'npm'. This may take several minutes...` to the **Output** window. We'll see this message when we run the project for the first time:

```
Output
Show output from: Build
1>------ Build started: Project: WebApplication1, Configuration: Debug Any CPU ------
1>WebApplication1 -> C:\code\WebApplication1\WebApplication1\bin\Debug\netcoreapp2.2\WebApplication1.dll
1>WebApplication1 -> C:\code\WebApplication1\WebApplication1\bin\Debug\netcoreapp2.2\WebApplication1.Views.dll
1>v10.13.0
1>Restoring dependencies using 'npm'. This may take several minutes...
```

Figure 1.11 – Restoring npm dependencies message when running a project for the first time

5. The final task that is carried out when the project is run in debug mode is another `Exec` task. This executes the following npm command:

```
> npm install
```

This command downloads all the packages that are listed as dependencies in `package.json` into a folder called `node_modules`:

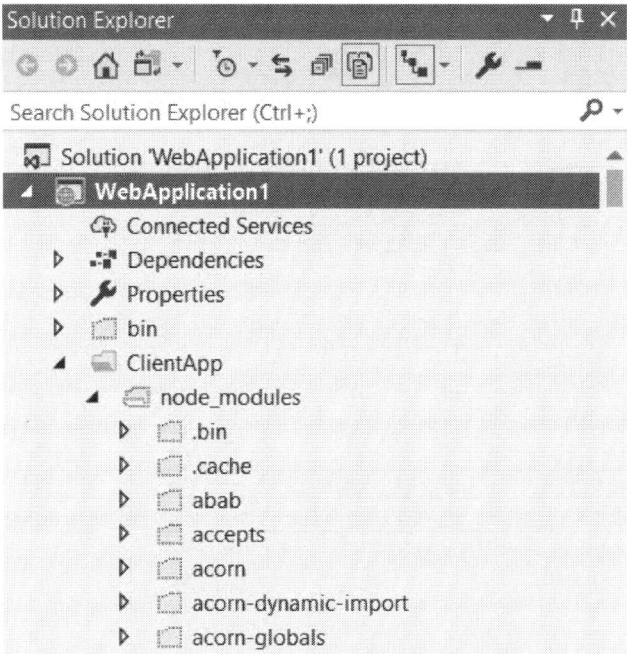

Figure 1.12 – The node_modules folder

We can see this in the **Solution Explorer** window if the **Show All Files** option is on. Notice that there are a lot more folders in node_modules than dependencies listed in package.json. This is because the dependencies will have dependencies. So, the packages in node_modules are all the dependencies in the dependency tree.

At the start of this section, we asked ourselves why it took such a long time for the project to run the app for the first time. The answer is that this last task takes a while because there are a lot of dependencies to download and install. On subsequent runs, node_modules will have been created, so these sets of tasks won't get invoked.

Earlier in this chapter, we learned that ASP.NET Core invokes an npm start command when the app is in development mode. If we look at the scripts section in package.json, we'll see the definition of this command:

```
"scripts": {
  "start": "rimraf ./build && react-scripts start",
  ...
}
```

This command deletes a folder called `build` and runs a **Webpack** development server.

> **Important Note**
> Webpack is a tool that transforms, bundles, and packages up files for use in a browser. Webpack also has a development server. The CRA tool has configured Webpack for us so that all the transformation and bundling configuration is already set up for us.

Why would we want to use the Webpack development server when we already have our ASP.NET Core backend running in IIS Express? The answer is a shortened feedback loop, which will increase our productivity. Later, we'll see that we can make a change to a React app running in the Webpack development server and that those changes are automatically loaded. There is no stopping and restarting the application, so there's a really quick feedback loop and great productivity.

Publishing process

The publishing process is the process of building artifacts to run an application in a production environment.

Let's continue and inspect the XML ASP.NET Core project file by looking at the `Target` element, which has a `Name` attribute of `PublishRunWebPack`. The following code executes a set of tasks when the Visual Studio project is published:

```xml
<Target Name="PublishRunWebpack"
AfterTargets="ComputeFilesToPublish">
  <!-- As part of publishing, ensure the JS resources are
  freshly built in production mode -->

  <Exec WorkingDirectory="$(SpaRoot)" Command="npm install"
  />
  <Exec WorkingDirectory="$(SpaRoot)" Command="npm run
  build" />

  <!-- Include the newly-built files in the publish output -->
  <ItemGroup>
    <DistFiles Include="$(SpaRoot)build\**" />
    <ResolvedFileToPublish Include="@(DistFiles-
    >'%(FullPath)')"
    Exclude="@(ResolvedFileToPublish)">
      <RelativePath>%(DistFiles.Identity)</RelativePath>
      <CopyToPublishDirectory>PreserveNewest
        </CopyToPublishDirectory>
```

```
        </ResolvedFileToPublish>
    </ItemGroup>
</Target>
```

The first task that is run is the execution of the npm install command via an Exec task. This will ensure that all the dependencies are downloaded and installed. Obviously, if we've already run our project in debug mode, then the dependencies should already be in place.

The next task is an Exec task that runs the following npm command:

```
> npm run build
```

This task will run an npm script called build. If we look in the package.json file again, we'll see this script in the scripts section:

```
"scripts": {
  "start": "rimraf ./build && react-scripts start",
  "build": "react-scripts build",
  "test": "cross-env CI=true react-scripts test --
   env=jsdom",
  "eject": "react-scripts eject",
  "lint": "eslint ./src/"
}
```

This references the create-react-app scripts, which bundle the React app ready for production, optimizing it for great performance, and outputting the content into a folder called build.

The next set of tasks defined in the ItemGroup element take their content from the build folder and place it in the publish location, along with the rest of the content to publish.

Let's give this a try and publish our app:

1. In the **Solution Explorer** window, right-click on the project and select the **Publish...** option.
2. Choose **Folder** as the target and click **Next**:

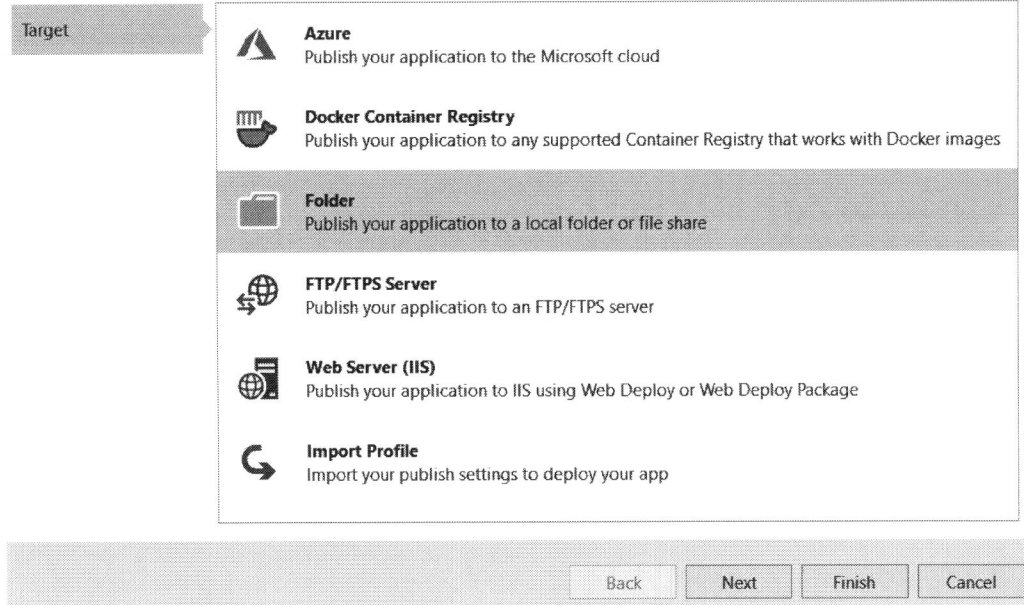

Figure 1.13 – Publishing to a folder

3. Enter a folder location to output the content to and click **Finish**:

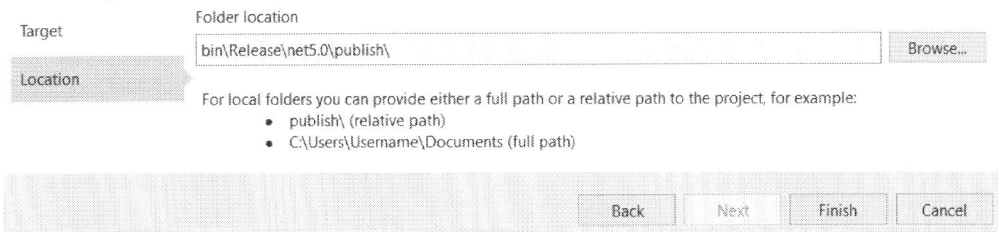

Figure 1.14 – Publish location

4. A publish profile is then created. Click the **Publish** button to start the publishing process on the screen that appears:

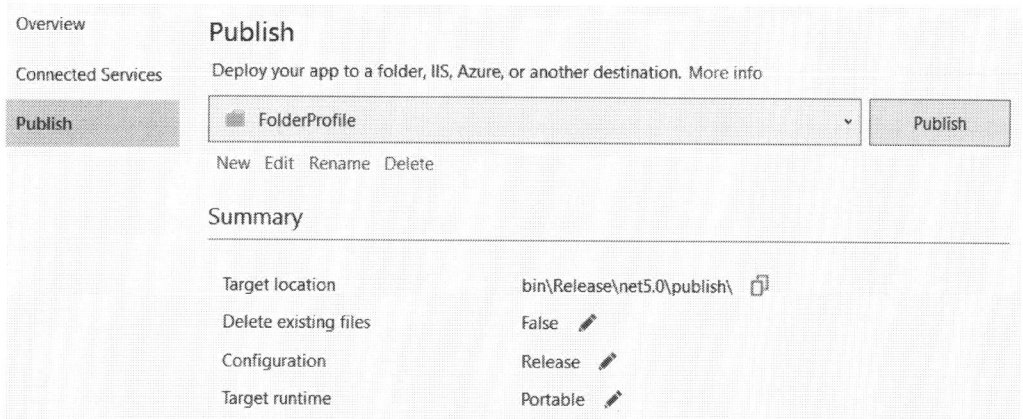

Figure 1.15 – Publish profile screen

After a while, we'll see the content appear in the folder we specified, including a `ClientApp` folder. If we look in this `ClientApp` folder, we'll see a `build` folder containing the React app, ready to be run in a production environment. Notice that the `build` folder contains `index.html`, which is the single page that will host the React app in production.

> **Important Note**
>
> It is important to note that publishing from a developer's machine is not ideal. Instead, it is good practice to carry out this process on a build server to make sure that built applications are consistent, and that code that's committed to the repository goes into the build. We'll cover this in *Chapter 15, Implementing CI and CD with Azure DevOps*.

Understanding the frontend dependencies

Earlier, we learned that frontend dependencies are defined in `package.json`. Why not just list all the dependencies as `script` tags in `index.html`? Why do we need the extra complexity of npm package management in our project? The answer is that a long list of dependencies is hard to manage. If we used `script` tags, we'd need to make sure these are ordered correctly. We'd also be responsible for downloading the packages, placing them locally in our project, and keeping them up to date. We have a huge list of dependencies in our scaffolded project already, without starting work on any functionality in our app. For these reasons, managing dependencies with npm has become an industry standard.

Let's open `package.json` again and look at the `dependencies` section:

```
"dependencies": {
  "bootstrap": "^4.1.3",
  "jquery": "3.4.1",
  "merge": "^1.2.1",
  "oidc-client": "^1.9.0",
  "react": "^16.0.0",
  "react-dom": "^16.0.0",
  "react-router-bootstrap": "^0.24.4",
  "react-router-dom": "^4.2.2",
  "react-scripts": "^3.0.1",
  "reactstrap": "^6.3.0",
  "rimraf": "^2.6.2"
},
```

We've already observed the `react` dependency, but what is the `react-dom` dependency? Well, React doesn't just target the web; it also targets native mobile apps. This means that `react` is the core React library that is used for both web and mobile, and `react-dom` is the library that's specified for targeting the web.

The `react-router-dom` package is the npm package for **React Router** and helps us manage the different pages in our app in the React frontend, without us needing to do a round trip to the server. We'll learn more about React Router in *Chapter 5*, *Routing with React Router*. The `react-router-bootstrap` package allows Bootstrap to work nicely with React Router.

We can see that this React app has a dependency for **Bootstrap 4.1** with the `bootstrap` npm package. So, Bootstrap CSS classes and components can be referenced to build the frontend in our project. The `reactstrap` package is an additional package that allows us to consume Bootstrap nicely in React apps. Bootstrap 4.1 has a dependency on jQuery, which is the reason why we have the `jquery` package dependency.

The `merge` package contains a function that merges objects together, while `oidc-client` is a package for interacting with **OpenID Connect** (**OIDC**) and OAuth2.

The final dependency that we haven't covered yet is `rimraf`. This simply allows files to be deleted, regardless of the host operating system. We can see that this is referenced in the `start` script:

```
"scripts": {
  "start": "rimraf ./build && react-scripts start",
  ...
}
```

Earlier in this chapter, we learned that this script is invoked when our app is running in development mode. So, `rimraf ./build` deletes the `build` folder and its contents before the development server starts.

If we look further down, we'll see a section called `devDependencies`. These are dependencies that are only used during development and not in production:

```
"devDependencies": {
  "ajv": "^6.9.1",
  "cross-env": "^5.2.0",
  "eslint": "^6.8.0",
  "eslint-config-react-app": "^5.2.1",
  "eslint-plugin-flowtype": "^4.6.0",
  "eslint-plugin-import": "^2.20.0",
  "eslint-plugin-jsx-a11y": "^6.2.3",
  "eslint-plugin-react": "^7.18.3"
},
```

The following is a brief description of these dependencies:

- `ajv` allows us to validate JSON files.
- `cross-env` allows us to set environment variables, regardless of the host operating system. If you look at the `test` script in the `scripts` section of the `package.json` file, you'll see that it uses `cross-env` to set a `CI` environment variable.
- The remaining dependencies are all designed to enable linting with **ESLint**. The linting process checks for problematic patterns in code according to a set of rules. We'll learn more about ESLint in *Chapter 3, Getting Started with React and TypeScript*.

Let's move on and learn how the single page is served and how the React app is injected into it.

Understanding how the single page is served

We know that the single page that hosts the React app is `index.html`, so let's examine this file. This file can be found in the `public` folder of the `ClientApp` folder. The React app will be injected into the `div` tag, which has an `id` of `root`:

```
<div id="root"></div>
```

Let's run our app again in Visual Studio to confirm that this is the case by pressing *F5*. If we open the developer tools in the browser page that opens and inspect the DOM in the **Elements** panel, we'll see this div tag with the React content inside it:

```html
▼<body>
    <noscript>
        You need to enable JavaScript to run this app.
    </noscript>
▶<div id="root">…</div> == $0
    <!--
        This HTML file is a template.
        If you open it directly in the browser, you will see an empty page.

        You can add webfonts, meta tags, or analytics to this file.
        The build step will place the bundled scripts into the <body> tag.

        To begin the development, run `npm start` or `yarn start`.
        To create a production bundle, use `npm run build` or `yarn build`.
    -->
    <script src="/static/js/bundle.js"></script>
    <script src="/static/js/0.chunk.js"></script>
    <script src="/static/js/main.chunk.js"></script>
</body>
```

Figure 1.16 – Root div element and script elements

Notice the script elements at the bottom of the body element. This contains all the JavaScript code for our React app, including the React library itself. However, these script elements don't exist in the source index.html file, so how did they get there in the served page? Webpack added them after bundling all the JavaScript together and splitting it up into optimal chunks that can be loaded on demand. If we look in the ClientApp folder and subfolders, we'll see that the static folder doesn't exist. The JavaScript files don't exist either. What's going on? These are virtual files that are created by the Webpack development server. Remember that when we run the app with Visual Studio debugger, the Webpack development server serves index.html. So, the JavaScript files are virtual files that the Webpack development server creates.

Now, what happens in production mode when the Webpack development server isn't running? Let's have a closer look at the app we published earlier in this chapter. Let's look in the `index.html` file in the `Build` folder, which can be found in the `ClientApp` folder. The `script` elements at the bottom of the `body` element will look something like the following:

```
<script>
  !function(e){...}([])
</script>
<script src="/static/js/2.f6873cc5.chunk.js"></script>
<script src="/static/js/main.61537c83.chunk.js"></script>
```

Carriage returns have been added in the preceding code snippet to make it more readable. The highlighted parts of the filenames may vary each time the app is published. The filenames are unique in order to break browser caching. If we look for these JavaScript files in our project, we'll find that they do exist. So, in production mode, the web server will serve this physical JavaScript file.

If we open this JavaScript file, we'll see it contains all the JavaScript for our app. This JavaScript is minified so that the file can be downloaded to the browser nice and quickly.

> **Important Note**
> Minification is the process of removing unnecessary characters in files without affecting how it is processed by the browser. This includes code comments and formatting, unused code, using shorter variable and function names, and so on.

However, the file isn't small and contains a lot of JavaScript. What's going on here? Well, the file contains not only our JavaScript app code but also the code from all the dependencies, including React itself.

Understanding how components fit together

Now, it's time to start looking at the React app code and how components are implemented. Remember that the root JavaScript file is `index.js` in the `ClientApp` folder. Let's open this file and look closely at the following block of code:

```
const rootElement = document.getElementById('root');

ReactDOM.render(
  <BrowserRouter basename={baseUrl}>
    <App />
  </BrowserRouter>,
  rootElement);
```

The first statement selects the `div` element we discovered earlier, which contains the `root` ID and stores it in a variable called `rootElement`.

The next statement extends over multiple lines and calls the `render` function from the React DOM library. It is this function that injects the React app content into the root `div` element. The `rootElement` variable, which contains a reference to the root `div` element, is passed into this function as the second parameter.

The first parameter that is passed into the `render` function is more interesting. In fact, it doesn't even look like legal JavaScript! This is, in fact, **JSX**, which we'll learn about in detail in *Chapter 3, Getting Started with React and TypeScript*.

> **Important Note**
> JSX is transformed into regular JavaScript by Webpack using a tool called **Babel**. This is one of many tasks that CRA configured for us when our app was scaffolded.

So, the first parameter passes in the root React component called `BrowserRouter`, which comes from the React Router library. We'll learn more about this component in *Chapter 5, Routing with React Router*.

Nested inside the `BrowserRouter` component is a component called `App`. If we look at the top of the `index.js` file, we will see that the `App` component is imported from a file called `App.js`:

```
import App from './App';
```

> **Important Note**
> `import` statements are used to import items that have been exported by another JavaScript module. The module is specified by its file location, with the `js` extension omitted.
>
> The `import` statements that import items from `npm` packages don't need the path to be specified. This is because CRA has configured a `resolver` in Webpack that automatically looks in the `node_modules` folder during the bundling process.

So, the `App` component is contained in the `App.js` file. Let's have a quick look. A class called `App` is defined in this file:

```
export default class App extends Component {
  static displayName = App.name;

  render () {
    return (
      <Layout>
        <Route exact path='/' component={Home} />
        <Route path='/counter' component={Counter} />
        <Route path='/fetch-data' component={FetchData} />
      </Layout>
    );
  }
}
```

Notice the `export` and `default` keywords before the `class` keyword.

> **Important Note**
>
> The `export` keyword is used to export an item from a JavaScript module. The `default` keyword defines the export as the default export, which means it can be imported without curly braces. So, a default export can be imported as `import App from './App'` rather than `import {App} from './App'`.

A method called `render` defines the output of the component. This method returns JSX, which, in this case, references a `Layout` component in our app code and a `Route` component from React Router.

So, we are starting to understand how React components can be composed together to form a UI.

Now, let's go through the React development experience by making a simple change:

1. Run the app in Visual Studio by pressing *F5*, if it's not already running.
2. Open the `Home.js` file, which can be found at `ClientApp\src\components`. This contains the component that renders the home page.

3. With the app still running, in the `render` method, change the h1 tag in the JSX so that it renders a different string:

```
render () {
  return (
    <div>
      <h1>Hello, React!</h1>
      <p>Welcome to your new single-page application,
        built with:
      </p>
      ...
    </div>
  );
}
```

4. Save the file and look at the running app:

Hello, React!

Welcome to your new single-page application, built with:

- ASP.NET Core and C# for cross-platform server-side code
- React for client-side code
- Bootstrap for layout and styling

Figure 1.17 – The home page is automatically updated in the browser

The app is automatically updated with our change. The Webpack development server automatically updated the running app with the change when the file was saved. The experience of seeing our changes implemented almost immediately gives us a really productive experience when developing our React frontend.

Understanding how components access the backend web API

The final topic we'll cover in this chapter is how the React frontend consumes the backend web API. If the app isn't running, then run it by pressing *F5* in Visual Studio. If we click on the **Fetch data** option in the top navigation bar in the app that opens in the browser, we'll see a page showing weather forecasts:

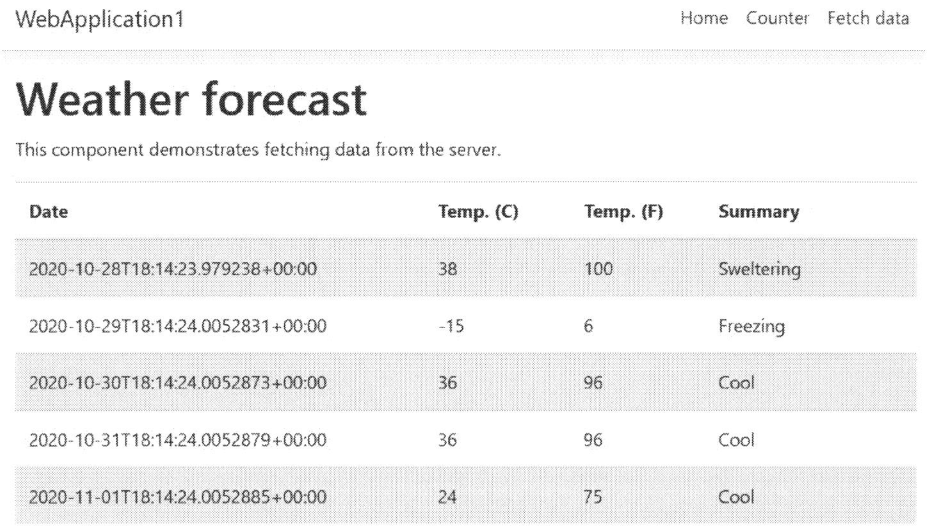

WebApplication1		Home Counter	Fetch data

Weather forecast

This component demonstrates fetching data from the server.

Date	Temp. (C)	Temp. (F)	Summary
2020-10-28T18:14:23.979238+00:00	38	100	Sweltering
2020-10-29T18:14:24.0052831+00:00	-15	6	Freezing
2020-10-30T18:14:24.0052873+00:00	36	96	Cool
2020-10-31T18:14:24.0052879+00:00	36	96	Cool
2020-11-01T18:14:24.0052885+00:00	24	75	Cool

Figure 1.18 – Weather forecast data

If we cast our minds back to earlier in this chapter, in the *Understanding controllers* section, we looked at an ASP.NET Core controller that surfaced a web API that exposed the data at `weatherforecast`. So, this is a great place to have a quick look at how a React app can call an ASP.NET Core web API.

The component that renders this page is in `FetchData.js`. Let's open this file and look at the `constructor` class:

```
constructor (props) {
  super(props);
  this.state = { forecasts: [], loading: true };
}
```

The `constructor` class in a JavaScript class is a special method that automatically gets invoked when a class instance is created. So, it's a great place to initialize class-level variables.

The constructor initializes a component state, which contains the weather forecast data, and a flag to indicate whether the data is being fetched. We'll learn more about component state in *Chapter 3*, *Getting Started with React and TypeScript*.

Let's have a look at the `componentDidMount` method:

```
componentDidMount() {
   this.populateWeatherData();
}
```

This method gets invoked by React when the component is inserted into the tree and is the perfect place to load data. This method calls a `populateWeatherData` method, so, let's have a look at that:

```
async populateWeatherData() {
   const response = await fetch('weatherforecast');
   const data = await response.json();
   this.setState({ forecasts: data, loading: false });
}
```

Notice the `async` keyword before the `populateWeatherData` function name. Also, notice the `await` keywords within the function.

> **Important Note**
>
> An `await` keyword is used to wait for an asynchronous function to complete. A function must be declared as asynchronous for us to use the `await` keyword within it. This can be done by placing the `async` keyword in front of the function name. This is very much like `async` and `await` in .NET.

We can see that a function called `fetch` is used within this method.

> **Important Note**
>
> The `fetch` function is a native JavaScript function for interacting with web APIs. The `fetch` function supersedes `XMLHttpRequest` and works a lot nicer with JSON-based web APIs.

The parameter that's passed into the `fetch` function is the path to the web API resource; that is, `weatherforecast`. A relative path can be used because the React app and web API are of the same origin.

Once the weather forecast data has been fetched from the web API and the response has been parsed, the data is placed in the component's state.

Hang on a minute, though – the native `fetch` function isn't implemented in **Internet Explorer** (**IE**). Does that mean our app won't work in IE? Well, the `fetch` function isn't available in IE, but CRA has set up a polyfill for this so that it works perfectly fine.

> **Important Note**
> A **polyfill** is a piece of code that implements a feature we expect the browser to provide natively. Polyfills allow us to develop against features that aren't supported in all browsers yet.

Now, let's turn our attention to the `render` method:

```
render () {
  let contents = this.state.loading
    ? <p><em>Loading...</em></p>
    : FetchData.renderForecastsTable(this.state.forecasts);

  return (
    <div>
      <h1 id="tabelLabel">Weather forecast</h1>
      <p>This component demonstrates fetching data from the
        server.</p>
      {contents}
    </div>
  );
}
```

The code may contain concepts you aren't familiar with, so don't worry if this doesn't make sense to you at this point. I promise that it will make sense as we progress through this book!

We already know that the `render` method in a React component returns JSX, and we can see that JSX is returned in this `render` method as well. Notice the `{contents}` reference in the JSX, which injects the `contents` JavaScript variable into the markup below the p tag, at the bottom of the `div` tag. The `contents` variable is set in the first statement in the `render` method and is set so that **Loading...** is displayed while the web API request is taking place, along with the result of `FetchData.renderForecastsTable` when the request has finished. We'll have a quick look at this now:

```
static renderForecastsTable (forecasts) {
  return (
    <table className='table table-striped' aria-
      labelledby="tabelLabel">
      <thead>
        <tr>
          <th>Date</th>
          <th>Temp. (C)</th>
          <th>Temp. (F)</th>
```

```
              <th>Summary</th>
            </tr>
          </thead>
          <tbody>
            {forecasts.map(forecast =>
              <tr key={forecast.dateFormatted}>
                <td>{forecast.dateFormatted}</td>
                <td>{forecast.temperatureC}</td>
                <td>{forecast.temperatureF}</td>
                <td>{forecast.summary}</td>
              </tr>
            )}
          </tbody>
        </table>
      );
    }
```

This function returns JSX, which contains an HTML table with the data from the `forecasts` data array injected into it. The `map` method on the `forecasts` array is used to iterate through the items in the array and render `tr` tags in the HTML table containing the data.

> **Important Note**
>
> The `map` method is a native JavaScript method that is available in an array. It takes in a function parameter that is called for each array element. The return values of the function calls then make up a new array. The `map` method is commonly used in JSX when iteration is needed.

Notice that we have applied a `key` attribute to each `tr` tag. What is this for? This isn't a standard attribute on an HTML table row, is it?

> **Important Note**
>
> The `key` attribute helps React detect when an element changes or is added or removed. So, it's not a standard HTML table row attribute. Where we output content in a loop, it is good practice to apply this attribute and set it to a unique value within the loop so that React can distinguish it from the other elements. Omitting keys can also lead to performance problems on large datasets as React will unnecessarily update the DOM when it doesn't need to.

Again, this is a lot to take in at this point, so don't worry if there are bits you don't fully understand. This will all become second nature to you by the end of this book.

Summary

In this chapter, we started off by learning that all the pages in a SPA are rendered in JavaScript with the help of a framework such as React, along with requests for data. This is handled by a backend API with the help of a framework such as ASP.NET Core. We now understand that the Startup class configures services that are used in the ASP.NET Core backend, as well as the request/response pipeline. Requests to specific backend API resources are handled by controller classes.

We also saw how CRA was leveraged by the ASP.NET Core React template to create the React app. This tool did a huge amount of setup and configuration for us, including creating a development server, bundling, linting, and even creating key polyfills for IE. We learned that the React app lives in the ClientApp folder in an ASP.NET Core React templated project, with a file called index.html being the single page. A file called package.json defines key project information for the React app, including its dependencies and the tasks that are used to run and build the React app.

This chapter has given us a great overview of all the basic parts of an ASP.NET Core React app and how they work together. We'll explore many of the topics we've covered in this chapter in greater depth throughout this book.

With the knowledge we've gained from this chapter, we are now ready to start creating the app we are going to build through this book, which we'll start to do in the next chapter.

Questions

Have a go at answering the following questions to test the knowledge that you have acquired in this chapter:

1. What is the entry point method in an ASP.NET Core app?
2. What is the single HTML page filename in an ASP.NET Core React app that's created by a template? What folder is this located in?
3. What file are React app dependencies defined in?
4. What npm command will run the React app in the Webpack development server?
5. What npm command builds the React app so that it's ready for production?
6. What is the method name in a React class component that renders the component?

7. Have a look at the following code snippet, which configures the request/response pipeline in an ASP.NET Core app:

    ```
    public void Configure(IApplicationBuilder app,
    IHostingEnvironment env)
    {
      app.UseAuthentication();
      app.UseHttpsRedirection();
      app.UseMvc();
    }
    ```

    Which is invoked first in the request/response pipeline – authentication or the MVC controllers?

8. Does the class that configures the services and request/response pipeline need to be called `Startup`? Can we give it a different name?

9. What browsers are supported by a React app created by CRA?

Answers

1. A method called `Main` in the `Program` class is the entry point method in an ASP.NET Core app.
2. A file called `index.html` is the single HTML page filename. This is located in the `public` folder, which can be found in the `ClientApp` folder.
3. The React app dependencies are defined in a file called `package.json` in the `ClientApp` folder.
4. `npm start` is the command that will run the React app in the WebPack development server.
5. `npm run build` is the command that builds the React app so that it's ready for production.
6. The `render` method renders a React class component.
7. Authentication will be invoked first in the request/response pipeline.

8. We can give the `Startup` class a different name by defining this class in `IHostBuilder`, as shown in the following example:

```
public static IHostBuilder CreateHostBuilder(string[] args) =>
  Host.CreateDefaultBuilder(args)
    .ConfigureWebHostDefaults(webBuilder =>
    {
        webBuilder.UseStartup<MyStartup>();
    });
```

9. All modern browsers, including IE, are supported by a React app created by CRA.

Further reading

The following are some useful links so that you can learn more about the topics that were covered in this chapter:

- **ASP.NET Core startup**: https://docs.microsoft.com/en-us/aspnet/core/fundamentals/startup
- **ASP.NET Core web API controllers**: https://docs.microsoft.com/en-us/aspnet/core/web-api
- **Create React app**: https://facebook.github.io/create-react-app/
- **WebPack development server**: https://webpack.js.org/configuration/dev-server/
- **npm**: https://docs.npmjs.com/
- **JSX**: https://reactjs.org/docs/introducing-jsx.html
- **JavaScript module import**: https://developer.mozilla.org/en-US/docs/Web/JavaScript/Reference/Statements/import
- **JavaScript module export**: https://developer.mozilla.org/en-US/docs/Web/JavaScript/Reference/Statements/export
- **JavaScript fetch**: https://developer.mozilla.org/en-US/docs/Web/API/Fetch_API
- **JavaScript array map**: https://developer.mozilla.org/en-US/docs/Web/JavaScript/Reference/Global_Objects/Array/map
- **React lists and keys**: https://reactjs.org/docs/lists-and-keys.html

2
Creating Decoupled React and ASP.NET 5 Apps

Throughout this book, we are going to develop a question-and-answer app; we will refer to it as the Q&A app. Users will be able to submit a question and other users will be able to submit answers. They will also be able to search for previous questions and view the answers that were given for them. In this chapter, we are going to start building this app by creating the ASP.NET Core and React projects.

In the previous chapter, we learned how to create an ASP.NET Core and React app using the template in Visual Studio. However, we'll create our app in a slightly different manner in this chapter and understand the reasoning behind this decision.

Our React app will use TypeScript, so we'll learn about the benefits of TypeScript and how to create a React and TypeScript app.

We will start this chapter by creating an ASP.NET Web API project before moving on to create a separate frontend project that uses React and TypeScript. We will then add a tool to the frontend project that identifies potential problematic code, as well as a tool that automatically formats the code.

We'll cover the following topics in this chapter:

- Creating an ASP.NET Core Web API project
- Creating a React and TypeScript app
- Adding linting to React and TypeScript
- Adding automatic code formatting to React and TypeScript

By the end of this chapter, we will be ready to start building the frontend of our Q&A app with React and TypeScript.

Technical requirements

We will need the following tools in this chapter:

- **Visual Studio 2019**: We'll use this to edit our ASP.NET Core code. This can be downloaded from `https://visualstudio.microsoft.com/vs/`.
- **.NET 5.0**: This can be downloaded from `https://dotnet.microsoft.com/download/dotnet/5.0`.
- **Visual Studio Code**: We'll use this to edit our React code. This can be downloaded from `https://code.visualstudio.com/`. If you already have this installed, make sure that it is at least version 1.52.
- **Node.js and npm**: These can be downloaded from `https://nodejs.org/`. If you already have these installed, make sure that Node.js is at least version 8.2 and that npm is at least version 5.2.

All the code snippets in this chapter can be found online at `https://github.com/PacktPublishing/ASP.NET-Core-5-and-React-Second-Edition`. In order to restore code from a chapter, download the relevant source code repository and open the relevant folder in the relevant editor. If the code is frontend code, then `npm install` can be entered into the Terminal to restore the dependencies.

Check out the following video to see the Code in Action: `https://bit.ly/2J7rc0k`.

Creating an ASP.NET Core Web API project

We are going to create the ASP.NET Core and React projects separately in this chapter. In *Chapter 1, Understanding the ASP.NET 5 React Template*, we discovered that old versions of React and `create-react-app` were used. Creating the React project separately allows us to use a more recent version of React and `create-react-app`. Creating the React project separately also allows us to use TypeScript with React, which will help us be more productive as the code base grows.

In this section, we will create our ASP.NET Core backend in Visual Studio.

Let's open Visual Studio and carry out the following steps:

1. In the startup dialog, select **Create a new project**:

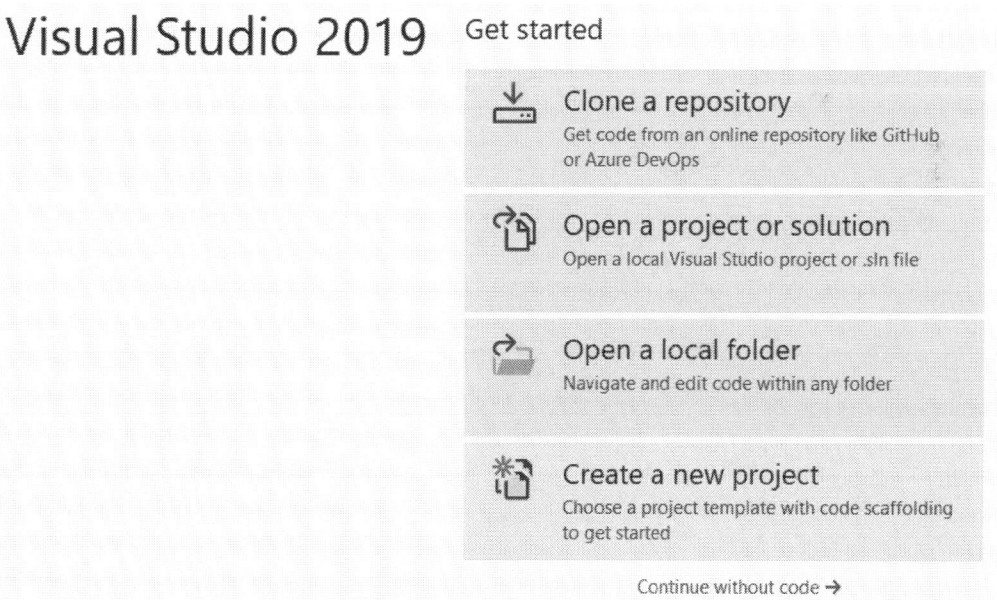

Figure 2.1 – Creating a new project

2. Choose **ASP.NET Core Web Application** in the wizard that opens and click the **Next** button:

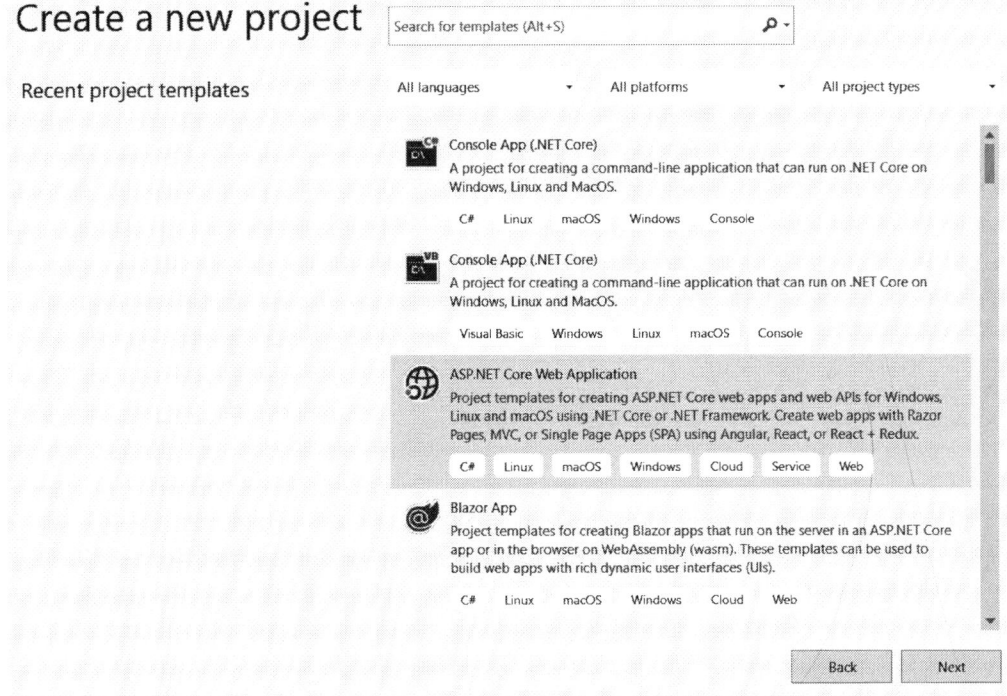

Figure 2.2 – Selecting a web application project

3. Create a folder called `backend` in an appropriate location.

4. Name the project `QandA` and choose the `backend` folder location to save the project. Tick **Place solution and project in the same directory** and click the **Create** button to create the project:

Technical requirements 61

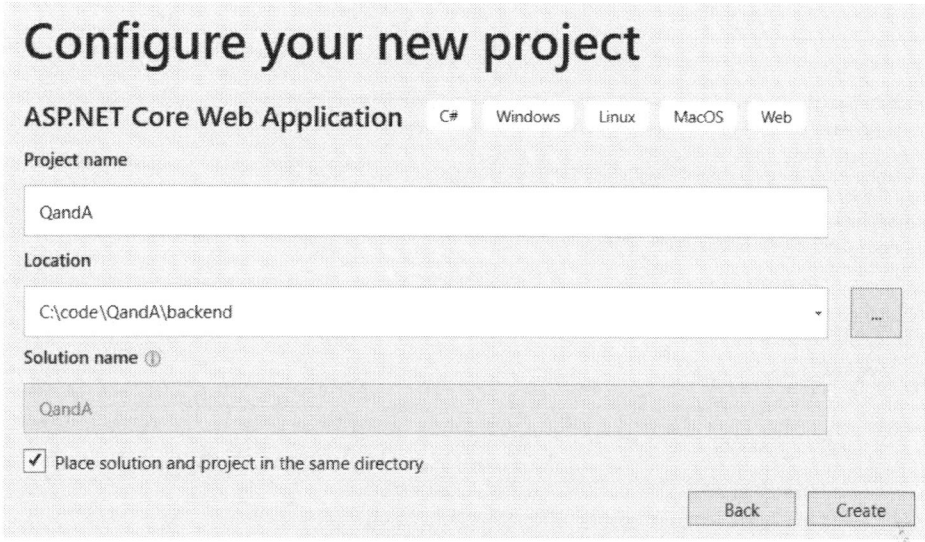

Figure 2.3 – Naming the project

Now, another dialog will appear that will allow us to specify the version of ASP.NET Core we want to use, as well as the specific type of project we want to create.

5. Select **ASP.NET Core 5.0** as the version and **ASP.NET Core Web API** in the dialog. Then, click the **Create** button, which will create the project:

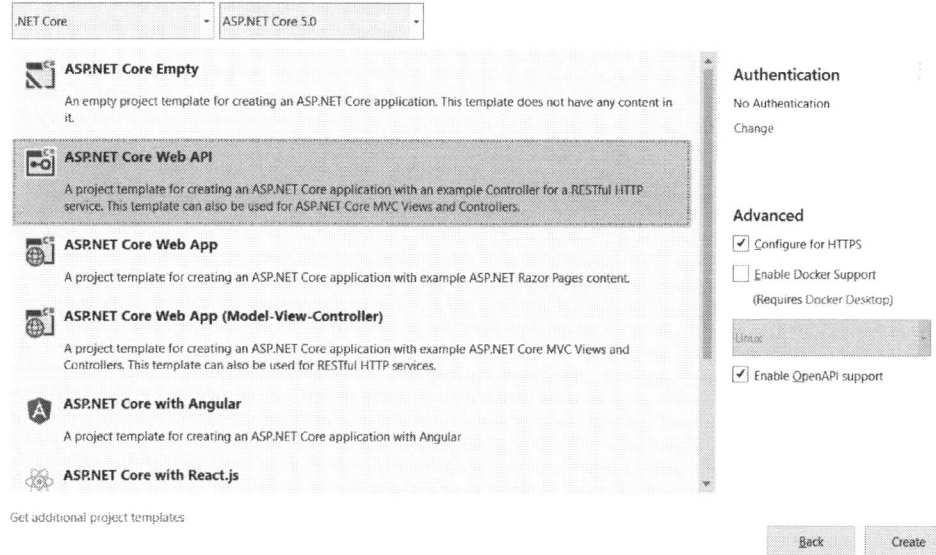

Figure 2.4 – Selecting an API project

6. Once the project has been created, open `Startup.cs` and move the `app.UseHttpsRedirection()` line of code so that it is not used while in development:

```
public void Configure(IApplicationBuilder app,
IWebHostEnvironment env)
{
  if (env.IsDevelopment())
  {
    ...
  }
  else
  {
    app.UseHttpsRedirection();
  }

  app.UseRouting();

  ...
}
```

We have made this change because, in development mode, our frontend will use the HTTP protocol. By default, the Firefox browser doesn't allow network requests for an app that has a different protocol to the backend. Due to this, we want the frontend and backend to use the HTTP protocol in development mode.

That's the only change we are going to make to our backend in this chapter. In the next section, we'll create the React frontend project.

Creating a React and TypeScript app

In *Chapter 1, Understanding the ASP.NET 5 React Template*, we discovered that **create-react-app** (**CRA**) was leveraged by the Visual Studio template to create the React app. We also learned that CRA did a lot of valuable setup and configuration for us. We are going to leverage CRA in this section to create our React app. CRA is a package in the npm registry that we will execute to scaffold a React and TypeScript project. First, we will take the time to understand the benefits of using TypeScript.

Understanding the benefits of TypeScript

TypeScript adds an optional static typing layer on top of JavaScript that we can use during our development. Static types allow us to catch certain problems earlier in the development process. For example, if we make a mistake when referencing a variable, TypeScript will spot this immediately once we've mistyped the variable, as shown in the following screenshot:

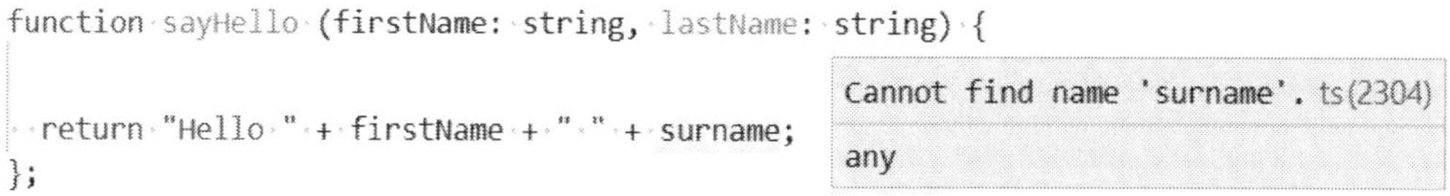

```
function sayHello (firstName: string, lastName: string) {

  return "Hello " + firstName + " " + surname;
};
```

> Cannot find name 'surname'. ts(2304)
> any

Figure 2.5 – TypeScript catching an unknown variable

Another example is that, if we forget to pass a required property when referencing a React component, TypeScript informs us of the mistake straight away:

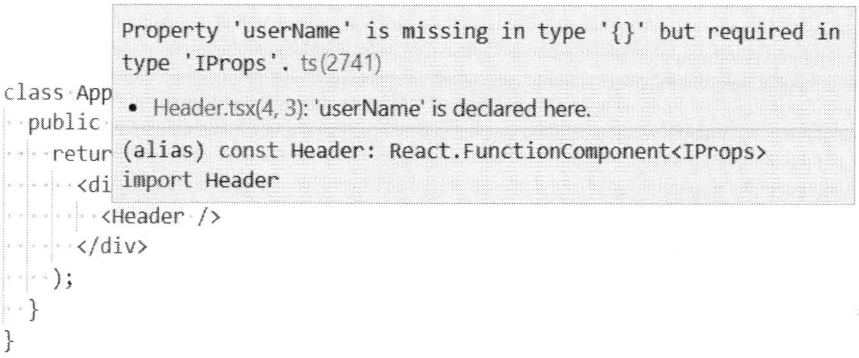

```
class App
  public
    retur
      <di
        <Header />
      </div>
    );
  }
}
```

> Property 'userName' is missing in type '{}' but required in type 'IProps'. ts(2741)
> • Header.tsx(4, 3): 'userName' is declared here.
> (alias) const Header: React.FunctionComponent<IProps>
> import Header

Figure 2.6 – TypeScript catching a missing React component property

This means we get a build-time error rather than a runtime error.

This also helps tools such as Visual Studio Code provide accurate IntelliSense; robust refactoring features, such as renaming a class; and great code navigation.

As we start building our frontend, we'll quickly experience the types of benefits that make us more productive.

Now that we are starting to understand the benefits of TypeScript, it's time to create a React project that uses TypeScript in the next subsection.

Creating the app with CRA

Let's create the React and TypeScript app with CRA by carrying out the following steps:

1. Open Visual Studio Code in the QandA folder we created earlier. Note that we should be at the same level as the backend folder and not inside it.

2. Open the Terminal in Visual Studio Code, which can be found in the **View** menu or by pressing *Ctrl + '*. Execute the following command in the Terminal:

   ```
   > npx create-react-app frontend --template typescript
   ```

   The npx tool is part of npm that temporarily installs the create-react-app npm package and uses it to create our project.

   We have told the create-react-app npm package to create our project in a folder called frontend.

   The --template typescript option has created our React project with TypeScript.

3. If we look in the src folder, we'll see that the App component has a tsx extension. This means that this is a TypeScript component.

4. Let's verify whether the app runs okay by executing the following commands in the Terminal:

   ```
   > cd frontend
   > npm start
   ```

5. The app will appear in our browser after a few seconds:

Figure 2.7 – App component in our React app

6. Press *Ctrl + C* to stop the running app and *Y* when you're asked to terminate the job.

So, why are we using Visual Studio Code to develop our React app and not Visual Studio? Well, the overall experience is a little better and faster when developing frontend code with Visual Studio Code.

So, we now have a React and TypeScript app using the latest version of CRA. In the next section, we are going to add more automated checks to our code by introducing **linting** into our project.

Adding linting to React and TypeScript

Linting is a series of checks that are used to identify code that is potentially problematic. A linter is a tool that performs linting, and it can be run in our code editor as well as in the **continuous integration** (**CI**) process. So, linting helps us write consistent and high-quality code as it is being written.

ESLint is the most popular linter in the React community and has already been installed in our project for us by CRA. Due to this, we will be using ESLint as our linting tool for our app.

> **Important Note**
>
> TSLint was a popular alternative to ESLint for linting TypeScript code but is now deprecated. More information can be found at `https://medium.com/palantir/tslint-in-2019-1a144c2317a9`.

In the following subsections, we will learn how to configure ESLints rules, as well as how to configure Visual Studio Code to highlight violations.

Configuring Visual Studio Code to lint TypeScript code

CRA has already installed ESLint and configured it for us.

> **Important Note**
>
> Note that ESLint doesn't appear in our `package.json` file. Instead, it is part of the CRA package. This can be confirmed by opening the `package.json` file in `node_modules\react-scripts`.

We need to tell Visual Studio Code to lint TypeScript code. Let's carry out the following steps to do this:

1. First, let's reopen Visual Studio Code in the `frontend` folder. This is required for an extension that we are going to install in a later step.

2. Go to the **Extensions** area in Visual Studio Code (*Ctrl + Shift + X*) and type `eslint` into the search box in the top-left corner. The extension we are looking for is called **ESLint** and is published by **Dirk Baeumer**:

Figure 2.9 – Visual Studio Code ESLint extension

3. Click on the **Install** button to install the extension.

4. Open **Settings** from the **Preferences** menu on the **File** menu. The shortcut keys to open **Settings** are *Ctrl + ,*.

5. Enter `eslint` in the search box and scroll down to the **Eslint: Probe** setting:

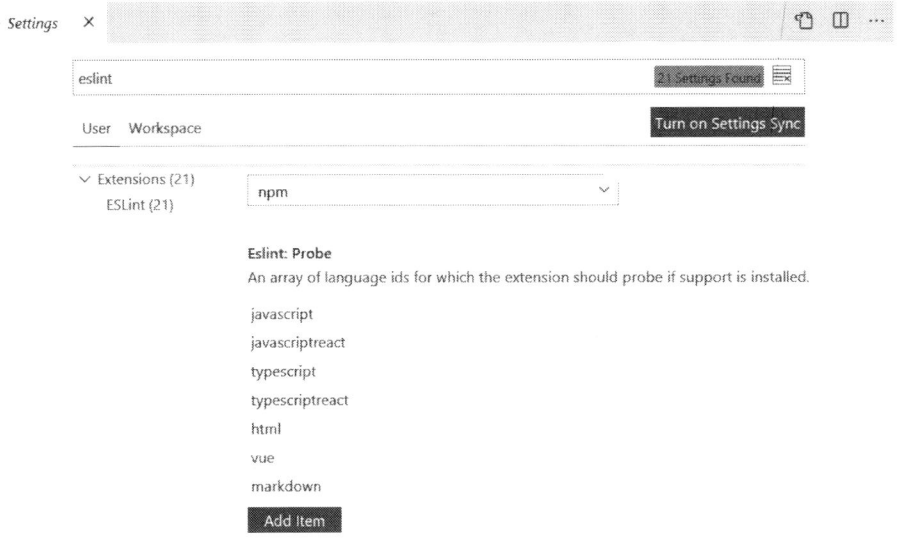

Figure 2.8 – ESLint: Probe setting

This setting tells Visual Studio Code which languages to run through ESLint while validating code.

6. Make sure that `typescript` and `typescriptreact` are in the list. If not, add them using the **Add Item** button.

> **Important Note**
>
> The preceding screenshot shows the setting being added to all the projects for the current user because it is in the **User** tab. If we just want to change a setting in the current project, we can find it in the **Workspace** tab and adjust it.

7. Now, we can go to the **Extensions** area in Visual Studio Code (*Ctrl + Shift + X*) and type `eslint` into the search box in the top-left corner. The extension we are looking for is called **ESLint** and is published by **Dirk Baeumer**:

Figure 2.9 – Visual Studio Code ESLint extension

8. Click on the **Install** button to install the extension.

Now, Visual Studio Code will be using ESLint to validate our code. Next, we will learn how to configure ESLint.

Configuring linting rules

Now that Visual Studio Code is linting our code, let's carry out the following steps to understand how we can configure the rules that ESLint executes:

1. Let's create a file called `.eslintrc.json` in the `frontend` folder with the following code:

```
{
    "extends": "react-app"
}
```

This file defines the rules that ESLint executes. We have just told it to execute all the rules that have been configured in CRA.

2. Let's check that Visual Studio Code is linting our code by adding the following highlighted line to `App.tsx`, just before the `return` statement:

```
const App: React.FC = () => {
  const unused = 'something';
  return (
    ...
  );
};
```

We'll see that ESLint immediately flags this line as being unused:

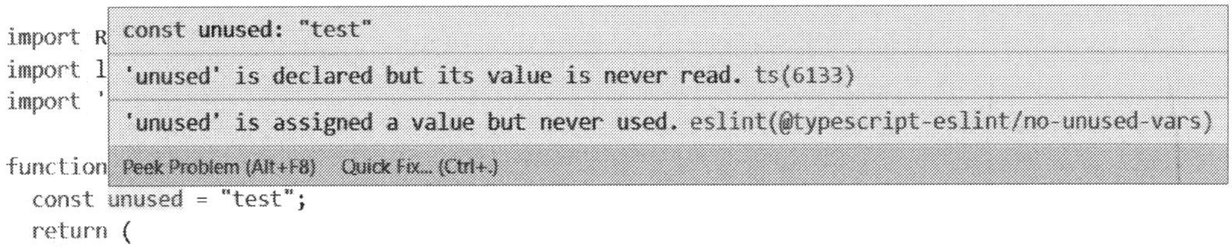

```
import R  const unused: "test"
import 1
import    'unused' is declared but its value is never read. ts(6133)
          'unused' is assigned a value but never used. eslint(@typescript-eslint/no-unused-vars)
function  Peek Problem (Alt+F8)   Quick Fix... (Ctrl+.)
  const unused = "test";
  return (
```

Figure 2.10 – ESLint catching an unused variable

That's great – this means our code is being linted.

3. Now, let's add a rule that CRA hasn't been configured to apply. In the `.eslintrc.json` file, add the following highlighted lines:

```
{
  "extends": "react-app",
  "rules": {
    "no-debugger":"warn"
  }
}
```

Here, we have told ESLint to warn us about the use of `debugger` statements.

> **Important Note**
>
> The list of available ESLint rules can be found at `https://eslint.org/docs/rules/`.

4. Let's add a `debugger` statement below our unused variable in `App.tsx`, like so:

```
const App: React.FC = () => {
  const unused = 'something';
  debugger;
  return (
    ...
  );
};
```

We will immediately see that ESLint flags this up:

```
fu  Unexpected 'debugger' statement. eslint(no-debugger)
    Peek Problem (Alt+F8)   Quick Fix... (Ctrl+.)
debugger;
```

Figure 2.11 – ESLint catching a debugger statement

Now, we have linting configured in our project. Let's clean up the code by performing the following steps:

1. Remove the unused line of code and `debugger` statement from `App.tsx`.
2. Remove the `no-debugger` rule from the `.eslintrc.json` file.

To quickly recap, CRA installs and configures ESLint for us. We can adjust the configuration using a `.eslintrc.json` file.

In the next section, we'll look at how we can autoformat the code.

Adding automatic code formatting to React and TypeScript

Enforcing a consistent code style improves the readability of the code base, but it can be a pain, even if ESLint reminds us to do it. Wouldn't it be great if those semicolons we forgot to add to the end of our statements were just automatically added for us? Well, that is what automatic code formatting tools can do for us, and **Prettier** is one of these great tools.

We will start this section by installing Prettier before configuring it to work nicely with ESLint and Visual Studio Code.

Adding Prettier

We are going to add Prettier to our project by following these steps in Visual Studio Code:

1. Make sure you are in the `frontend` directory. Execute the following command to install Prettier:

   ```
   > npm install prettier --save-dev
   ```

2. Now, we want Prettier to take responsibility for the style rules from ESLint. Let's install some npm packages that will do this:

   ```
   > npm install eslint-config-prettier eslint-plugin-prettier --save-dev
   ```

   `eslint-config-prettier` disables ESLint rules that conflict with Prettier. `eslint-plugin-prettier` is an ESLint rule that formats code using Prettier.

3. Now, let's tell ESLint to let Prettier take care of the code formatting by adding the following highlighted changes to `.eslintrc.json`:

   ```
   {
     "extends": ["react-app", "plugin:prettier/recommended"],
     "rules": {
       "prettier/prettier": [
         "error",
         {
           "endOfLine": "auto"
         }
       ]
     }
   }
   ```

4. Now, let's specify the formatting rules we want in a `.prettierrc` file in the `frontend` folder. Create a file with the following content:

   ```
   {
     "printWidth": 80,
     "singleQuote": true,
     "semi": true,
     "tabWidth": 2,
     "trailingComma": "all",
     "endOfLine": "auto"
   }
   ```

These rules will result in lines over 80 characters long being sensibly wrapped, double quotes being automatically converted into single quotes, semicolons being automatically added to the end of statements, indentations automatically being set to two spaces, and trailing commas being automatically added wherever possible to items such as arrays on multiple lines.

5. Now, go to the **Extensions** area in Visual Studio Code (*Ctrl* + *Shift* + *X*) and type `prettier` into the search box in the top-left corner. The extension we are looking for is called **Prettier – Code formatter** and is published by **Esben Petersen**:

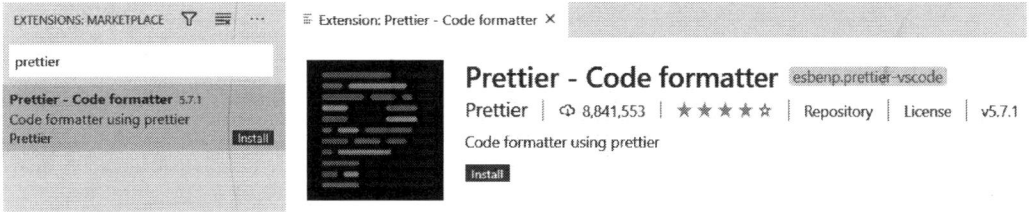

Figure 2.12 – Visual Studio Code Prettier extension

6. Click on the **Install** button to install the extension.

7. We can get Prettier to format our code when a file is saved in Visual Studio Code with some settings. Open **Settings** from the **Preferences** menu on the **File** menu. Enter `format` into the search box and make sure **Default Formatter** is set to **esbenp.prettier-vscode** and **Format on Save** is ticked:

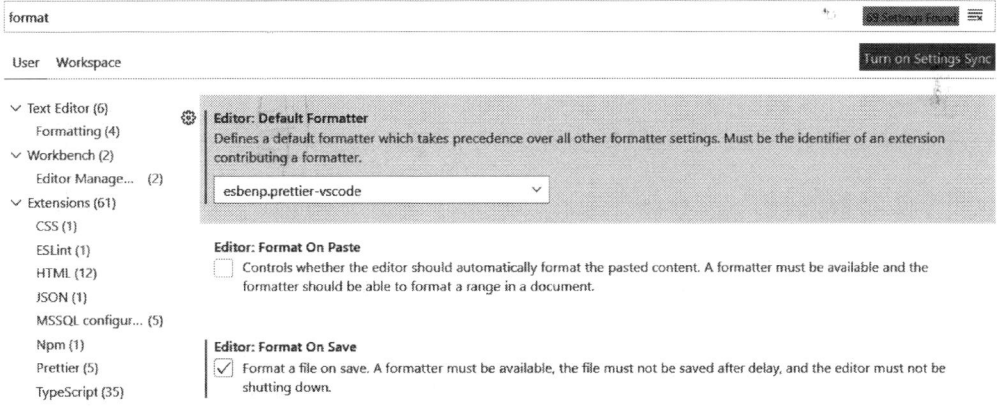

Figure 2.13 – Settings for Prettier to format on save

So, that's Prettier set up. Whenever we save a file in Visual Studio Code, it will be automatically formatted.

Resolving errors

Once Prettier has been installed, the following error may appear on the React import:

```
Failed to compile

C:/QandA/frontend/src/App.tsx
TypeScript error in C:/QandA/frontend/src/App.tsx(1,19):
Could not find a declaration file for module 'react'. 'C:/QandA/frontend/node_modules/react/index.js' implicitly has an 'any' type.
  If the 'react' package actually exposes this module, consider sending a pull request to amend
'https://github.com/DefinitelyTyped/DefinitelyTyped/tree/master/types/react'  TS7016

  > 1 | import React from 'react';
      |                   ^
    2 | import logo from './logo.svg';
    3 | import './App.css';
    4 |
```

Figure 2.14 – Error with React once Prettier has been installed

To resolve this, run the following command:

```
> npm install
```

Once the command has finished running, the problem will be resolved.

Some of the files may not be formatted as per our Prettier settings. Start the frontend by running the following command:

```
> npm start
```

Some errors will appear in the browser:

```
Failed to compile

src\reportWebVitals.ts
  Line 6:27:  Delete `··`   prettier/prettier
  Line 13:2:  Insert `;`    prettier/prettier

Search for the keywords to learn more about each error.
```

Figure 2.15 – Prettier error

To resolve these errors, simply go to each problem file and press *Ctrl + S* to save it. Each file will then be formatted as per our rules.

To quickly recap, we installed Prettier to automatically format our frontend code with the `eslint-config-prettier` and `eslint-plugin-prettier` packages to make it play nicely with ESLint. The formatting can be configured in a file called `.prettierrc`.

Summary

In this chapter, we created our projects for the Q&A app that we are going to build throughout this book. We created the backend using the Web API ASP.NET Core template and the frontend using Create React App. We included TypeScript so that our frontend code is strongly typed, which will help us catch problems earlier and help Visual Studio Code provide a better development experience.

We added linting to our frontend code to drive quality and consistency into our code base. ESLint is our linter and its rules are configured in a file called `.eslintrc.json`. We also added Prettier to our frontend code, which automatically formats our code. This is really helpful in code reviews. We then configured the formatting rules in a `.prettierrc` file and used `eslint-config-prettier` to stop ESLint conflicting with Prettier.

So, we now have two separate projects for the frontend and backend, unlike what we had with the SPA template. This makes sense, mainly because we'll be using Visual Studio to develop the backend and Visual Studio Code to develop the frontend. So, there isn't any need to start both the frontend and backend together from within Visual Studio.

In the next chapter, we are going to start building the frontend in React and TypeScript.

Questions

Have a go at answering the following questions to test what you have learned in this chapter:

1. What option from the `create-react-app` command did we use to create a React app with a TypeScript project?
2. What ESLint rule could we use to help prevent `console.log` statements being added to our code?
3. What setting in `.prettierrc` could we set to use single quotes in our code?
4. What setting in Visual Studio Code tells the ESLint extension to check React and TypeScript code?
5. What settings in Visual Studio tell it to use the Prettier extension to automatically format the code when it's saved?

Answers

1. We used the `--template typescript` option on the `create-react-app` command to create a React app with a TypeScript project.
2. We could use the `no-console` rule to prevent `console.log` statements being added to our code.
3. We can use the `"singleQuote": true` setting in `.prettierrc` to use single quotes in our code.
4. The **Eslint: Probe** setting in Visual Studio Code tells the ESLint extension to check React and TypeScript code if it contains `typescript` and `typescriptreact`.
5. **Default Formatter** must be set to **esbenp.prettier-vscode** and **Format on Save** must be ticked for Prettier to automatically format the code when it's saved.

Further reading

The following are some useful links for learning more about the topics that were covered in this chapter:

- **ASP.NET Core API controllers**: https://docs.microsoft.com/en-us/aspnet/core/web-api
- **npx**: https://www.npmjs.com/package/npx
- **Create React app**: https://create-react-app.dev/docs/getting-started
- **ESLint**: https://eslint.org/
- **Prettier**: https://prettier.io/

Section 2: Building a Frontend with React and TypeScript

In this section, we will build the frontend of our Q&A app using React and TypeScript. We will learn different approaches to styling, how to implement client-side routes, how to implement forms efficiently, and also how to manage complex state.

This section comprises the following chapters:

- *Chapter 3, Getting Started with React and TypeScript*
- *Chapter 4, Styling Components with Emotion*
- *Chapter 5, Routing with React Router*
- *Chapter 6, Working with Forms*
- *Chapter 7, Managing State with Redux*

3
Getting Started with React and TypeScript

In this chapter, we will start to build the Q&A React frontend with TypeScript by creating a function-based component that shows the home page in the app. This will show the most recent questions being asked in a list. As part of this, we'll take the time to understand strict mode and JSX. We'll then move on and create more components using props to pass data between them. At the end of the chapter, we'll start to understand component state and how it can make components interactive, along with events.

We'll cover the following topics in this chapter:

- Understanding JSX
- Understanding and enabling React Strict Mode
- Creating function-based components
- Implementing component props
- Implementing component state

Let's get started!

Technical requirements

We will need the following tools in this chapter:

- **Visual Studio Code**: We'll use this to edit our React code. This can be downloaded and installed from `https://code.visualstudio.com/`. If you already have this installed, make sure that it is at least version 1.52.
- **Node.js and npm**: These can be downloaded from `https://nodejs.org/`. If you already have these installed, make sure that Node.js is at least version 8.2 and that npm is at least version 5.2. Installation steps can be found at `https://treehouse.github.io/installation-guides/windows/node-windows.html`.
- **Babel REPL**: We'll use this online tool briefly to explore JSX. This can be found at `https://babeljs.io/repl`.
- **Q&A**: We'll start with the Q&A frontend starter project for this chapter. This is the project we finished in *Chapter 2, Creating Decoupled React and ASP.NET 5 Apps*, and provides an icon that we need for this chapter. This is available on GitHub at `https://github.com/PacktPublishing/ASP.NET-Core-5-and-React-Second-Edition` in the `chapter-03/start` folder.

All the code snippets in this chapter can be found online at `https://github.com/PacktPublishing/ASP.NET-Core-5-and-React-Second-Edition`. In order to restore code from a chapter, you can download the source code repository and open the relevant folder in the relevant editor. If the code is frontend code, then you can use `npm install` in the Terminal to restore the dependencies.

Check out the following video to see the code in action: `https://bit.ly/3mzfoSp`.

Understanding JSX

In this section, we're going to understand JSX, which we briefly touched on in *Chapter 1, Understanding the ASP.NET 5 React Template*. We already know that JSX isn't valid JavaScript and that we need a preprocessor step to convert it into JavaScript. We are going to use the Babel REPL to play with JSX to get an understanding of how it maps to JavaScript by carrying out the following steps:

1. Open a browser, go to `https://babeljs.io/repl`, and enter the following JSX in the left-hand pane:

   ```
   <span>Q and A</span>
   ```

The following appears in the right-hand pane, which is what our JSX has compiled down to:

```
React.createElement("span", null, "Q and A");
```

2. We can see that it compiles down to a call to `React.createElement`, which has three parameters:

- The element type, which can be an HTML tag name (such as `span`), a React component type, or a React fragment type.
- An object containing the properties to be applied to the element.
- The children of the element.

3. Let's expand our example by putting a `header` tag around our `span`:

```
<header><span>Q and A</span></header>
```

4. This compiles down to two calls with `React.createElement`, with `span` being passed in as a child to the `header` element that's created:

```
React.createElement(
  "header",
  null,
  React.createElement(
    "span",
    null,
    "Q and A"
  )
);
```

Note that the format of the code snippet will be slightly different to the format shown in the Babel REPL. The preceding snippet is more readable and allows us to clearly see the nested `React.createElement` statements.

5. Let's change the `span` tag to an anchor tag and add an `href` attribute:

```
<header><a href="/">Q and A</a></header>
```

6. In the compiled JavaScript, we can see that the nested `React.createElement` call has changed to have `"a"` passed in as the element type, along with a properties object containing `href` as the second parameter:

```
React.createElement(
  "header",
  null,
  React.createElement(
    "a",
    { href: "/" },
    "Q and A"
  )
);
```

7. This is starting to make sense, but so far, our JSX only contains HTML. Let's start to mix in some JavaScript. We'll do this by declaring and initializing a variable and referencing it inside the anchor tag:

```
var appName = "Q and A";
<header><a href="/">{appName}</a></header>
```

We can see that this compiles to the following with the JavaScript code:

```
var appName = "Q and A";
React.createElement(
  "header",
  null,
  React.createElement(
    "a",
    { href: "/" },
    appName
  )
);
```

So, the `appName` variable is declared in the first statement, exactly how we defined it, and is passed in as the children parameter in the nested `React.createElement` call.

8. The key point to note here is that we can inject JavaScript into HTML in JSX by using curly braces. To further illustrate this point, let's add the word `app` to the end of `appName`:

```
const appName = "Q and A";
<header><a href="/">{appName + " app"}</a></header>
```

This compiles down to the following:

```
var appName = "Q and A";
React.createElement(
  "header",
  null,
  React.createElement(
    "a",
    { href: "/" },
    appName + " app"
  )
);
```

So, JSX can be thought of as HTML with JavaScript mixed in using curly braces. This makes it incredibly powerful since regular JavaScript can be used to conditionally render elements, as well as render elements in a loop.

Now that we have an understanding of JSX, we are going to learn about React strict mode in the next section.

Understanding and enabling strict mode

React **strict mode** helps us write better React components by carrying out certain checks. This includes checks on class component *life cycle methods*.

React components can either be implemented using a class or a function. Class components have special methods called *life cycle methods* that can execute logic at certain times in the component's life cycle.

Strict mode checks that the life cycle methods will function correctly in React **concurrent mode**.

> **Important Note**
> React concurrent mode is a set of features that help React apps stay responsive, even when network speeds are slow. More information on concurrent mode can be found at `https://reactjs.org/docs/concurrent-mode-intro.html`.

Strict mode checks life cycle methods in third-party libraries, as well as the life cycle methods we have written. So, even if we build our app using function components, we may still get warnings about problematic life cycle methods.

Strict mode checks also warn about usage of old APIs, such as the old context API. We will learn about the recommended context API in *Chapter 12, Interacting with RESTful APIs*.

The last category of checks that strict mode performs are checks for unexpected side effects. Memory leaks and invalid application state are also covered in these checks.

> **Important Note**
> Strict mode checks only happen in development mode – they do not impact a production build.

Strict mode can be turned on by using a `StrictMode` component from React. Create React App has already enabled strict mode for the entirety of our app in `index.tsx`:

```
ReactDOM.render(
  <React.StrictMode>
    <App />
  </React.StrictMode>,
  document.getElementById('root')
);
```

The `StrictMode` component is wrapped around all the React components in the component tree that will be checked. So, the `StrictMode` component is usually placed right at the top of the component tree.

Let's temporarily add usage of an old API to `App.tsx`. If the frontend project isn't open in Visual Studio Code, open it and carry out the following steps:

1. Add the following code at the bottom of `App.tsx`:

   ```
   class ProblemComponent extends React.Component {
     render() {
       return <div ref="div" />;
     }
   }
   ```

   This is a class component that uses an old **refs** API in React. *Refs* is short for *references* but is more often referred to as refs within the React community. Don't worry about fully understanding the syntax of this component – the key point is that it uses an API, which isn't recommended.

> **Important Note**
> A React ref is a feature that allows us to access the DOM node. More information on React refs can be found at `https://reactjs.org/docs/refs-and-the-dom.html`.

2. Reference this component in the `App` component:

   ```
   <div className="App">
     <header className="App-header">
       <ProblemComponent />
       ...
     </header>
   </div>
   ```

3. Start the application by running the following command in the Terminal:

   ```
   npm start
   ```

4. Open the browser console; the following message will be displayed:

Figure 3.1 – Strict mode warning

Strict mode has output a warning to the console about an old API being used.

5. Remove `ProblemComponent` and the reference to it from `App.tsx`.

6. Press *Ctrl+C* and press *Y* when prompted to stop the app from running.

Now that we have a good understanding of strict mode, we are going to start creating the components for the home page in our app.

Creating function-based components

In this section, we are going to start by creating a component for the header of our app, which will contain our app name and the ability to search for questions. Then, we'll implement some components so that we can start to build the home page of the app, along with some mock data.

Creating a Header component

We can create a basic `Header` component and reference it within our `App` component by carrying out the following steps:

1. Create a new file called `Header.tsx` in the `src` folder.
2. Import `React` into the file with the following `import` statement:

   ```
   import React from 'react';
   ```

   We need to import `React` because, as we learned at the start of this chapter, JSX is transpiled into JavaScript `React.createElement` statements. So, without `React`, these statements will error out.

3. Our component is just going to render the word `header` initially. So, enter the following as our initial `Header` component:

   ```
   export const Header = () => <div>header</div>;
   ```

Congratulations! We have implemented our first function-based React component!

The preceding component is actually an arrow function that is set to the `Header` variable.

> **Important Note**
> An arrow function is an alternative function syntax that was introduced in ES6. The arrow function syntax is a little shorter than the original syntax and it also preserves the lexical scope of `this`. The function parameters are defined in parentheses and the code that the function executes follows a =>, which is often referred to as a fat arrow. More information can be found at https://developer.mozilla.org/en-US/docs/Web/JavaScript/Reference/Functions/Arrow_functions.

Notice that there are no curly braces or a `return` keyword. Instead, we just define the JSX that the function should return directly after the fat arrow. This is called an **implicit return**.

We use the `const` keyword to declare and initialize the `Header` variable.

> **Important Note**
>
> The const keyword can be used to declare and initialize a variable where its reference won't change later in the program. Alternatively, the let keyword can be used to declare a variable whose reference can change later in the program. More information can be found at https://developer.mozilla.org/en-US/docs/Web/JavaScript/Reference/Statements/const.

We can now use the Header component within the App component.

1. The export keyword allows the component to be used in other files. So, let's use this in our App component by importing it into App.tsx. Add the following import statement beneath the other import statements in App.tsx:

   ```
   import { Header } from './Header';
   ```

2. Now, we can reference the Header component in the App component's return statement. Let's replace the header tag that Create React App created for us with our Header component. Let's remove the redundant logo import as well:

   ```
   import React from 'react';
   import './App.css';
   import { Header } from './Header';

   function App() {
     return (
       <div className="App">
         <Header />
       </div>
     );
   };

   export default App;
   ```

3. In the Visual Studio Code Terminal, enter npm start to run the app. We'll see that the word **header** appears at the top of the page, centered like so:

Figure 3.2 – Header component

Congratulations again – we have just consumed our first React component!

So, the arrow function syntax is a really nice way of implementing function-based components. The implicit return feature reduces the number of characters we need to type in. We'll use arrow functions with implicit returns heavily throughout this book.

Adding elements to the Header component

We're going to work on the `Header` component a little more so that it eventually looks as follows:

Figure 3.3 – All the elements in the Header component

So, the `Header` component will contain the app name, which will be **Q & A**, a search input, and a **Sign In** link.

With the app still running, carry out the following steps to modify the `Header` component:

1. Add the app name inside an anchor tag inside the `div` tag by replacing the word `header`, which was previously used inside `div`:

   ```
   export const Header = () => (
     <div>
       <a href="./">Q & A</a>
     </div>
   );
   ```

   Notice that the implicit return statement containing the JSX is now in parentheses.

   > **Important Note**
   >
   > When an implicit return statement is on multiple lines, parentheses are required. When an implicit return is on just a single line, we can get away without the parentheses.
   >
   > Prettier automatically adds parentheses to an implicit return if they are needed, so we don't need to worry about remembering this rule.

2. Add an `input` to allow the user to perform a search:

   ```
   <div>
     <a href="./">Q & A</a>
     <input type="text" placeholder="Search..." />
   </div>
   ```

3. Add a link to allow users to sign in:

```
<div>
  <a href="./">Q & A</a>
  <input type="text" placeholder="Search..." />
  <a href="./signin"><span>Sign In</span></a>
</div>
```

4. The **Sign In** link needs a user icon next to it. We're going to use `user.svg` for this, which should already be in our project.

> **Important Note**
> `user.svg` was in the starter project for this chapter. You can download it from `https://github.com/PacktPublishing/NET-5-and-React-17---Second-Edition/blob/master/chapter-03/start/frontend/src/user.svg` if you didn't start this chapter with the start project.

5. We are going to create a component to host this icon, so create a file called `Icons.tsx` in the `src` folder and enter the following content into it:

```
import React from 'react';
import user from './user.svg';

export const UserIcon = () => (
  <img src={user} alt="User" width="12px" />
);
```

Here, we have created a component called `UserIcon` that renders an `img` tag, with the `src` attribute set to the `svg` file we imported from `user.svg`.

6. Let's go back to `Header.tsx` and import the icon component we just created:

```
import { UserIcon } from './Icons';
```

7. Now, we can place an instance of the `UserIcon` component in the `Header` component inside `button`, before `span`:

```
export const Header = () => (
  <div>
    <a href="./">Q & A</a>
    <input type="text" placeholder="Search..." />
    <a href="./signin">
      <UserIcon />
      <span>Sign In</span>
```

88 Getting Started with React and TypeScript

```
      </a>
    </div>
  );
```

8. Let's look at the header in the running app:

Figure 3.4 – Updated Header component

Our header doesn't look great, but we can see the elements in the `Header` component we just created. We'll style our `Header` component in the next chapter, *Chapter 4, Styling React Components with Emotion*.

Creating a HomePage component

Let's create another component to get more familiar with this process. This time, we'll create a component for the home page by carrying out the following steps:

1. Create a file called `HomePage.tsx` in the `src` folder with the following content:

```
import React from 'react';

export const HomePage = () => (
  <div>
    <div>
      <h2>Unanswered Questions</h2>
      <button>Ask a question</button>
    </div>
  </div>
);
```

Our home page simply consists of a title containing the text, **Unanswered Questions**, and a button to submit a question.

2. Open `App.tsx` and import our `HomePage` component:

```
import { HomePage } from './HomePage';
```

3. Now, we can add an instance of `HomePage` under the `Header` component in the `render` method:

```
<div className="App">
  <Header />
  <HomePage />
</div>
```

4. If we look at the running app, we'll see the title and button under the content of the `Header` component:

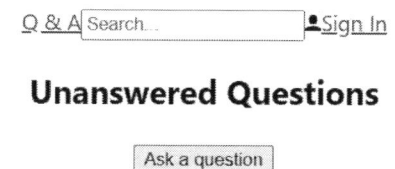

Figure 3.5 – Page title with the Ask a question button

We have made a good start on the `HomePage` component. In the next section, we will create some mock data that will be used within it.

Creating mock data

We desperately need some data so that we can develop our frontend. In this section, we'll create some mock data in our frontend. We will also create a function that components will call to get data. Eventually, this function will call our real ASP.NET Core backend. Follow these steps:

1. Create a new file in the `src` folder called `QuestionsData.ts` with the following interface:

```
export interface QuestionData {
  questionId: number;
  title: string;
  content: string;
  userName: string;
  created: Date;
}
```

Before moving on, let's understand the code we have just entered since we have just written some TypeScript.

> **Important Note**
>
> An **interface** is a type that defines the structure for an object, including all its properties and methods. Interfaces don't exist in JavaScript, so they are purely used by the TypeScript compiler during the type checking process. We create an interface with the `interface` keyword, followed by its name, followed by the properties and methods that make up the interface in curly braces. More information can be found at https://www.typescriptlang.org/docs/handbook/interfaces.html.

So, our interface is called `QuestionData` and it defines the structure of the questions we expect to be working with. We have exported the interface so that it can be used throughout our app when we interact with question data.

Notice what appear to be types after the property names in the interface. These are called **type annotations** and is a TypeScript feature that doesn't exist in JavaScript.

> **Important Note**
>
> **Type annotations** lets us declare variables, properties, and function parameters with specific types. This allows the TypeScript compiler to check that the code adheres to these types. In short, type annotations allow TypeScript to catch bugs where our code is using the wrong type much earlier than if we were writing our code in JavaScript.

Notice that we have specified that the `created` property has a `Date` type.

> **Important Note**
>
> The `Date` type is a special type in TypeScript that represents the `Date` JavaScript object. This `Date` object represents a single moment in time and is specified as the number of milliseconds since midnight on January 1, 1970, UTC. More information can be found at `https://developer.mozilla.org/en-US/docs/Web/JavaScript/Reference/Global_Objects/Date`.

2. Under `QuestionData`, let's create another interface for the structure of the answers we expect:

```
export interface AnswerData {
  answerId: number;
  content: string;
  userName: string;
  created: Date;
}
```

3. Now, we can adjust the `QuestionData` interface so that it includes an array of answers:

```
export interface QuestionData {
  questionId: number;
  title: string;
  content: string;
  userName: string;
  created: Date;
```

```
  answers: AnswerData[];
}
```

Notice the square brackets in the type annotation for the `answers` property.

> **Important Note**
> Square brackets after a type denote an array of the type. More information can be found at https://www.typescriptlang.org/docs/handbook/basic-types.html#array.

4. Let's create some mock questions below the interfaces. You can copy the code at https://github.com/PacktPublishing/NET-5-and-React-17---Second-Edition/blob/master/chapter-03/finish/frontend/src/QuestionsData.ts to save yourself typing it all out:

```
const questions: QuestionData[] = [
  {
    questionId: 1,
    title: 'Why should I learn TypeScript?',
    content:
      'TypeScript seems to be getting popular so I
        wondered whether it is worth my time learning
        it? What benefits does it give
          over JavaScript?',
    userName: 'Bob',
    created: new Date(),
    answers: [
      {
        answerId: 1,
        content: 'To catch problems earlier speeding
         up your developments',

        userName: 'Jane',
        created: new Date(),
      },
      {
        answerId: 2,
        content:
          'So, that you can use the JavaScript
            features of tomorrow, today',

        userName: 'Fred',
        created: new Date(),
      },
```

```
    ],
  },
  {
    questionId: 2,
    title: 'Which state management tool should
    I use?',
    content:
      'There seem to be a fair few state management
        tools around for React - React, Unstated, ...
        Which one should I use?',
    userName: 'Bob',
    created: new Date(),
    answers: [],
  },
];
```

Notice that we typed out our `questions` variable, which contains the array of the `QuestionData` interface we have just created. If we miss a property out or misspell it, the TypeScript compiler will complain.

5. Let's create a function that returns unanswered questions:

```
export const getUnansweredQuestions = (): QuestionData[]
=> {
  return questions.filter(q => q.answers.length ===
    0);
};
```

This function returns the question array items we have just created, which contains no answers, by making use of the `array.filter` method.

> **Important Note**
>
> The `array.filter` method in an array executes the function that was passed into it for each array item, and then creates a new array with all the elements that return truthy from the function. A truthy value is any value other than `false`, `0`, `""`, `null`, `undefined`, or NaN. More information can be found at https://developer.mozilla.org/en-US/docs/Web/JavaScript/Reference/Global_Objects/Array/filter.

Notice that we defined the return type, `QuestionData[]`, for the function after the function parameters.

In the next section, we are going to use the `getUnansweredQuestions` function to provide the home page with data.

Implementing component props

Components can have properties that allow consumers to pass parameters into them, just like when we pass parameters into a JavaScript function. React function components accept a single parameter named `props`, which holds its properties. The word **props** is short for properties.

In this section, we'll learn all about how to implement strongly typed props, including optional and default props. Then, we'll implement the rest of the home page to assist in our learning.

Creating HomePage child components

We are going to implement some child components that the `HomePage` component will use. We will pass the unanswered questions data to the child components via props.

Creating the QuestionList component

Let's go through the following steps to implement the `QuestionList` component:

1. Let's create a file called `QuestionList.tsx` in the `src` folder and add the following `import` statements:

   ```
   import React from 'react';
   import { QuestionData } from './QuestionsData';
   ```

2. Now, let's define the interface for the component props underneath the `import` statements:

   ```
   interface Props {
     data: QuestionData[];
   }
   ```

   We have called the props interface `Props` and it contains a single property to hold an array of questions.

3. Let's start by implementing the `QuestionList` component:

   ```
   export const QuestionList = (props: Props) => <ul></ul>;
   ```

Notice the parameter, `props`, in the function component. We have given it a `Props` type with a type annotation. This means we can pass a `data` prop into `QuestionList` when we reference it in JSX.

4. Now, we can inject the data into the list:

```
export const QuestionList = (props: Props) => (
  <ul>
    {props.data.map((question) => (
      <li key={question.questionId}>
      </li>
    ))}
  </ul>
);
```

We are using the `map` method within the `data` array to iterate through the data that's been passed into the component.

> **Important Note**
>
> `map` is a standard method that is available in a JavaScript array. The method iterates through the items in the array, invoking the function that's passed into it for each array item. The function is expected to return an item that will form a new array. In summary, it is a way of *mapping* an array to a new array. More information can be found at https://developer.mozilla.org/en-US/docs/Web/JavaScript/Reference/Global_Objects/Array/map.

So, we iterate through the questions that are passed into `QuestionList` and render a `li` HTML element for each array item.

Notice the `key` prop we pass into the `li` element.

> **Important Note**
>
> The `key` prop helps React detect when the element changes or is added or removed. When we output content in a loop, in React, it is good practice to apply this prop and set it to a unique value within the loop. This helps React distinguish it from the other elements during the rendering process. If we don't provide a key prop, React will make unnecessary changes to the DOM that can impact performance. More information can be found at https://reactjs.org/docs/lists-and-keys.html.

5. Our `QuestionList` component will work perfectly fine, but we are going to make one small change that will make the implementation a little more succinct. Here, we are going to destructure the props into a `data` variable in the function parameter:

```
export const QuestionList = ({ data }: Props) => (
  <ul>
    {data.map((question) => (
      <li key={question.questionId} >
      </li>
    ))}
  </ul>
);
```

> **Important Note**
> **Destructuring** is a special syntax that allows us to unpack objects or arrays into variables. More information on destructuring can be found at https://developer.mozilla.org/en-US/docs/Web/JavaScript/Reference/Operators/Destructuring_assignment.

Notice that we directly reference the data variable in the JSX and not through the props variable, like we did in the previous example. This is a nice pattern to use, particularly when there are more props.

Before we can complete the `QuestionList` component, we must create its child component, `Question`, which we'll do next.

Creating the Question component

Follow these steps to implement the `Question` component:

1. Create a file called `Question.tsx` in the `src` folder, which contains the following `import` statements:

    ```
    import React from 'react';
    import { QuestionData } from './QuestionsData';
    ```

2. Let's create the props type for the `Question` component, which will simply contain a prop for the question data:

    ```
    interface Props {
      data: QuestionData;
    }
    ```

3. Now, we can create the component:

```
export const Question = ({ data }: Props) => (
  <div>
    <div>
      {data.title}
    </div>
    <div>
      {`Asked by ${data.userName} on
        ${data.created.toLocaleDateString()} ${data.
        created.toLocaleTimeString()}`}
    </div>
  </div>
);
```

So, we are rendering the question title, who asked the question, and when it was asked.

Notice that we are using
the `toLocaleDateString` and `toLocaleTimeString` functions on the `data.created` Date object to output when the question was asked.

> **Important Note**
>
> Dates are often displayed in different formats in different countries. For example, February 1, 2021 can be displayed as 02/01/21 or 01/02/21 in different countries. `toLocaleDateString` and `toLocaleTimeString` are methods on the `Date` object that format the date and time according to the browser's locale. More information can be found at https://developer.mozilla.org/en-US/docs/Web/JavaScript/Reference/Global_Objects/Date/toLocaleDateString and https://developer.mozilla.org/en-US/docs/Web/JavaScript/Reference/Global_Objects/Date/toLocaleTimeString.

That completes our `Question` component nicely.

Wiring up the components

Now, we can wire up the components we have just created using our props so that we get the unanswered questions rendered on the home page. Follow these steps to do so:

1. Let's go back to `QuestionList.tsx` and import the `Question` component we just created:

```
import { Question } from './Question';
```

2. Now, we can place an instance of the `Question` component inside the `QuestionList` JSX that's nested within the `li` element:

```
{data.map((question) => (
  <li key={question.questionId}>
    <Question data={question} />
  </li>
))}
```

3. Moving on to the `HomePage` component in `HomePage.tsx`, let's import the `QuestionList` component. Let's also import the `getUnansweredQuestions` function we created earlier, which returns unanswered questions:

```
import { QuestionList } from './QuestionList';
import { getUnansweredQuestions } from './QuestionsData';
```

4. Now, we can place an instance of `QuestionList` inside the `HomePage` component JSX, inside the outermost `div` tag:

```
<div>
  <div>
    <h2>Unanswered Questions</h2>
    <button>Ask a question</button>
  </div>
  <QuestionList data={getUnansweredQuestions()} />
</div>
```

Notice that we pass the array of questions into the `data` prop by calling the `getUnansweredQuestions` function we created and imported earlier in this chapter.

5. If we look at the running app now, we'll see one unanswered question output:

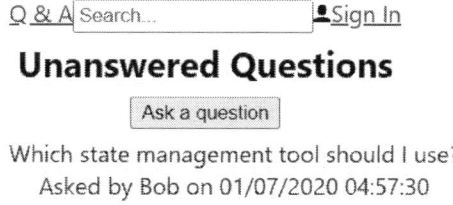

Figure 3.6 – Unanswered questions

If we had more than one unanswered question in our mock data, they would be the output on our home page.

We are going to finish this section on props by understanding optional and default props, which can make our components more flexible for consumers.

Optional and default props

A prop can be optional so that the consumer doesn't necessarily have to pass it into a component. For example, we could have an optional prop in the `Question` component that allows a consumer to change whether the content of the question is rendered or not. We'll do this now:

1. We need to add the content to the `Question` component, so add the following code beneath the question title in the JSX:

```
export const Question = ({ data }: Props) => (
  <div>
    <div>
      {data.title}
    </div>
    <div>
      {data.content.length > 50
        ? `${data.content.substring(0, 50)}...`
        : data.content}
    </div>
    <div>
      {`Asked by ${data.userName} on
        ${data.created.toLocaleDateString()} ${data.
        created.toLocaleTimeString()}`}
    </div>
  </div>
);
```

Here, we have used a JavaScript **ternary operator** to truncate the content if it is longer than 50 characters.

> **Important Note**
>
> A JavaScript ternary is a short way of implementing a conditional statement that results in one of two branches of logic being executed. The statement contains three operands separated by a question mark (?) and a colon (:). The first operand is a condition, the second is what is returned if the condition is `true`, and the third is what is returned if the condition is `false`. The ternary operator is a popular way of implementing conditional logic in JSX. More information can be found at https://developer.mozilla.org/en-US/docs/Web/JavaScript/Reference/Operators/Conditional_Operator.

We have also used **template literals** and **interopolation** in this code snippet.

> **Important Note**
>
> JavaScript template literals are strings contained in backticks (`` ` ``). A template literal can include expressions that inject data into the string. Expressions are contained in curly brackets after a dollar sign. This is often referred to as *interpolation*. More information can be found at https://developer.mozilla.org/en-US/docs/Web/JavaScript/Reference/Template_literals.

2. Create an additional property in the `Props` interface in `Question.tsx` to represent whether the question's content is shown:

```tsx
interface Props {
  data: QuestionData;
  showContent: boolean;
}
```

3. Let's destructure the `showContent` prop in the `Question` component parameter:

```tsx
export const Question = ({ data, showContent }: Props) =>
```

4. Let's change where we render the question content to the following:

```tsx
<div>
  {data.title}
</div>
{showContent && (
  <div>
    {data.content.length > 50
      ? `${data.content.substring(0, 50)}...`
      : data.content}
  </div>
```

```
  )}
  <div>
    {`Asked by ${data.userName} on
      ${data.created.toLocaleDateString()} ${data.created.
        toLocaleTimeString()}`}
  </div>
```

We have just changed the component so that it only renders the question's content if the `showContent` prop is `true` using the short-circuit operator, `&&`.

> **Important Note**
>
> The short-circuit operator (`&&`) is another way of expressing conditional logic. It has two operands, with the first being the condition and the second being the logic to execute if the condition evaluates to `true`. It is often used in JSX to conditionally render an element if the condition is `true`.

5. If we go back to `QuestionList.tsx`, we'll see a TypeScript compilation error where the `Question` component is referenced:

```
(alias) const Question: ({ data, showContent }: Props) => JSX.Element
import Question

Property 'showContent' is missing in type '{ data: QuestionData; }' but required in type
'Props'. ts(2741)

Question.tsx(6, 3): 'showContent' is declared here.

Peek Problem   No quick fixes available
<Question data={question} />
```

Figure 3.7 – TypeScript compilation error on the Question component

This is because `showContent` is a required prop in the `Question` component and we haven't passed it in. It can be a pain to always have to update consuming components when a prop is added. Couldn't `showContent` just default to `false` if we don't pass it in? Well, this is exactly what we are going to do next.

6. Move back into `Question.tsx` and make the `showContent` prop optional by adding a question mark after the name of the prop in the interface:

```
interface Props {
  data: QuestionData;
  showContent?: boolean;
}
```

> **Important Note**
> Optional properties are actually a TypeScript feature. Function parameters can also be made optional by putting a question mark at the end of the parameter name before the type annotation; for example, (`duration?:number`).

Now, the compilation error in `QuestionList.tsx` has gone away and the app will render the unanswered questions without their content.

What if we wanted to show the question's content by default and allow consumers to suppress this if required? We'll do just this using two different approaches to default props.

7. We can set a special object literal called `defaultProps` on the component to define the default values:

```
export const Question = ({ data, showContent }: Props) =>
(
  ...
);
Question.defaultProps = {
  showContent: true,
};
```

If we look at the running app, we'll see the question content being rendered as expected:

Unanswered Questions

Ask a question

Which state management tool should I use?
There seem to be a fair few state management tools...
Asked by Bob on 01/07/2020 05:24:54

Figure 3.8 – Unanswered questions with content

8. There is another way of setting default props that's arguably neater. Let's remove the `defaultProps` object literal and specify the default after the destructured component's `showContent` parameter:

```
export const Question = ({ data, showContent = true }:
Props) => ( ... )
```

This arguably makes the code more readable because the default is right next to its parameter. This means our eyes don't need to scan right down to the bottom of the function to see that there is a default value for a parameter.

So, our home page is looking good in terms of code structure. However, there are a couple of components in `HomePage.tsx` that can be extracted so that we can reuse them as we develop the rest of the app. We'll do this next.

Children prop

The `children` prop is a magical prop that all React components automatically have. It can be used to render child elements. It's magical because it's automatically there, without us having to do anything, as well as being extremely powerful. In the following steps, we'll use the `children` prop when creating `Page` and `PageTitle` components:

1. First, let's create a file called `PageTitle.tsx` in the `src` folder with the following content:

   ```
   import React from 'react';

   interface Props {
     children: React.ReactNode;
   }
   export const PageTitle = ({
     children,
   }: Props) => <h2>{children}</h2>;
   ```

   We define the `children` prop with a type annotation of `ReactNode`. This will allow us to use a wide range of child elements, such as other React components and plain text.

   We have referenced the `children` prop inside the `h2` element. This means that the child elements that consuming components specify will be placed inside the `h2` element.

2. Let's create a file called `Page.tsx` with the following content:

   ```
   import React from 'react';
   import { PageTitle } from './PageTitle';

   interface Props {
     title?: string;
     children: React.ReactNode;
   }
   export const Page = ({ title, children }: Props) => (
     <div>
       {title && <PageTitle>{title}</PageTitle>}
       {children}
     </div>
   );
   ```

Here, the component takes in an optional `title` prop and renders this inside the `PageTitle` component.

The component also takes in a `children` prop. In the consuming component, the content nested within the `Page` component will be rendered where we have just placed the `children` prop.

3. Let's move back to `HomePage.tsx` now and import the `Page` and `PageTitle` components:

    ```
    import { Page } from './Page';
    import { PageTitle } from './PageTitle';
    ```

4. Let's use the `Page` and `PageTitle` components in the `HomePage` component, as follows:

    ```
    export const HomePage = () => (
      <Page>
        <div>
          <PageTitle>Unanswered Questions</PageTitle>
          <button>Ask a question</button>
        </div>
        <QuestionList data={getUnansweredQuestions()} />
      </Page>
    );
    ```

Notice that we aren't taking advantage of the `title` prop in the `Page` component in `HomePage`. This is because this page needs to have the **Ask a question** button to the right of the title, so we are rendering this within `HomePage`. However, other pages that we implement will take advantage of the `title` prop we have implemented.

So, the `children` prop allows a consumer to render custom content within the component. This gives the component flexibility and makes it highly reusable, as we'll discover when we use the `Page` component throughout our app. Something you may not know, however, is that the `children` prop is actually a function prop. We'll learn about function props in the next section.

Function props

Props can consist of primitive types, such as the `boolean showContent` prop we implemented in the `Question` component. Props can also be objects and arrays, as we have seen with the `Question` and `QuestionList` components. This in itself is powerful. However, props can also be functions, which allows us to implement components that are extremely flexible.

Using the following steps, we are going to implement a function prop on the `QuestionList` component that allows the consumer to render the question as an alternative to `QuestionList` rendering it:

1. In `QuestionList.tsx`, add a `renderItem` function prop to the `Props` interface, as follows:

   ```
   interface Props {
     data: QuestionData[];
     renderItem?: (item: QuestionData) => JSX.Element;
   }
   ```

2. So, the `renderItem` prop is a function that takes in a parameter containing the question and returns a JSX element. Notice that we have made this an optional prop so that our app will continue to run just as it was previously.

3. Let's destructure the function parameters into a `renderItem` variable:

   ```
   export const QuestionList = ({ data, renderItem }: Props) => ...
   ```

4. Now, we can call the `renderItem` function prop in the JSX if it has been passed and, if not, render the `Question` component:

   ```
   {data.map((question) => (
     <li key={question.questionId} >
       {renderItem ? renderItem(question) : <Question
         data={question} />}
     </li>
   ))}
   ```

5. Notice that we are using `renderItem` in the ternary condition, even though it isn't a boolean.

> **Important Note**
>
> Conditions in `if` statements and ternaries will execute the second operand if the condition evaluates to **truthy**, and the third operand if the condition evaluates to **falsy**. `true` is only one of many truthy values. In fact, `false`, `0`, `""`, `null`, `undefined`, and `NaN` are falsy values and everything else is truthy.

So, `renderItem` will be truthy and will execute if it has been passed as a prop.

6. Our app will render the unanswered questions, just like it did previously, by rendering the `Question` component. Let's try our `renderItem` prop out by opening `HomePage.tsx` and setting this to the following in the `QuestionList` element:

```
<QuestionList
  data={getUnansweredQuestions()}
  renderItem={(question) => <div>{question.title}</div>}
/>
```

If we look at the running app, we'll see this effect:

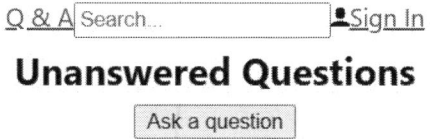

Figure 3.9 – Custom rendered question

> **Important Note**
>
> The pattern of implementing a function prop to allow consumers to render an internal piece of the component is often referred to as a **render prop**. It makes the component extremely flexible and useable in many different scenarios.

7. Now that we understand what a render prop is, we are going to revert this change and have `QuestionList` take back control of rendering the questions. So, remove the following highlighted line from the JSX:

```
<QuestionList
  data={getUnansweredQuestions()}
  renderItem={(question) => <div>{question.title}</div>}
/>
```

We can already see that function props are extremely powerful. We'll use these again when we cover handling events later in this chapter. Before we look at events, however, we are going to cover another fundamental part of a component, which is state.

Implementing component state

Components can use what is called **state** to have the component re-render when a variable in the component changes. This is crucial for implementing interactive components. For example, when filling out a form, if there is a problem with a field value, we can use state to render information about that problem. State can also be used to implement behavior when external things interact with a component, such as a web API. We are going to do this in this section after changing the `getUnansweredQuestions` function in order to simulate a web API call.

Changing getUnansweredQuestions so that it's asynchronous

The `getUnansweredQuestions` function doesn't simulate a web API call very well because it isn't asynchronous. In this section, we are going to change this. Follow these steps to do so:

1. Open `QuestionsData.ts` and create an asynchronous `wait` function that we can use in our `getUnansweredQuestions` function:

   ```
   const wait = (ms: number): Promise<void> => {
     return new Promise(resolve => setTimeout(resolve, ms));
   };
   ```

   This function will wait asynchronously for the number of milliseconds we pass into it. The function uses the native JavaScript `setTimeout` function internally so that it returns after the specified number of milliseconds. Notice that the function returns a `Promise` object.

   > **Important Note**
   >
   > A **promise** is a JavaScript object that represents the eventual completion (or failure) of an asynchronous operation and its resulting value.
   > The `Promise` type in TypeScript is like the `Task` type in .NET. More information can be found at `https://developer.mozilla.org/en-US/docs/Web/JavaScript/Reference/Global_Objects/Promise`.

Notice `<void>` after the `Promise` type in the return type annotation. Angle brackets after a TypeScript type indicate that this is a generic type.

> **Important Note**
>
> **Generic types** are a mechanism for allowing the consumer's own type to be used in the internal implementation of the generic type. The angle brackets allow the consumer type to be passed in as a parameter. Generics in TypeScript is very much like generics in .NET. More information can be found at https://www.typescriptlang.org/docs/handbook/generics.html.

We are passing a `void` type into the generic `Promise` type. But what is the `void` type?

The `void` type is another TypeScript-specific type that is used to represent a non-returning function. So, `void` in TypeScript is like `void` in .NET.

2. Now, we can use the `wait` function in our `getUnansweredQuestions` function to wait half a second:

```
export const getUnansweredQuestions = async ():
Promise<QuestionData[]> => {
  await wait(500);
  return questions.filter(q => q.answers.length ===
    0);
};
```

Notice the `await` keyword before the call to the `wait` function and the `async` keyword before the function signature.

`async` and `await` are two JavaScript keywords we can use to make asynchronous code read almost identically to synchronous code. `await` stops the next line from executing until the asynchronous statement has completed, while `async` simply indicates that the function contains asynchronous statements. So, these keywords are very much like `async` and `await` in .NET.

We return `Promise<QuestionData[]>` rather than `QuestionData[]` because the function doesn't return the questions straight away. Instead, it returns the questions eventually.

3. So, the `getUnansweredQuestions` function is now asynchronous. If we open `HomePage.tsx`, which is where this function is consumed, we'll see a compilation error:

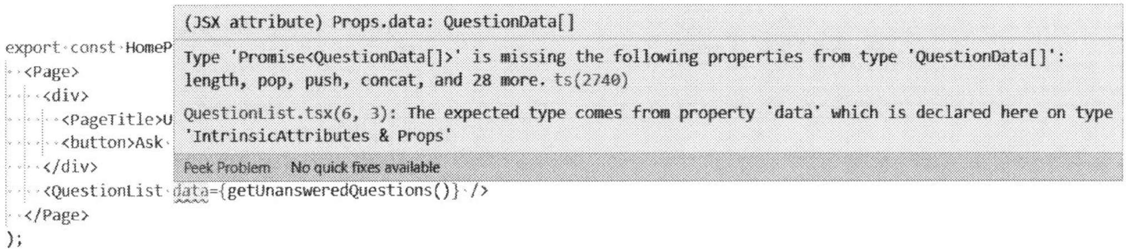

```
export const HomeP
  <Page>
    <div>
      <PageTitle>U
      <button>Ask
    </div>
    <QuestionList data={getUnansweredQuestions()} />
  </Page>
);
```

(JSX attribute) Props.data: QuestionData[]
Type 'Promise<QuestionData[]>' is missing the following properties from type 'QuestionData[]': length, pop, push, concat, and 28 more. ts(2740)
QuestionList.tsx(6, 3): The expected type comes from property 'data' which is declared here on type 'IntrinsicAttributes & Props'
Peek Problem   No quick fixes available

Figure 3.10 – Type error on the data prop

This is because the return type of the function has changed and no longer matches what we defined in the `QuestionList` props interface.

4. For now, let's comment the instance of `QuestionList` out so that our app compiles:

```
{/* <QuestionList data={getUnansweredQuestions()} /> */}
```

> **Important Note**
> Lines of code can be commented out in Visual Studio Code by highlighting the lines and pressing *Ctrl + /* (forward slash).

Eventually, we're going to change `HomePage` so that we can store the questions in the local state and then use this value in the local state to pass to `QuestionList`. To do this, we need to invoke `getUnansweredQuestions` when the component is first rendered and set the value that's returned to state. We'll do this in the next section.

Using useEffect to execute logic

So, how do we execute logic when a function-based component is rendered? Well, we can use a `useEffect` hook in React, which is what we are going to do in the following steps:

1. We need to change `HomePage` so that it has an explicit `return` statement since we want to write some JavaScript logic in the component, as well as return JSX:

```
export const HomePage = () => {
  return (
    <Page>
      ...
    </Page>
```

```
    );
};
```

2. Now, we can call the `useEffect` hook before we return the JSX:

```
export const HomePage = () => {
  React.useEffect(() => {
    console.log('first rendered');
  }, []);
  return (
    ...
  );
};
```

> **Important Note**
>
> The `useEffect` hook is a function that allows a side effect, such as fetching data, to be performed in a component. The function takes in two parameters, with the first parameter being a function to execute. The second parameter determines when the function in the first parameter should be executed. This is defined in an array of variables that, if changed, results in the first parameter function being executed. If the array is empty, then the function is only executed once the component has been rendered for the first time. More information can be found at https://reactjs.org/docs/hooks-effect.html.

So, we output **first rendered** into the console when the `HomePage` component is first rendered.

3. In the running app, let's open the browser developer tools and inspect the console:

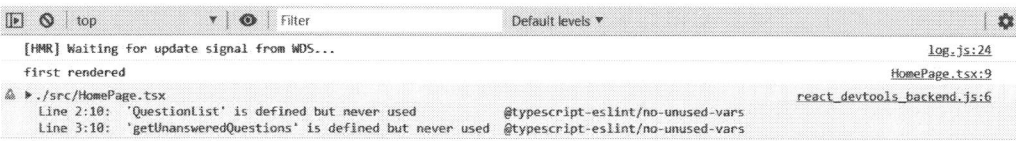

Figure 3.11 – useEffect being executed

So, our code is executed when the component is first rendered, which is great.

Note that we shouldn't worry about the ESLint warnings about the unused `QuestionList` component and the `getUnansweredQuestions` variable. This is because these will be used when we uncomment the reference to the `QuestionList` component.

Using useState to implement component state

The time has come to implement state in the `HomePage` component so that we can store any unanswered questions. But how do we do this in function-based components? Well, the answer is to use another React hook called `useState`. Follow the steps listed in `HomePage.tsx` to do this:

1. Add the `QuestionData` interface to the `QuestionsData` import:

    ```
    import {
      getUnansweredQuestions,
      QuestionData
    } from './QuestionsData';
    ```

2. We'll use this hook just above the `useEffect` statement in the `HomePage` component to declare the state variable:

    ```
    const [
      questions,
      setQuestions,
    ] = React.useState<QuestionData[]>([]);

    React.useEffect(() => {
      console.log('first rendered');
    }, []);
    ```

> **Important Note**
>
> The `useState` function returns an array containing the state variable in the first element and a function to set the state in the second element. The initial value of the state variable is passed into the function as a parameter. The TypeScript type for the state variable can be passed to the function as a generic type parameter. More information can be found at https://reactjs.org/docs/hooks-state.html.

Notice that we have destructured the array that's returned from `useState` into a state variable called `questions`, which is initially an empty array, and a function to set the state called `setQuestions`. We can destructure arrays to unpack their contents, just like we did previously with objects.

So, the type of the `questions` state variable is an array of `QuestionData`.

3. Let's add a second piece of state called `questionsLoading` to indicate whether the questions are being fetched:

```
const [
  questions,
  setQuestions,
] = React.useState<QuestionData[]>([]);
const [
  questionsLoading,
  setQuestionsLoading,
] = React.useState(true);
```

We have initialized this state to `true` because the questions are being fetched immediately in the first rendering cycle. Notice that we haven't passed a type into the generic parameter. This is because, in this case, TypeScript can cleverly infer that this is a `boolean` state from the default value, `true`, that we passed into the `useState` parameter.

4. Now, we need to set these pieces of state when we fetch the unanswered questions. First, we need to call the `getUnansweredQuestions` function asynchronously in the `useEffect` hook. Let's add this and remove the `console.log` statement:

```
React.useEffect(() => {
  const questions = await getUnansweredQuestions();
}, []);
```

We immediately get a compilation error:

```
'await' expression is only allowed within an async function. ts(1308)
HomePage.tsx(24, 19): Did you mean to mark this function as 'async'?
React.useEffect(() =  Peek Problem   Quick Fix...
  const questions = await getUnansweredQuestions();
}, []);
```

Figure 3.12 – useEffect error

5. This error has occurred because the `useEffect` function callback isn't flagged as `async`. So, let's try to make it `async`:

```
React.useEffect(async () => {
  const questions = await getUnansweredQuestions();
}, []);
```

6. Unfortunately, we get another error:

```
Argument of type '() => Promise<void>' is not assignable to parameter of type 'EffectCallback'.
  Type 'Promise<void>' is not assignable to type 'void | (() => void | undefined)'.
    Type 'Promise<void>' is not assignable to type '() => void | undefined'.
      Type 'Promise<void>' provides no match for the signature '(): void | undefined'. ts(2345)
Effect callbacks are synchronous to prevent race conditions. Put the async function inside:

useEffect(() => {
  async function fetchData() {
    // You can await here
    const response = await MyAPI.getData(someId);
    // ...
  }
  fetchData();
React.useEffect(async () => {
  const questions = await getUnansweredQuestions();
}, []);
```

Figure 3.13 – Another useEffect error

Unfortunately, we can't specify an asynchronous callback in the `useEffect` parameter.

7. The error message guides us to a solution. We can create a function that calls `getUnansweredQuestions` asynchronously and call this function within the `useEffect` callback function:

```
React.useEffect(() => {
  const doGetUnansweredQuestions = async () => {
    const unansweredQuestions = await
    getUnansweredQuestions();
  };
  doGetUnansweredQuestions();
}, []);
```

8. Now, we need to set the `questions` and `questionsLoading` states once we have retrieved the data:

```
useEffect(() => {
  const doGetUnansweredQuestions = async () => {
    const unansweredQuestions = await
     getUnansweredQuestions();
    setQuestions(unansweredQuestions);
    setQuestionsLoading(false);
  };
  doGetUnansweredQuestions();
}, []);
```

9. In the `HomePage` JSX, we can uncomment the `QuestionList` reference and pass in our `question` state:

   ```
   <Page>
     <div ... >
       ...
     </div>
     <QuestionList data={questions} />
   </Page>
   ```

   If we look at the running app, we'll see that the questions are being rendered nicely again.

10. We haven't made use of the `questionsLoading` state yet. So, let's change the `HomePage` JSX to the following:

    ```
    <Page>
      <div>
        ...
      </div>
      {questionsLoading ? (
         <div>Loading...</div>
      ) : (
         <QuestionList data={questions || []} />
      )}
    </Page>
    ```

    Here, we are rendering a **Loading...** message while the questions are being fetched. Our home page will render nicely again in the running app, and we should see a **Loading...** message while the questions are being fetched.

11. Before we move on, let's take some time to understand when components are re-rendered. Still in `HomePage.tsx`, let's add a `console.log` statement before the `return` statement and comment out `useEffect`:

    ```
    // React.useEffect(() => {
    //   ...
    // }, []);

    console.log('rendered');
    return ...
    ```

114   Getting Started with React and TypeScript

Every time the `HomePage` component is rendered, we'll see a rendered message in the console:

```
[HMR] Waiting for update signal from WDS...      log.js:24
rendered                                         HomePage.tsx:28
rendered                                         HomePage.tsx:28
```

Figure 3.14 – Rendered twice with no state changes

So, the component is rendered twice when no state is set.

In development mode, components are rendered twice if in strict mode and if the component contains state. This is so that React can detect unexpected side effects.

12. Comment `useEffect` back in but leave one of the state setter functions commented out:

```
React.useEffect(() => {
  const doGetUnansweredQuestions = async () => {
    const unansweredQuestions = await
    getUnansweredQuestions();
    setQuestions(unansweredQuestions);
    // setQuestionsLoading(false);
  };
  doGetUnansweredQuestions();
}, []);
```

The component is rendered four times:

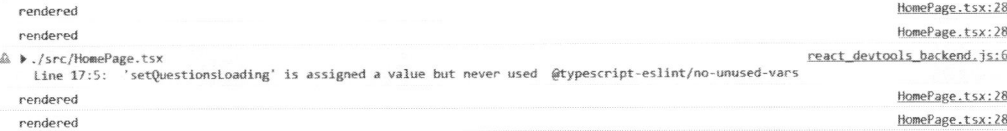

Figure 3.15 – Rendered four times with a state change

React renders a component when state is changed and because we are in strict mode, we get a double render.

We get a double render when the component first loads and a double render after the state change. So, we get four renders in total.

13. Comment the other state setter back in:

```
React.useEffect(() => {
  const doGetUnansweredQuestions = async () => {
    const unansweredQuestions = await
     getUnansweredQuestions();
    setQuestions(unansweredQuestions);
```

```
    setQuestionsLoading(false);
  };
  doGetUnansweredQuestions();
}, []);
```

The component is rendered six times:

rendered	HomePage.tsx:28
rendered	HomePage.tsx:28
rendered	HomePage.tsx:28
rendered	HomePage.tsx:28
rendered	HomePage.tsx:28
rendered	HomePage.tsx:28

Figure 3.16 – Rendered six times when two pieces of state are changed

14. Let's remove the `console.log` statement before continuing.

So, we are starting to understand how we can use state to control what is rendered when external things such as users or a web API interact with components. A key point that we need to take away is that when we change state in a component, React will automatically re-render the component.

> **Important Note**
>
> The `HomePage` component is what is called a **container** component, with `QuestionList` and `Question` being **presentational** components. Container components are responsible for how things work, fetching any data from a web API, and managing state. Presentational components are responsible for how things look. Presentational components receive data via their props, and also have property event handlers so that their containers can manage user interactions.

Structuring a React app into a container and presentational components often allows presentation components to be used in different scenarios. Later in this book, we'll see that we can easily reuse `QuestionList` on other pages in our app.

In the next section, we are going to learn how to implement logic when users interact with components using events.

Handling events

JavaScript events are invoked when a user interacts with a web app. For example, when a user clicks a button, a `click` event will be raised from that button. We can implement a JavaScript function to execute some logic when the event is raised. This function is often referred to as an **event listener**.

> **Important Note**
>
> In JavaScript, event listeners are attached to an element using its `addEventListener` method and removed using its `removeEventListener` method.

React allows us to declaratively attach events in JSX using function props, without the need to use `addEventListener` and `removeEventListener`. In this section, we are going to implement a couple of event listeners in React.

Handling a button click event

In this section, we are going to implement an event listener on the **Ask a question** button in the `HomePage` component. Follow these steps to do so:

1. Open `HomePage.tsx` and add a `click` event listener to the `button` element in the JSX:

   ```
   <button onClick={handleAskQuestionClick}>
     Ask a question
   </button>
   ```

   > **Important Note**
   >
   > Event listeners in JSX can be attached using a function prop that is named with `on` before the native JavaScript event name in camel case. So, a native `click` event can be attached using an `onClick` function prop. React will automatically remove the event listener for us before the element is destroyed.

2. Let's implement the `handleAskQuestionClick` function, just above the `return` statement in the `HomePage` component:

```
const handleAskQuestionClick = () => {
  console.log('TODO - move to the AskPage');
};

return ...
```

3. If we click on the **Ask a question** button in the running app, we'll see the following message in the console:

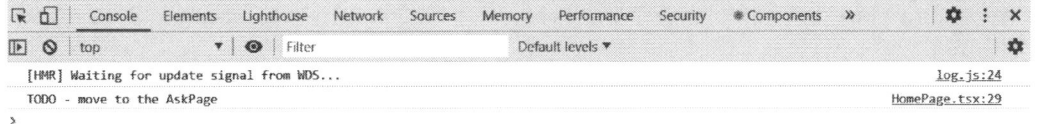

Figure 3.17 – Click event

So, handling events in React is super easy! In *Chapter 5, Routing with React Router*, we'll finish off the implementation of the `handleAskQuestionClick` function and navigate to the page where a question can be asked.

Handling an input change event

In this section, we are going to handle the `change` event on the `input` element and interact with the event parameter in the event listener. Follow these steps to do so:

1. Open `Header.tsx` and add a `change` event listener to the `input` element in the JSX:

```
<input
  type="text"
  placeholder="Search..."
  onChange={handleSearchInputChange}
/>
```

2. Let's change the `Header` component so that it has an explicit `return` statement and implement the `handleSearchInputChange` function just above it:

```
export const Header = () => {
  const handleSearchInputChange = (
    e: React.ChangeEvent<HTMLInputElement>
  ) => {
    console.log(e.currentTarget.value);
  };
  return ( ... );
};
```

3. Notice the type annotation, `React.ChangeEvent<HTMLInputElement>`, for the event parameter. This ensures the interactions with the event parameter are strongly typed.

4. If we type something into the search box in the running app, we'll see each change in the console:

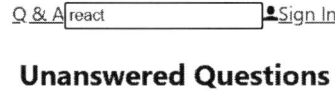

Figure 3.18 – Change event

In this section, we've learned that we can implement strongly typed event listeners, which will help us avoid making mistakes when using the `event` parameter. We'll finish off the implementation of the search input in *Chapter 6, Working with Forms*.

Summary

In this chapter, we learned that JSX compiles JavaScript nested calls into `createElement` functions in React, which allows us to mix HTML and JavaScript.

We learned that we can create a React component using functions with strongly typed props passed in as parameters. Now, we know that a prop can be a function, which is how events are handled.

The component state is used to implement behavior when users or other external things interact with it. Due to this, we understand that a component and its children are re-rendered when the state is changed.

By completing this chapter, we understand that React can help us discover problems in our app when it is run in strict mode. We also understand that a component is double rendered in strict mode when it contains state.

In the next chapter, we are going to style the home page.

Questions

Try to answer the following questions to test your knowledge of this chapter:

1. Does a component re-render when its props change?
2. How can we create some state called `rating` that is initially set to `0`?
3. What function prop name would we use to add a `keydown` event listener?
4. A component has the following props interface:

   ```
   interface Props {
     name: string;
     active: boolean;
   }
   ```

   How can we destructure the `Props` parameter and default `active` to `true`?
5. How can we use the `useEffect` hook to call a synchronous function called `getItems` when a piece of state called `category` changes while we're passing `category` to `getItems`?

Answers

1. Yes, when the props of a component change, it will rerender.
2. The state can be defined as follows:

   ```
   const [rating, setRating] = React.useState(0);
   ```

3. We would use the `onKeyDown` prop to handle the `keydown` event.

4. We could destructure the props parameter and set `active` to `true`, as follows:

```
export const myComponent = ({name, active = true}: Props)
=> ...
```

5. The `useEffect` hook would be as follows:

```
React.useEffect(() => {
  getItems(category)
}, [category]);
```

Further reading

The following are some useful links so that you can learn more about the topics that were covered in this chapter:

- React getting started: https://reactjs.org/docs/getting-started.html.
- React strict mode: https://reactjs.org/docs/strict-mode.html.
- TypeScript: https://www.typescriptlang.org/.
- Components and props: https://reactjs.org/docs/components-and-props.html.
- React lists and keys: https://reactjs.org/docs/lists-and-keys.html.
- `useState` hook: https://reactjs.org/docs/hooks-state.html.
- `useEffect` hook: https://reactjs.org/docs/hooks-effect.html.

4
Styling React Components with Emotion

In this chapter, we will style the Q&A app we have built so far with a popular CSS-in-JS library called Emotion. We will start by understanding how you can style components with plain CSS and its drawbacks. Next, we will move on to understanding how CSS-in-JS addresses the problems that plain CSS has before installing Emotion. Finally, we will style components using Emotion's `css` prop before creating some reusable styled components.

We'll cover the following topics in this chapter:

- Styling components with CSS
- Styling components with CSS modules
- Styling components with Emotion
- Styling pseudo-classes and nested elements with Emotion
- Creating a reusable styled component with Emotion
- Completing the home page styling

Technical requirements

The following tools are required for this chapter:

- **Visual Studio Code**: We'll use this to edit our React code. This can be downloaded and installed from `https://code.visualstudio.com/`. If you already have this installed, make sure that it is at least version 1.52.
- **Node.js and npm**: These can be downloaded from `https://nodejs.org/`. If you already have these installed, make sure that Node.js is at least version 8.2 and that `npm` is at least version 5.2.
- **Q&A**: We'll start with the Q&A frontend starter project for this chapter. This is the project we finished in *Chapter 3, Getting Started with React and TypeScript*. It is available on GitHub at `https://github.com/PacktPublishing/ASP.NET-Core-5-and-React-Second-Edition` in the `chapter-04/start` folder.

All the code snippets in this chapter can be found online at `https://github.com/PacktPublishing/ASP.NET-Core-5-and-React-Second-Edition`. In order to restore code from a chapter, the source code repository can be downloaded and the relevant folder can be opened in the relevant editor. If the code is frontend code, then you can use `npm install` in the terminal to restore the dependencies.

Check out the following video to see the Code in Action: `https://bit.ly/2WALbb2`

Styling components with CSS

In this section, we're going to style the body, app container, and header container with regular CSS and understand the drawbacks of this approach.

Styling the document body

We are going to use the traditional approach to style the document's body. Follow these steps to do so:

1. Open `index.tsx`. Remember that `index.tsx` is the root of the React component tree. Notice how the CSS file is referenced:

   ```
   import './index.css';
   ```

To reference a CSS file in a React component, we specify the location of the file after the `import` statement. `index.css` is in the same folder as `index.tsx`, so the import path is `./`.

2. Open `index.css`. Notice that we already have CSS in place for the `body` tag. Let's remove everything apart from `margin` and add a background color:

```
body {
  margin: 0;
  background-color: #f7f8fa;
}
```

3. Let's also remove the redundant `code` CSS class in `index.css`.

   Congratulations, we have just applied some styles to our app!

4. Let's run the app by entering the following command in the terminal:

```
> npm start
```

The app looks like the following:

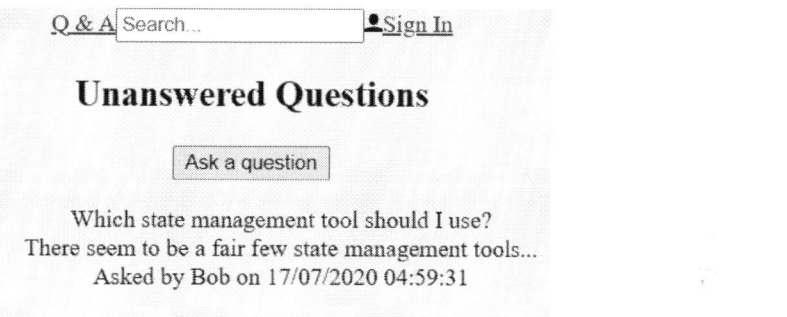

Figure 4.1 – Styled HTML body

The background color of the app is now light gray. Leave the app running as we progress to styling our `App` component.

Styling the App component

We are going to apply a CSS class to the `App` component in the following steps:

1. Open `App.tsx` and change the class name to `container` on the `div` element:

```
function App() {
  return (
    <div className="container">
      <Header />
```

```
        <HomePage />
    </div>
  );
}
```

Why is a `className` attribute used to reference CSS classes? Shouldn't we use the `class` attribute? Well, we already know that JSX compiles down to JavaScript, and since `class` is a keyword in JavaScript, React uses a `className` attribute instead. React converts `className` to `class` when it adds elements to the HTML DOM.

> **Important Note**
> The React team is currently working on allowing `class` attributes to be used instead of `className`. See https://github.com/facebook/react/issues/13525 for more information.

2. Open `App.css`, delete all the CSS in this file, and add the following CSS class:

```
.container {
  font-family: 'Segoe UI', 'Helvetica Neue',
    sans-serif;
  font-size: 16px;
  color: #5c5a5a;
}
```

3. Look at the app in the browser. It looks as in the following screenshot:

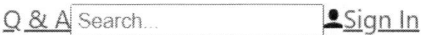

Unanswered Questions

Ask a question

- Which state management tool should I use?
  There seem to be a fair few state management tools...
  Asked by Bob on 06/07/2020 17:28:37

Figure 4.2 – App component styled with CSS

We see that the text content within the app has the font, size, and color we specified. Leave the app running while we apply more CSS in the next subsection.

Styling the Header component

We are going to apply a CSS class to the `Header` component in the following steps:

1. Create a file called `Header.css` in the `src` folder and add the following CSS class:

   ```css
   .container {
     position: fixed;
     box-sizing: border-box;
     top: 0;
     width: 100%;
     display: flex;
     align-items: center;
     justify-content: space-between;
     padding: 10px 20px;
     background-color: #fff;
     border-bottom: 1px solid #e3e2e2;
     box-shadow: 0 3px 7px 0 rgba(110, 112, 114, 0.21);
   }
   ```

   This style will fix the element it is applied to the top of the page. The elements within it will flow horizontally across the page and be positioned nicely.

2. Open `Header.tsx` and import the CSS file we just created:

   ```
   import './Header.css';
   ```

3. Add a `container` class to the `div` element in the JSX:

   ```
   <div className="container">
   ```

4. Look at the running app and open the browser's DevTools to the **Elements** panel.

5. We can see that the container style has leaked out of the `Header` component into the `App` component because the `div` element in the `App` component has a drop shadow:

Figure 4.3 – Header component styled with CSS

6. Press *Ctrl + C* in the terminal and press *Y* if prompted to stop the app from running.

7. We have just experienced a common problem with CSS. CSS is global in nature. So, if we use a CSS class name called `container` within a component, it would collide with another CSS class called `container` in a different CSS file if a page references both CSS files.

We can resolve this issue by being careful when naming and structuring our CSS by using something such as BEM. For example, we could have named the CSS classes `app-container` and `header-container` so that they don't collide. However, there's still some risk of the chosen names colliding, particularly in large apps and when new members join a team.

> **Important Note**
> **BEM** stands for **Block, Element, Modifier** and is a popular naming convention for CSS class names. More information can be found at https://css-tricks.com/bem-101/.

In the next section, we will learn how to resolve this issue with CSS modules.

Styling components with CSS modules

CSS modules are a mechanism for scoping CSS class names. The scoping happens as a build step rather than in the browser. In fact, CSS modules are already available in our app because Create React App has configured them in webpack.

We are going to update the styles on the Header and App components to CSS modules in the following steps:

1. Rename Header.css to Header.module.css and App.css to App.module.css. Create React App is configured to treat files ending with module.css as CSS modules.

2. Open App.tsx and change the App.css import statement to the following:

   ```
   import styles from './App.module.css'
   ```

3. Update the className prop on the div element to the following:

   ```
   <div className={styles.container}>
   ```

   This references the container class with the App CSS module.

4. Open Header.tsx and change the Header.css import statement to the following:

   ```
   import styles from './Header.module.css'
   ```

5. Update the className prop on the div element to the following:

   ```
   <div className={styles.container}>
   ```

6. Let's run the app by entering the following command in the terminal:

   ```
   npm start
   ```

7. Open the browser's DevTools to the **Elements** panel:

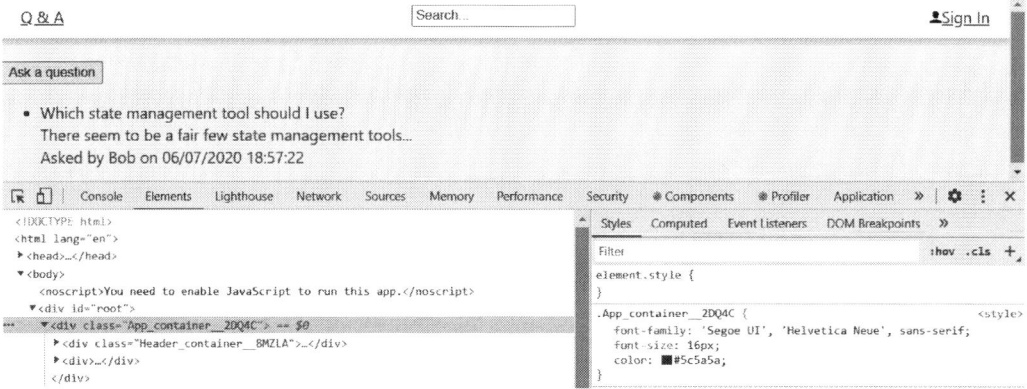

Figure 4.4 – Styling with CSS modules

We can see that styles from the `Header` component no longer leak into the `App` component. We can see that the CSS modules have updated the class names on the elements, prefixing them with the component name and adding random-looking characters to the end.

8. Look in the HTML `head` tag. We can see the CSS from the CSS modules in `style` tags:

Figure 4.5 – CSS modules in a head tag

9. Press *Ctrl* + *C* in the terminal and press *Y* if prompted to stop the app from running.

This is great! CSS modules automatically scope CSS that is applied to React components without us having to be careful with the class naming.

In the next section, we are going to learn about another approach to styling React components, which is arguably more powerful.

Styling components with Emotion

In this section, we're going to style the `App`, `Header`, and `HomePage` components with a popular CSS-in-JS library called Emotion. Along the way, we will discover the benefits of CSS-in-JS over CSS modules.

Installing Emotion

With our frontend project open in Visual Studio Code, let's install Emotion into our project by carrying out the following steps:

1. Open the terminal, make sure you are in the `frontend` folder, and execute the following command:

   ```
   > npm install @emotion/react @emotion/styled
   ```

2. There is a nice Visual Studio Code extension that will provide CSS syntax highlighting and IntelliSense for Emotion. Open the **Extensions** area (*Ctrl + Shift + X* on Windows or *Cmd + Shift + X* on Mac) and type `styled components` in the search box at the top left. The extension we are looking for is called `vscode-styled-components` and was published by **Julien Poissonnier**:

Figure 4.6 – Styled components Visual Studio Code extension

> **Important Note**
> This extension was primarily developed for the Styled Components CSS in the JS library. CSS highlighting and IntelliSense work for Emotion as well, though.

3. Click on the **Install** button to install the extension.
4. To show the **Explorer** panel again, press *Ctrl + Shift + E* on Windows or *Cmd + Shift + E* on Mac.

That's Emotion installed within our project and set up nicely in Visual Studio Code.

Styling the App component

Let's style the `App` component with Emotion by carrying out the following steps:

1. Start by removing the `App.module.css` file by right-clicking on it and selecting the **Delete** option.
2. In `App.tsx`, remove the line that says `import styles from './App.module.css'`.
3. Remove the React `import` statement from `App.tsx`.

> Important Note
>
> In React 17 and beyond, it is no longer necessary to include the React `import` statement to render JSX, as is the case in `App.tsx`. However, the React `import` statement is still required if we want to use functions from the library, such as `useState` and `useEffect`.

4. Add the following imports from the Emotion library at the top of `App.tsx`:

```
/** @jsxImportSource @emotion/react */
import { css } from '@emotion/react';
```

The `css` function is what we'll use to style an HTML element. The comment above the `import` statement tells Babel to use this `jsx` function to transform JSX into JavaScript.

> Important Note
>
> It is important to include the `/** @jsxImportSource @emotion/react */` comment; otherwise, the transpilation process will error out. It is also important that this is placed right at the top of the file.

5. On the App component's `div` element, remove the `className` prop and use the `css` function to specify the style:

```
<div css={css`
  font-family: 'Segoe UI', 'Helvetica Neue', sans-serif;
  font-size: 16px;
  color: #5c5a5a;
`}>
  <Header />
  <HomePage />
</div>
```

We put the styles in a `css` prop on an HTML element in what is called a tagged template literal.

> **Important Note**
>
> A template literal is a string enclosed by backticks (` `` `) that can span multiple lines and can include a JavaScript expression in curly braces, prefixed with a dollar sign (`${expression}`). Template literals are great when we need to merge static text with variables.
>
> A tagged template literal is a template string that is executed through a function that is specified immediately before the template literal string. The function is executed on the template literal before the string is rendered in the browser.

So, Emotion's `css` function is being used in a tagged template literal to render the styles defined in backticks (` `` `) on the HTML element.

6. We actually want to specify the font family, size, and color in various components in our app. To do this, we are going to extract these values into variables in a separate file. Let's create a file called `Styles.ts` in the `src` folder that contains the following variables:

```
export const gray1 = '#383737';
export const gray2 = '#5c5a5a';
export const gray3 = '#857c81';
export const gray4 = '#b9b9b9';
export const gray5 = '#e3e2e2';
export const gray6 = '#f7f8fa';

export const primary1 = '#681c41';
export const primary2 = '#824c67';

export const accent1 = '#dbb365';
export const accent2 = '#efd197';
```

```
export const fontFamily = "'Segoe UI', 'Helvetica
Neue',sans-serif";
export const fontSize = '16px';
```

Here, we have defined six shades of gray, two shades of the primary color for our app, two shades of an accent color, as well as the font family we'll use with the standard font size.

7. Let's import the variables we need into `App.tsx`:

```
import { fontFamily, fontSize, gray2 } from './Styles';
```

8. Now, we can use these variables inside the CSS template literal using interpolation:

```
<div
  css={css`
    font-family: ${fontFamily};
    font-size: ${fontSize};
    color: ${gray2};
  `}
>
  <Header />
  <HomePage />
</div>
```

Congratulations – we have just styled our first component with Emotion!

Let's explore the styling in the running app. This will help us understand how Emotion is applying styles:

1. Let's run the app by executing `npm start` in the terminal.
2. Let's inspect the DOM on the browser page by pressing *F12*:

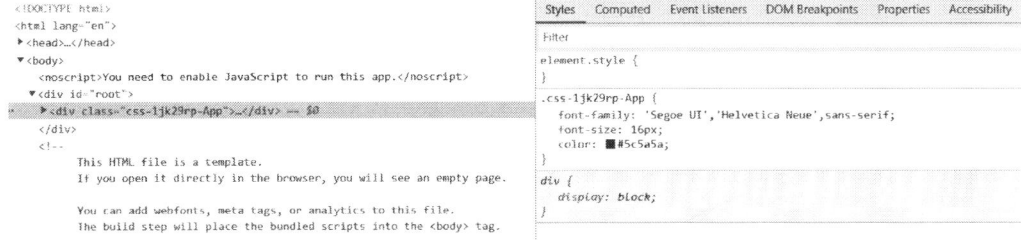

Figure 4.7 – App component styled with Emotion

We can see that the `div` element we styled has a class name that starts with `css` and ends with the component name, with a unique name in the middle. The styles in the CSS class are the styles we defined in our component with Emotion. So, Emotion doesn't generate inline styles as we might have thought. Instead, Emotion generates styles that are held in unique CSS classes. If we look in the HTML header, we'll see the CSS class defined in a `style` tag:

```
▼<style data-emotion="css">
   .css-1jk29rp-App{font-family:'Segoe UI','Helvetica Neue',sans-serif;font-
   size:16px;color:#5c5a5a;}
  </style>
</head>
```

Figure 4.8 – Emotion styles in the head tag

So, during the app's build process, Emotion has transformed the styles into a real CSS class.

3. Press *Ctrl + C* in the terminal and press *Y* if prompted to stop the app from running.

4. An advantage of using Emotion over CSS modules is the ability to use variables in CSS. We have just used this to define some common style properties and use them in the `App` component. We will use variables in styles throughout this book where logic drives styles on components.

Styling the Header component

We can style the `Header` component with Emotion by carrying out the following steps:

1. Start by removing the `Header.module.css` file.

2. In `Header.tsx`, remove the `Header.module.css import` statement and add the following imports for Emotion and some of the style variables we set up previously. Add these `import` statements right at the top of the file:

   ```
   /** @jsxImportSource @emotion/react */
   import { css } from '@emotion/react';
   import { fontFamily, fontSize, gray1, gray2, gray5 } from
   './Styles';
   ```

3. Now, we can remove the `className` property and define the following style on the `div` container element:

   ```
   <div
     css={css`
       position: fixed;
   ```

```
    box-sizing: border-box;
    top: 0;
    width: 100%;
    display: flex;
    align-items: center;
    justify-content: space-between;
    padding: 10px 20px;
    background-color: #fff;
    border-bottom: 1px solid ${gray5};
    box-shadow: 0 3px 7px 0 rgba(110, 112, 114, 0.21);
  `}
>
  ...
</div>
```

We are applying the same styles as were in the CSS module.

4. The `App` and `Header` components are now styled as they were with the CSS modules approach. In the next section, we will continue to style the `Header` component, learning about more features in Emotion.

Styling pseudo-classes and nested elements with Emotion

In this section, we will learn how to style pseudo-classes with Emotion. We will then move on to learn how to style nested elements:

1. In `Header.tsx`, implement the following styles on the anchor tag:

```
<a
  href="./"
  css={css`
    font-size: 24px;
    font-weight: bold;
    color: ${gray1};
    text-decoration: none;
  `}
>
  Q & A
</a>
```

Here, we are making the app name fairly big, bold, and dark gray, and also removing the underline.

2. Let's move on and style the search box:

```
<input
  type="text"
  placeholder="Search..."
  onChange={handleSearchInputChange}
  css={css`
    box-sizing: border-box;
    font-family: ${fontFamily};
    font-size: ${fontSize};
    padding: 8px 10px;
    border: 1px solid ${gray5};
    border-radius: 3px;
    color: ${gray2};
    background-color: white;
    width: 200px;
    height: 30px;
  `}
/>
```

Here, we are using the standard font family and size and giving the search box a light-gray, rounded border.

3. We are going to continue to style the `input` element. We want to change its outline color for when it has focus to a gray color. We can achieve this with a `focus` pseudo-class selector, as follows:

```
<input
  type="text"
  placeholder="Search..."
  css={css`
    ...
    :focus {
      outline-color: ${gray5};
    }
  `}
/>
```

The pseudo-class is defined by being nested within the CSS for the input. The syntax is the same as in regular CSS with a colon (:) before the pseudo-class name and its CSS properties within curly brackets.

4. Let's move on to the **Sign In** link element now. Let's start to style it as follows:

```
<a
  href="./signin"
  css={css`
    font-family: ${fontFamily};
    font-size: ${fontSize};
    padding: 5px 10px;
    background-color: transparent;
    color: ${gray2};
    text-decoration: none;
    cursor: pointer;
    :focus {
      outline-color: ${gray5};
    }
  `}
>
  <UserIcon />
  <span>Sign In</span>
</a>
```

The styles have added some space around the icon and the text inside the link and removed the underline from it. We have also changed the color of the line around the link when it has focus using a pseudo-class selector.

5. Let's style the `span` element within the **Sign In** link by adding the following to the end of the template literal:

```
<a
  href="./signin"
  css={css`
    ...
    span {
      margin-left: 7px;
    }
  `}
>
  <UserIcon />
  <span>Sign In</span>
</a>
```

We have chosen to use a nested element selector on the anchor tag to style the `span` element. This is equivalent to applying the style directly on the `span` element, as follows:

```
<span
  css={css`
    margin-left: 7px;
  `}
>
  Sign In
</span>
```

6. Next up is styling the `UserIcon` component in the `Icons.tsx` file. Let's add the following to the top of the file:

```
/** @jsxImportSource @emotion/react */
import { css } from '@emotion/react';
```

7. Now, we can define the styles on the `img` element, replacing the `width` attribute:

```
<img
  src={user}
  alt="User"
  css={css`
    width: 12px;
    opacity: 0.6;
  `}
/>
```

We've moved the width from the attribute on the `img` tag into its CSS style. Now, the icon is a nice size and appears to be a little lighter in color.

8. Let's run the app by executing `npm start` in the terminal.

9. If we look at the running app, we'll see that our app header is looking much nicer now:

Figure 4.9 – Fully styled header

We are getting the hang of Emotion now.

The syntax for defining the styling properties is exactly the same as defining properties in CSS, which is nice if we already know CSS well. We can even nest CSS properties in a similar manner to how we can do this in SCSS.

The remaining component to style is `HomePage` – we'll look at that next.

Creating a reusable styled component with Emotion

In this section, we are going to learn how to create reusable styled components while styling the `HomePage` component. Let's carry out the following steps:

1. We will start with the `Page` component in `Page.tsx` and add the following lines to the top of the file:

   ```
   /** @jsxImportSource @emotion/react */
   import { css } from '@emotion/react';
   ```

2. Let's style the `div` element and place the page content in the center of the screen:

   ```
   export const Page = ({ title, children }: Props) => (
     <div
       css={css`
         margin: 50px auto 20px auto;
         padding: 30px 20px;
         max-width: 600px;
       `}
     >
       ...
     </div>
   );
   ```

3. Let's move to `HomePage.tsx` and add the following lines to the top of the file:

   ```
   /** @jsxImportSource @emotion/react */
   import { css } from '@emotion/react';
   ```

4. Next, we will style the `div` element that wraps the page title and the **Ask a question** button:

   ```
   <Page>
     <div
       css={css`
         display: flex;
         align-items: center;
         justify-content: space-between;
       `}
     >
       <PageTitle>Unanswered Questions</PageTitle>
       <button onClick={handleAskQuestonClick}>Ask a
   ```

```
      question</button>
    </div>
  </Page>
```

This puts the page title and the **Ask a question** button on the same line.

5. Now, let's open `PageTitle.tsx` and style the page title. Add the following lines to the top of the file:

```
/** @jsxImportSource @emotion/react */
import { css } from '@emotion/react';
```

6. We can then apply the following styles to the h2 element:

```
<h2
  css={css`
    font-size: 15px;
    font-weight: bold;
    margin: 10px 0px 5px;
    text-align: center;
    text-transform: uppercase;
  `}
>
  {children}
</h2>
```

This reduces the size of the page title and makes it uppercase, which will make the page's content stand out more.

7. Finally, we have the **Ask a question** button, which is the primary button on the home page. Eventually, we are going to have primary buttons on several pages, so let's create a reusable `PrimaryButton` styled component in the `Styles.ts` file. First, we need to import the styled function from Emotion. So, add this line to the top of the file:

```
import styled from '@emotion/styled';
```

8. Now, we can create the primary button styled component:

```
export const PrimaryButton = styled.button`
  background-color: ${primary2};
  border-color: ${primary2};
  border-style: solid;
  border-radius: 5px;
  font-family: ${fontFamily};
  font-size: ${fontSize};
  padding: 5px 10px;
```

```
    color: white;
    cursor: pointer;
    :hover {
      background-color: ${primary1};
    }
    :focus {
      outline-color: ${primary2};
    }
    :disabled {
      opacity: 0.5;
      cursor: not-allowed;
    }
`;
```

Here, we've created a styled component in Emotion by using a **tagged template literal**.

> **Important Note**
>
> A **tagged template literal** is a template literal to be parsed with a function. The template literal is contained in backticks (` `) and the parsing function is placed immediately before it. More information can be found at `https://developer.mozilla.org/en-US/docs/Web/JavaScript/Reference/Template_literals`.

In a styled component, the parsing function before the backticks (` `) references a function within Emotion's `styled` function. The function is named with the HTML element name that will be created and is styled with the provided style. This is `button` in this example.

So, this styled component creates a flat, slightly rounded button with our chosen primary color.

9. Let's import this into the `HomePage.tsx` file:

```
import { PrimaryButton } from './Styles';
```

10. Now, we can replace the `button` tag in the `HomePage` JSX with our `PrimaryButton` styled component:

```
<Page>
  <div ... >
    <PageTitle>...</PageTitle>
    <PrimaryButton onClick={handleAskQuestionClick}>
      Ask a question
    </PrimaryButton>
```

```
    </div>
  </Page>
```

11. If we look at the running app, we'll see that it's looking much nicer:

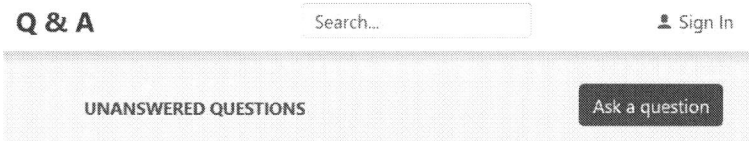

Figure 4.10 – Styled page title and primary button

There is still work to do on the home page's styling, such as rendering the list of unanswered questions. We'll do this in the next section.

Completing the home page styling

In this section, we are going to complete the styling on the home page.

Styling the QuestionList component

Let's go through the following steps to style the `QuestionList` component:

1. Open `QuestionList.tsx` and add the following lines at the top of the file:

    ```
    /** @jsxImportSource @emotion/react */
    import { css } from '@emotion/react';
    ```

2. Also import the following common styles:

    ```
    import { accent2, gray5 } from './Styles';
    ```

3. Style the `ul` element in the JSX as follows:

    ```
    <ul
      css={css`
        list-style: none;
        margin: 10px 0 0 0;
        padding: 0px 20px;
        background-color: #fff;
        border-bottom-left-radius: 4px;
        border-bottom-right-radius: 4px;
        border-top: 3px solid ${accent2};
        box-shadow: 0 3px 5px 0 rgba(0, 0, 0, 0.16);
      `}
    ```

```
  >
    ...
  </ul>
```

So, the `ul` element will appear without bullet points and with a rounded border. The top border will be slightly thicker and in the accent color. We've added a box shadow to make the list pop out a bit.

4. Now, let's style the list items:

```
<ul ...
>
  <li key={question.questionId}
    css={css`
      border-top: 1px solid ${gray5};
      :first-of-type {
        border-top: none;
      }
    `}
  >
    ...
  </li>
</ul>
```

The style on the list items adds a light-gray top border. This will act as a line separator between each list item.

5. If we look at the running app, the unanswered questions container is looking nice:

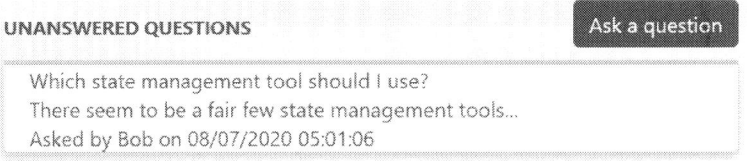

Figure 4.11 – Styled unanswered questions container

Next, we will add styling to the questions.

Styling the Question component

Follow these steps to style the `Question` component:

1. Open `Question.tsx` and add the following lines to the top of the file:

   ```
   /** @jsxImportSource @emotion/react */
   import { css } from '@emotion/react';
   import { gray2, gray3 } from './Styles';
   ```

2. Let's add some padding to the outermost `div` element, as follows:

   ```
   <div
     css={css`
       padding: 10px 0px;
     `}
   >
     <div>
       {data.title}
     </div>
     ...
   </div>
   ```

3. Add some padding to the question title and increase its font size:

   ```
   <div
     css={css`
       padding: 10px 0px;
       font-size: 19px;
     `}
   >
     {data.title}
   </div>
   ```

4. Add the following styles to the optional question content:

   ```
   {showContent && (
     <div
       css={css`
         padding-bottom: 10px;
         font-size: 15px;
         color: ${gray2};
       `}
     >
       ...
     </div>
   )}
   ```

5. Lastly, add the following styles around the text for who asked the question:

```
<div
  css={css`
    font-size: 12px;
    font-style: italic;
    color: ${gray3};
  `}
>
  {`Asked by ${data.userName} on
    ${data.created.toLocaleDateString()} ${data.created.
      toLocaleTimeString()}`}
</div>
```

6. If we look at the running app now, we'll see the styles on the home page:

Figure 4.12 – Completed home page styling

That completes the styling on the home page. It is looking much nicer now.

Summary

In this chapter, we learned about different approaches to styling a React app. We now understand that CSS-in-JS libraries automatically scope styles to components and allow us to use dynamic variables within styles.

We understand how to use the Emotion CSS-in-JS library to style React components using its `css` prop. We can style a pseudo-class by nesting it within the `css` prop style string.

We know how to create reusable styled components using the `styled` function in Emotion. These can be consumed as regular React components in our app.

In the next chapter, we are going to add more pages to our app and learn how to implement client-side routing to these pages.

Questions

Try to answer the following questions to test your knowledge of this chapter:

1. In Create React App, what is the filename convention for a CSS module?

2. The submit button component in the following code block has its background color set from a constant in a `Color.ts` file. The button background color isn't being set, though, when the component is rendered on the page. What is the problem?

   ```
   import React from 'react';

   /** @jsxImportSource @emotion/react */
   import { css } from '@emotion/react';

   import { primaryAccent1 } from './Colors';

   interface Props {
     children: React.ReactNode
   }
   export const SubmitButton = ({ children }: Props) => {
     return (
       <button
         css={css`
           background-color: primaryAccent1;
         `}
       >
         {children}
       </button>
     );
   };
   ```

3. In the `SubmitButton` component from the last question, how can we remove the outline when it has focus?

4. In our Q&A app, we created a `PageTitle` component that only contains styles. How could we change this to be a reusable styled component?

5. We have the following input element in some JSX. How can we style the placeholder text so that it has the `#dcdada` color?

   ```
   <input
     type="text"
     placeholder="Enter your name"
   />
   ```

Answers

1. The file naming convention is `ComponentName.module.css`. For example, `Footer.module.css` would be a CSS module for the `Footer` component.

2. The problem is that the background color is set to the `'primaryAccent'` string rather than the constant. The `css` prop should be set to the following:

```
<button
  css={css`
    background-color: ${primaryAccent1};
  `}
>
  {children}
</button>
```

3. We can use the `focus` pseudo-class as follows:

```
<button
  css={css`
    background-color: ${primaryAccent1};
    :focus {
      outline: none;
    }
  `}
>
  {children}
</button>
```

4. We can use the following styled component:

```
export const PageTitle = styled.h2`
  font-size: 15px;
  font-weight: bold;
  margin: 10px 0px 5px;
  text-align: center;
  text-transform: uppercase;
`;
```

5. We can style the placeholder pseudo-element as follows:

```
<input
  type="text"
  placeholder="Enter your name"
  css={css`
    ::placeholder {
      color: #dcdada;
```

```
        }
      `}
/>
```

Further reading

The following are some useful links so that you can learn more about the topics that were covered in this chapter:

- **CSS modules**: `https://github.com/css-modules/css-modules`
- **CSS modules in Create React App**: `https://create-react-app.dev/docs/adding-a-css-modules-stylesheet`
- **Emotion**: `https://emotion.sh/docs/introduction`

5
Routing with React Router

So far, our Q&A app only contains one page, so the time has come to add more pages to the app. In *Chapter 1, Understanding the ASP.NET 5 React Template*, we learned that pages in a **Single Page Application** (**SPA**) are constructed in the browser without any request for the HTML to the server.

React Router is a great library that helps us to implement client-side pages and the navigation between them. So, we are going to bring it into our project in this chapter.

In this chapter, we will declaratively define the routes that are available in our app. We learn how to provide feedback to users when they navigate to paths that don't exist. We'll implement a page that displays the details of a question, along with its answers. This is where we will learn how to implement route parameters. We'll begin by implementing the question search feature, where we will learn how to handle query parameters. We will also start to implement the page for asking a question and optimize this so that its JavaScript is loaded on demand rather than when the app loads.

We'll cover the following topics in this chapter:

- Installing React Router
- Declaring routes
- Handling routes not found
- Implementing links
- Using route parameters
- Using query parameters
- Lazy loading routes

Technical requirements

We'll use the following tools in this chapter:

- **Visual Studio Code**: We'll use this to edit our React code. This can be downloaded from `https://code.visualstudio.com/`. If you already have this installed, make sure that it is at least version 1.52.

- **Node.js and npm**: These can be downloaded from `https://nodejs.org/`. If you already have these installed, make sure that Node.js is at least version 8.2 and that npm is at least version 5.2.

- **Q&A**: We'll start with the Q&A frontend starter project for this chapter. This is the project we finished in *Chapter 4*, *Styling React Components with Emotion*. This is available on GitHub at `https://github.com/PacktPublishing/ASP.NET-Core-5-and-React-Second-Edition` in the `chapter-05/start` folder.

All the code snippets in this chapter can be found online at `https://github.com/PacktPublishing/ASP.NET-Core-5-and-React-Second-Edition`. In order to restore code from a chapter, the source code repository can be downloaded and the relevant folder opened in the relevant editor. If the code is frontend code, then `npm install` can be entered in the terminal to restore the dependencies.

Check out the following video to see the code in action: `http://bit.ly/34XoKyz`

Installing React Router

In this section, we are going to install React Router with the corresponding TypeScript types by carrying out the following steps:

1. Make sure the frontend project is open in Visual Studio Code and enter the following command to install React Router in the terminal:

   ```
   > npm install react-router-dom
   ```

   > **Important note**
   > Make sure `react-router-dom` version 6+ has been installed and listed in `package.json`. If version 5 has been installed, then version 6 can be installed by running `npm install react-router-dom@next`.

2. React router has a peer dependency on the `history` package, so let's install this using the terminal as well:

   ```
   > npm install history
   ```

   A peer dependency is a dependency that is not automatically installed by npm. This is why we have installed it in our project.

That's it—nice and simple! We'll start to declare the routes in our app in the next section.

Declaring routes

We declare the pages in our app using `BrowserRouter`, `Routes`, and `Route` components. `BrowserRouter` is the top-level component that performs navigation between pages. Paths to pages are defined in `Route` components nested within a `Routes` component. The `Routes` component decides which `Route` component should be rendered for the current browser location.

We are going to start this section by creating blank pages that we'll eventually implement throughout this book. Then, we'll declare these pages in our app using `BrowserRouter`, `Routes`, and `Route` components.

Creating some blank pages

Let's create blank pages for signing in, asking a question, viewing search results, and viewing a question with its answers by carrying out the following steps:

1. Create a file called `SignInPage.tsx` with the following content:

    ```
    import React from 'react';
    import { Page } from './Page';

    export const SignInPage = () => (
      <Page title="Sign In">{null}</Page>
    );
    ```

    Here, we have used the `Page` component we created in the previous chapter to create an empty page that has the title **Sign In**. We are going to use a similar approach for the other pages we need to create.

    Notice that we are rendering `null` in the content of the `Page` component at the moment. This is a way of telling React to render nothing.

2. Create a file called `AskPage.tsx` with the following content:

    ```
    import React from 'react';
    import { Page } from './Page';

    export const AskPage = () => (
      <Page title="Ask a question">{null}</Page>
    );
    ```

3. Create a file called `SearchPage.tsx` with the following content:

    ```
    import React from 'react';
    import { Page } from './Page';

    export const SearchPage = () => (
      <Page title="Search Results">{null}</Page>
    );
    ```

4. Create a file called `QuestionPage.tsx` with the following content:

    ```
    import React from 'react';
    import { Page } from './Page';

    export const QuestionPage = () => (
      <Page>Question Page</Page>
    );
    ```

The title on the question page is going to be styled differently, which is why we are not using the `title` prop on the `Page` component. We have simply added some text on the page for the time being so that we can distinguish this page from the other pages.

So, that's our pages created. Now, it's time to define all the routes to these pages.

Creating a component containing routes

We are going to define all of the routes to the pages we created by carrying out the following steps:

1. Open `App.tsx` and add the following `import` statements under the existing `import` statements:

   ```
   import { BrowserRouter, Routes, Route } from 'react-router-dom';
   import { AskPage } from './AskPage';
   import { SearchPage } from './SearchPage';
   import { SignInPage } from './SignInPage';
   ```

2. In the `App` component's JSX, add `BrowserRouter` as the outermost element:

   ```
   <BrowserRouter>
     <div css={ ... } >
       <Header />
       <HomePage />
     </div>
   </BrowserRouter>
   ```

3. Let's define the routes in our app under the `Header` component, replacing the previous reference to `HomePage`:

   ```
   <BrowserRouter>
     <div css={ ... } >
       <Header />
       <Routes>
         <Route path="" element={<HomePage/>} />
         <Route path="search" element={<SearchPage/>} />
         <Route path="ask" element={<AskPage/>} />
         <Route path="signin" element={<SignInPage/>} />
       </Routes>
     </div>
   </BrowserRouter>
   ```

Each route is defined in a `Route` component that defines what should be rendered in an `element` prop for a given path in a `path` prop. The route with the path that best matches the browser's location is rendered.

For example, if the browser location is `http://localhost:3000/search`, then the second `Route` component (that has `path` set to `"search"`) will be the best match. This will mean that the `SearchPage` component is rendered.

Notice that we don't need a preceding slash (`/`) on the path because React Router performs relative matching by default.

4. Run the app by entering the `npm start` command in the Visual Studio Code terminal. We'll see that the home page renders just like it did before, which is great.

5. Now, enter `/search` at the end of the browser location path:

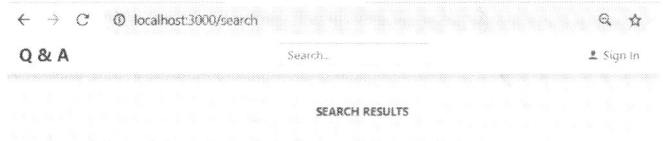

Figure 5.1 – Search page

Here, we can see that React Router has decided that the best match is the `Route` component with a path of `"search"`, and so renders the `SearchPage` component.

Feel free to visit the other pages as well – they will render fine now.

So, that's our basic routing configured nicely. What happens if the user enters a path in the browser that doesn't exist in our app? We'll find out in the next section.

Handling routes not found

In this section, we'll handle paths that aren't handled by any of the `Route` components. By following these steps, we'll start by understanding what happens if we put an unhandled path in the browser:

1. Enter a path that isn't handled in the browser and see what happens:

Figure 5.2 – Unhandled path

So, nothing is rendered beneath the header when we browse to a path that isn't handled by a `Route` component. This makes sense if we think about it.

2. We'd like to improve the user experience of routes not found and inform the user that this is the case. Let's add the following highlighted route inside the `Routes` component:

```
<Routes>
  <Route path="" element={<HomePage/>} />
  <Route path="search" element={<SearchPage/>} />
  <Route path="ask" element={<AskPage/>} />
  <Route path="signin" element={<SignInPage/>} />
  <Route path="*" element={<NotFoundPage/>} />
</Routes>
```

In order to understand how this works, let's think about what the `Routes` component does again – it renders the `Route` component that best matches the browser location. Path * will match any browser location, but isn't very specific. So, * won't be the best match for a browser location of /, /search, /ask, or /signin, but will catch invalid routes.

3. `NotFoundPage` hasn't been implemented yet, so let's create a file called `NotFoundPage.tsx` with the following content:

```
import React from 'react';
import { Page } from './Page';

export const NotFoundPage = () => (
  <Page title="Page Not Found">{null}</Page>
);
```

4. Back in `App.tsx`, let's import the `NotFoundPage` component:

```
import { NotFoundPage } from './NotFoundPage';
```

5. Now, if we enter an /invalid path in the browser, we'll see that our `NotFoundPage` component has been rendered:

Figure 5.3 – Unhandled path

So, once we understand how the `Routes` component works, implementing a not-found page is very easy. We simply use a `Route` component with a path of `*` inside the `Routes` component.

At the moment, we are navigating to different pages in our app by manually changing the location in the browser. In the next section, we'll learn how to implement links to perform navigation within the app itself.

Implementing links

In this section, we are going to use the `Link` component from React Router to declaratively perform navigation when clicking the app name in the app header. Then, we'll move on to programmatically performing navigation when clicking the **Ask a question** button to go to the ask page.

Using the Link component

At the moment, when we click on **Q and A** in the top-left corner of the app, it is doing an HTTP request that returns the whole React app, which, in turn, renders the home page. We are going to change this by making use of React Router's `Link` component so that navigation happens in the browser without an HTTP request. We are also going to make use of the `Link` component for the link to the sign-in page as well. We'll learn how to achieve this by performing the following steps:

1. In `Header.tsx`, import the `Link` component from React Router. Place the following line under the existing `import` statements:

   ```
   import { Link } from 'react-router-dom';
   ```

2. Let's change the anchor tag around the `Q & A` text to a `Link` element. The `href` attribute also needs to change to a `to` attribute:

   ```
   <Link
     to="/"
     css={ ... }
   >
     Q & A
   </Link>
   ```

3. Let's also change the sign-in link to the following:

```
<Link
  to="signin"
  css={ ... }
>
  <UserIcon />
  <span>Sign In</span>
</Link>
```

4. If we go to the running app and click the **Sign In** link, we'll see the sign-in page rendered. Now, click on **Q & A** in the app header. We will be taken back to the home page, just like we wanted.

5. Execute *step 4* again, but this time with the browser developer tools open and look at the **Network** tab. We'll find that, when clicking on the **Sign In** and **Q & A** links, no network requests are made.

So, the `Link` component is a great way of declaratively providing client-side navigation options in JSX. The task we performed in the last step confirms that all the navigation happens in the browser without any server requests, which is great for performance.

Navigating programmatically

Sometimes, it is necessary to do navigation programmatically. Follow these steps to programmatically navigate to the ask page when the **Ask a question** button is clicked:

1. Import `useNavigate` from React Router into `HomePage.tsx`:

   ```
   import { useNavigate } from 'react-router-dom';
   ```

   This is a hook that returns a function that we can use to perform a navigation.

2. Assign the `useNavigate` hook to a function called `navigate` just before the `handleAskQuestionClick` event handler:

   ```
   const navigate = useNavigate();
   const handleAskQuestionClick = () => {
     ...
   };
   ```

3. In `handleAskQuestionClick`, we can replace the `console.log` statement with the navigation:

```
const handleAskQuestionClick = () => {
  navigate('ask');
};
```

4. In the running app, if we give this a try and click the **Ask a question** button, it will successfully navigate to the ask page.

So, we can declaratively navigate by using the `Link` component and programmatically navigate using the `useNavigate` hook in React Router. We will continue to make use of the `Link` component in the next section.

Using route parameters

In this section, we are going to define a `Route` component for navigating to the question page. This will contain a variable called `questionId` at the end of the path, so we will need to use what is called a **route parameter**. We'll implement more of the question page content in this section as well.

Adding the question page route

Let's carry out the following steps to add the question page route:

1. In `App.tsx`, import the `QuestionPage` component we created earlier in this chapter:

```
import { QuestionPage } from './QuestionPage';
```

2. In the `App` component's JSX, add a `Route` component for navigation to the question page inside the `Routes` component just above the wildcard route:

```
<Routes>
  ...
  <Route path="questions/:questionId"
    element={<QuestionPage />} />
  <Route path="*" element={<NotFoundPage/>} />
</Routes>
```

Note that the path we entered contains `:questionId` at the end.

> **Important note**
> Route parameters are defined in the path with a colon in front of them. The value of the parameter is then available to destructure in the `useParams` hook.

The `Route` component could be placed in any position within the `Routes` component. It is arguably more readable to keep the wildcard route at the bottom because this is the least specific path and therefore will be the last to be matched.

3. Let's go to `QuestionPage.tsx` and import `useParams` from React Router:

   ```
   import { useParams } from 'react-router-dom';
   ```

4. We can destructure the value of the `questionId` route parameter from the `useParams` hook:

   ```
   export const QuestionPage = () => {
     const { questionId } = useParams();
     return <Page>Question Page</Page>;
   };
   ```

   We have also changed `QuestionPage` to have an explicit return statement.

5. For now, we are going to output `questionId` on the page as follows in the JSX:

   ```
   <Page>Question Page {questionId}</Page>;
   ```

   We'll come back and fully implement the question page in *Chapter 6*, *Working with Forms*. For now, we are going to link to this page from the `Question` component.

6. So, in `Question.tsx`, add the following `import` statement to import the `Link` component:

   ```
   import { Link } from 'react-router-dom';
   ```

7. Now, we can wrap a `Link` component around the title text in the `Question` JSX while specifying the path to navigate to:

```
<div
  css={css`
    padding: 10px 0px;
    font-size: 19px;
  `}
>
  <Link
    css={css`
      text-decoration: none;
      color: ${gray2};
    `}
    to={`/questions/${data.questionId}`}
  >
    {data.title}
  </Link>
</div>
```

8. Go to the running app and try clicking on the **Which state management tool should I use?** question. It will successfully navigate to the question page, showing the correct `questionId`:

Figure 5.4 – Question page with route parameter

So, we implement route parameters by defining variables in the route path with a colon in front and then picking the value up with the `useParams` hook.

Implementing more of the question page

Let's carry out some more steps to implement the question page a little more:

1. In `QuestionsData.ts`, add a function that will simulate a web request to get a question:

   ```
   export const getQuestion = async (
     questionId: number
   ): Promise<QuestionData | null> => {
     await wait(500);
     const results
       = questions.filter(q => q.questionId ===
         questionId);
     return results.length === 0 ? null : results[0];
   };
   ```

   We have used the array `filter` method to get the question for the passed-in `questionId`.

   Notice the type annotation for the function's return type. The type passed into the `Promise` generic type is `Question | null`, which is called a **union type**.

   > **Important note**
   >
   > A union type is a mechanism for defining a type that contains values from multiple types. If we think of a type as a set of values, then the union of multiple types is the same as the union of the sets of values. More information is available at `https://www.typescriptlang.org/docs/handbook/unions-and-intersections.html#union-types`.

   So, the function is expected to asynchronously return an object of the `QuestionData` or `null` type.

2. Moving on to `QuestionPage.tsx`, let's import the function we just created, along with the question interface:

   ```
   import { QuestionData, getQuestion } from './
   QuestionsData';
   ```

3. Add the emotion `import` statement and import a couple of gray colors from our standard colors. Add the following lines at the top of `QuestionPage.tsx`:

```
/** @jsxImportSource @emotion/react */
import { css } from '@emotion/react';
import { gray3, gray6 } from './Styles';
```

4. In the `QuestionPage` component, create a state for the question:

```
export const QuestionPage = () => {
  const [
    question,
    setQuestion,
  ] = React.useState<QuestionData | null>(null);

  const { questionId } = useParams();
  return <Page>Question Page {questionId}</Page>;
};
```

We are going to store the question in the state when the component is initially rendered.

Note that we are using a union type for the state because the state will be `null` initially while the question is being fetched, and also `null` if the question isn't found.

5. We want to call the `getQuestion` function during the initial render, so let's call it inside a call to the `useEffect` hook:

```
export const QuestionPage = () => {
  ...
  const { questionId } = useParams();

  React.useEffect(() => {
    const doGetQuestion = async (
      questionId: number,
    ) => {
      const foundQuestion = await getQuestion(
        questionId,
      );
      setQuestion(foundQuestion);
    };
    if (questionId) {
      doGetQuestion(Number(questionId));
    }
  }, [questionId]);
```

```
  return ...
};
```

So, when it is first rendered, the question component will fetch the question and set it in the state that will cause a second render of the component. Note that we use the `Number` constructor to convert `questionId` from a `string` into a `number`.

Also, note that the second parameter in the `useEffect` function has `questionId` in an array. This is because the function that `useEffect` runs (the first parameter) is dependent on the `questionId` value and should rerun if this value changes. If `[questionId]` wasn't provided, it would get into an infinite loop because every time it called `setQuestion`, it causes a re-render, which, without `[questionId]`, would always rerun the method.

6. Let's start to implement the JSX for the `QuestionPage` component by adding a container element for the page and the question title:

```
<Page>
  <div
    css={css`
      background-color: white;
      padding: 15px 20px 20px 20px;
      border-radius: 4px;
      border: 1px solid ${gray6};
      box-shadow: 0 3px 5px 0 rgba(0, 0, 0, 0.16);
    `}
  >
    <div
      css={css`
        font-size: 19px;
        font-weight: bold;
        margin: 10px 0px 5px;
      `}
    >
      {question === null ? '' : question.title}
    </div>
  </div>
</Page>
```

164　Routing with React Router

We don't render the title until the `question` state has been set. The `question` state is null while the question is being fetched, and it remains null if the question isn't found. Note that we use a triple equals (`===`) to check whether the `question` variable is `null` rather than a double equals (`==`).

> **Important note**
> When using triple equals (`===`), we are checking for strict equality. This means both the type and the value we are comparing have to be the same. When using a double equals (`==`), the type isn't checked. Generally, it is good practice to use the triple equals (`===`) to perform a strict equality check.

If we look at the running app, we will see that the question title has been rendered in a nice white card:

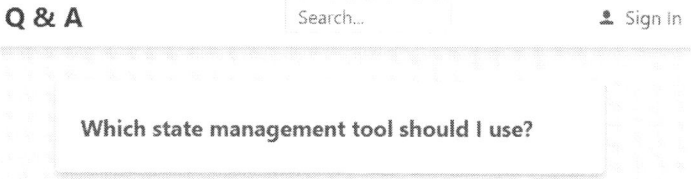

Figure 5.5 – Question page title

7. Let's now implement the question content:

```
<Page>
  <div ... >
    <div ... >
      {question === null ? '' : question.title}
    </div>
    {question !== null && (
      <React.Fragment>
        <p
          css={css`
            margin-top: 0px;
            background-color: white;
          `}
        >
          {question.content}
        </p>
      </React.Fragment>
    )}
  </div>
</Page>
```

So, we show the output content from the question in JSX if the `question` state has been set from the fetched data. Note that this is nested within a `Fragment` component—what is this for?

> **Important note**
> In React, a component can only return a single element. This rule applies to conditional rendering logic where there can be only a single parent React element being rendered. React `Fragment` allows us to work around this rule because we can nest multiple elements within it without creating a DOM node.

We can see the problem that `Fragment` solves if we try to return two elements after the short circuit operator:

```
57          {question !== null && (
58            <p
59              css={css`
60                margin-top: 0px;
61                background-color: white;
62              `}
63            >
64              {question.content}
65            </p>
66            <span>2nd element</span>
67          )}
68        </div>
69      </Page>
70    );
71  };
72
```

PROBLEMS (3)   OUTPUT   DEBUG CONSOLE   TERMINAL

Failed to compile.

/src/QuestionPage.tsx
  Line 68:10: Parsing error: JSX expressions must have one parent element

Figure 5.6 – Reason for react fragment

8. Let's add when the question was asked and who asked it into the `Fragment`:

```
{question !== null && (
  <React.Fragment>
    <p ... >
      {question.content}
    </p>
    <div
      css={css`
        font-size: 12px;
        font-style: italic;
```

```
          color: ${gray3};
        `}
      >
        {`Asked by ${question.userName} on 
    ${question.created.toLocaleDateString()} 
    ${question.created.toLocaleTimeString()}`}
      </div>
    </React.Fragment>
  )}
```

Now, all the details of the question will render in a nice white card in the running app on the question page:

Figure 5.7 – Question page

So, the question page is looking nice now. We aren't rendering any answers yet though, so let's look at that next.

Creating an AnswerList component

Follow these steps to create a component that will render a list of answers:

1. Create a new file called `AnswerList.tsx` with the following `import` statements:

    ```
    /** @jsxImportSource @emotion/react */
    import { css } from '@emotion/react';
    import React from 'react';
    import { AnswerData } from './QuestionsData';
    import { Answer } from './Answer';
    import { gray5 } from './Styles';
    ```

    So, we are going to use an unordered list to render the answers without the bullet points. We have referenced a component, `Answer`, that we'll create later in these steps.

2. Let's define the interface so that it contains a `data` prop for the array of answers:

   ```
   interface Props {
     data: AnswerData[];
   }
   ```

3. Let's create the `AnswerList` component, which outputs the answers:

   ```
   export const AnswerList = ({ data }: Props) => (
     <ul
       css={css`
         list-style: none;
         margin: 10px 0 0 0;
         padding: 0;
       `}
     >
       {data.map(answer => (
         <li
           css={css`
             border-top: 1px solid ${gray5};
           `}
           key={answer.answerId}
         >
           <Answer data={answer} />
         </li>
       ))}
     </ul>
   );
   ```

   Each answer is output in an unordered list in an `Answer` component, which we'll implement next.

4. Let's move on and implement the `Answer` component by creating a file called `Answer.tsx` with the following `import` statements:

   ```
   /** @jsxImportSource @emotion/react */
   import { css } from '@emotion/react';
   import React from 'react';
   import { AnswerData } from './QuestionsData';
   import { gray3 } from './Styles';
   ```

5. The interface for the `Answer` component is simply going to contain the answer data:

   ```
   interface Props {
     data: AnswerData;
   }
   ```

6. Now, the `Answer` component will simply render the answer content, along with who answered it and when it was answered:

```
export const Answer = ({ data }: Props) => (
  <div
    css={css`
      padding: 10px 0px;
    `}
  >
    <div
      css={css`
        padding: 10px 0px;
        font-size: 13px;
      `}
    >
      {data.content}
    </div>
    <div
      css={css`
        font-size: 12px;
        font-style: italic;
        color: ${gray3};
      `}
    >
      {`Answered by ${data.userName} on
      ${data.created.toLocaleDateString()}
      ${data.created.toLocaleTimeString()}`}
    </div>
  </div>
);
```

7. Let's now go back to `QuestionPage.tsx` and import `AnswerList`:

```
import { AnswerList } from './AnswerList';
```

8. Now, we can add `AnswerList` to the `Fragment` element:

```
{question !== null && (
  <React.Fragment>
    <p ... >
      {question.content}
    </p>
    <div ... >
      {`Asked by ${question.userName} on
      ${question.created.toLocaleDateString()}
      ${question.created.toLocaleTimeString()}`}
```

```
    </div>
    <AnswerList data={question.answers} />
  </React.Fragment>
)}
```

If we look at the running app on the question page at `questions/1`, we'll see the answers rendered nicely:

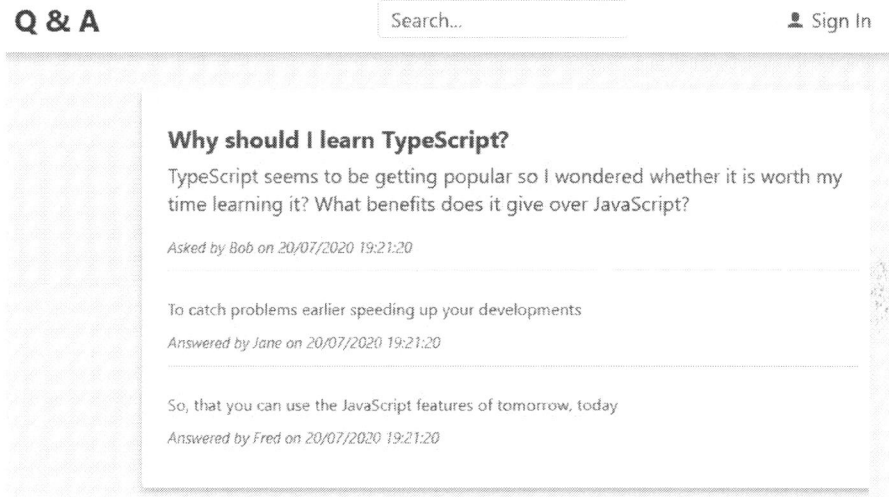

Figure 5.8 – Question page with answers

That completes the work we need to do on the question page in this chapter. However, we need to allow users to submit answers to a question, which we'll cover in *Chapter 6, Working with Forms*.

Next up, we'll look at how we can work with query parameters with React Router.

Using query parameters

A query parameter is part of the URL that allows additional parameters to be passed into a path. For example, `/search?criteria=typescript` has a query parameter called `criteria` with a value of `typescript`. Query parameters are sometimes referred to as a search parameter.

In this section, we are going to implement a query parameter on the search page called `criteria`, which will drive the search. We'll implement the search page along the way. Let's carry out the following steps to do this:

1. We are going to start in `QuestionsData.ts` by creating a function to simulate a search via a web request:

   ```
   export const searchQuestions = async (
     criteria: string,
   ): Promise<QuestionData[]> => {
     await wait(500);
     return questions.filter(
       q =>
         q.title.toLowerCase()
           .indexOf(criteria.toLowerCase()) >= 0 ||
         q.content.toLowerCase()
           .indexOf(criteria.toLowerCase()) >= 0,
     );
   };
   ```

   So, the function uses the array `filter` method and matches the criteria to any part of the question title or content.

2. Let's import this function, along with the other items we need, into `SearchPage.tsx`. Place these statements above the existing `import` statements in `SearchPage.tsx`:

   ```
   /** @jsxImportSource @emotion/react */
   import { css } from '@emotion/react'
   import { useSearchParams } from 'react-router-dom';
   import { QuestionList } from './QuestionList';
   import { searchQuestions, QuestionData } from './QuestionsData';
   ```

   The `useSearchParams` hook from React Router is used to access query parameters.

3. Add an explicit `return` statement to the `SearchPage` component and destructure the object from `useSearchParams` that contains the search parameters:

   ```
   export const SearchPage = () => {
     const [searchParams] = useSearchParams();
     return (
       <Page title="Search Results">{null}</Page>
     );
   };
   ```

The `useSearchParams` hook returns an array with two elements. The first element is an object containing the search parameters, and the second element is a function to update the query parameters. We have only destructured the first element in our code because we don't need to update query parameters in this component.

4. We are now going to create some state to hold the matched questions in the search:

```
export const SearchPage = () => {
  const [searchParams] = useSearchParams();
  const [
    questions,
    setQuestions,
  ] = React.useState<QuestionData[]>([]);
  return ...
};
```

5. Next, we are going to get the `criteria` query parameter value:

```
export const SearchPage = () => {
  const [searchParams] = useSearchParams();
  const [
    questions,
    setQuestions,
  ] = React.useState<QuestionData[]>([]);

  const search = searchParams.get('criteria') || "";

  return ...
};
```

The `searchParams` object contains a `get` method that can be used to get the value of a query parameter.

6. We are going to invoke the search when the component first renders and when the `search` variable changes using the `useEffect` hook:

```
const search = searchParams.get('criteria') || '';
React.useEffect(() => {
  const doSearch = async (criteria: string) => {
    const foundResults = await searchQuestions(
      criteria,
    );
    setQuestions(foundResults);
  };
  doSearch(search);
}, [search]);
```

7. We can now render the search criteria under the page title. Replace `{null}` with the highlighted code:

```
<Page title="Search Results">
  {search && (
    <p
      css={css`
        font-size: 16px;
        font-style: italic;
        margin-top: 0px;
      `}
    >
      for "{search}"
    </p>
  )}
</Page>
```

8. The last task is to use the `QuestionList` component to render the questions that are returned from the search:

```
<Page title="Search Results">
  {search && (
    <p ... >
      for "{search}"
    </p>
  )}
  <QuestionList data={questions} />
</Page>
```

Our `QuestionList` component is now used in both the home and search pages with different data sources. The reusability of this component has been made possible because we have followed the container pattern we briefly mentioned in *Chapter 3, Getting Started with React and TypeScript*.

9. In the running app, enter `/search?criteria=type` in the browser. The search will be invoked and the results will be rendered as we would expect:

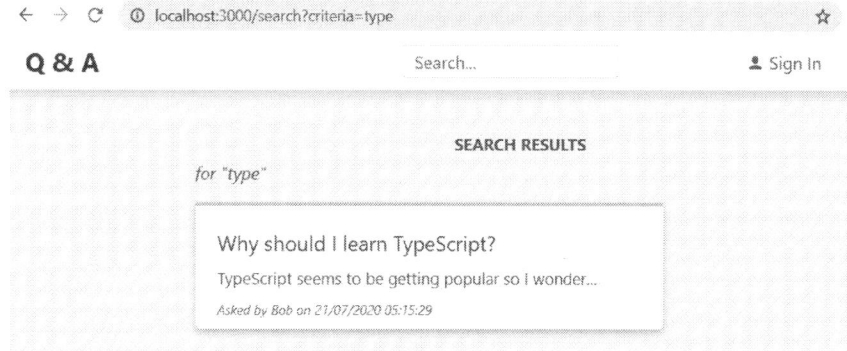

Figure 5.9 – Search results

So, the `useSearchParams` hook in React Router makes interacting with query parameters nice and easy.

In *Chapter 6*, *Working with Forms*, we'll wire up the search box in the header to our search form.

In the next section, we'll learn how we can load components on demand.

Lazy loading routes

At the moment, all the JavaScript for our app is loaded when the app first loads. This is fine for small apps, but for large apps, this can have a negative impact on performance. There may be large pages that are rarely used in the app that we want to load the JavaScript for on demand. This process is called **lazy loading**.

We are going to lazy load the ask page in this section. It isn't a great use of lazy loading because this is likely to be a popular page in our app, but it will help us learn how to implement this. Let's carry out the following steps:

1. First, we are going to add a default export to the `AskPage` component in `AskPage.tsx`:

   ```
   export const AskPage = () => <Page title="Ask a question" />;
   export default AskPage;
   ```

2. Open `App.tsx` and remove the current `import` statement for the `AskPage` component.

3. Add an `import` statement for React:

    ```
    import React from 'react';
    ```

4. Add a new `import` statement for the `AskPage` component after all the other `import` statements:

    ```
    const AskPage = React.lazy(() => import('./AskPage'));
    ```

    It is important that this is the last `import` statement in the file because, otherwise, ESLint may complain that the `import` statements beneath it are in the body of the module.

    The `lazy` function in React lets us render a *dynamic import* as a regular component. A dynamic import returns a promise for the requested module that is resolved after it has been fetched, instantiated, and evaluated.

5. So, the `AskPage` component is being loaded on demand now, but the `App` component is expecting this component to be loaded immediately. If we enter the `ask` path in the browser's address bar and press the *Enter* key, we may receive an error with a clue of how to resolve this:

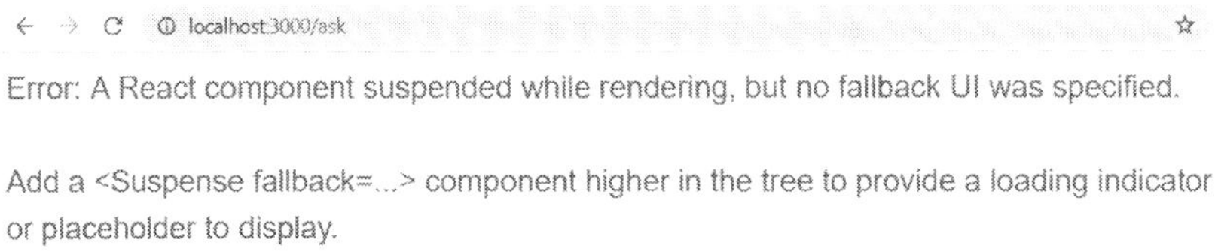

    Error: A React component suspended while rendering, but no fallback UI was specified.

    Add a <Suspense fallback=...> component higher in the tree to provide a loading indicator or placeholder to display.

    Figure 5.10 – No Suspense component warning

6. As suggested by the error message, we are going to use the `Suspense` component from React to resolve this issue. For `ask` `Route`, we wrap the `Suspense` component around the `AskPage` component:

    ```
    <Route
      path="ask"
      element={
        <React.Suspense
          fallback={
            <div
              css={css`
                margin-top: 100px;
                text-align: center;
              `}
            >
              Loading...
    ```

```
            </div>
        }
    >
        <AskPage />
    </React.Suspense>
  }
/>
```

The `Suspense fallback` prop allows us to render a component while `AskPage` is loading. So, we are rendering a **Loading...** message while the `AskPage` component is being loaded.

7. Let's go to the running app on the home page and open the browser developer tools by pressing *F12*.

8. On the **Network** tab, let's clear the previous network activity by clicking the *no entry* icon. Then, if we click the **Ask a question** button, we will see confirmation that additional JavaScript has been downloaded in order to render the `AskPage` component:

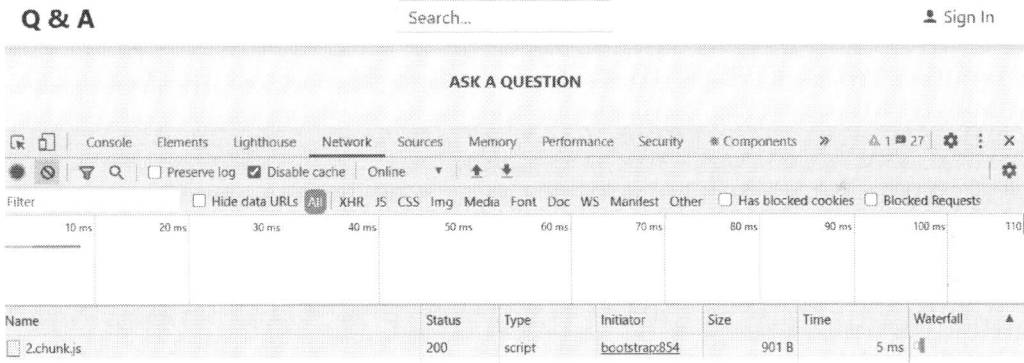

Figure 5.11 – AskPage component loaded on demand

9. The `AskPage` component loads so fast that we are unlikely to see the `Loading` component being rendered. In the Chrome browser developer tools, there is an option to simulate a **Slow 3G** network in the **Network** tab:

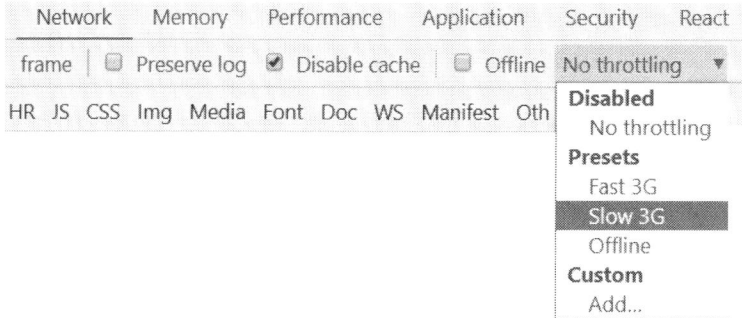

Figure 5.12 – Slow 3G option

10. If we turn this on, load the app again by pressing *F5* on the home page, and click the **Ask a question** button, we will see the **Loading...** message being rendered temporarily:

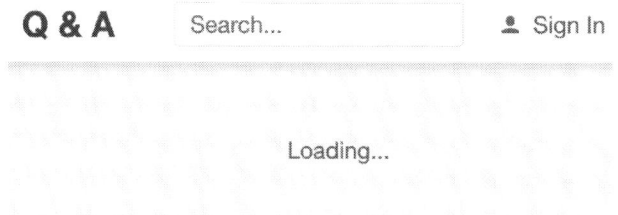

Figure 5.13 – Suspense fallback

In this example, the `AskPage` component is small in size, so this approach doesn't really positively impact performance. However, loading larger components on demand can really help performance, particularly on slow connections.

Summary

React Router gives us a comprehensive set of components for managing the navigation between pages in our app. We learned that the top-level component is `BrowserRouter`, which looks for `Route` components within a `Routes` component beneath it where we define what components should be rendered for certain paths. The `path` in a `Route` component that best matches the current browser location is the one that is rendered.

The `useParams` hook gives us access to route parameters, and the `useSearchParams` hook gives us access to query parameters. These hooks are available in any React component under `BrowserRouter` in the component tree.

We learned that the React `lazy` function, along with its `Suspense` component, can be used on large components that are rarely used by users to load them on demand. This helps the performance of the startup time of our app.

In the next chapter, we are going to continue building the frontend of the Q&A app, this time focusing on implementing forms.

Questions

The following questions will cement your knowledge of what you have just learned about in this chapter:

1. We have the following routes defined:

   ```
   <BrowserRouter>
     <Routes>
       <Route path="search" element={<SearchPage/>} />
       <Route path="" element={<HomePage/>} />
     </Routes>
   </BrowserRouter>
   ```

   Answer the following questions:

   - What component(s) will be rendered when the `/` location is entered in the browser?
   - What about when the `/search` location is entered in the browser?

2. In our Q&A app, we want a `/login` path to navigate to the sign-in page, as well as the `/signin` path. How can we implement this?

3. We have the following routes defined:

   ```
   <BrowserRouter>
     <Routes>
       <Route path="search" element={<SearchPage/>} />
       <Route path="" element ={<HomePage/>} />
       <Route path="*" element={<NotFoundPage/>} />
     </Routes>
   </BrowserRouter>
   ```

   What component will be rendered when the `/signin` location is entered in the browser?

4. We have the following route defined:

   ```
   <Route path="users/:userId" component={UserPage} />
   ```

   How can we reference the `userId` route parameter in a component?

5. How can we get the value of an `id` query parameter from a path such as `/users?id=1`?

6. We have an option that navigates to another page when clicked. The JSX for this option is as follows:

   ```
   <a href="/products">Products</a>
   ```

   At the moment, the navigation makes a server request. How can we change this so that the navigation happens only within the browser?

7. We have a requirement to programmatically navigate to a `/success` path when a process has completed. How can we do this?

Answers

1. The `HomePage` component will be rendered when the browser location is `/`, and the `SearchPage` component will be rendered when the browser location is `/search`.

2. To enable a path of `/login` to render the sign-in page, we can define an additional `Route` component as follows:

   ```
   <Route path="signin" element={<SignInPage />} />
   <Route path="login" element={<SignInPage />} />
   ```

3. The `NotFoundPage` component will be rendered.

4. We can reference the `userId` route parameter using the `useParams` hook as follows:

   ```
   const { userId } = useParams();
   ```

5. We can reference the `id` query parameter using the `useSearchParams` hook as follows:

   ```
   const [searchParams] = useSearchParams();
   const id = searchParams.get('id');
   ```

6. The `Link` component can be used so that navigation only happens on the client:

   ```
   <Link to="products">Products</Link>
   ```

7. In order to programmatically navigate, we first need to get a function from the `useNavigate` hook that can perform the navigation:

   ```
   const navigate = useNavigate();
   ```

   We can then use this function at the appropriate place in code to navigate to the `/success` path:

   ```
   navigate('success');
   ```

Further reading

The following are some useful links for learning more about the topics that have been covered in this chapter:

- **React Router**: `https://reacttraining.com/react-router`
- **JavaScript array filter**: `https://developer.mozilla.org/en-US/docs/Web/JavaScript/Reference/Global_Objects/Array/filter`
- **TypeScript union types**: `https://www.typescriptlang.org/docs/handbook/advanced-types.html`
- **React fragments**: `https://reactjs.org/docs/fragments.html`
- **React lazy**: `https://reactjs.org/docs/code-splitting.html#reactlazy`

6
Working with Forms

Forms are an important topic because they are extremely common in the apps we build. In this chapter, we'll learn how to build forms using React controlled components and discover that there is a fair amount of boilerplate code involved. We will use a popular library to reduce the boilerplate code. This will also help us to build several forms in our app.

Client-side validation is critical to the user experience of the forms we build, so we'll cover this topic in a fair amount of depth. We will also cover how to submit forms.

We'll cover the following topics in this chapter:

- Understanding controlled components
- Reducing boilerplate code with React Hook Form
- Implementing validation
- Submitting forms

By the end of this chapter, you will have learned how to efficiently create forms with their key ingredients.

Technical requirements

We'll use the following tools in this chapter:

- **Visual Studio Code**: We'll use this to edit our React code. This can be downloaded and installed from `https://code.visualstudio.com/`. If you already have this installed, make sure that it is at least version 1.52.

- **Node.js** and **npm**: These can be downloaded from `https://nodejs.org/`. If you already have these installed, make sure that Node.js is at least version 8.2 and that `npm` is at least version 5.2.

- **Q and A**: We'll start with the Q and A frontend project we finished in *Chapter 5, Routing with React Router*. This is available on GitHub at `https://github.com/PacktPublishing/ASP.NET-Core-5-and-React-Second-Edition` in the `chapter-06/start` folder.

All the code snippets in this chapter can be found online at `https://github.com/PacktPublishing/ASP.NET-Core-5-and-React-Second-Edition`. To restore code from a chapter, you can download the source code repository, and the relevant folder can be opened in the relevant editor. If the code is frontend code, then `npm install` can be entered in the Terminal to restore the required dependencies.

Check out the following video to see the code in action: `https://bit.ly/3pherQp`.

Understanding controlled components

In this section, we are going to learn how to use what are called **controlled components** to implement a form. A controlled component has its value synchronized with the state in React. This will make more sense when we've implemented our first controlled component.

Let's open our project in Visual Studio Code and change the search box in our app header to a controlled component. Follow these steps:

1. Open `Header.tsx` and add the following imports:

    ```
    import {
      Link,
      useSearchParams,
    } from 'react-router-dom';
    ```

2. The default value for the search box is going to be the `criteria` route query parameter. So, let's use the `useSearchParams` hook from React Router to get this:

   ```
   export const Header = () => {
     const [searchParams] = useSearchParams();
     const criteria = searchParams.get('criteria') || '';

     const handleSearchInputChange = ...
   }
   ```

3. Let's create a state that we can store the search value in, defaulting it to the `criteria` variable we have just set:

   ```
   const searchParams = new URLSearchParams(location.search);
   const criteria = searchParams.get('criteria') || '';

   const [search, setSearch] = React.useState(criteria);
   ```

4. Now, let's drive the search box value from this `search` state:

   ```
   <input
     type="text"
     placeholder="Search..."
     value={search}
     onChange={handleSearchChange}
     css={ ... }
   />
   ```

5. Start the app by running the `npm start` command in Visual Studio Code's Terminal.

6. Try to type something into the search box in the app header.

   You'll notice that nothing seems to happen; something is preventing us from entering the value. We have just set the value to some React state, so React is now controlling the value of the search box. This is why we no longer appear to be able to type into it.

   We are part way through creating our first controlled input. However, controlled inputs aren't much use if users can't enter anything into them. So, how can we make our `input` editable again? The answer is that we need to listen to changes that have been made to the `input` value and update the state accordingly. React will then render the new value from the state.

7. We are already listening to changes with the `handleSearchInputChange` function. So, all we need to do is update the state in the following function, replacing the previous `console.log` statement with the following:

```
const handleSearchChange = (e:
ChangeEvent<HTMLInputElement>) => {
  setSearch(e.currentTarget.value);
};
```

Now, if we go to the running app and enter something into the search box, this time, it will behave as expected, allowing us to enter characters into it.

8. Now, add a `form` element that's wrapped around the `input` element:

```
<form>
  <input
    type="text"
    placeholder="Search..."
    onChange={handleSearchInputChange}
    value={search}
    css={ ... }
  />
</form>
```

Eventually, this will allow a user to invoke the search when the *Enter* key is pressed.

9. Add the following `onSubmit` prop to the form element:

```
<form onSubmit={handleSubmit}>
```

10. Add the implementation of the submit handler just above the `return` statement:

```
const handleSubmit = (e: React.FormEvent) => {
  e.preventDefault();
  console.log(search);
};
return ...
```

11. In the running app, type something into the search box in the app header and press *Enter*. Open the browser's DevTools and look at the console:

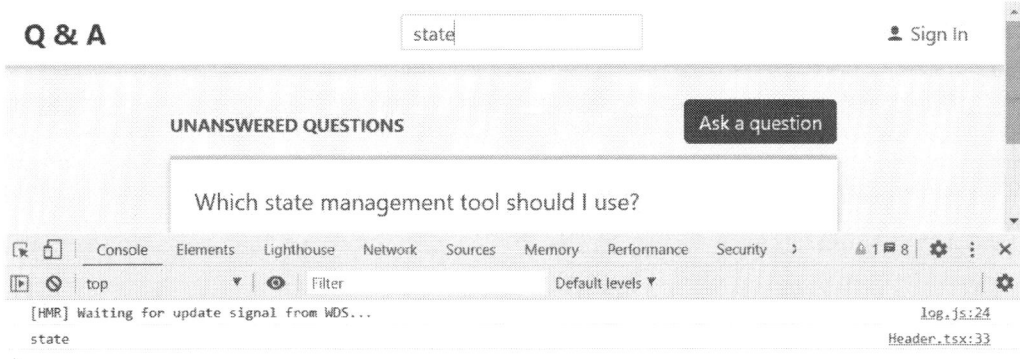

Figure 6.1 – Controlled component

Now, if we type characters into the search box and press *Enter*, we will see the submitted search criteria in the console.

12. Press *Ctrl + C* in the Terminal and press *Y* when prompted to stop the app from running.

In summary, controlled components have their values managed by React's state. It is important that we implement a change handler that updates the state; otherwise, our users won't be able to interact with the component.

If we were to implement a form with several controlled components, we would have to create the state and a change event listener to update the state for each field. That's quite a lot of boilerplate code to write when implementing forms. Is there a forms library that we can use to reduce the amount of repetitive code we must write? Yes! We'll do just this in the next section.

Reducing boilerplate code with React Hook Form

In this section, we are going to use a popular forms library called **React Hook Form**. This library reduces the amount of code we need to write when implementing forms. Once we have installed React Hook Form, we will refactor the search form we created in the previous section. We will then use React Hook Form to implement forms for asking a question and answering a question.

Installing React Hook Form

Let's install React Hook Form by entering the following command into the Terminal:

```
> npm install react-hook-form
```

After a few seconds, React Hook Form will be installed.

The `react-hook-form` package includes TypeScript types, so these aren't in a separate package that we need to install.

Next, we will start to use React Hook Form for the search form in the `Header` component.

Refactoring the Header component to use React Hook Form

We are going to use React Hook Form to reduce the amount of code in the `Header` component. Open `Header.tsx` and follow these steps:

1. Remove the line where the `search` state is declared. The line you must remove is shown here:

   ```
   const [search, setSearch] = React.useState(criteria);
   ```

   React Hook Form will manage the field state, so we don't have to write explicit code for this.

2. Add the following name property to the `input` element:

   ```
   <input
     name="search"
     type="text"
     ...
   />
   ```

   The `name` property is required by React Hook Form and must have a unique value for a given form. We will eventually be able to access this value from the `input` element using this name.

3. Remove the `value` and `onChange` properties from the `input` element and add a `defaultValue` property, which is set to the `criteria` query parameter value:

   ```
   <input
     name="search"
     type="text"
     placeholder="Search..."
     defaultValue={criteria}
     css={ ... }
   />
   ```

   React Form Hook will eventually manage the value of the input.

   Note that `defaultValue` is a property of the `input` element for setting its initial value.

4. Remove the `handleSearchInputChange` function handler for the input's change event.

5. Remove the `console.log` statement from the `handleSubmit` function:

   ```
   const handleSubmit = (e: React.FormEvent) => {
     e.preventDefault();
   };
   ```

6. Now that we have removed the boilerplate form code, it's time to use React Hook Form. Let's start by importing the `useForm` hook from React Hook Form:

   ```
   import { useForm } from 'react-hook-form';
   ```

7. Add a type that will represent the form data just above the `Header` component definition and below the `import` statements:

   ```
   type FormData = {
     search: string;
   };
   ```

8. Pass the form data type into the `useForm` hook and destructure the `register` function from it:

   ```
   export const Header = () => {
     const { register } = useForm<FormData>();
     const [searchParams] = useSearchParams();
     ...
   ```

9. Add a `ref` property to the `input` element in the `Header` component's JSX and set this to the `register` function from React Hook Form:

```
<input
  ref={register}
  name="search"
  type="text"
  placeholder="Search..."
  defaultValue={criteria}
  css={ ... }
/>
```

The `register` function allows an `input` element to be registered with React Hook Form and then be managed by it. It needs to be set to the `ref` property on the element.

> **Important note**
> The `ref` property is a special property that React adds to elements that enables the underlying DOM node to be accessed.

The code for our form is a lot shorter now. This is because React Hook Form holds the field state and manages updates to it.

We used the `register` function from the `useForm` hook to tell React Hook Form which fields to manage. There are other useful functions and objects in the `useForm` hook that we will learn about and use in this chapter.

React Form Hook is now controlling the search input field. We will return to this and implement the search submission ability in the *Submitting forms* section.

Next, will turn our attention to styling our forms.

Creating form styled components

In this section, we are going to create some styled components that can be used in the forms that we will eventually implement. Open `Styles.ts` and follow these steps:

1. Import the `css` function from emotion:

   ```
   import { css } from '@emotion/react';
   ```

2. Add a styled component for a `fieldset` element:

   ```
   export const Fieldset = styled.fieldset`
     margin: 10px auto 0 auto;
     padding: 30px;
     width: 350px;
     background-color: ${gray6};
     border-radius: 4px;
     border: 1px solid ${gray5};
     box-shadow: 0 3px 5px 0 rgba(0, 0, 0, 0.16);
   `;
   ```

   We will eventually use a `fieldset` element inside our forms.

3. Add a styled component for the field container:

   ```
   export const FieldContainer = styled.div`
     margin-bottom: 10px;
   `;
   ```

4. Add a styled component for the `label` element:

   ```
   export const FieldLabel = styled.label`
     font-weight: bold;
   `;
   ```

5. The field editor elements will have many common CSS properties. Create a variable that contains the following code:

   ```
   const baseFieldCSS = css`
     box-sizing: border-box;
     font-family: ${fontFamily};
     font-size: ${fontSize};
     margin-bottom: 5px;
     padding: 8px 10px;
     border: 1px solid ${gray5};
     border-radius: 3px;
     color: ${gray2};
     background-color: white;
     width: 100%;
     :focus {
       outline-color: ${gray5};
     }
     :disabled {
       background-color: ${gray6};
     }
   `;
   ```

6. Use the following variable in a styled component for an `input` element:

   ```
   export const FieldInput = styled.input`
     ${baseFieldCSS}
   `;
   ```

   This causes the input element to include the CSS from the `baseFieldCSS` variable in the new styled component we are creating.

7. Now, create a styled component for the `textarea` element:

   ```
   export const FieldTextArea = styled.textarea`
     ${baseFieldCSS}
     height: 100px;
   `;
   ```

8. Add a styled component for the validation error message:

   ```
   export const FieldError = styled.div`
     font-size: 12px;
     color: red;
   `;
   ```

9. Add a styled component for a container for the form submit button:

   ```
   export const FormButtonContainer = styled.div`
     margin: 30px 0px 0px 0px;
     padding: 20px 0px 0px 0px;
     border-top: 1px solid ${gray5};
   `;
   ```

   The last styled components we are going to create are the submission messages:

   ```
   export const SubmissionSuccess = styled.div`
     margin-top: 10px;
     color: green;
   `;
   export const SubmissionFailure = styled.div`
     margin-top: 10px;
     color: red;
   `;
   ```

With that, we've implemented all the styled components that we will use in our forms.

Now that we have implemented these styled components, we will use these to implement our next form.

Implementing the ask form

Now, it's time to implement the form so that our users can ask a question. We'll do this by leveraging React Hook Form and our form's styled components. Follow these steps:

1. Open `AskPage.tsx` and add the following `import` statements:

   ```
   import {
     Fieldset,
     FieldContainer,
     FieldLabel,
     FieldInput,
     FieldTextArea,
     FormButtonContainer,
     PrimaryButton,
   } from './Styles';
   import { useForm } from 'react-hook-form';
   ```

2. Add a type to represent the form data just above the `AskPage` component definition and just below the `import` statements:

   ```
   type FormData = {
     title: string;
     content: string;
   };
   ```

3. Add an explicit `return` statement to the `AskPage` component, pass in the `FormData` type to the `useForm` hook, and destructure the register function
4. from it:

   ```
   export const AskPage = () => {
     const { register } = useForm<FormData>();
     return (
       <Page title="Ask a question">
         {null}
       </Page>
     );
   }
   ```

5. Add the `form` and `Fieldset` elements, replacing the `null` output:

   ```
   <Page title="Ask a question">
     <form>
       <Fieldset>
       </Fieldset>
     </form>
   </Page>
   ```

6. Now, let's add a field that will capture the question's title:

   ```
   <Fieldset>
     <FieldContainer>
       <FieldLabel htmlFor="title">
         Title
       </FieldLabel>
       <FieldInput
         id="title"
         name="title"
         type="text"
         ref={register}
       />
     </FieldContainer>
   </Fieldset>
   ```

   Notice how we have tied the label to the input using the `htmlFor` attribute. This means a screen reader will read out the label when the input has focus. In addition, clicking on the label will automatically set focus on the input.

7. Add a field that will capture the question's content:

   ```
   <Fieldset>
     <FieldContainer>
       ...
     </FieldContainer>
     <FieldContainer>
       <FieldLabel htmlFor="content">
         Content
       </FieldLabel>
       <FieldTextArea
         id="content"
         name="content"
         ref={register}
       />
     </FieldContainer>
   </Fieldset>
   ```

8. Finally, add a button for submitting the question using the `FormButtonContainer` and `PrimaryButton` styled components:

```
<Fieldset>
  <FieldContainer>
    ...
  </FieldContainer>
  <FormButtonContainer>
    <PrimaryButton type="submit">
      Submit Your Question
    </PrimaryButton>
  </FormButtonContainer>
</Fieldset>
```

9. Start the app by running the `npm start` command in Visual Studio Code's Terminal.

10. Let's give this a try in the running app by clicking the **Ask a question** button on the home page:

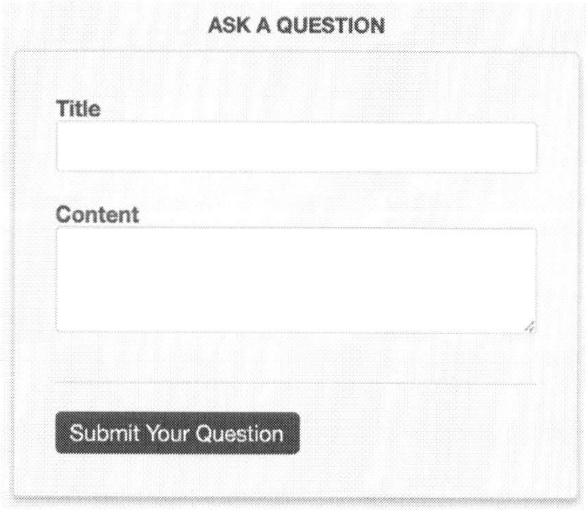

Figure 6.2 – Form for asking a question

Our form renders as expected.

React Hook Form and the styled form components made that job pretty easy. Now, let's try implementing another form, which is none other than the answer form.

Implementing the answer form

Let's implement an answer form on the question page. Follow these steps:

1. Open `QuestionPage.tsx` and update the following `import` statement:

   ```
   import {
     gray3,
     gray6,
     Fieldset,
     FieldContainer,
     FieldLabel,
     FieldTextArea,
     FormButtonContainer,
     PrimaryButton,
   } from './Styles';
   ```

2. Add an import statement for React Hook Form:

   ```
   import { useForm } from 'react-hook-form';
   ```

3. Add a type that will represent the form data:

   ```
   type FormData = {
     content: string;
   };
   ```

4. Pass the form data type to the `useForm` hook and destructure the `register` function from it:

   ```
   export const QuestionPage = () => {
     ...
     const { register } = useForm<FormData>();
     return ...
   }
   ```

5. Let's create our form in the JSX, just beneath the list of answers:

   ```
   <AnswerList data={question.answers} />
   <form
     css={css`
       margin-top: 20px;
     `}
   >
     <Fieldset>
       <FieldContainer>
         <FieldLabel htmlFor="content">
           Your Answer
   ```

```
        </FieldLabel>
        <FieldTextArea
          id="content"
          name="content"
          ref={register}
        />
      </FieldContainer>
      <FormButtonContainer>
        <PrimaryButton type="submit">
          Submit Your Answer
        </PrimaryButton>
      </FormButtonContainer>
    </Fieldset>
  </form>
```

So, the form will contain a single field for the answer content and the submit button will have the caption **Submit Your Answer**.

6. Let's give this a try in the running app by clicking a question on the home page:

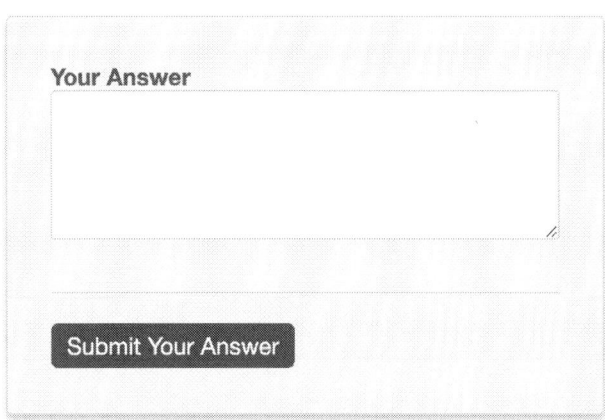

Figure 6.3 – Answer form

Our form renders as expected.

We have now built three forms with React Hook Form and experienced first-hand how it simplifies building fields. We also built a handy set of styled form components along the way.

Our forms are looking good, but there is no validation yet. For example, we could submit a blank answer to a question, and it wouldn't be verified since there no such mechanism has been implemented yet. We will enhance our forms with validation in the next section.

Implementing validation

Including validation on a form improves the user experience as you can provide immediate feedback on whether the information that's been entered is valid. In this section, we are going to add validation rules to the forms for asking and answering questions. These validation rules will include checks to ensure a field is populated and that it contains a certain number of characters.

Implementing validation on the ask form

We are going to implement validation on the ask form by following these steps:

1. In `AskPage.tsx`, we are going to make sure that the title and content fields are populated by the user with a minimum number of characters. First, import the `FieldError` styled component:

   ```
   import {
     ...
     FieldError,
   } from './Styles';
   ```

2. Destructure the form error messages from the `useForm` hook:

   ```
   const { register, errors } = useForm<FormData>();
   ```

3. Next, configure the form so that it invokes the validation rules when the field elements lose focus (that is, the element's `blur` event):

   ```
   const { register, errors } = useForm<FormData>({
     mode: 'onBlur',
   });
   ```

   It is important to note that the fields will be validated when the form is submitted as well.

4. Specify the validation rules in the register function, as follows:

```
<FieldInput
  id="title"
  name="title"
  type="text"
  ref={register({
    required: true,
    minLength: 10,
  })}
/>
```

The highlighted code states that the `title` field is required and must be at least 10 characters long.

5. Let's conditionally render the validation error messages for both these rules beneath the `input` element:

```
<FieldInput
  ...
/>
{errors.title &&
  errors.title.type ===
    'required' && (
    <FieldError>
      You must enter the question title
    </FieldError>
  )}
{errors.title &&
  errors.title.type ===
    'minLength' && (
    <FieldError>
      The title must be at least 10 characters
    </FieldError>
  )}
</FieldContainer>
```

`errors` is an object that React Hook Form maintains for us. The keys in the object correspond to the name property in `FieldInput`. The `type` property within each error specifies which rule the error is for.

6. Add validation to the `content` field to make it mandatory. It should contain at least 50 characters:

```
<FieldTextArea
  id="content"
  name="content"
  ref={register({
    required: true,
    minLength: 50,
  })}
/>
```

7. Add a validation error message to the `content` field:

```
<FieldTextArea
  ...
/>
{errors.content &&
  errors.content.type ===
    'required' && (
    <FieldError>
      You must enter the question content
    </FieldError>
  )}
{errors.content &&
  errors.content.type ===
    'minLength' && (
    <FieldError>
      The content must be at least 50 characters
    </FieldError>
  )}
</FieldContainer>
```

The `errors` object will contain a `content` property when the content field fails a validation check. The type property within the `content` property indicates which rule has been violated. So, we use this information in the `errors` object to render the appropriate validation messages.

8. Let's give this a try. In the running app, go to the ask page by clicking on the **Ask a question** button at the bottom of the home screen.

Without entering anything in the form, click into and out of the fields. You'll see that the form has rendered validation errors, meaning the mechanism that we implemented has worked successfully. Don't type anything in the title field and then enter content that is less than 50 characters:

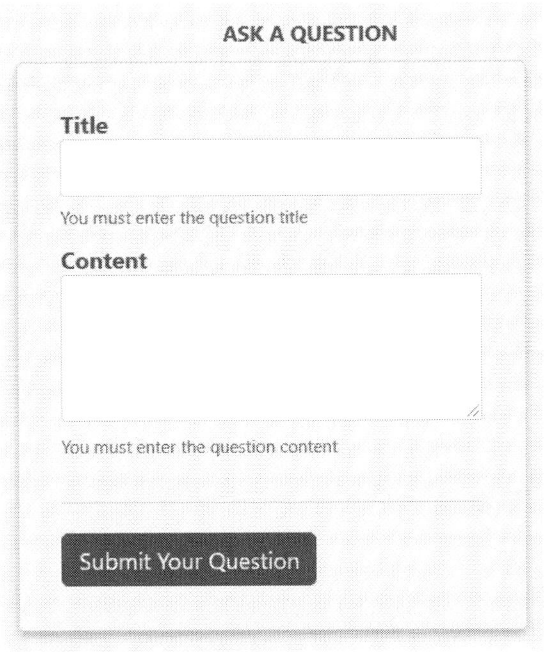

Figure 6.4 – Validation on the ask form

Here, we can see that the validation errors render as we tab out of the fields.

Implementing validation on the answer form

Let's implement validation on the answer form. We are going to validate that the content has been filled in with at least 50 characters. To do this, follow these steps:

1. Open `QuestionPage.tsx` and import the `FieldError` styled component:

   ```
   import {
     ...
     FieldError,
   } from './Styles';
   ```

2. In the `useForm` hook, destructure the `errors` object and configure the form to validate when its fields lose focus:

```
const { register, errors } = useForm<FormData>({
  mode: 'onBlur',
});
```

3. Specify the validation rules on the answer field, as follows:

```
<FieldTextArea
  id="content"
  name="content"
  ref={register({
      required: true,
      minLength: 50,
    })}
/>
```

Here, we've specified that the answer needs to be mandatory and must be at least 50 characters long.

4. Let's conditionally render the validation error messages for both these rules beneath the text area element:

```
<FieldTextArea
  ...
/>
{errors.content &&
  errors.content.type ===
    'required' && (
    <FieldError>
      You must enter the answer
    </FieldError>
  )}
{errors.content &&
  errors.content.type ===
    'minLength' && (
    <FieldError>
      The answer must be at least 50 characters
    </FieldError>
  )}
</FieldContainer>
```

5. In the running app, we can check that this is working as expected by clicking on a question on the home page and entering `Some answer`:

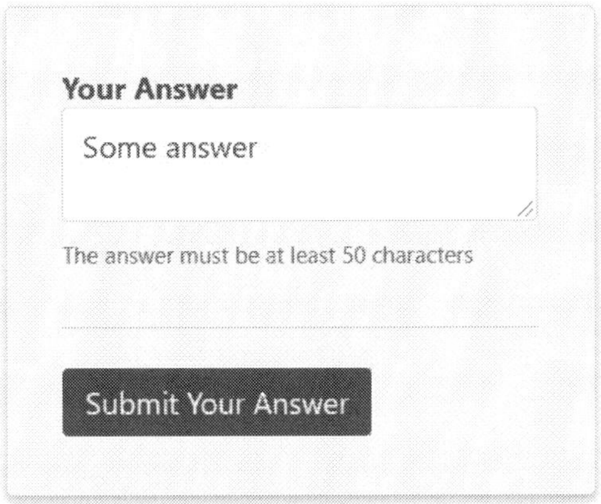

Figure 6.5 – Validation on the answer form

With that, we've finished implementing validation on our forms. React Hook Form has a useful set of validation rules that can be applied to its `register` function. The `errors` object from React Hook Form gives us all the information we need to output informative validation error messages. More information on React Hook Form validation can be found at `https://react-hook-form.com/get-started#Applyvalidation`.

Our final task is to perform submission logic when the user submits our forms. We'll do this in the next section.

Submitting forms

Submitting the form is the final part of the form's implementation. We are going to implement form submission logic in all three of our forms, starting with the search form.

Submission logic is logic that performs a task with the data from the form. Often, this task will involve posting the data to a web API to perform a server-side task, such as saving the data to a database table. In this section, our submission logic will simply call functions that will simulate web API calls.

Implementing form submission in the search form

In `Header.tsx`, carry out the following steps to implement form submission on the search form:

1. Import the `useNavigate` hook from React Router:

   ```
   import {
     Link,
     useSearchParams,
     useNavigate,
   } from 'react-router-dom';
   ```

2. Inside the `Header` component, on the first line, assign a function to the result of the `useNavigate` hook:

   ```
   const navigate = useNavigate();
   ```

3. Destructure a `handleSubmit` function from the `useForm` hook:

   ```
   const { register, handleSubmit } = useForm<FormData>();
   ```

   This conflicts with the existing `handleSubmit`, which we'll resolve later in *step 5*.

4. Use the `handleSubmit` function to handle the `submit` event in the form:

   ```
   <form onSubmit={handleSubmit(submitForm)}>
   ```

   The `handleSubmit` function from React Hook Form includes boilerplate code such as stopping the browser posting the form to the server.

   Notice that we have passed `submitForm` to `handleSubmit`. This is a function that we will implement next that contains our submission logic.

5. Overwrite the existing `handleSubmit` function with the following `submitForm` function:

   ```
   const submitForm = ({ search }: FormData) => {
     navigate(`search?criteria=${search}`);
   };
   ```

   React Hook Form passes the function the form data. We destructure the `search` field value from the form data.

   The submission logic programmatically navigates to the search page, setting the `criteria` query parameter to the `search` field value.

6. Let's try this out in the running app. In the search box, enter the word `typescript` and press *Enter*, as follows:

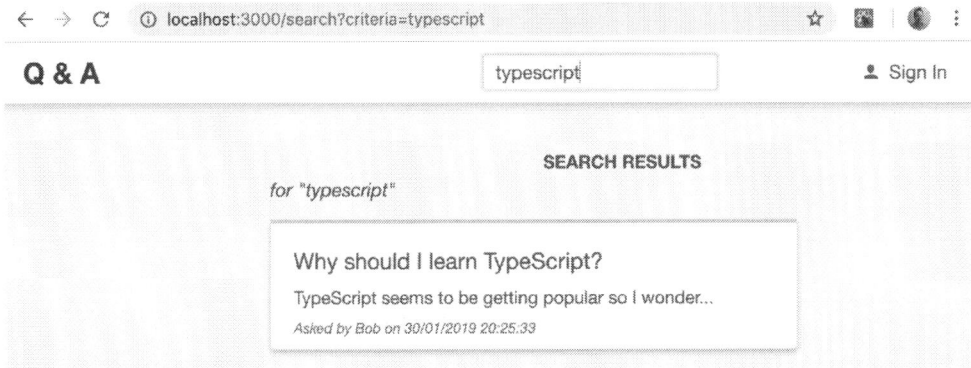

Figure 6.6 – Search submission

The browser location query parameter is set as expected, with the correct result rendering in the search form.

That's the submission implemented in our first form. Now, we will continue to implement the submission logic in our other forms.

Implementing form submission in the ask form

Let's carry out the following steps to implement submission in the ask form:

1. In `QuestionsData.ts`, create a function that will simulate posting a question:

```
export interface PostQuestionData {
  title: string;
  content: string;
  userName: string;
  created: Date;
}

export const postQuestion = async (
  question: PostQuestionData,
): Promise<QuestionData | undefined> => {
  await wait(500);
  const questionId =
    Math.max(...questions.map(q => q.questionId)) + 1;
  const newQuestion: QuestionData = {
    ...question,
    questionId,
    answers: [],
```

Working with Forms

```
  };
  questions.push(newQuestion);
  return newQuestion;
};
```

This function adds the question to the `questions` array using the `Math.max` method to set `questionId` to the next number.

2. In `AskPage.tsx`, import the function we just added to `QuestionData.ts`:

```
import { postQuestion } from './QuestionsData';
```

Also, import the `SubmissionSuccess` message styled component:

```
import {
  ...,
  SubmissionSuccess,
} from './Styles';
```

3. Add some state for whether the form has been successfully submitted within the `AskPage` component:

```
const [
  successfullySubmitted,
  setSuccessfullySubmitted,
] = React.useState(false);
```

4. Destructure the `handleSubmit` function from the `useForm` hook:

```
const {
  register,
  errors,
  handleSubmit,
} = useForm<FormData>({
  mode: 'onBlur',
});
```

5. Also, destructure `formState` from the `useForm` hook:

```
const {
  register,
  errors,
  handleSubmit,
  formState,
} = useForm<FormData>({
  mode: 'onBlur',
});
```

`formState` contains information such as whether the form is being submitted and whether the form is valid.

6. Use the `handleSubmit` function to handle the `submit` event in the form:

   ```
   <form onSubmit={handleSubmit(submitForm)}>
   ```

7. Create a `submitForm` function just above the component's `return` statement, as follows:

   ```
   const submitForm = async (data: FormData) => {
     const result = await postQuestion({
       title: data.title,
       content: data.content,
       userName: 'Fred',
       created: new Date()
     });
     setSuccessfullySubmitted(result ? true : false);
   };
   ```

   The preceding code calls the `postQuestion` function asynchronously, passing in the title and content from the form data with a hardcoded username and created date.

8. Disable the form if the submission is in progress or successfully completed:

   ```
   <Fieldset
     disabled={
       formState.isSubmitting ||
       successfullySubmitted
     }
   >
   ```

   `isSubmitting` is a flag within `formState` that indicates whether form submission is taking place.

   You may notice an `isSubmitted` flag within `formState`. This indicates whether a form has been submitted and is `true`, even if the form is invalid. This is why we use our own state (`successfullySubmitted`) to indicate that a valid form has been submitted.

9. After `FormButtonContainer` in the JSX, add the following submission success message:

```
{successfullySubmitted && (
  <SubmissionSuccess>
    Your question was successfully submitted
  </SubmissionSuccess>
)}
```

This message is rendered once the form has been successfully submitted.

10. In the running app, on the home page, click the **Ask a question** button and fill out the question form. Then, click the **Submit Your Question** button:

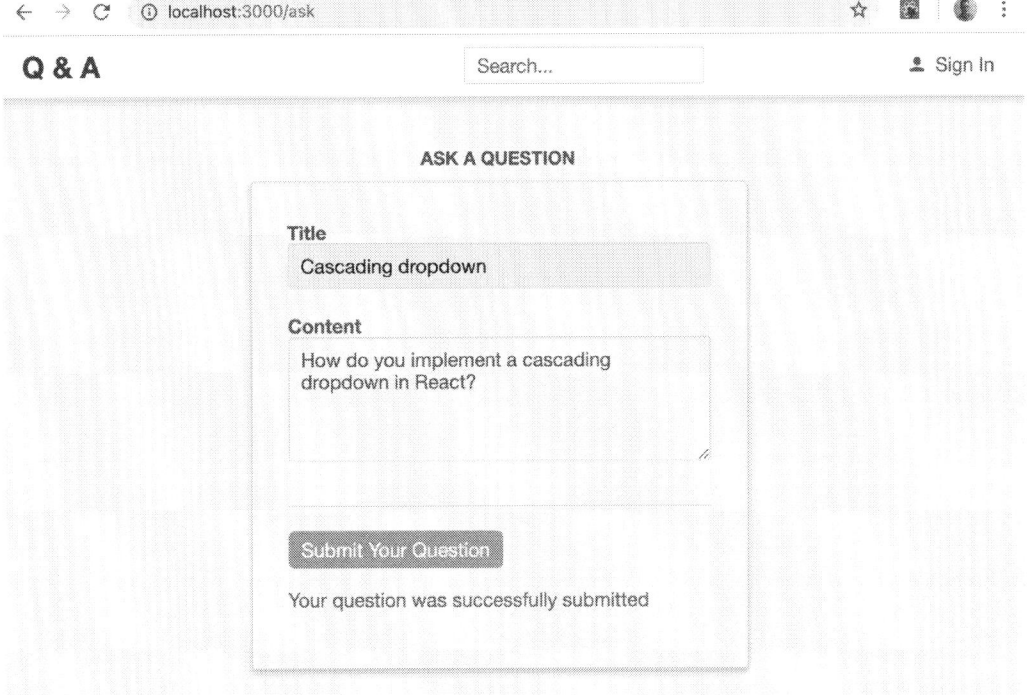

Figure 6.7 – Ask a question submission

The form is disabled during and after a successful submission, and we receive the expected success message.

Next, we'll implement form submission in the answer form.

Implementing form submission in the answer form

Carry out the following steps to implement form submission in the answer form:

1. In `QuestionsData.ts`, create a function that simulates posting an answer:

```ts
export interface PostAnswerData {
  questionId: number;
  content: string;
  userName: string;
  created: Date;
}

export const postAnswer = async (
  answer: PostAnswerData,
): Promise<AnswerData | undefined> => {
  await wait(500);
  const question = questions.filter(
    q => q.questionId === answer.questionId,
  )[0];
  const answerInQuestion: AnswerData = {
    answerId: 99,
    ...answer,
  };
  question.answers.push(answerInQuestion);
  return answerInQuestion;
};
```

The function finds the question in the `questions` array and adds the answer to it. The remainder of the preceding code contains straightforward types for the answer to post and the function's result.

2. In `QuestionPage.tsx`, import the function we just created, along with the `Styles` component for a success message:

```tsx
import {
  ...,
  postAnswer
} from './QuestionsData';
import {
  ...,
  SubmissionSuccess,
} from './Styles';
```

3. Add a state for whether the form has been successfully submitted in the `QuestionPage` component:

```
const [
  successfullySubmitted,
  setSuccessfullySubmitted,
] = React.useState(false);
```

4. Destructure `handleSubmit` and `formState` from the `useForm` hook:

```
const {
  register,
  errors,
  handleSubmit,
  formState
} = useForm<FormData>({
  mode: 'onBlur',
});
```

5. Use the `handleSubmit` function to handle the `submit` event in the form:

```
<form
  onSubmit={handleSubmit(submitForm)}
  css={...}
>
```

6. Create a `submitForm` function just above the component's `return` statement, as follows:

```
const submitForm = async (data: FormData) => {
  const result = await postAnswer({
    questionId: question!.questionId,
    content: data.content,
    userName: 'Fred',
    created: new Date(),
  });
  setSuccessfullySubmitted(
    result ? true : false,
  );
};
```

So, this calls the `postAnswer` function, asynchronously passing in the content from the field values with a hardcoded username and the created date.

Notice `!` after the reference to the `question` state variable. This is a **non-null assertion operator**.

> **Important note**
>
> A non-null assertion operator (!) tells the TypeScript compiler that the variable before it cannot be `null` or `undefined`. This is useful in situations where the TypeScript compiler isn't smart enough to figure this fact out itself.

So, `!` in `question!.questionId` stops the TypeScript from complaining that `question` could be `null`.

7. Disable the form if the submission is in progress or successfully completed:

```
<Fieldset
  disabled={
    formState.isSubmitting ||
    successfullySubmitted
  }
>
```

8. After `FormButtonContainer` in the JSX, add the following submission success message:

```
{successfullySubmitted && (
  <SubmissionSuccess>
    Your answer was successfully submitted
  </SubmissionSuccess>
)}
```

9. In the running app, on the home page, click on a question. Fill in an answer and submit it:

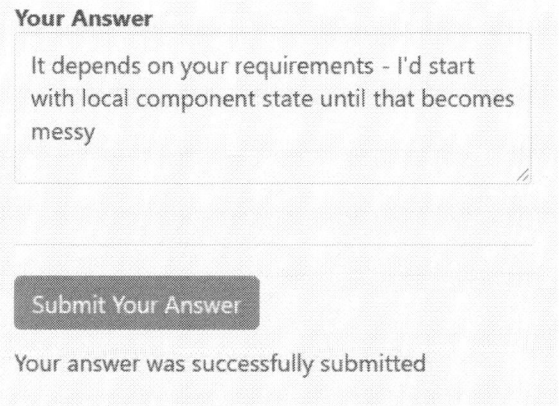

Figure 6.8 – Answer submission

Like the ask form, the answer form is disabled during and after submission, and we receive the expected success message.

So, that's our three forms complete and working nicely.

Summary

In this chapter, we learned that forms can be implemented using controlled components in React. With controlled components, React controls the field component values via state, and we are required to implement boilerplate code to manage this state.

React Hook Form is a popular forms library in the React community. This removes the need for boilerplate code, which you need with controlled components.

We now understand that the `register` function can be set to a React element's `ref` property to allow React Hook Form to manage that element. Validation rules can be specified within the `register` function parameter.

We can pass form submission logic into the `handleSubmit` function from React Hook Form. We learned that `isSubmitting` is a useful flag within `formState` that we can use to disable a form while submission is taking place.

In the next chapter, we are going to focus heavily on state management in our app and leverage Redux.

Questions

Check whether all of that information about forms has stuck by answering the following questions:

1. What property on an uncontrolled `input` element can be used to set its initial value?

2. The following JSX is a controlled `input` element:
   ```
   <input
     id="firstName"
     value={firstName}
   />
   ```
   However, users are unable to enter characters in the input. What is the problem here?

3. When we implement a form field as follows, why do we tie `label` to `input` using the `htmlFor` attribute?

   ```
   <label htmlFor="title">{label}</label>
   <input id="title" … />
   ```

4. What object in React Hook Form allows us to access validation errors?

5. What can we use from React Hook Form to determine whether the form is being submitted?

6. Why don't we use the `isSubmitted` flag with `formState` to determine whether a form has been successfully submitted?

Answers

1. The `defaultValue` property on an `input` element can be used to set its initial value.

2. The problem is that the change that's been made to the `firstName` state needs to be managed:

   ```
   <input
     id="firstName"
     value={firstName}
     onChange={e => setFirstName(e.currentTarget.value)}
   />
   ```

3. When we tie a `label` to `input` using the `htmlFor` attribute, it makes it accessible to tools such as screen readers. Also, when a user clicks on the label, the focus will automatically be set on the input.

4. The `errors` object in React Hook Form allows us to access validation errors.

5. We can use the `isSubmitting` flag within `formState` to determine whether a form is being submitted.

6. The `isSubmitted` flag with `formState` indicates whether a form has been submitted, irrespective of whether the submission was successful.

Further reading

Here are some useful links so that you can learn more about the topics that were covered in this chapter:

- **React forms**: `https://reactjs.org/docs/forms.html`
- **React Hook Form**: `https://react-hook-form.com/`

7
Managing State with Redux

So far, in our app, the state is held locally within our React components. This approach works well for simple applications. React Redux helps us to handle complex state scenarios robustly. It shines when user interactions result in several changes to state, perhaps some that are conditional, and mainly when the interaction results in web service calls. It's also great when there's lots of shared state across the application.

We'll start this chapter by understanding the Redux pattern and the different terms, such as **actions** and **reducers**. We'll follow the principles of Redux and the benefits it brings.

We are going to change the implementation of our app and use Redux to manage unanswered questions. We'll implement a Redux store with a state containing unanswered questions, searched questions, and the question being viewed. We will interact with the store in the home, search, and question pages. These implementations will give us a good grasp of how to use Redux in a React app.

In this chapter, we'll cover the following topics:

- Understanding the Redux pattern
- Installing Redux
- Creating the state

- Creating actions
- Creating a reducer
- Creating the store
- Connecting components to the store

By the end of the chapter, we'll understand the Redux pattern and will be comfortable implementing a state using it in React apps.

Technical requirements

We'll use the following tools in this chapter:

- **Visual Studio Code**: We'll use this to edit our React code. This can be downloaded and installed from `https://code.visualstudio.com/`. If you already have this installed, make sure that it is at least version 1.52.

- **Node.js and npm**: These can be downloaded from `https://nodejs.org/`. If you already have these installed, make sure that Node.js is at least version 8.2 and that npm is at least version 5.2.

- **Q and A**: We'll start with the Q&A frontend project we finished in *Chapter 6, Working with Forms*. This is available on GitHub at `https://github.com/PacktPublishing/ASP.NET-Core-5-and-React-Second-Edition` in the `chapter-07/start` folder.

All the code snippets in this chapter can be found online at `https://github.com/PacktPublishing/ASP.NET-Core-5-and-React-Second-Edition`. In order to restore the code from a chapter, the source code repository can be downloaded and the relevant folder opened in the relevant editor. If the code is frontend code, then `npm install` can be entered in the terminal to restore the dependencies.

Check out the following video to see the Code in Action: `https://bit.ly/3h5fjVc`

Understanding the Redux pattern

Redux is a predictable state container that can be used in React apps. In this section, we'll start by going through the three principles in Redux before understanding the benefits of Redux and the situations it works well in. Then, we will dive into the core concepts so that we understand the terminology and the steps that happen as the `state` is updated. By doing this, we will be well equipped to implement Redux in our app.

Principles

Let's take a look at the three principles of Redux:

- **Single source of truth**: This means that the whole application state is stored in a single object. In a real app, this object is likely to contain a complex tree of nested objects.
- **The state is read-only**: This means that the state can't be changed directly. In Redux, the only way to change the state is to dispatch what's called an action.
- **Changes are made with pure functions**: The functions that are responsible for changing the state are called reducers.

Redux shines when many components need access to the same data because the state and its interactions are stored in a single place. Having the state read-only and only updatable with a function makes the interactions easier to understand and debug. It is particularly useful when many components are interacting with the state and some of the interactions are asynchronous.

In the following sections, we'll dive into actions and reducers a little more, along with the thing that manages them, which is called a store.

Key concepts

The whole state of the application lives inside what is called a **store**. The state is stored in a JavaScript object like the following one:

```
{
  questions: {
    loading: false,
    unanswered: [{
      questionId: 1, title: ...
    }, {
      questionId: 2, title: ...
    }]
  }
}
```

In this example, the single object contains an array of unanswered questions, along with whether the questions are being fetched from a web API.

The state won't contain any functions or setters or getters. It's a simple JavaScript object. The store also orchestrates all the moving parts in Redux. This includes pushing actions through reducers to update the state.

So, the first thing that needs to happen in order to update the state in a store is to dispatch an **action**. An action is another simple JavaScript object like the one in the following code snippet:

```
{ type: 'GettingUnansweredQuestions' }
```

The `type` property determines the kind of action that needs to be performed. The `type` property is an important part of the action because the reducer won't know how to change the state without it. In the previous example, the action doesn't contain anything other than the `type` property. This is because the reducer doesn't need any more information in order to make changes to the `state` for this action. The following example is another action:

```
{
  type: 'GotUnansweredQuestions',
  questions: [{
    questionId: 1, title: ...
  }, {
    questionId: 2, title: ...
  }]
}
```

This time, an additional bit of information is included in the action in a `questions` property. This additional information is needed by the reducer to make the change to the state for this kind of action.

Reducers are pure functions that make the actual state changes.

> Important note
> A **pure function** always returns the same result for a given set of parameters. So, these functions don't depend on any variables outside the scope of the function that isn't passed into the function. Pure functions also don't change any variables outside the scope of the function.

The following is an example of a reducer:

```
const questionsReducer = (state, action) => {
  switch (action.type) {
    case 'GettingUnansweredQuestions': {
      return {
        ...state,
        loading: true
      };
    }
    case 'GotUnansweredQuestions': {
      return {
        ...state,
        unanswered: action.questions,
        loading: false
      };
    }
  }
};
```

Here are some key points regarding reducers:

- Reducers take in two parameters for the current state and the action that is being performed.
- A `switch` statement is used on the action type and creates a new state object appropriately for each action type in each of its branches.
- To create the new state, we spread the current state into a new object and then overwrite it with properties that have changed.
- The new state is returned from the reducer.

You'll notice that the actions and reducer we have just seen didn't have TypeScript types. Obviously, we'll include the necessary types when we implement these in the following sections.

The following diagram shows the Redux pieces we have just learned about and how a component interacts with them to get and update a state:

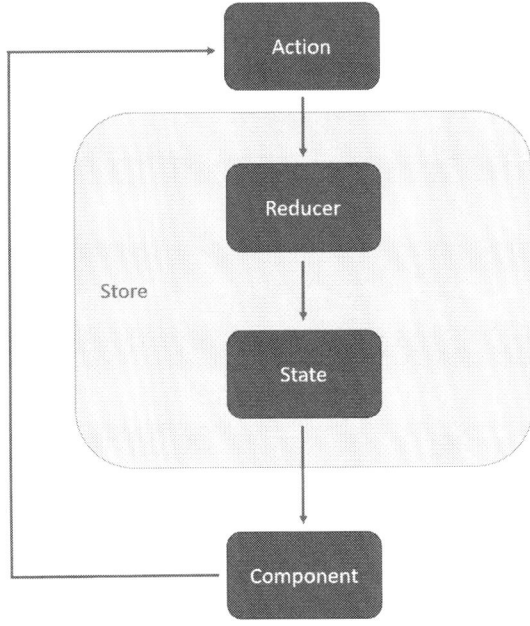

Figure 7.1 – How components interact with Redux to get and update a state

Components get a state from the store. Components update the state by dispatching an action that is fed into a reducer that updates the state. The store passes the new state to the component when it is updated.

Now that we have started to get an understanding of what Redux is, it's time to put this into practice in our app.

Installing Redux

Before we can use Redux, we need to install it, along with the TypeScript types. Let's perform the following steps to install Redux:

1. If we haven't already done so, let's open our project in Visual Studio Code from where we left off in the previous chapter. We can install the core Redux library via the terminal with the following command:

```
> npm install redux
```

Note that the core Redux library contains TypeScript types within it, so there is no need for an additional install for these.

2. Now, let's install the React-specific bits for Redux in the terminal with the following command:

```
> npm install react-redux
```

These bits allow us to connect our React components to the Redux store.

3. Let's also install the TypeScript types for React Redux:

```
> npm install @types/react-redux --save-dev
```

With all the Redux bits now installed, we can start to build our Redux store.

Creating the state

In this section, we are going to implement the type for the state object in our store, along with the initial value for the state. Perform the following steps to do so:

1. Create a new file called `Store.ts` in the `src` folder with the following `import` statement:

```
import { QuestionData } from './QuestionsData';
```

2. Let's create the TypeScript types for the state of our store:

```
interface QuestionsState {
  readonly loading: boolean;
  readonly unanswered: QuestionData[];
  readonly viewing: QuestionData | null;
  readonly searched: QuestionData[];
}
export interface AppState {
  readonly questions: QuestionsState;
}
```

So, our store is going to have a `questions` property that is an object containing the following properties:

- `loading`: Whether a server request is being made
- `unanswered`: An array containing unanswered questions
- `viewing`: The question the user is viewing
- `searched`: An array containing questions matched in the search

3. Let's define the initial state for the store so that it has an empty array of unanswered questions:

```
const initialQuestionState: QuestionsState = {
  loading: false,
  unanswered: [],
  viewing: null,
  searched: [],
};
```

So, we have defined the types for the state object and created the initial state object. We have made the state read-only by using the `readonly` keyword before the state property names.

Let's now move on and define types to represent our actions.

Creating actions

Actions initiate changes to our store state. In this section, we are going to create functions that create all the actions in our store. We will start by understanding all the actions that will be required in our store.

Understanding the actions in the store

The three processes that will interact with the store are as follows:

- Fetching and rendering the unanswered questions on the home page
- Fetching and rendering the question being viewed on the question page
- Searching questions and showing the matches on the search page

Each process comprises the following steps:

1. When the process starts, the store's `loading` state is set to `true`.
2. The request to the server is then made.
3. When the response from the server is received, the data is put into the appropriate place in the store's state and `loading` is set to `false`.

Each process has two state changes. This means that each process requires two actions:

1. An action representing the start of the process
2. An action representing the end of the process, which will contain the data from the server request

So, our store will have six actions in total.

Getting unanswered questions

We are going to create the actions in `Store.ts`. Let's create the two actions for the process that gets unanswered questions. Perform the following steps:

1. Let's start by creating a constant to hold the action type for our first action, which is indicating that unanswered questions are being fetched from the server:

   ```
   export const GETTINGUNANSWEREDQUESTIONS =
      'GettingUnansweredQuestions';
   ```

2. Create a function that returns this action:

   ```
   export const gettingUnansweredQuestionsAction = () =>
   ({
      type: GETTINGUNANSWEREDQUESTIONS,
   } as const);
   ```

   Notice the **as const** keywords after the object is being returned. This is a TypeScript *const assertion*.

   > **Important note**
   >
   > A **const assertion** on an object will give it an immutable type. It also will result in string properties having a narrow string literal type rather than the wider string type.

   The type of this action without the const assertion would be as follows:

   ```
   {
      type: string
   }
   ```

The type of this action with the type assertion is as follows:

```
{
  readonly type: 'GettingUnansweredQuestions'
}
```

So, the `type` property can only be `'GettingUnansweredQuestions'` and no other string value because we have typed it to that specific string literal. Also, the `type` property value can't be changed because it is read-only.

3. Create a function that returns the action for when the unanswered questions have been retrieved from the server:

```
export const GOTUNANSWEREDQUESTIONS =
  'GotUnansweredQuestions';
export const gotUnansweredQuestionsAction = (
  questions: QuestionData[],
) =>
  ({
    type: GOTUNANSWEREDQUESTIONS,
    questions: questions,
  } as const);
```

This time, the action contains a property called `questions` to hold the unanswered questions, as well as the fixed `type` property. We are expecting the questions to be passed into the function in the `questions` parameter.

That completes the implementation of the action types for getting unanswered questions.

Viewing a question

Let's add the two actions for viewing a question using a similar approach:

```
export const GETTINGQUESTION = 'GettingQuestion';
export const gettingQuestionAction = () =>
  ({
    type: GETTINGQUESTION,
  } as const);

export const GOTQUESTION = 'GotQuestion';
export const gotQuestionAction = (
  question: QuestionData | null,
) =>
  ({
    type: GOTQUESTION,
    question: question,
  } as const);
```

Notice that the action `type` property is given a unique value. This is required so that the reducer can determine what changes to make to the store's state.

We also make sure that the `type` property is given a value that is meaningful. This helps the readability of the code.

The data returned from the server can be a question or can be `null` if the question isn't found. This is why a union type is used.

Searching questions

The final actions in the store are for searching questions. Let's add these now:

```
export const SEARCHINGQUESTIONS =
  'SearchingQuestions';
export const searchingQuestionsAction = () =>
  ({
    type: SEARCHINGQUESTIONS,
  } as const);

export const SEARCHEDQUESTIONS =
  'SearchedQuestions';
export const searchedQuestionsAction = (
  questions: QuestionData[],
) =>
  ({
    type: SEARCHEDQUESTIONS,
    questions,
  } as const);
```

The action types are again given unique and meaningful values. The data returned from the server search is an array of questions.

In summary, we have used the `Action` type from Redux to create interfaces for our six actions. This ensures that the action contains the required type property.

Our Redux store is shaping up nicely now. Let's move on and create a reducer.

Creating a reducer

A reducer is a function that will make the necessary changes to the state. It takes in the current state and the action being processed as parameters and returns the new state. In this section, we are going to implement a reducer. Let's perform the following steps:

1. One of the parameters in the reducer is the action that invoked the state change. Let's create a union type containing all the action types that will represent the reducer action parameter:

   ```
   type QuestionsActions =
     | ReturnType<typeof gettingUnansweredQuestionsAction>
     | ReturnType<typeof gotUnansweredQuestionsAction>
     | ReturnType<typeof gettingQuestionAction>
     | ReturnType<typeof gotQuestionAction>
     | ReturnType<typeof searchingQuestionsAction>
     | ReturnType<typeof searchedQuestionsAction>;
   ```

   We have used the `ReturnType` utility type to get the return type of the action functions. `ReturnType` expects a function type to be passed into it, so we use the `typeof` keyword to get the type of each function.

   > **Important note**
   > When `typeof` is used for a type, TypeScript will infer the type from the variable after the `typeof` keyword.

2. Next, create the skeleton reducer function:

   ```
   const questionsReducer = (
     state = initialQuestionState,
     action: QuestionsActions
   ) => {
     // TODO - Handle the different actions and return
        // new state
     return state;
   };
   ```

   The reducer takes in two parameters, one for the current state and another for the action that is being processed. The state will be `undefined` the first time the reducer is called, so we default this to the initial state we created earlier.

   The reducer needs to return the new state object for the given action. We're simply returning the initial state at the moment.

It is important that a reducer always returns a value because a store may have multiple reducers. In this case, all the reducers are called, but won't necessarily process the action.

3. Now, add a `switch` statement to handle the different actions:

```
const questionsReducer = (
  state = initialQuestionState,
  action: QuestionsActions,
) => {
  switch (action.type) {
    case GETTINGUNANSWEREDQUESTIONS: {
    }
    case GOTUNANSWEREDQUESTIONS: {
    }
    case GETTINGQUESTION: {
    }
    case GOTQUESTION: {
    }
    case SEARCHINGQUESTIONS: {
    }
    case SEARCHEDQUESTIONS: {
    }
  }
  return state;
};
```

Notice that the `type` property in the `action` parameter is strongly typed and that we can only handle the six actions we defined earlier.

Let's handle the `GettingUnansweredQuestions` question first:

```
case GETTINGUNANSWEREDQUESTIONS: {
  return {
    ...state,
    loading: true,
  };
}
```

We use the spread syntax to copy the previous state into a new object and then set the `loading` state to `true`.

> **Important note**
>
> The **spread** syntax allows an object to expand into a place where key-value pairs are expected. The syntax consists of three dots followed by the object to be expanded. More information can be found at `https://developer.mozilla.org/en-US/docs/Web/JavaScript/Reference/Operators/Spread_syntax`.

The spread syntax is commonly used in reducers to copy old state into the new state object without mutating the state passed into the reducer. This is important because the reducer must be a pure function and not change values outside its scope.

4. Let's now move on to the `GotUnansweredQuestions` action:

   ```
   case GOTUNANSWEREDQUESTIONS: {
     return {
       ...state,
       unanswered: action.questions,
       loading: false,
     };
   }
   ```

   We use the spread syntax to copy the previous state into a new object and set the `unanswered` and `loading` properties. Notice how we get IntelliSense only for the properties in the `GotUnansweredQuestions` action:

   ```
   case "GotUnansweredQuestions": {
     return {
       ...state,
       unanswered: action.,
       loading: false      ● questions    (property) GotUnansweredQuestionsAction...
     };                    ● type
   }
   ```

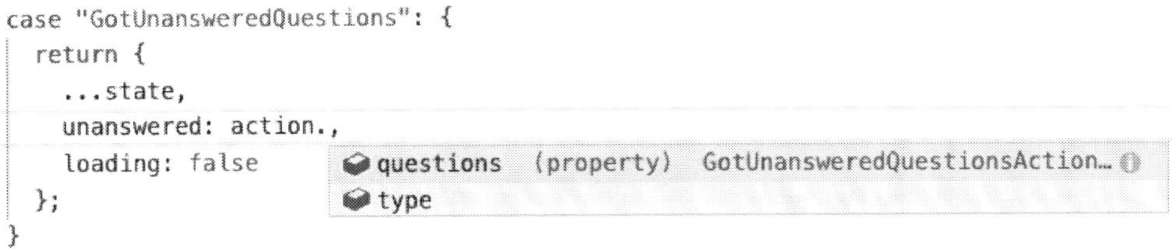

   Figure 7.2 – Narrowed action type

   TypeScript has smartly narrowed down the type in the switch branch from the union type that was passed into the reducer for the `action` parameter.

5. Handle the action getting a question by using the same approach:

   ```
   case GETTINGQUESTION: {
     return {
       ...state,
       viewing: null,
       loading: true,
     };
   }
   ```

The question being viewed is reset to `null` and the `loading` state is set to `true` while the server request is being made.

6. Handle the action for receiving a question:

   ```
   case GOTQUESTION: {
     return {
       ...state,
       viewing: action.question,
       loading: false,
     };
   }
   ```

   The question being viewed is set to the question from the action and the `loading` state is reset to `false`.

7. Handle the action for searching questions:

   ```
   case SEARCHINGQUESTIONS: {
     return {
       ...state,
       searched: [],
       loading: true,
     };
   }
   ```

   The search results are initialized to an empty array and the `loading` state is set to `true` while the server request is being made.

8. Let's handle the last action, which is for receiving matched questions from the search:

   ```
   case SEARCHEDQUESTIONS: {
     return {
       ...state,
       searched: action.questions,
       loading: false,
     };
   }
   ```

That's the reducer complete. We used a `switch` statement to handle the different action types. Within the switch branches, we used the spread syntax to copy the previous state and update the relevant values.

Now, we have all the different pieces implemented for our Redux store, so we are going to create a function to create the store in the next section.

Creating the store

The final task in `Store.ts` is to create a function that creates the Redux store so that it can be provided to the React components. We need to feed all the store reducers into this function as well. Let's do this by performing the following steps:

1. First, let's import the `Store` type and the `createStore` and `combineReducers` functions from Redux:

   ```
   import { Store, createStore, combineReducers } from
     'redux';
   ```

   `Store` is the top-level type representing the Redux store.

   We will use the `createStore` function to create the store later.

   `combineReducers` is a function we can use to put multiple reducers together into a format required by the `createStore` function.

2. Let's use the `combineReducers` function to create what is called a *root reducer*:

   ```
   const rootReducer = combineReducers<AppState>({
     questions: questionsReducer
   });
   ```

   An object literal is passed into `combineReducers`, which contains the properties in our app state, along with the reducer that is responsible for that state. We only have a single property in our app state called `questions`, and a single reducer managing changes to that state called `questionsReducer`.

3. Create a function to create the store:

   ```
   export function configureStore(): Store<AppState> {
     const store = createStore(
       rootReducer,
       undefined
     );
     return store;
   }
   ```

   This function uses the `createStore` function from Redux by passing in the combined reducers and `undefined` as the initial state.

   We use the generic `Store` type as the return type for the function passing in the interface for our app state, which is `AppState`.

That's all we need to do to create the store.

We have created all the bits and pieces in our store in a single file called `Store.ts`. For larger stores, it may help maintainability to structure the store across different files. Structuring the store by feature where you have all the actions and the reducer for each feature in a file works well because we generally read and write our code by feature.

In the next section, we will connect our store to the components we implemented in the previous chapters.

Connecting components to the store

In this section, we are going to connect the existing components in our app to our store. We will start by adding what is called a store *provider* to the root of our component tree, which allows components lower in the tree to consume the store. We will then connect the home, question, and search pages to the Redux store using hooks from React Redux.

Adding a store provider

Let's provide the store to the root of our component tree. To do that, perform the following steps:

1. In `App.tsx`, import the `Provider` component from React Redux and the `configureStore` function we created in the previous section. Add these import statements just after the React import statement:

   ```
   import React from 'react';
   import { Provider } from 'react-redux';
   import { configureStore } from './Store';
   ```

   This is the first time we have referenced anything from React-Redux. Remember that this library helps React components interact with a Redux store.

2. Just before the `App` component is defined, create an instance of our store using our `configureStore` function:

   ```
   const store = configureStore();
   function App() {
     ...
   }
   ```

3. In the `App` component's JSX, wrap a `Provider` component around the `BrowserRouter` component by passing in our store instance:

   ```
   return (
     <Provider store={store}>
       <BrowserRouter>
         ...
       </BrowserRouter>
     </Provider>
   );
   ```

Components lower in the component tree can now connect to the store.

Connecting the home page

Let's connect the home page to the store. To do that, perform the following steps:

1. In `HomePage.tsx`, let's add the following `import` statement:

   ```
   import { useSelector, useDispatch } from 'react-redux';
   ```

   We will eventually use the `useSelector` function to get state from the store. The `useDispatch` function will be used to invoke actions.

2. We are going to use the Redux store for the unanswered questions, so let's import the action functions for this, along with the type for the store's state:

   ```
   import {
     gettingUnansweredQuestionsAction,
     gotUnansweredQuestionsAction,
     AppState,
   } from './Store';
   ```

3. Let's remove the `QuestionData` type from the `import` statement from `QuestionsData.ts` so that it now looks like the following:

   ```
   import {
     getUnansweredQuestions,
   } from './QuestionsData';
   ```

   The `QuestionData` type will be inferred in our revised implementation.

4. The `useDispatch` hook from React Redux returns a function that we can use to dispatch actions. Let's assign this to a function called `dispatch`:

   ```
   export const HomePage = () => {
     const dispatch = useDispatch();
     ...
   }
   ```

5. The `useSelector` hook from React Redux returns state from the store if we pass it a function that selects the state. Use the `useSelector` hook to get the unanswered questions state from the store:

   ```
   export const HomePage = () => {
     const dispatch = useDispatch();
     const questions = useSelector(
       (state: AppState) =>
         state.questions.unanswered,
     );
     ...
   }
   ```

   The function passed to `useSelector` is often referred to as a *selector*. It takes in the store's state object and contains logic to return the required part of the state from the store.

6. Use the `useSelector` hook again to get the `loading` state from the store:

   ```
   const questions = useSelector(
     (state: AppState) =>
       state.questions.unanswered,
   );
   const questionsLoading = useSelector(
     (state: AppState) => state.questions.loading,
   );
   ```

7. Our local component state is now redundant, so let's remove it by deleting the highlighted lines:

   ```
   const questionsLoading = useSelector(
     (state: AppState) => state.questions.loading,
   );
   const [
     questions,
     setQuestions,
   ] = React.useState<QuestionData[]>([]);
   const [
     questionsLoading,
   ```

232   Managing State with Redux

```
  setQuestionsLoading,
] = React.useState(true);
```

8. Invoke the action for getting unanswered questions at the start of the `useEffect` function:

```
React.useEffect(() => {
  const doGetUnansweredQuestions = async () => {
    dispatch(gettingUnansweredQuestionsAction());
    const unansweredQuestions = await
      getUnansweredQuestions();
    setQuestions(unansweredQuestions);
    setQuestionsLoading(false);
  };
  doGetUnansweredQuestions();
}, []);
```

We dispatch the action to the store using the `dispatch` function.

9. Invoke the action for receiving unanswered questions after the call to `getUnansweredQuestions`:

```
React.useEffect(() => {
  const doGetUnansweredQuestions = async () => {
    dispatch(gettingUnansweredQuestionsAction());
    const unansweredQuestions = await
      getUnansweredQuestions();
    dispatch(gotUnansweredQuestionsAction(unansweredQuesti
    ons));
    setQuestions(unansweredQuestions);
    setQuestionsLoading(false);
  };
  doGetUnansweredQuestions();
}, []);
```

We pass in the unanswered questions to the function that creates this action. We then dispatch the action using the `dispatch` function.

10. Remove the references that set the local state from the `useEffect` function by removing the highlighted lines:

```
React.useEffect(() => {
  const doGetUnansweredQuestions = async () => {
    ...
    setQuestions(unansweredQuestions);
    setQuestionsLoading(false);
  };
```

```
    doGetUnansweredQuestions();
}, []);
```

11. ESLint is warning us that the `dispatch` function might be a missing dependency in the `useEffect` hook. We only want the `useEffect` function to trigger when the component is first mounted and not subsequently if the reference to the `dispatch` function changes. So, let's suppress this warning by adding the following line:

```
React.useEffect(() => {
    ...
    // eslint-disable-next-line react
    hooks/exhaustive-deps
}, []);
```

12. If the app isn't running, type `npm start` in the terminal to start it. The app will run fine and the unanswered questions will be rendered on the home page, just as they were before we added the Redux store:

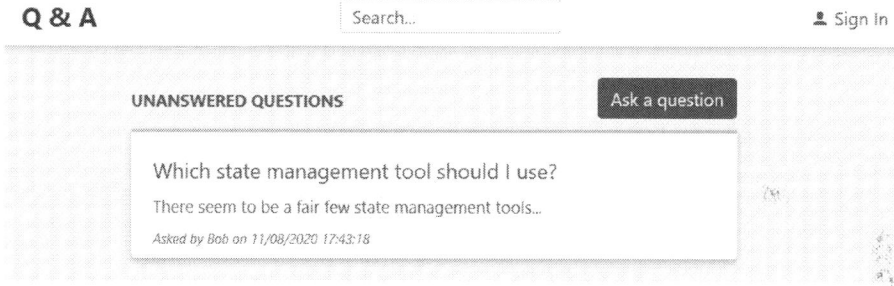

Figure 7.3 – HomePage component connected to the Redux store

Congratulations! We have just connected our first component to a Redux store!

The key parts of connecting a component to the store are using the `useSelector` hook to select the required state and using the `useDispatch` hook to dispatch actions.

We'll use a similar approach to connect another component to the store.

Connecting the question page

Let's connect the question page to the store. To do that, perform the following steps:

1. In `QuestionPage.tsx`, let's add the following `import` statements to import the hooks we need from React Redux and action functions from our store:

   ```
   import {
     useSelector,
     useDispatch,
   } from 'react-redux';
   import {
     AppState,
     gettingQuestionAction,
     gotQuestionAction,
   } from './Store';
   ```

2. Remove the `QuestionData` type from the `import` statement from `QuestionsData.ts` so that it now looks like the following:

   ```
   import { getQuestion, postAnswer } from './
   QuestionsData';
   ```

3. Assign a `dispatch` function to the `useDispatch` hook:

   ```
   export const QuestionPage = () => {
     const dispatch = useDispatch();
     ...
   }
   ```

4. Use the `useSelector` hook with a selector to get the question being viewed from the state from the store:

   ```
   const dispatch = useDispatch();
   const question = useSelector(
     (state: AppState) => state.questions.viewing,
   );
   ```

5. Our local `question` state is now redundant, so let's remove it by removing the highlighted lines:

   ```
   const [
     question,
     setQuestion,
   ] = React.useState<QuestionData | null>(null);
   ```

6. Inside the `useEffect` function, remove the reference to the local `question` state and dispatch the appropriate actions from the store:

```
React.useEffect(() => {
  const doGetQuestion = async (
    questionId: number,
  ) => {
    dispatch(gettingQuestionAction());
    const foundQuestion = await
      getQuestion(questionId);
    dispatch(gotQuestionAction(foundQuestion));
  };
  if (questionId) {
    doGetQuestion(Number(questionId));
  }
  // eslint-disable-next-line react
  hooks/exhaustive-deps
}, [questionId]);
```

7. In the running app, browse to the question page as follows:

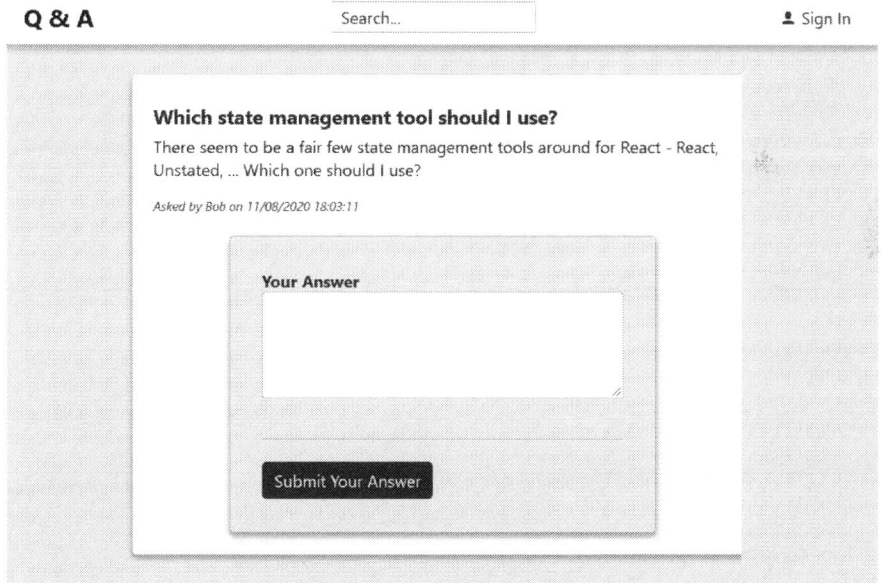

Figure 7.4 – QuestionPage component connected to the Redux store

The page will render correctly.

The question page is now connected to the store. Next, we'll connect our final component to the store.

Connecting the search page

Let's connect the search page to the store. To do that, perform the following steps:

1. In `SearchPage.tsx`, let's add the following `import` statements to import the hooks we need from React Redux and types from our store:

   ```
   import { useSelector, useDispatch } from 'react-redux';
   import {
     AppState,
     searchingQuestionsAction,
     searchedQuestionsAction,
   } from './Store';
   ```

2. Remove the `QuestionData` type from the `import` statement from `QuestionsData.ts:` so that it now looks like the following:

   ```
   import { searchQuestions } from './QuestionsData';
   ```

3. Assign a `dispatch` function to the `useDispatch` hook:

   ```
   export const SearchPage = () => {
     const dispatch = useDispatch();
     ...
   }
   ```

4. Use the `useSelector` hook with a selector to get the searched questions state from the store:

   ```
   const dispatch = useDispatch();
   const questions = useSelector(
     (state: AppState) => state.questions.searched,
   );
   ```

5. Our local `questions` state is now redundant, so let's remove it by removing the highlighted lines:

   ```
   const [
     questions,
     setQuestions,
   ] = React.useState<QuestionData[]>([]);
   ```

6. Inside the `useEffect` function, remove the reference to the local `question` state and dispatch the appropriate actions from the store:

```
React.useEffect(() => {
  const doSearch = async (criteria: string) => {
    dispatch(searchingQuestionsAction());
    const foundResults = await searchQuestions(
      criteria,
    );
    dispatch(searchedQuestionsAction(foundResults));
  };
  doSearch(search);
  // eslint-disable-next-line react
  hooks/exhaustive-deps
}, [search]);
```

7. In the running app, perform a search operation by entering `typescript`, as shown in the following screenshot:

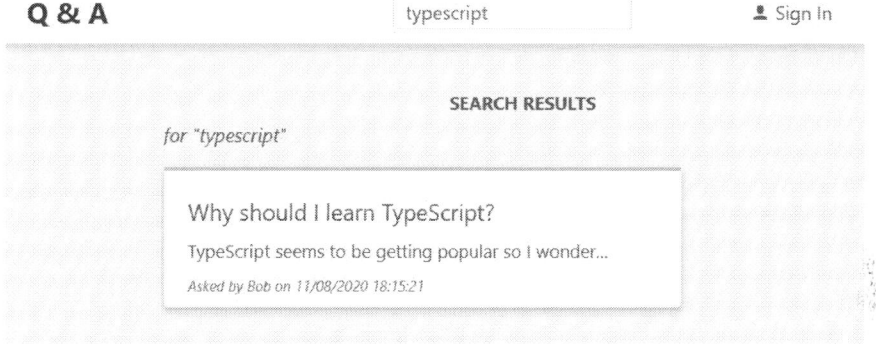

Figure 7.5 – SearchPage component connected to the Redux store

The page will render correctly.

The search page is now connected to the store.

That completes connecting the required components to our Redux store.

We accessed the Redux store state by using the `useSelector` hook from React Redux. We passed a function into this that retrieved the appropriate piece of state we needed in the React component.

To begin the process of a state change, we invoked an action using a function returned from the `useDispatch` hook from React Redux. We passed the relevant action object into this function, containing information to make the state change.

Summary

In this chapter, we learned that the state in a Redux store is stored in a single place, is read-only, and is changed with a pure function called a reducer. Our components don't talk directly to the reducer; instead, they dispatch objects called actions that describe the change to the reducer. We now know how to create a strongly typed type Redux store containing a read-only state object with the necessary reducer functions.

We learned that React components can access a Redux store if they are children of a Redux `Provider` component. We also know how to get state from the store from a component using the `useSelector` hook and create a dispatcher to dispatch actions with `useDispatch` as the hook.

There are lots of bits and pieces to get our heads around when implementing Redux within a React app. It does shine in scenarios where the state management is complex because Redux forces us to break the logic up into separate pieces that are easy to understand and maintain. It is also very useful for managing global state, such as user information, because it is easily accessible below the `Provider` component.

Now, we have built the majority of the frontend in our app, which means it's time to turn our attention to the backend. In the next chapter, we'll focus on how we can interact with the database in ASP.NET.

Questions

Before we end this chapter, let's test our knowledge with some questions:

1. When implementing an action object, how many properties can it contain?
2. How did we make the state in our store read-only?
3. Does the `Provider` component from React Redux need to be placed at the top of the component tree?
4. What hook from React Redux allows a component to select the state from the Redux store?
5. What is wrong with the following code that dispatches an action to the store?

   ```
   useDispatch(gettingQuestionAction);
   ```

6. Is a component that consumes the Redux store allowed to have a local state?

Answers

1. An action can contain as many properties as we like! It needs to include at least one for the `type` property. It can then include as many other properties as we need for the reducer to change the state, but this is generally lumped into one additional property usually called `payload`. So, generally, an action will have one or two properties.

2. We used the `readonly` keyword in the properties in the interface for the state to make it read-only.

3. The `Provider` component needs to be placed above the components that need access to the store. So, it doesn't need to be right at the top of the tree.

4. The `useSelector` hook allows a component to select state from the store.

5. The `useDispatch` hook returns a function that can be used to dispatch an action – it can't be used to dispatch an action directly. Here's the correct way to dispatch an action:

   ```
   const dispatch = useDispatch();
   ...
   dispatch(gettingQuestionAction);
   ```

6. Yes, a component can have a local state as well as a Redux state. If the state is not useful outside the component, then it is perfectly acceptable to have this state locally within the component.

Further reading

Here are some useful links so that you can learn more about the topics that were covered in this chapter:

- **Getting started with Redux**: https://redux.js.org/introduction/getting-started
- **React Redux**: https://react-redux.js.org/
- **Never type**: https://www.typescriptlang.org/docs/handbook/basic-types.html

Section 3: Building an ASP.NET Backend

In this section, we will build the backend of our Q&A app by creating a REST API for interacting with questions and answers. We'll use Dapper behind the REST API to interact with the SQL Server database. We will learn techniques to make our backend perform and scale well. We will learn how to secure the REST API before consuming it from the frontend.

This section comprises the following chapters:

- *Chapter 8, Interacting with the Database with Dapper*
- *Chapter 9, Creating REST API Endpoints*
- *Chapter 10, Improving Performance and Scalability*
- *Chapter 11, Securing the Backend*
- *Chapter 12, Interacting with RESTful APIs*

8
Interacting with the Database with Dapper

It's time to start working on the backend of our Q&A app. In this chapter, we are going to build the database for the app and interact with it from ASP.NET Core with a library called Dapper.

We'll start by understanding what Dapper is and the benefits it brings over the Entity Framework. We'll create the data access layer in our app by learning how to read data from the database into model classes using Dapper. We'll then move on to writing data to the database from model classes.

Deploying database changes during releases of our app is an important and non-trivial task. So, we'll set up the management of database migrations using a library called DbUp toward the end of this chapter.

In this chapter, we'll cover the following topics:

- Implementing the database
- Understanding what Dapper is and its benefits
- Installing and configuring Dapper
- Reading data using Dapper
- Writing data using Dapper
- Managing migrations with `DbUp`

By the end of this chapter, we will have created a SQL Server database that stores questions and answers and the implemented performant data layer that interacts with it.

Technical requirements

We will need to use the following tools in this chapter:

- **Visual Studio 2019**: We'll use this to edit our ASP.NET Core code. This can be downloaded and installed from `https://visualstudio.microsoft.com/vs/`.
- **.NET 5.0**: This can be downloaded from `https://dotnet.microsoft.com/download/dotnet/5.0`.
- **SQL Server 2019 Express Edition**: We'll use this for our database. This can be downloaded and installed from `https://www.microsoft.com/en-gb/sql-server/sql-server-editions-express`.
- **SQL Server Management Studio**: We'll use this to create our database. This can be downloaded and installed from `https://docs.microsoft.com/en-us/sql/ssms/download-sql-server-management-studio-ssms`.
- **Q and A**: We'll start with the QandA backend project we created and finished in *Chapter 2*, *Creating Decoupled React and ASP.NET 5 Apps*. This is available on GitHub at `https://github.com/PacktPublishing/ASP.NET-Core-5-and-React-Second-Edition`.

All of the code snippets in this chapter can be found online at `https://github.com/PacktPublishing/ASP.NET-Core-5-and-React-Second-Edition`. To restore code from a chapter, you can download the necessary source code repository and open the relevant folder in the relevant editor. If the code is frontend code, then `npm install` can be entered in the Terminal to restore any dependencies.

Check out the following video to see the code in action: `http://bit.ly/2EVDsv6`.

Implementing the database

In this section, we are going to create a SQL Server database for our Q&A app. We will then create tables in the database that will store questions and answers. After that, we will create stored procedures that read and write records in these tables.

Creating the database

We are going to create the database using **SQL Server Management Studio (SSMS)** by carrying out the following steps:

1. Open SSMS and connect to the SQL Server instance:

Figure 8.1 – Connecting to SQL Server Express

2. In **Object Explorer**, right-click on **Databases** and click on the **New Database...** option.

3. Enter QandA for the name of the database and click **OK**:

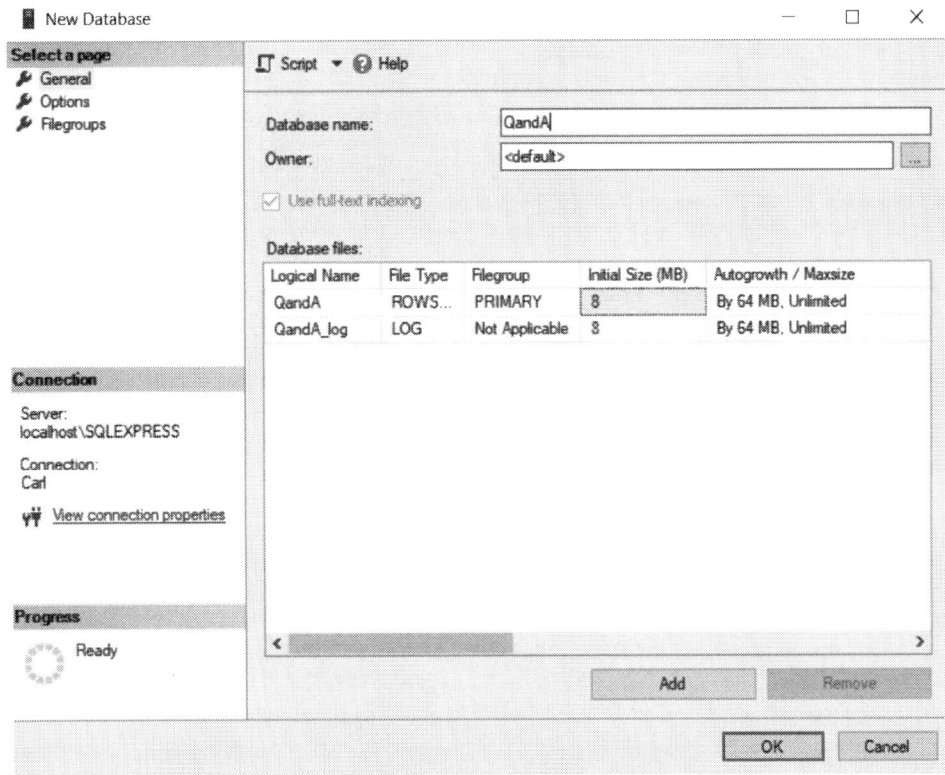

Figure 8.2 – Creating the Q&A database

4. Once the database has been created, we'll see it listed in **Object Explorer**:

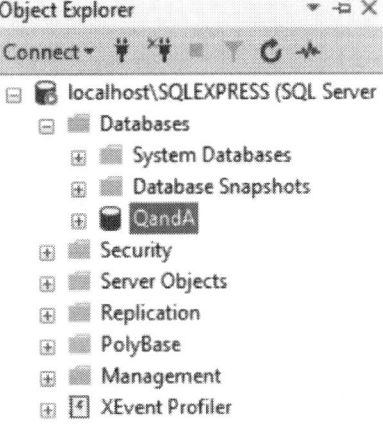

Figure 8.3 – The Q&A database in Object Explorer

Nice and easy! We are going to create database tables for the questions and answers in the following section.

Creating database tables

Let's create some tables for the users, questions, and answers in our new database in SSMS:

1. Copy the contents of the SQL Script at `https://github.com/PacktPublishing/ASP.NET-Core-5-and-React-Second-Edition/blob/master/chapter-08/start/backend/SQLScripts/01-Tables.sql`.
2. In SSMS, with the **QandA** database highlighted, click **New Query** on the toolbar to create a new SQL query and paste in the contents from the copied script.
3. Click the **Execute** option on the toolbar or press *F5* to execute the query.
4. If we look under **Tables** in **Object Explorer**, we should see that several tables have been created:

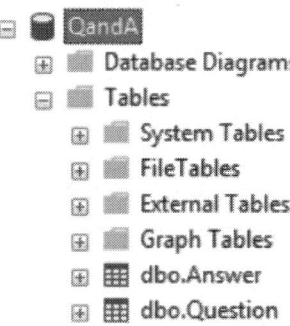

Figure 8.4 – The Q&A database in Object Explorer

Here, a `Question` table has been created. This holds questions that have been asked and contains the following fields:

- An integer-based field called `QuestionId`, which is the primary key Unicode-based `Title` and `Content` fields.
- `UserId` and `UserName` fields, which reference the user who asked the question.
- A field called `Created`, which will hold the date and time the question was asked.

An `Answer` table has also been created. This holds answers to the questions and contains the following fields:

- An integer-based `AnswerId` field, which is the primary key.
- An integer-based `QuestionId` field, which references the question being answered.
- A Unicode-based `Content` field.
- `UserId` and `UserName` fields, which reference the user who answered the question.
- A field called `Created`, which will hold the date and time the answer was submitted.

The SQL Script has added some example data. If we right-click on the **Question** table in **Object Explorer** and choose the **Edit Top 200 rows** option, we'll see the data in our table:

	QuestionId	Title	Content	UserId	UserName	Created
1	1	Why should I learn TypeScript?	TypeScript seems to be getting popular so I wond...	1	bob.test@test.com	2021-01-1
2	2	Which state management tool should I use?	There seem to be a fair few state management to...	2	jane.test@test.com	2021-01-1

Figure 8.5 – Questions in the Q&A database

So, we now have a database that contains our tables and have some nice data to work with.

Creating stored procedures

Let's create some stored procedures that our app will use to interact with the database tables.

Copy the contents of the SQL Script at `https://github.com/PacktPublishing/ASP.NET-Core-5-and-React-Second-Edition/blob/master/chapter-08/start/backend/SQLScripts/02-Sprocs.sql`. Now, follow these steps:

1. Click **New Query** to create a new SQL query and paste in the contents from the copied script.
2. Click the **Execute** option on the toolbar.
3. If we look under **Stored Procedures** under **Programmability** in **Object Explorer**, we should see that several stored procedures have been created:

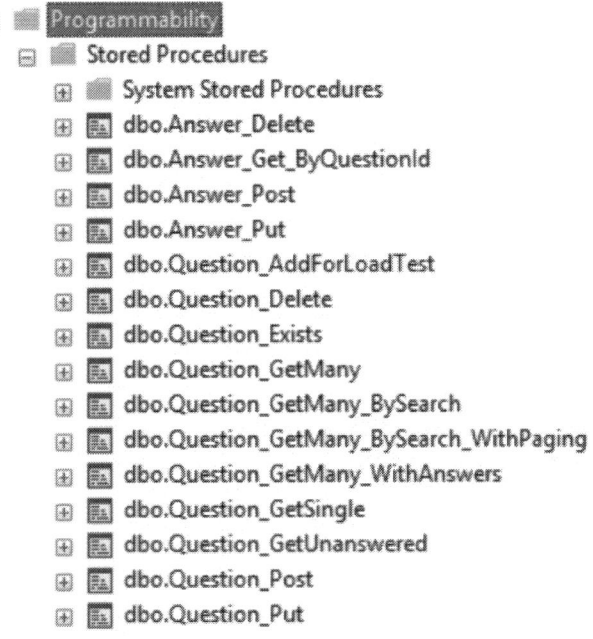

Figure 8.6 – Stored procedures in the Q&A database

We'll be using these stored procedures to interact with the database from the ASP.NET Core app.

4. Before we finish this section, let's try to run one of the stored procedures. Click **New Query** to create a new SQL query and enter the following:

```
EXEC dbo.Question_GetMany_BySearch @Search = 'type'
```

So, this SQL command will execute the `Question_GetMany_BySearch` stored procedure by passing in the `@Search` parameter with a `type` value. This stored procedure returns questions that have the value of the `@Search` parameter in the title of its content.

5. Click the **Execute** option on the toolbar. We should get the following results:

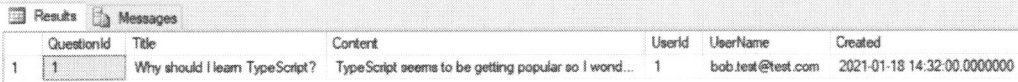

Figure 8.7 – Results from running the stored procedure

With our SQL Server database in place, we can now turn our attention to Dapper.

Understanding what Dapper is and its benefits

Dapper is a performance-focused simple object mapper for .NET that helps map SQL query output to instances of a C# class. It is built and maintained by the Stack Overflow team, has been released as open source, and is a popular alternative to Microsoft's Entity Framework.

So, why use Dapper rather than Entity Framework? The goal of Entity Framework is to abstract away the database, so it trades learning SQL for Entity Framework-specific objects such as `DBSet` and `DataContext`. We generally don't write SQL with Entity Framework – instead, we write LINQ queries, which are translated into SQL by Entity Framework.

If we are implementing a large database that serves a large number of users, Entity Framework can be a challenge because the queries it generates can be inefficient. We need to understand Entity Framework well to make it scale, which can be a significant investment. When we find Entity Framework queries that are slow, we need to understand SQL to properly understand the root cause. So, it makes sense to invest time in learning SQL really well rather than the abstraction that the Entity Framework provides. Also, if we have a team with good database and SQL skills, it doesn't make sense to not use these.

Dapper is much simplier than Entity Framework. Later in this chapter, we'll see that we can read and write data from a SQL database with just a few lines of C# code. This allows us to interact with stored procedures in the database, thus automatically mapping C# class instances to SQL parameters, along with the results of the query. In the next section, we will install and start using Dapper to access our data.

Installing and configuring Dapper

In this section, we are going to install and configure Dapper. We will also install the Microsoft SQL Server client package that Dapper uses. Let's carry out the following steps:

1. Let's open the backend project in Visual Studio. Go to the **Tools** menu and then **NuGet Package Manager** and choose **Manage NuGet Packages for Solution...**.

   > **Important Note**
   > NuGet is a tool that downloads third-party and Microsoft libraries and manages the references to them so that the libraries can easily be updated.

2. On the **Browse** tab, enter `Dapper` into the search box.

3. Select the **Dapper** package by Sam Saffron, Marc Gravell, and Nick Craver. Tick our project and click the **Install** button with the latest stable version selected. Refer to the following screenshot:

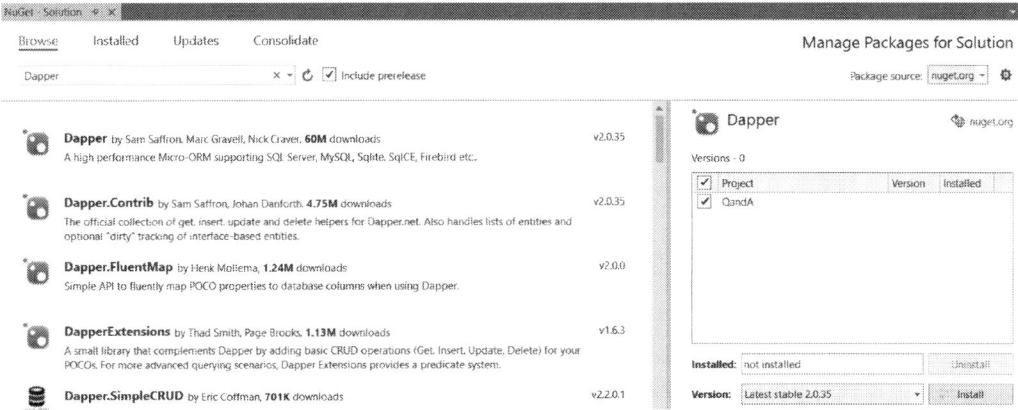

Figure 8.8 – Installing Dapper in the NuGet manager

We may be asked to accept a licensing agreement before Dapper can be downloaded and installed into our project.

4. Still in the NuGet package manager, search for the `Microsoft.Data.SqlClient` package and install the latest stable version. Refer to the following screenshot:

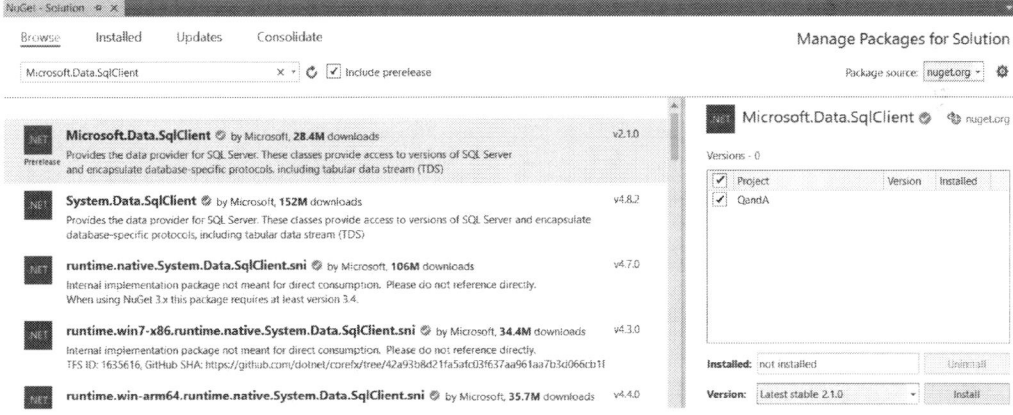

Figure 8.9 – Installing Microsoft.Data.Client

5. Next, we are going to define a connection string in our ASP.NET Core project that goes to our database. In **Solution Explorer**, open up a file called `appsettings.json` to add a `ConnectionStrings` field that contains our connection string:

```
{
  "ConnectionStrings": {
    "DefaultConnection":
      "Server=localhost\\SQLEXPRESS;Database=QandA;
        Trusted_Connection=True;"
  },
  ...
}
```

> **Important Note**
>
> The `appsettings.json` file is a JSON-formatted file that contains various configuration settings for an ASP.NET Core app.

Obviously, change the connection string so that it references your SQL Server and database.

So, that's Dapper installed, along with a connection string to our database in place. Next, we will learn how to read data from the database using Dapper.

Reading data using Dapper

In this section, we are going to write some C# code that reads data from the database.

We are going to use the popular repository design pattern to structure our data access code. This will allow us to provide a nice, centralized abstraction of the data layer.

We are going to start by creating a data repository class that will hold all of the queries we are going to make to the data. We are going to create C# classes that hold the data we get from the database, called models.

We will implement methods for getting all the questions, getting questions from a search, getting unanswered questions, getting a single question, getting information stating whether a question exists, and getting an answer.

Creating the repository class

Let's create a class that will hold all of the methods for interacting with the database:

1. In **Solution Explorer**, right-click on our project, select the **Add** menu, and then choose the **New Folder** option.

2. A new folder will be created in the solution tree. Name the folder Data.

3. Right-click on the Data folder and select the **Add** menu. Then, choose the **Class...** option.

4. In the dialog box that appears, enter DataRepository for the name of the file and click the **Add** button.

5. A skeleton DataRepository class will be created:

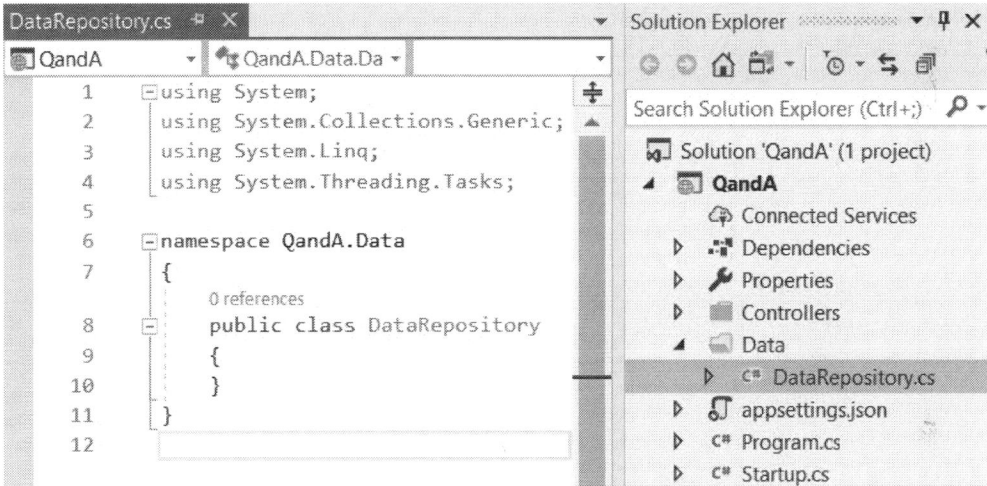

Figure 8.10 – Skeleton DataRepository class

6. Now, we are going to create an interface for the data repository so that it can be mocked when we write unit tests. Right-click on the Data folder and select the **Add** menu. Then, choose the **Class...** option.

7. This time, choose the **Interface** option in the dialog box that appears and name it IDataRepository before pressing the **Add** button.

8. Change the modifier for the interface to public and add the following methods:

```
public interface IDataRepository
{
    IEnumerable<QuestionGetManyResponse> GetQuestions();

    IEnumerable<QuestionGetManyResponse>
```

```
    GetQuestionsBySearch(string search);

    IEnumerable<QuestionGetManyResponse>
      GetUnansweredQuestions();

    QuestionGetSingleResponse
      GetQuestion(int questionId);

    bool QuestionExists(int questionId);

    AnswerGetResponse GetAnswer(int answerId);
}
```

Here, we are going to have six methods in the data repository that will read different bits of data from our database. Note that this won't compile yet because we are referencing classes that don't exist.

9. Moving back to `DataRepository.cs`, specify that the class must implement the interface we just created:

```
public class DataRepository: IDataRepository
{
}
```

10. If we click on the class name, a light bulb icon will appear. Click on the light bulb menu and choose **Implement interface**:

Figure 8.11 – Automatically implementing the IDataRepository interface

Skeleton methods will be added to the repository class that satisfy the interface.

11. Create a class-level private variable called `_connectionString` that will store the database connection string:

    ```
    public class DataRepository : IDataRepository
    {
        private readonly string _connectionString;
        ...
    }
    ```

    > **Important Note**
    > The `readonly` keyword prevents the variable from being changed outside of the class constructor, which is what we want in this case.

12. Let's create a constructor for the repository class that will set the value of the connection string from the `appsettings.json` file:

    ```
    public class DataRepository : IDataRepository
    {
        private readonly string _connectionString;

        public DataRepository(IConfiguration configuration)
        {
            _connectionString =
            configuration["ConnectionStrings:DefaultConnection"];
        }

        ...
    }
    ```

    The `configuration` parameter in the constructor gives us access to items within the `appsettings.json` file. The key we use when accessing the `configuration` object is the path to the item we want from the `appsettings.json` file, with colons being used to navigate the fields in the JSON.

    How does the `configuration` parameter get passed into the constructor? The answer is dependency injection, which we'll cover in the next chapter.

13. Our class doesn't recognize `IConfiguration` yet, so, let's click on it, click on the light bulb menu that appears, and choose **using Microsoft.Extensions. Configuration;**:

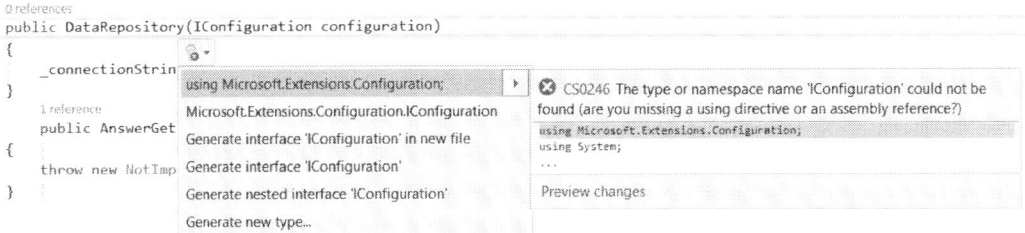

Figure 8.12 – Referencing the Microsoft.Extensions.Configuration namespace

We've made a good start on the repository class. We do have compile errors, but these will disappear as we fully implement the methods.

Creating a repository method to get questions

Let's implement the `GetQuestions` method first:

1. Let's add a couple of `using` statements at the top of the file for the Microsoft SQL client library, as well as Dapper:

   ```
   using Microsoft.Data.SqlClient;;
   using Dapper;
   ```

2. In the `GetQuestions` method, overwrite the statement that throws a `NotImplementedException` by declaring a new database connection:

   ```
   public IEnumerable<QuestionGetManyResponse>
   GetQuestions()
   {
     using (var connection = new
       SqlConnection(_connectionString))
     {

     }
   }
   ```

   Notice that we've used a `using` block to declare the database connection.

> **Important Note**
>
> A `using` block automatically disposes of the object defined in the block when the program exits the scope of the block. This includes whether a `return` statement is invoked within the block, as well as errors occurring within the block.

So, the `using` statement is a convenient way of ensuring the connection is disposed of. Notice that we are using a `SqlConnection` from the Microsoft SQL client library because this is what the Dapper library extends.

3. Next, let's open the connection:

   ```
   public IEnumerable<QuestionGetManyResponse>
   GetQuestions()
   {
     using (var connection = new
       SqlConnection(_connectionString))
     {
       connection.Open();
     }
   }
   ```

4. Now, we can execute the query:

   ```
   public IEnumerable<QuestionGetManyResponse>
   GetQuestions()
   {
     using (var connection = new
       SqlConnection(_connectionString))
     {
       connection.Open();
       return connection.Query<QuestionGetManyResponse>(
         @"EXEC dbo.Question_GetMany"
       );
     }
   }
   ```

We've used a `Query` extension method from Dapper on the `connection` object to execute the `Question_GetMany` stored procedure. We then simply return the results of this query from our method. Nice and simple!

Notice how we pass in a class, `QuestionGetManyResponse`, into the generic parameter of the `Query` method. This defines the model class the query results should be stored in. We'll define `QuestionGetManyResponse` in the next step.

5. In **Solution Explorer**, right-click on the `Data` folder, choose **Add**, and then choose the **New Folder** option. Enter `Models` as the name of the new folder. We are going to place all of our models here.

6. In **Solution Explorer**, right-click on the **Models** folder and select **Add**. Then, choose the **Class...** option.

7. In the dialog that appears, enter `QuestionGetManyResponse` for the name of the file that will be created and click the **Add** button. A skeleton class will be created for us.

8. Add the following properties to the class:

   ```
   public class QuestionGetManyResponse
   {
     public int QuestionId { get; set; }
     public string Title { get; set; }
     public string Content { get; set; }
     public string UserName { get; set; }
     public DateTime Created { get; set; }
   }
   ```

   The property names match the fields that have been output from the `Question_GetMany` stored procedure. This allows Dapper to automatically map the data from the database to this class. The property types have also been carefully chosen so that this Dapper mapping process works.

   > **Important Note**
   > Note that the class doesn't need to contain properties for all of the fields that are output from the stored procedure. Dapper will ignore fields that don't have the corresponding properties in the class.

9. Moving back to `DataRepository.cs`, add a `using` statement so that the class can get access to the models:

   ```
   using QandA.Data.Models;
   ```

10. Let's also add this `using` statement to `IDataRepository.cs`:

    ```
    using QandA.Data.Models;
    ```

Congratulations – we have implemented our first repository method! This consisted of just a few lines of code that opened a database connection and executed a query. This has shown us that writing data access code in Dapper is super simple.

Creating a repository method to get questions by a search

Let's implement the `GetQuestionsBySearch` method, which is similar to the `GetQuestions` method, but this time, the method and stored procedure have a parameter. Let's carry out the following steps:

1. Start by creating and opening the connection in the same way as we did when we implemented the last method:

   ```
   public IEnumerable<QuestionGetManyResponse>
   GetQuestionsBySearch(string search)
   {
     using (var connection = new
       SqlConnection(_connectionString))
     {
       connection.Open();
       // TODO - execute Question_GetMany_BySearch stored
       // procedure
     }
   }
   ```

2. Now, we can execute the `Question_GetMany_BySearch` stored procedure:

   ```
   public IEnumerable<QuestionGetManyResponse>
   GetQuestionsBySearch(string search)
   {
     using (var connection = new SqlConnection(_
   connectionString))
     {
       connection.Open();
       return connection.Query<QuestionGetManyResponse>(
         @"EXEC dbo.Question_GetMany_BySearch @Search =
         @Search",
         new { Search = search }
       );
     }
   }
   ```

Notice how we pass in the stored procedure parameter value.

> **Important Note**
> Parameter values are passed into a Dapper query using an object where its property names match the parameter names. Dapper will then create and execute a parameterized query.

In this case, we've used an anonymous object for the parameters to save us defining a class for the object.

Why do we have to pass a parameter to Dapper? Why can't we just do the following?

```
return connection.Query<QuestionGetManyResponse>($"EXEC dbo.
Question_GetMany_BySearch '{search}'");
```

Well, there are several reasons, but the main one is that the preceding code is vulnerable to a SQL injection attack. So, it's always best to pass parameters into Dapper rather than trying to construct the SQL ourselves.

That's our second repository method complete. Nice and simple!

Creating a repository method to get unanswered questions

Let's implement the `GetUnansweredQuestions` method, which is very similar to the `GetQuestions` method:

```
public IEnumerable<QuestionGetManyResponse> 
GetUnansweredQuestions()
{
  using (var connection = new
    SqlConnection(_connectionString))
  {
    connection.Open();
    return connection.Query<QuestionGetManyResponse>(
      "EXEC dbo.Question_GetUnanswered"
    );
  }
}
```

Here, we opened the connection, executed the `Question_GetUnanswered` stored procedure, and returned the results in the `QuestionGetManyResponse` class we had already created.

Creating a repository method to get a single question

Let's implement the `GetQuestion` method now:

1. Start by opening the connection and executing the `Question_GetSingle` stored procedure:

   ```
   public QuestionGetSingleResponse GetQuestion(int
   questionId)
   {
     using (var connection = new
       SqlConnection(_connectionString))
     {
       connection.Open();
       var question =
         connection.QueryFirstOrDefault<
           QuestionGetSingleResponse>(
           @"EXEC dbo.Question_GetSingle @QuestionId =
             @QuestionId",
           new { QuestionId = questionId }
         );

         // TODO - Get the answers for the question

         return question;
     }
   }
   ```

   This method is a little different from the previous methods because we are using the `QueryFirstOrDefault` Dapper method to return a single record (or `null` if the record isn't found) rather than a collection of records.

2. We need to execute a second stored procedure to get the answers for the question, so let's do that now:

   ```
   public QuestionGetSingleResponse GetQuestion(int
   questionId)
   {
     using (var connection = new
       SqlConnection(_connectionString))
     {
       connection.Open();
       var question =
         connection.QueryFirstOrDefault<
           QuestionGetSingleResponse>(
           @"EXEC dbo.Question_GetSingle @QuestionId =
   ```

```
            @QuestionId",
          new { QuestionId = questionId }
        );
    question.Answers =
      connection.Query<AnswerGetResponse>(
        @"EXEC dbo.Answer_Get_ByQuestionId
            @QuestionId = @QuestionId",
          new { QuestionId = questionId }
        );

    return question;
  }
}
```

3. The question may not be found and return `null`, so let's handle this case and only add the answers if the question is found:

```
public QuestionGetSingleResponse GetQuestion(int questionId)
{
  using (var connection = new
    SqlConnection(_connectionString))
  {
    connection.Open();
    var question =
      connection.QueryFirstOrDefault<
        QuestionGetSingleResponse>(
          @"EXEC dbo.Question_GetSingle @QuestionId =
            @QuestionId",
          new { QuestionId = questionId }
        );
    if (question != null)
    {
      question.Answers =
        connection.Query<AnswerGetResponse>(
          @"EXEC dbo.Answer_Get_ByQuestionId
            @QuestionId = @QuestionId",
          new { QuestionId = questionId }
        );
    }
    return question;
  }
}
```

4. Let's create the `QuestionGetSingleResponse` class we referenced in the method in a file called `QuestionGetSingleResponse.cs` in the `Models` folder:

```csharp
public class QuestionGetSingleResponse
{
    public int QuestionId { get; set; }
    public string Title { get; set; }
    public string Content { get; set; }
    public string UserName { get; set; }
    public string UserId { get; set; }
    public DateTime Created { get; set; }
    public IEnumerable<AnswerGetResponse> Answers { get; set; }
}
```

These properties match up with the data that was returned from the `Question_GetSingle` stored procedure.

5. Let's also create the `AnswerGetResponse` class we referenced in the method in a file called `AnswerGetResponse.cs` in the `Models` folder:

```csharp
public class AnswerGetResponse
{
    public int AnswerId { get; set; }
    public string Content { get; set; }
    public string UserName { get; set; }
    public DateTime Created { get; set; }
}
```

These properties match up with the data that was returned from the `Answer_Get_ByQuestionId` stored procedure.

The `GetQuestion` method should now compile fine.

Creating a repository method to check whether a question exists

Now, let's implement the `QuestionExists` method by following the same approach we followed for the previous methods:

```csharp
public bool QuestionExists(int questionId)
{
    using (var connection = new
        SqlConnection(_connectionString))
    {
```

```csharp
    connection.Open();
    return connection.QueryFirst<bool>(
      @"EXEC dbo.Question_Exists @QuestionId = 
        @QuestionId",
      new { QuestionId = questionId }
    );
  }
}
```

We are using the Dapper `QueryFirst` method rather than `QueryFirstOrDefault` because the stored procedure will always return a single record.

Creating a repository method to get an answer

The last method we will implement in this section is `GetAnswer`:

```csharp
public AnswerGetResponse GetAnswer(int answerId)
{
  using (var connection = new 
    SqlConnection(_connectionString))
  {
    connection.Open();
    return connection.QueryFirstOrDefault<
      AnswerGetResponse>(
      @"EXEC dbo.Answer_Get_ByAnswerId @AnswerId = 
        @AnswerId",
      new { AnswerId = answerId }
    );
  }
}
```

There is nothing new here – the implementation follows the same pattern as the previous methods.

We have now implemented all of the methods in the data repository for reading data. In the next section, we'll turn our attention to writing data.

Writing data using Dapper

In this section, we are going to implement methods in our data repository that will write to the database. We will start by extending the interface for the repository and then do the actual implementation.

The stored procedures that perform the write operations are already in the database. We will be interacting with these stored procedures using Dapper.

Adding methods to write data to the repository interface

We'll start by adding the necessary methods to the repository interface:

```
public interface IDataRepository
{
  ...
  QuestionGetSingleResponse
    PostQuestion(QuestionPostRequest question);

  QuestionGetSingleResponse
    PutQuestion(int questionId, QuestionPutRequest
      question);

  void DeleteQuestion(int questionId);

  AnswerGetResponse PostAnswer(AnswerPostRequest answer);
}
```

Here, we must implement some methods that will add, change, and delete questions, as well as adding an answer.

Creating a repository method to add a new question

Let's create the `PostQuestion` method in `DataRepository.cs` in order to add a new question:

```
public QuestionGetSingleResponse
  PostQuestion(QuestionPostRequest question)
{
  using (var connection = new
    SqlConnection(_connectionString))
  {
    connection.Open();
```

```
    var questionId = connection.QueryFirst<int>(
      @"EXEC dbo.Question_Post
        @Title = @Title, @Content = @Content,
        @UserId = @UserId, @UserName = @UserName,
        @Created = @Created",
      question
    );

    return GetQuestion(questionId);
  }
}
```

This is a very similar implementation to the methods that read data. We are using the `QueryFirst` Dapper method because the stored procedure returns the ID of the new question after inserting it into the database table. Our method returns the saved question by calling the `GetQuestion` method with `questionId`, which was returned from the `Question_Post` stored procedure.

We've used a model class called `QuestionPostRequest` for Dapper to map to the SQL parameters. Let's create this class in the `models` folder:

```
public class QuestionPostRequest
{
  public string Title { get; set; }
  public string Content { get; set; }
  public string UserId { get; set; }
  public string UserName { get; set; }
  public DateTime Created { get; set; }
}
```

Great stuff! That's our first write method created.

Creating a repository method to change a question

Let's create the `PutQuestion` method in `DataRepository.cs` to change a question. This is very similar to the `PostQuestion` method we have just implemented:

```
public QuestionGetSingleResponse PutQuestion(int questionId,
QuestionPutRequest question)
{
  using (var connection = new SqlConnection(_connectionString))
  {
    connection.Open();
    connection.Execute(
      @"EXEC dbo.Question_Put
```

```
        @QuestionId = @QuestionId, @Title = @Title,
          @Content = @Content",
      new { QuestionId = questionId, question.Title,
        question.Content }
    );
    return GetQuestion(questionId);
  }
}
```

Notice that we are using the Dapper `Execute` method because we are simply executing a stored procedure and not returning anything.

We've created the SQL parameters from a model class called `QuestionPutRequest` and the `questionId` parameters that were passed into the method. Let's create the `QuestionPutRequest` class in the `models` folder:

```
public class QuestionPutRequest
{
  public string Title { get; set; }
  public string Content { get; set; }
}
```

That's another method implemented.

Creating a repository method to delete a question

Moving on, let's implement a method for deleting a question:

```
public void DeleteQuestion(int questionId)
{
  using (var connection = new
    SqlConnection(_connectionString))
  {
    connection.Open();
    connection.Execute(
      @"EXEC dbo.Question_Delete
        @QuestionId = @QuestionId",
      new { QuestionId = questionId }
    );
  }
}
```

Again, we are using the Dapper `Execute` method because nothing is returned from the stored procedure.

Creating a repository method to add an answer

The last method we are going to implement will allow us to add an answer to a question:

```
public AnswerGetResponse PostAnswer(AnswerPostRequest answer)
{
  using (var connection = new
    SqlConnection(_connectionString))
  {
    connection.Open();
    return connection.QueryFirst<AnswerGetResponse>(
      @"EXEC dbo.Answer_Post
        @QuestionId = @QuestionId, @Content = @Content,
        @UserId = @UserId, @UserName = @UserName,
        @Created = @Created",
      answer
    );
  }
}
```

As well as inserting the answer into the database table, the stored procedure returns the saved answer. Here, we are using the Dapper `QueryFirst` method to execute the stored procedure and return the saved answer.

We also need to create the `AnswerPostRequest` model class in the `models` folder:

```
public class AnswerPostRequest
{
  public int QuestionId { get; set; }
  public string Content { get; set; }
  public string UserId { get; set; }
  public string UserName { get; set; }
  public DateTime Created { get; set; }
}
```

That completes our data repository. We've chosen to have a single method containing all of the methods that will read and write data. We can, of course, create multiple repositories for different areas of the database, which would be a good idea if the app was larger.

As we add features to our app that involve database changes, we'll need a mechanism for deploying these database changes. We'll look at this in the next section.

Managing migrations using DbUp

DbUp is an open source library that helps us deploy changes to SQL Server databases. It keeps track of SQL Scripts embedded within an ASP.NET Core project, along with which ones have been executed on the database. It contains methods that we can use to execute the SQL Scripts that haven't been executed yet on the database.

In this section, we are going to add DbUp to our project and configure it to do our database migrations when our app starts up.

Installing DbUp into our project

Let's start by installing DbUp by carrying out the following steps in our backend project, in Visual Studio:

1. Go to the **Tools** menu and then **NuGet Package Manager**. Then, choose **Manage NuGet Packages for Solution...**.

2. On the **Browse** tab, enter DbUp into the search box.

3. Select the **dbup** package by Paul Stovell, Jim Burger, Jake Ginnivan, and Damian Maclennan. Tick our project and click the **Install** button, with the latest stable version selected:

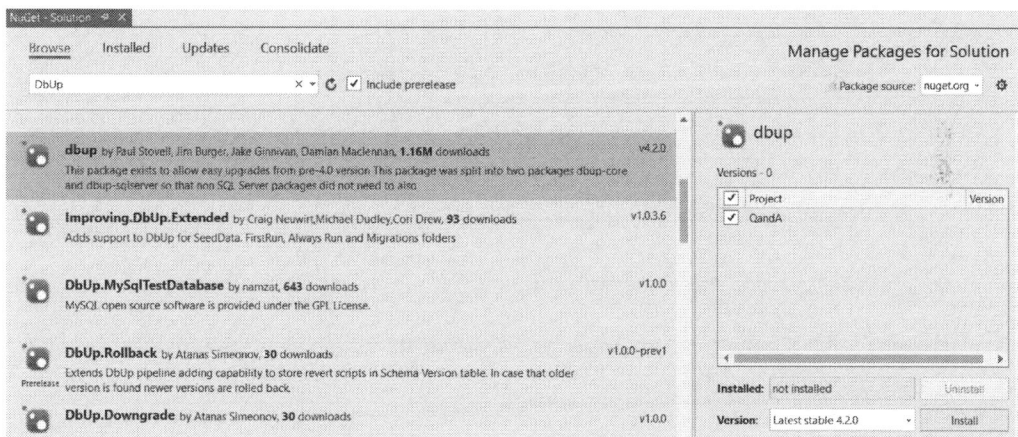

Figure 8.13 – Adding DbUp in NuGet Manager

270　Interacting with the Database with Dapper

We may be asked to accept a licensing agreement before DbUp can be downloaded and installed in our project.

Configuring DbUp to do migrations on app startup

Now that we have DbUp installed in our project, let's get it to do database migrations when the app starts up:

1. Open up `Startup.cs`. We know from *Chapter 1*, *Understanding the ASP.NET 5 React Template*, that the code in this file executes when an ASP.NET Core app runs. We'll start by adding a `using` statement so that we can reference the DbUp library:

   ```
   using DbUp;
   ```

2. At the top of the `ConfigureServices` method, add the following two lines:

   ```
   public void ConfigureServices(IServiceCollection services)
   {
     var connectionString =
       Configuration.GetConnectionString("DefaultConnection");

     EnsureDatabase.For.SqlDatabase(connectionString);

     // TODO - Create and configure an instance of the
     // DbUp upgrader
     // TODO - Do a database migration if there are any
     // pending SQL
     //Scripts

     ...
   }
   ```

   This gets the database connection from the `appsettings.json` file and creates the database if it doesn't exist.

3. Let's create and configure an instance of the DbUp upgrader:

   ```
   public void ConfigureServices(IServiceCollection services)
   {
     var connectionString =
       Configuration.GetConnectionString("DefaultConnection");
   ```

```
    EnsureDatabase.For.SqlDatabase(connectionString);

    var upgrader = DeployChanges.To
      .SqlDatabase(connectionString, null)
      .WithScriptsEmbeddedInAssembly(
        System.Reflection.Assembly.GetExecutingAssembly()
      )
      .WithTransaction()
      .Build();

    // TODO - Do a database migration if there are any pending SQL
    //Scripts

    ...
}
```

We've told DbUp where the database is and to look for SQL Scripts that have been embedded in our project. We've also told DbUp to do the database migrations in a transaction.

4. The final step is to get DbUp to do a database migration if there are any pending SQL Scripts:

```
public void ConfigureServices(IServiceCollection services)
{
  var connectionString =
    Configuration.GetConnectionString("DefaultConnection");

  EnsureDatabase.For.SqlDatabase(connectionString);

  var upgrader = DeployChanges.To
    .SqlDatabase(connectionString, null)
    .WithScriptsEmbeddedInAssembly(
      System.Reflection.Assembly.GetExecutingAssembly()
    )
    .WithTransaction()
    .LogToConsole()
    .Build();

  if (upgrader.IsUpgradeRequired())
  {
    upgrader.PerformUpgrade();
  }
```

```
        ...
}
```

We are using the `IsUpgradeRequired` method in the DbUp upgrade to check whether there are any pending SQL Scripts, and using the `PerformUpgrade` method to do the actual migration.

Embedding SQL Scripts in our project

In the previous subsection, we told DbUp to look for SQL Scripts that have been embedded in our project. Now, we are going to embed SQL Scripts for the tables and stored procedures in our project so that DbUp will execute them if they haven't already been executed when our app loads:

1. In **Solution Explorer**, right-click on the project and choose **Add | New Folder**. Enter `SQLScripts` as the folder name.

2. Right-click on the `SQLScripts` folder and choose **Add | New Item…**.

3. In the dialog box that appears, select the **General** tab and then **Text File** and enter `01-Tables.sql` as the filename:

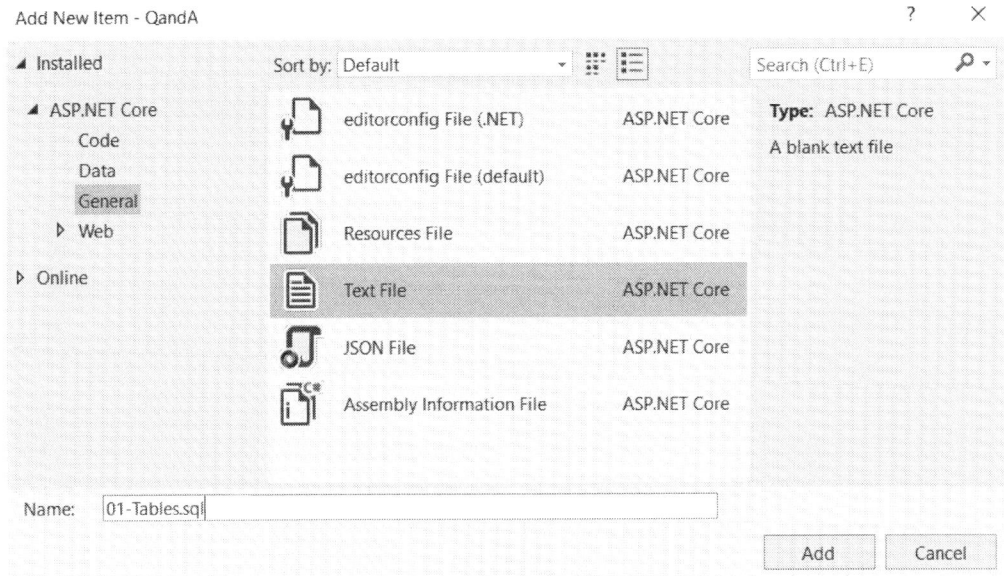

Figure 8.14 – Adding a SQL file to a Visual Studio project

4. Copy the contents of the script from `https://github.com/PacktPublishing/ASP.NET-Core-5-and-React-Second-Edition/blob/master/chapter-08/start/backend/SQLScripts/01-Tables.sql` and paste it into the file we just created.

5. Right-click on **01-Tables.sql** in **Solution Explorer** and choose **Properties** to view the properties of this file.

6. Change the **Build Action** property to **Embedded resource**:

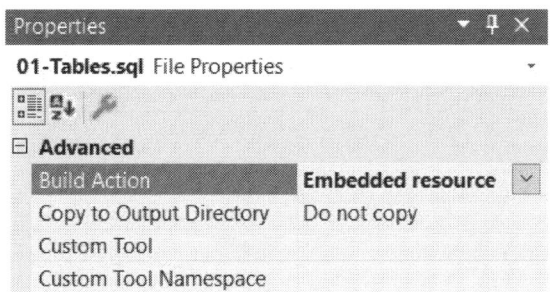

Figure 8.15 – Changing a file to an embedded resource

This embeds the SQL Script in our project so that `DbUp` can find it.

7. Let's repeat this process for the stored procedures by creating a file called `02-Sprocs.sql` in the `SQLScripts` folder with the content from `https://github.com/PacktPublishing/ASP.NET-Core-5-and-React-Second-Edition/blob/master/chapter-08/start/backend/SQLScripts/02-Sprocs.sql`. Let's not forget to embed this file as a project resource.

> **Important Note**
> DbUp will run SQL Scripts in name order, so it's important to have a script naming convention that caters to this. In our example, we are prefixing the script name with a two-digit number.

So, those are the SQL Scripts that make up our database. They have been saved within our project.

Performing a database migration

Now that the database migration code is in place, it is time to test a migration. To do this, we will remove the database tables and stored procedures and expect them to be recreated when our API runs.

Let's carrying out the following steps:

1. The database that we are working with already contains the tables and stored procedures in our scripts, so we are going to be brave and delete our database. In SSMS, in **Object Explorer**, right-click the database and choose **Delete**:

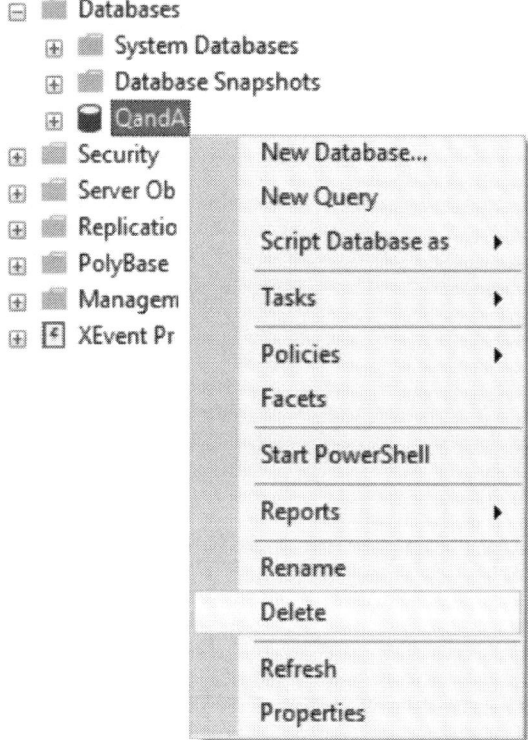

Figure 8.16 – Deleting a database

2. We are going to create the database again with the same name. So, in **Object Explorer**, right-click on **Databases** and click on the **New Database...** option. Enter QandA for the name of the database and click **OK**:

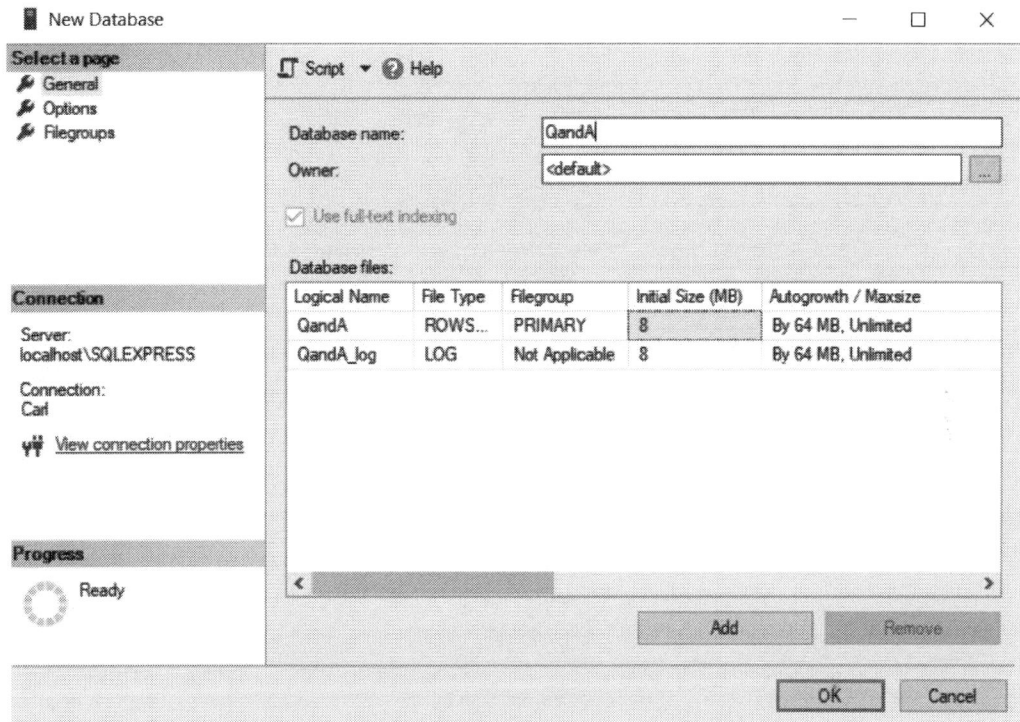

Figure 8.17 – Adding a database

3. Back in Visual Studio, press *F5* to run the app.

4. Once the app has started, go to SSMS. In **Object Explorer**, we'll see that the tables and stored procedures have been created. We'll also see a table called SchemaVersions:

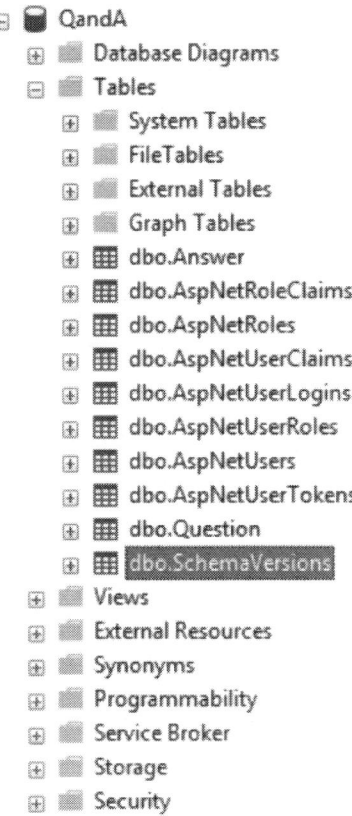

Figure 8.18 – The SchemaVersions table in Object Explorer

5. Right-click on **dbo.SchemaVersions** and choose **Edit Top 200 Rows**:

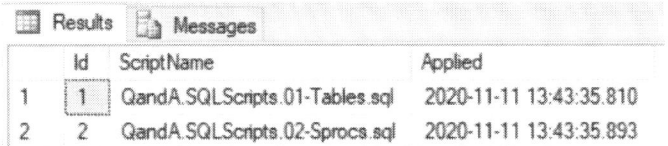

Figure 8.19 – SchemaVersions data

This is a table that DbUp uses to manage what scripts have been executed. So, we'll see our two scripts listed in this table.

6. Back in Visual Studio, stop the app by pressing *Shift + F5*.

7. Run the app again. The app will run up just fine.
8. Inspect the database objects in **Object Explorer** in SSMS. The objects will be unchanged.
9. Examine the contents of the SchemaVersions table. We'll find that no new scripts have been added.
10. We can now stop the app again in Visual Studio.

With that, our project has been set up to handle database migrations. All we need to do is add the necessary SQL Script files in the SQLScripts folder, remembering to embed them as a resource. DbUp will then perform the migration when the app runs again.

Summary

We now understand that Dapper is a simple way of interacting with a database in a performant manner. It's a great choice when our team already has SQL Server skills because it doesn't abstract the database away from us.

In this chapter, we learned that Dapper adds various extension methods to the Microsoft SqlConnection object for reading and writing to the database. Dapper maps the results of a query to instances of a C# class automatically by matching the field names in the query result to the class properties. Query parameters can be passed in using a C# class, with Dapper automatically mapping properties in the C# class to the SQL parameters.

We then discovered that DbUp is a simple open source tool that can be used to manage database migrations. We can embed SQL Scripts within our project and write code that is executed when our app loads to instruct DbUp to check and perform any necessary migrations.

In the next chapter, we are going to create the RESTful API for our app by leveraging the data access code we have written in this chapter.

Questions

Answer the following questions to test the knowledge you have gained from this chapter:

1. What Dapper method can be used to execute a stored procedure that returns no results?
2. What Dapper method can be used to read a single record of data, where the record is guaranteed to exist?

3. What Dapper method can be used to read a collection of records?

4. What is wrong with the following statement, which calls the Dapper `Query` method?

   ```
   return connection.Query<BuildingGetManyResponse>(
     @"EXEC dbo.Building_GetMany_BySearch
       @Search = @Search",
     new { Criteria = "Fred"}
   );
   ```

5. We have the following stored procedure:

   ```
   CREATE PROC dbo.Building_GetMany
   AS
   BEGIN
      SET NOCOUNT ON

      SELECT BuildingId, Name
      FROM dbo.Building
   END
   ```

   We have the following statement, which calls the Dapper `Query` method:

   ```
   return connection.Query<BuildingGetManyResponse>(
     "EXEC dbo.Building_GetMany"
   );
   ```

   We also have the following model, which is referenced in the preceding statement:

   ```
   public class BuildingGetManyResponse
   {
      public int Id{ get; set; }
      public string Name { get; set; }
   }
   ```

   When our app is run, we find that the `Id` property within the `BuildingGetManyResponse` class instance is not populated. Can you spot the problem?

6. Can DbUp be used to deploy new reference data within a table?

Answers

1. `Execute` is the Dapper method that executes a stored procedure, returning no results.
2. `QueryFirst` is the Dapper method for reading a single record of data where the record is guaranteed to exist.
3. `Query` is the Dapper method for reading a collection of records.
4. The problem with the query is that it expects a parameter called `Search` but we have passed it a parameter called `Criteria`. So, Dapper won't be able to map the SQL parameter.
5. The problem is that the stored procedure returns a field called `BuildingId`, which won't automatically get mapped to the `Id` property in the class because the names are different.
6. Yes! DbUp can execute any SQL script, and can also deploy new reference data for a table.

Further reading

Here are some useful links if you wish to learn more about the topics that were covered in this chapter:

- **Creating a SQL Server database**: https://docs.microsoft.com/en-us/sql/relational-databases/databases/create-a-database
- **Creating SQL Server tables**: https://docs.microsoft.com/en-us/sql/t-sql/statements/create-table-transact-sql
- **Creating SQL Server stored procedures**: https://docs.microsoft.com/en-us/sql/relational-databases/stored-procedures/create-a-stored-procedure
- **The C# using statement**: https://docs.microsoft.com/en-us/dotnet/csharp/language-reference/keywords/using-statement
- **Dapper**: https://github.com/StackExchange/Dapper
- **DbUp**: https://dbup.readthedocs.io/en/latest/

9
Creating REST API Endpoints

In *Chapter 1, Understanding the ASP.NET 5 React Template*, we learned that a RESTful endpoint is implemented using an API controller in ASP.NET. In this chapter, we'll implement an API controller for our Q&A app that will eventually allow the frontend to read and write questions and answers. We'll implement a range of controller action methods that handle different HTTP request methods returning appropriate responses.

We'll learn about dependency injection and use this to inject the data repository we created in the previous chapter into the API controller. We'll validate requests so that we can be sure the data is valid before it reaches the data repository.

At the end of the chapter, we'll ensure we aren't asking for unnecessary information in the API requests. This will prevent potential security issues as well as improve the experience for API consumers.

In this chapter, we'll cover the following topics:

- Creating an API controller
- Creating controller action methods
- Adding model validation
- Removing unnecessary request fields

Technical requirements

We'll use the following tools in this chapter:

- **Visual Studio 2019**: We'll use this to edit our ASP.NET code. This can be downloaded from `https://visualstudio.microsoft.com/vs/`.
- **.NET 5**: This can be downloaded from `https://dotnet.microsoft.com/download/dotnet/5.0`.
- **Postman**: We'll use this to try out the REST API endpoint we'll implement in this chapter. This can be downloaded from `https://www.getpostman.com/downloads/`.
- **Q&A**: We'll start with the Q&A backend project we finished in the previous chapter. This is available on GitHub at `https://github.com/PacktPublishing/ASP.NET-Core-5-and-React-Second-Edition` in the `chapter-09/start` folder.

All the code snippets in this chapter can be found online at `https://github.com/PacktPublishing/ASP.NET-Core-5-and-React-Second-Edition`. In order to restore code from a chapter, the source code repository can be downloaded and the relevant folder opened in the relevant editor. If the code is frontend code then `npm install` can be entered in the terminal to restore the dependencies.

Check out the following video to see the Code in Action: `https://bit.ly/34xLwzq`.

Creating an API controller

An API controller is a class that handles HTTP requests for an endpoint in a REST API and sends responses back to the caller.

In this section, we are going to create an API controller to handle requests to an `api/questions` endpoint. The controller will call into the data repository we created in the previous chapter. We'll also create an instance of the data repository in the API controller using dependency injection.

Creating an API controller for questions

Let's create a controller for the `api/questions` endpoint. If we don't have our backend project open in Visual Studio, let's do so and carry out the following steps:

1. In **Solution Explorer**, right-click on the `Controllers` folder, choose **Add**, and then **Class...**.

2. In the left-hand panel, find and select **ASP.NET Core** and then **API Controller - Empty** in the middle panel. Enter `QuestionsController.cs` for the name of the file and click **Add**:

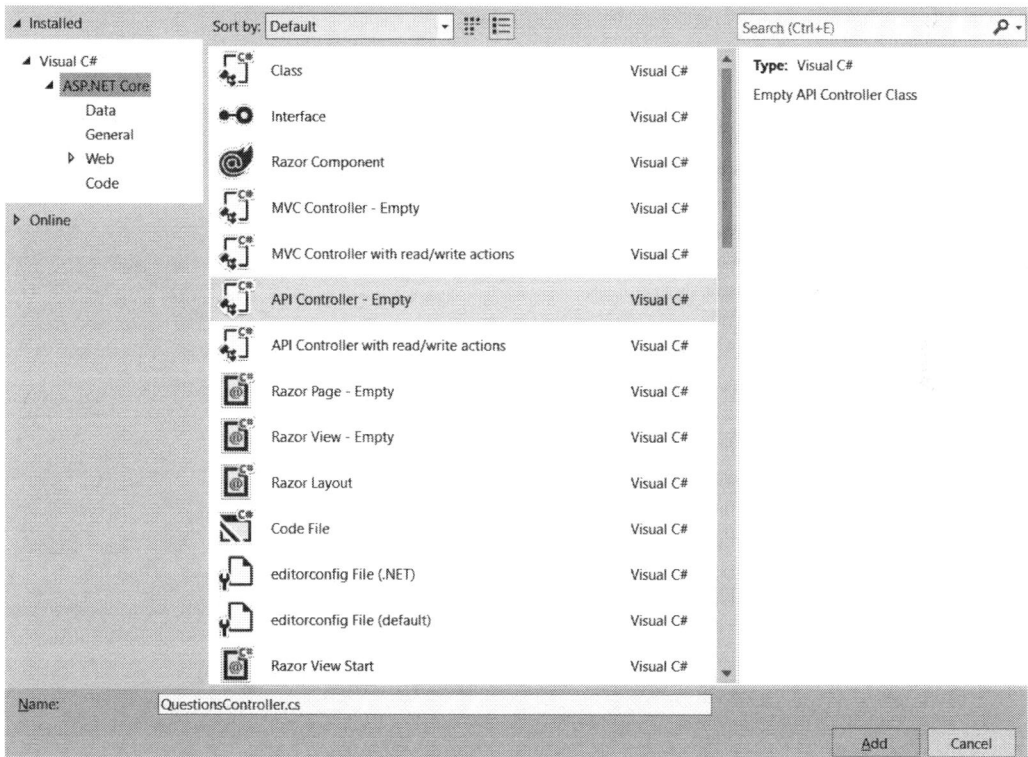

Figure 9.1 – Creating a new API controller

3. A `QuestionsController.cs` file will appear in the `Controllers` folder in **Solution Explorer**. Open this file by double-clicking on it in **Solution Explorer**. The file will contain the following class in the `QandA.Controllers` namespace:

```
[Route("api/[controller]")]
[ApiController]
public class QuestionsController : ControllerBase
{
}
```

The `Route` attribute defines the path that our controller will handle. In our case, the path will be `api/questions` because `[controller]` is substituted with the name of the controller minus the word `Controller`.

The `ApiController` attribute includes behavior such as automatic model validation, which we'll take advantage of later in this chapter.

The class also inherits from `ControllerBase`. This gives us access to more API-specific methods in our controller.

Next, we will learn how to interact with the data repository from the API controller.

Injecting the data repository into the API controller

We want to interact with an instance of the data repository we created in the previous chapter into our API controller. Let's carry out the following steps to do this:

1. We'll start by adding `using` statements to the `QuestionsController.cs` file so that the data repository and its models can be referenced. Add the following statements under the `using` statements that were generated automatically:

```
using QandA.Data;
using QandA.Data.Models;
```

2. Create a `private` class-level variable to hold a reference to our repository:

```
[Route("api/[controller]")]
[ApiController]
public class QuestionsController : ControllerBase
{
    private readonly IDataRepository _dataRepository;
}
```

We've used the `readonly` keyword to make sure the variable's reference doesn't change outside the constructor.

3. Let's create the constructor as follows beneath the _dataRepository variable declaration:

   ```
   private readonly IDataRepository _dataRepository;

   public QuestionsController()
   {
       // TODO - set reference to _dataRepository
   }
   ```

   We need to set up the reference to _dataRepository in the constructor. We could try the following:

   ```
   public QuestionsController()
   {
       _dataRepository = new DataRepository();
   }
   ```

   However, the DataRepository constructor requires the connection string to be passed in. Recall that we used something called **dependency injection** in the previous chapter to inject the configuration object into the data repository constructor to give us access to the connection string. Maybe we could use dependency injection to inject the data repository into our API controller? Yes, this is exactly what we are going to do.

   > **Important note**
   >
   > **Dependency injection** is the process of injecting an instance of a class into another object. The goal of dependency injection is to decouple a class from its dependencies so that the dependencies can be changed without changing the class. ASP.NET has its own dependency injection facility that allows class dependencies to be defined when the app starts up. These dependencies are then available to be injected into other class constructors.

4. Change the constructor to the following:

   ```
   public QuestionsController(IDataRepository dataRepository)
   {
       _dataRepository = dataRepository;
   }
   ```

   So, our constructor now expects the data repository to be passed into the constructor as a parameter. We then simply set our private class-level variable to the data repository passed in.

Unlike the `configuration` object that was injected into the data repository, the data repository isn't automatically available for dependency injection. ASP.NET already sets up the `configuration` object for dependency injection for us because it is responsible for this class. However, `DataRepository` is our class, so we must register this for dependency injection.

5. Let's go to `startup.cs` and add a `using` statement so that we can reference our data repository. Add the following statement after the existing `using` statements:

```
using QandA.Data;
```

6. Enter the following highlighted line at the bottom of the `ConfigureServices` class to make the data repository available for dependency injection:

```
public void ConfigureServices(IServiceCollection services)
{
    ...
    services.AddScoped<IDataRepository,
      DataRepository>();
}
```

This tells ASP.NET that whenever `IDataRepository` is referenced in a constructor, substitute an instance of the `DataRepository` class.

> **Important note**
>
> The `AddScoped` method means that only one instance of the `DataRepository` class is created in a given HTTP request. This means the lifetime of the class that is created lasts for the whole HTTP request.

So, if ASP.NET encounters a second constructor that references `IDataRepository` in the same HTTP request, it will use the instance of the `DataRepository` class it created previously.

> **Important note**
>
> As well as `AddScoped`, there are other methods for registering dependencies that result in different lifetimes for the generated class. `AddTransient` will generate a new instance of the class each time it is requested. `AddSingleton` will generate only one class instance for the lifetime of the whole app.

To recap, we can use dependency injection to have dependent class instances injected into the constructor of an API controller. Classes that are used in dependency injection need to be registered in the `ConfigureServices` method in the `StartUp` class.

So, we now have access to our data repository in our API controller with the help of dependency injection. Next, we are going to implement methods that are going to handle specific HTTP requests.

Creating controller action methods

Action methods are where we can write code to handle requests to a resource. In this section, we are going to implement action methods that will handle requests to the questions resource. We will cover the `GET`, `POST`, `PUT`, and `DELETE` HTTP methods.

Creating an action method for getting questions

Let's implement our first action method, which is going to return an array of all the questions. Open `QuestionsController.cs` and carry out the following steps:

1. Let's create a method called `GetQuestions` at the bottom of the `QuestionsController` class:

    ```
    [HttpGet]
    public IEnumerable<QuestionGetManyResponse>
    GetQuestions()
    {
        // TODO - get questions from data repository
        // TODO - return questions in the response
    }
    ```

    We decorate the method with the `HttpGet` attribute to tell ASP.NET that this will handle HTTP `GET` requests to this resource.

    We use the specific `IEnumerable<QuestionGetManyResponse>` type as the return type.

2. We can get the questions from the data repository using the `GetQuestions` method as follows:

```
[HttpGet]
public IEnumerable<QuestionGetManyResponse>
GetQuestions()
{
    var questions = _dataRepository.GetQuestions();
    // TODO - return questions in the response
}
```

3. Let's return the questions in the response:

```
[HttpGet]
public IEnumerable<QuestionGetManyResponse>
GetQuestions()
{
    var questions = _dataRepository.GetQuestions();
    return questions;
}
```

ASP.NET will automatically convert the `questions` object to JSON format and put this in the response body. It will also automatically return `200` as the HTTP status code. Nice!

4. Let's try this by first pressing *F5* in Visual Studio to start our app.

5. In the browser that opens, change the path to end with `api/questions`:

```
[{"questionId":1,"title":"Why should I learn TypeScript?","content":"TypeScript seems to be getting popular so I wondered whether it is worth my time learning it? What benefits does it give over JavaScript?","userName":"bob.test@test.com","created":"2020-12-04T14:32:00"},
{"questionId":2,"title":"Which state management tool should I use?","content":"There seem to be a fair few state management tools around for React Redux, Recoil, ... Which one should I use?","userName":"jane.test@test.com","created":"2020-12-04T15:03:00"}]
```

Figure 9.2 – Getting all questions

We'll see the questions from our database output in JSON format. Great, that's our first action method implemented!

6. We are going to change the default path that invokes when the app is run to the `api/questions` path in the next step. First, we need to make sure the `Properties` folder is available in **Solution Explorer**. If the `Properties` folder isn't visible in **Solution Explorer**, then switch to **Show All Files** in the toolbar:

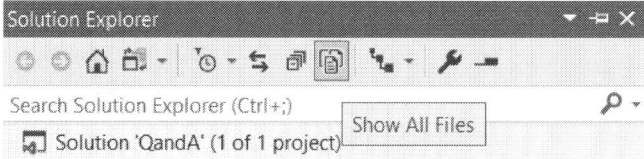

Figure 9.3 – Show all files in Solution Explorer

7. Open up the `launchSettings.json` file in the `Properties` folder in **Solution Explorer** and change the `launchUrl` fields to be `api/questions`:

```
...
"profiles": {
  "IIS Express": {
    "commandName": "IISExpress",
    "launchBrowser": true,
    "launchUrl": "api/questions",
    "environmentVariables": {
      "ASPNETCORE_ENVIRONMENT": "Development"
    }
  },
  "QandA": {
    "commandName": "Project",
    "launchBrowser": true,
    "launchUrl": "api/questions",
    "applicationUrl":
      "https://localhost:5001;http://localhost:5000",
    "environmentVariables": {
      "ASPNETCORE_ENVIRONMENT": "Development"
    }
  }
}
...
```

8. Press *Shift* + *F5* to stop the app, and then *F5* to start it again. Our `api/questions` path will now be invoked by default in the browser.

9. Press *Shift* + *F5* again to stop the app. Now, we are ready for implementing more code in our next task.

That completes the action method that will handle `GET` requests to `api/questions`.

In summary, `GET` request action methods have an `HttpGet` attribute decorator. The return type of the method is the type of data we want in the response body, which is automatically converted to JSON for us.

We will continue implementing handlers for more HTTP methods in the following subsections.

Extending the GetQuestions action method for searching

We don't always want all of the questions to be returned in the `api/questions` endpoint. Recall that our frontend had a search feature that returned questions that matched the search criteria. Let's extend our `GetQuestions` method to handle a search request. To do that, follow these steps:

1. Add a `search` parameter to the `GetQuestions` method:

    ```
    [HttpGet]
    public IEnumerable<QuestionGetManyResponse>
      GetQuestions(string search)
    {
        var questions = _dataRepository.GetQuestions();
        return questions;
    }
    ```

2. Put a breakpoint on the statement that gets the questions from the repository and press *F5* to run the app:

    ```
    public IEnumerable<QuestionGetManyResponse> GetQuestions(string search)
    {                                                              search null
        var questions = _dataRepository.GetQuestions();
        return questions;
    }
    ```

    Figure 9.4 – Model binding with no search query parameter

    We'll see that the search parameter is `null`. Press *F5* to let the app continue.

3. With the breakpoint still in place, change the URL in the browser to end with `questions?search=type`:

    ```
    public IEnumerable<QuestionGetManyResponse> GetQuestions(string search)
    {                                                              search Q ▼ "type"
        var questions = _dataRepository.GetQuestions();  ≤6,711ms elapsed
        return questions;
    }
    ```

    Figure 9.5 – Model binding with a search query parameter value

    This time the `search` parameter is set to the value of the `search` query parameter we put in the browser URL. This process is called **model binding**.

> **Important note**
>
> Model binding is a process in ASP.NET that maps data from HTTP requests to action method parameters. Data from query parameters is automatically mapped to action method parameters that have the same name. We'll see later in this section that model binding can also map data from the HTTP request body. So, a [FromQuery] attribute could be placed in front of the action method parameter to instruct ASP.NET to map only from the query parameter.

4. Now stop the running app by pressing *Shift + F5*.

5. Let's branch our code on whether the search parameter contains a value and get and return all the questions if it doesn't. Replace the code inside GetQuestions with the following highlighted code:

```
[HttpGet]
public IEnumerable<QuestionGetManyResponse>
  GetQuestions(string search)
{
    if (string.IsNullOrEmpty(search))
    {
        return _dataRepository.GetQuestions();
    }
    else
    {
        // TODO - call data repository question search
    }
}
```

If there is no search value, we get and return all the questions as we did before, but this time in a single statement.

6. Let's add a call to the data repository question search method if we have a search value:

```
[HttpGet]
public IEnumerable<QuestionGetManyResponse>
  GetQuestions(string search)
{
    if (string.IsNullOrEmpty(search))
    {
        return _dataRepository.GetQuestions();
    }
    else
    {
        return
        _dataRepository.GetQuestionsBySearch(search);
```

```
    }
}
```

7. Let's run the app and give this a try. All the questions will be returned in the browser when it opens up. Let's add a `search` query parameter with a value of `type`:

```
[{"questionId":1,"title":"Why should I learn TypeScript?","content":"TypeScript seems to be getting popular so I wondered whether it is worth my time learning it? What benefits does it give over JavaScript?","userName":"bob.test@test.com","created":"2020-12-04T14:32:00"}]
```

Figure 9.6 – Searching questions

We'll see that the TypeScript question is returned as we would expect.

8. Stop the app running by pressing *Shift* + *F5* so that we can write more code for our next task.

We have started to take advantage of model binding in ASP.NET. Model binding automatically binds the query parameters in a request to action method parameters. We'll continue to use model binding throughout this chapter.

Creating an action method for getting unanswered questions

Recall that the home screen of our app, as implemented in *Chapter 3, Getting Started with React and TypeScript*, shows the unanswered questions. We will create an action method that will handle the `api/questions/unanswered` path and return unanswered questions. Follow the steps given here.

Let's implement an action method that provides this functionality:

1. Add the following action method below the `GetQuestions` action method:

```
[HttpGet("unanswered")]
public IEnumerable<QuestionGetManyResponse>
  GetUnansweredQuestions()
{
    return _dataRepository.GetUnansweredQuestions();
}
```

The implementation simply calls into the data repository `GetUnansweredQuestions` method and returns the results.

Notice that the `HttpGet` attribute contains the string `"unanswered"`. This is an additional path to concatenate to the controller's root path. So, this action method will handle `GET` requests to the `api/questions/unanswered` path.

2. Let's give this a try by running the app in a browser by entering the `api/questions/unanswered` path:

```
[{"questionId":2,"title":"Which state management tool should I use?","content":"There seem to be a fair few state management tools around for React - Redux, Recoil, ... Which one should I use?","userName":"jane.test@test.com","created":"2020-12-04T15:03:00"}]
```

Figure 9.7 – Unanswered questions

We get the unanswered question about state management as expected.

3. Stop our app running by pressing *Shift + F5* so that we can write another action method.

That completes the implementation of the action method that handles `GET` requests to `api/questions/unanswered`. To handle a subpath in an action method, we pass the subpath in the `HttpGet` attribute parameter.

Creating an action method for getting a single question

Let's move on to implementing the action method for getting a single question. To do that, follow these steps:

1. Add the following skeleton method underneath the `GetUnansweredQuestions` method:

```
[HttpGet("{questionId}")]
public ActionResult<QuestionGetSingleResponse>
  GetQuestion(int questionId)
{
    // TODO - call the data repository to get the
    // question
    // TODO - return HTTP status code 404 if the
    // question isn't found
    // TODO - return question in response with status
    // code 200
}
```

Note the `HttpGet` attribute parameter.

> **Important note**
> The curly brackets tell ASP.NET to put the endpoint subpath in a variable that can be referenced as a method parameter.

In this method, the `questionId` parameter will be set to the subpath on the endpoint. So, for the `api/questions/3` path, `questionId` would be set to 3.

Notice that the return type is `ActionResult<QuestionGetSingleResponse>` rather than just `QuestionGetSingleResponse`. This is because our action method won't return `QuestionGetSingleResponse` in all cases—there will be a case that will return `NotFoundResult` when the question can't be found. `ActionResult` gives us the flexibility to return these different types.

2. Let's call into the repository to get the question:

```
[HttpGet("{questionId}")]
public ActionResult<QuestionGetSingleResponse>
  GetQuestion(int questionId)
{
    var question =
      _dataRepository.GetQuestion(questionId);
    // TODO - return HTTP status code 404 if the
    // question isn't found
    // TODO - return question in response with status
    // code 200
}
```

3. Next, we can check whether the question has been found and return HTTP status code 404 if it hasn't:

```
[HttpGet("{questionId}")]
public ActionResult<QuestionGetSingleResponse>
GetQuestion(int questionId)
{
    var question =
      _dataRepository.GetQuestion(questionId);
    if (question == null)
    {
        return NotFound();
    }
    // TODO - return question in response with status
    // code 200
}
```

If the question isn't found, the result from the repository call will be `null`. So, we check for `null` and return a call to the `NotFound` method in `ControllerBase`, which returns HTTP status code 404.

4. The last implementation step is to `return` the question that has been found:

```
[HttpGet("{questionId}")]
public ActionResult<QuestionGetSingleResponse>
GetQuestion(int questionId)
{
    var question =
      _dataRepository.GetQuestion(questionId);
    if (question == null)
    {
        return NotFound();
    }
    return question;
}
```

This will result in HTTP status code `200` being returned in the response with the question in JSON format in the response body.

5. Let's give this a try by running the app and requesting question `1`:

```
{"questionId":1,"title":"Why should I learn TypeScript?","content":"TypeScript seems to be getting popular so I wondered whether it is worth my time learning it? What benefits does it give over JavaScript?","userName":"bob.test@test.com","userId":"1","created":"2020-12-04T14:32:00","answers":
[{"answerId":1,"content":"To catch problems earlier speeding up your developments","userName":"jane.test@test.com","created":"2020-12-04T14:40:00"},
{"answerId":2,"content":"So, that you can use the JavaScript features of tomorrow, today","userName":"fred.test@test.com","created":"2020-12-06T10:04:00"}]}
```

Figure 9.8 – Getting a question

The question is returned as expected.

6. Let's try requesting a question that doesn't exist by putting `1000` as the requested question number:

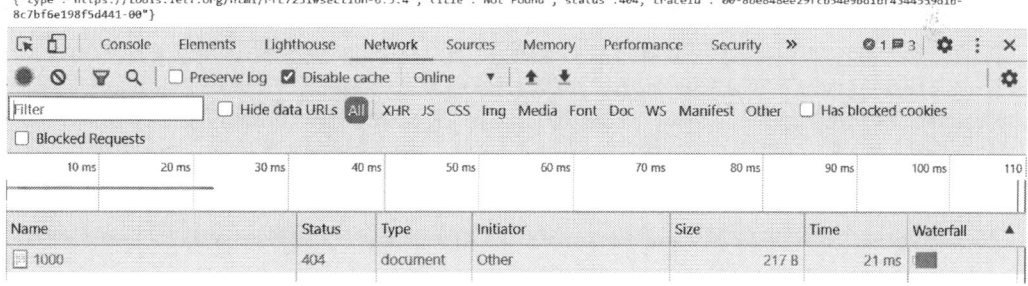

Figure 9.9 – Requesting a question that doesn't exist

We can get confirmation that a `404` status code is returned by pressing *F12* to open the DevTools and looking at the **Network** panel to see the status of the response.

7. Stop our app running so that we are ready to implement another action method.

That completes the action method for getting a question.

We now understand that endpoint subpath parameters can be implemented by putting the parameter name inside curly brackets inside the HTTP method attribute decorator. We have also learned that there is a handy `NotFound` method in `ControllerBase`, which returns an HTTP status code `404` that we can use for requested resources that don't exist.

We've implemented a range of action methods that handle `GET` requests. It's time to implement action methods for the other HTTP methods next.

Creating an action method for posting a question

Let's implement an action method for posting a question:

1. We'll start with the skeleton method. Add the following after the `GetQuestion` method:

   ```
   [HttpPost]
   public ActionResult<QuestionGetSingleResponse>
     PostQuestion(QuestionPostRequest questionPostRequest)
   {
       // TODO - call the data repository to save the
         // question
       // TODO - return HTTP status code 201
   }
   ```

   Note that we use an `HttpPost` attribute to tell ASP.NET that this method handles HTTP `POST` requests.

   Note that the method parameter type for `questionPostRequest` is a class rather than a primitive type. Earlier, in the *Extending the GetQuestions action method for searching* section, we introduced ourselves to model binding and explained how it maps data from an HTTP request to method parameters. Well, model binding can map data from the HTTP body as well as the query parameters. Model binding can also map to properties in parameters. This means that the data in the HTTP request body will be mapped to properties in the instance of the `QuestionPostRequest` class.

2. Let's call into the data repository to post the question:

   ```
   [HttpPost]
   public ActionResult<QuestionGetSingleResponse>
     PostQuestion(QuestionPostRequest questionPostRequest)
   {
       var savedQuestion =
           _dataRepository.
             PostQuestion(questionPostRequest);
   ```

```
            // TODO - return HTTP status code 201
    }
```

3. The last step in the implementation is to return status code `201` to signify that the resource has been created:

```
[HttpPost]
public ActionResult<QuestionGetSingleResponse>
    PostQuestion(QuestionPostRequest questionPostRequest)
{
    var savedQuestion =
        _dataRepository.PostQuestion(questionPostRequest);
    return CreatedAtAction(nameof(GetQuestion),
        new { questionId = savedQuestion.QuestionId },
        savedQuestion);
}
```

We return a call to `CreatedAtAction` from `ControllerBase`, which will return status code `201` with the question in the response. In addition, it also includes a `Location` HTTP header that contains the path to get the question.

4. Let's try this out. First, we'll run the app by pressing *F5*.

5. This time we'll use Postman to check whether the action method is working. Postman is a great tool for testing REST APIs. Open Postman and create a new request by clicking the + icon on the tabs bar:

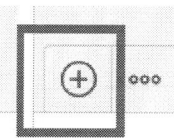

Figure 9.10 – Creating a new request

6. Set the HTTP method to `POST` and enter the path to the questions resource:

Figure 9.11 – Setting the HTTP method and path in Postman

7. Go to the **Body** tab, select **raw**, and then select **JSON** to specify the request body type:

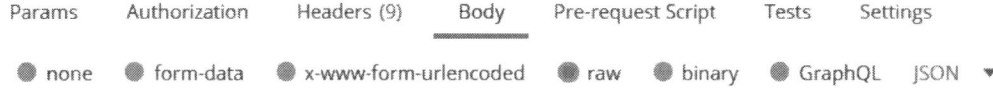

Figure 9.12 – Setting the request body type to JSON in Postman

8. Enter the request body in the box provided, as shown in the following screenshot:

```
{
    "title": "Accessing HttpContext in a service class",
    "content": "How do you access HttpContext",
    "userId": "1",
    "userName": "bob.test@test.com",
    "created": "2020-12-06T17:39:00"
}
```

Figure 9.13 – Adding the request body in Postman

9. Click the **Send** button to send the request and look at the response panel underneath the request body:

Figure 9.14 – Response body from posting a question

The expected `201` HTTP status code is returned with the saved question in the response.

Note how the question in the response has the generated `questionId`, which will be useful for the consumer when interacting with the question.

10. If we look at the response headers, we can see that ASP.NET has also included a `Location` HTTP header that contains the path to get the question:

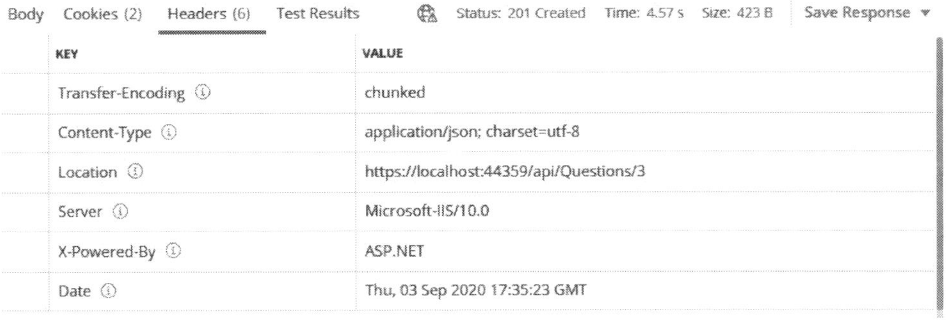
Body
Cookies (2)
Headers (6)
Test Results
Status: 201 Created
Time: 4.57 s
Size: 423 B
Save Response
KEY
VALUE
Transfer-Encoding
chunked
Content-Type
application/json; charset=utf-8
Location
https://localhost:44359/api/Questions/3
Server
Microsoft-IIS/10.0
X-Powered-By
ASP.NET
Date
Thu, 03 Sep 2020 17:35:23 GMT

Figure 9.15 – Response headers from posting a question

That's a nice touch.

11. Stop our app running so that we are ready to implement another action method.

That completes the implementation of the action method that will handle `POST` requests to `api/questions`.

We use the `HttpPost` attribute decorator to allow an action method to handle `POST` requests. Executing the `CreatedAtAction` method from `ControllerBase` in the action method's return statement will automatically add an HTTP location header containing the path to get the resource as well adding HTTP status code `201` to the response.

Creating an action method for updating a question

Let's move on to updating a question. To do that, implement the following steps:

1. Add the following skeleton for the action method:

```
[HttpPut("{questionId}")]
public ActionResult<QuestionGetSingleResponse>
  PutQuestion(int questionId,
    QuestionPutRequest questionPutRequest)
{
    // TODO - get the question from the data
     // repository
    // TODO - return HTTP status code 404 if the
      // question isn't found
    // TODO - update the question model
    // TODO - call the data repository with the
     // updated question model to update the question
```

```
            // in the database
        // TODO - return the saved question
}
```

We use the `HttpPut` attribute to tell ASP.NET that this method handles HTTP PUT requests. We are also putting the route parameter for the question ID in the `questionId` method parameter.

The ASP.NET model binding will populate the `QuestionPutRequest` class instance from the HTTP request body.

2. Let's get the question from the data repository and return HTTP status code 404 if the question isn't found:

```
[HttpPut("{questionId}")]
public ActionResult<QuestionGetSingleResponse>
  PutQuestion(int questionId,
    QuestionPutRequest questionPutRequest)
{
    var question = _dataRepository.
     GetQuestion(questionId);
    if (question == null)
    {
        return NotFound();
    }

    // TODO - update the question model
    // TODO - call the data repository with the
      // updated question
    //model to update the question in the database
    // TODO - return the saved question
}
```

3. Now let's update the `question` model:

```
[HttpPut("{questionId}")]
public ActionResult<QuestionGetSingleResponse>
  PutQuestion(int questionId,
    QuestionPutRequest questionPutRequest)
{
    var question = _dataRepository.
     GetQuestion(questionId);
    if (question == null)
    {
        return NotFound();
    }
```

```
        questionPutRequest.Title =
          string.IsNullOrEmpty(questionPutRequest.Title) ?
            question.Title :
            questionPutRequest.Title;
        questionPutRequest.Content =
          string.IsNullOrEmpty(questionPutRequest.Content) ?
            question.Content :
            questionPutRequest.Content;

        // TODO - call the data repository with the
        // updated question model to update the question
           // in the database
        // TODO - return the saved question
    }
```

We use ternary expressions to update the request model with data from the existing question if it hasn't been supplied in the request.

> **Important note**
>
> Allowing the consumer of the API to submit just the information that needs to be updated (rather than the full record) makes our API easy to consume.

4. The final steps in the implementation are to call the data repository to update the question and then return the saved question in the response:

```
[HttpPut("{questionId}")]
public ActionResult<QuestionGetSingleResponse>
  PutQuestion(int questionId,
    QuestionPutRequest questionPutRequest)
{
    var question =
      _dataRepository.GetQuestion(questionId);
    if (question == null)
    {
        return NotFound();
    }
    questionPutRequest.Title =
      string.IsNullOrEmpty(questionPutRequest.Title) ?
        question.Title :
        questionPutRequest.Title;
    questionPutRequest.Content =
      string.IsNullOrEmpty(questionPutRequest.Content) ?
        question.Content :
        questionPutRequest.Content;
    var savedQuestion =
```

```
    _dataRepository.PutQuestion(questionId,
        questionPutRequest);
    return savedQuestion;
}
```

5. Let's try this out by running the app and using Postman. Create a new request and set the HTTP method to PUT and enter the path to question 3 that we
6. recently added:

Figure 9.16 – PUT request path

7. Go to the **Body** tab, select **raw**, and then select **JSON** to specify the request body type.
8. Enter the request body in the box provided, as shown in the following screenshot:

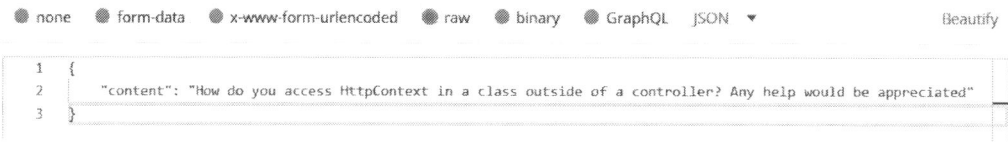

Figure 9.17 – PUT request body

So, we are requesting that question 3 is updated with the new content we have provided.

9. Click the **Send** button to send the request:

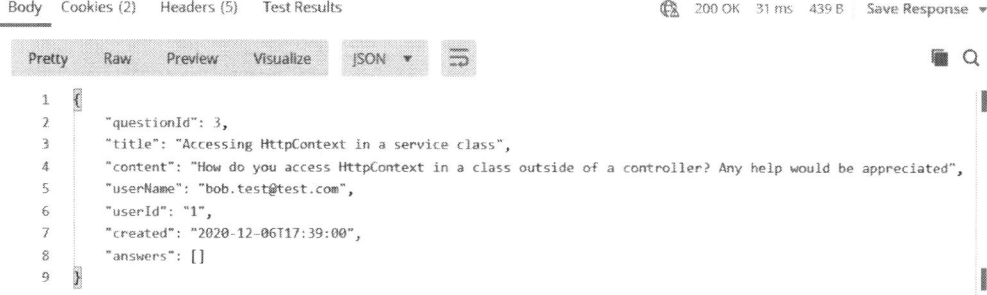

Figure 9.18 – PUT response body

The question is updated just as we expect.

10. Stop our app running so that we are ready to implement another action method.

The `PutQuestion` action method we implemented was arguably a handler for `PATCH` requests because it doesn't require the full record to be submitted. To handle `PATCH` requests, the `HttpPut` attribute decorator can be changed to `HttpPatch`. Note that handling `PATCH` requests properly requires a `NewtonsoftJson` NuGet package and registering a special input formatter. More information can be found at https://docs.microsoft.com/en-us/aspnet/core/web-api/jsonpatch.

To handle both `PUT` and `PATCH` requests, the method can be decorated with both the `HttpPut` and `HttpPatch` attribute decorators. We will leave our implementation with just `HttpPut`.

That completes the implementation of the action method that will handle `PUT` requests to `api/questions`.

Creating an action method for deleting a question

Let's implement deleting a question. This follows a similar pattern to the previous methods:

1. We'll add the action method in a single step as it's similar to what we've done before:

    ```
    [HttpDelete("{questionId}")]
    public ActionResult DeleteQuestion(int questionId)
    {
        var question =
          _dataRepository.GetQuestion(questionId);
        if (question == null)
        {
            return NotFound();
        }
        _dataRepository.DeleteQuestion(questionId);
        return NoContent();
    }
    ```

    We use the `HttpDelete` attribute to tell ASP.NET that this method handles HTTP `DELETE` requests. The method expects the question ID to be included at the end of the path.

    The method checks that the question exists before deleting it, and returns an HTTP `404` status code if it doesn't exist.

    The method returns HTTP status code `204` if the deletion is successful.

304 Creating REST API Endpoints

2. Let's try this out by running the app and using Postman. Set the HTTP method to `DELETE` and enter the path to question 3. Click the **Send** button to send the request:

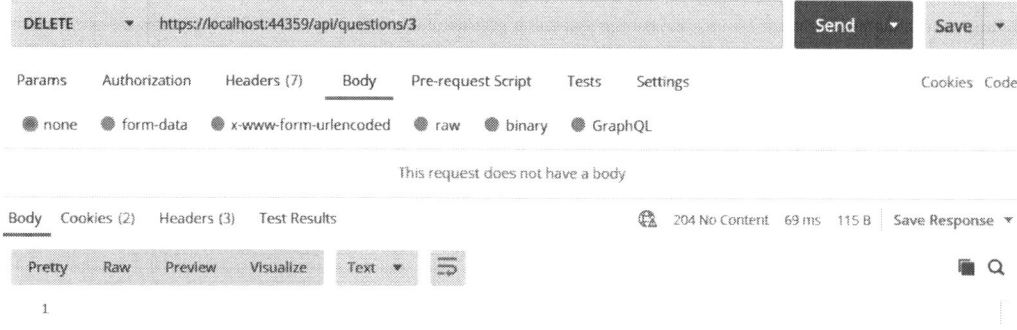

Figure 9.19 – DELETE request

A response with HTTP status code `204` is returned as expected.

3. Stop our app running so that we are ready to implement our final action method.

That completes the implementation of the action method that will handle `DELETE` requests to `api/questions`.

Creating an action method for posting an answer

The final action method we are going to implement is a method for posting an answer to a question:

1. This method will handle an HTTP `POST` request to the `api/question/answer` path:

```
[HttpPost("answer")]
public ActionResult<AnswerGetResponse>
  PostAnswer(AnswerPostRequest answerPostRequest)
{
    var questionExists =
      _dataRepository.QuestionExists(
        answerPostRequest.QuestionId);
    if (!questionExists)
    {
        return NotFound();
    }
    var savedAnswer =
      _dataRepository.PostAnswer(answerPostRequest);
```

```
            return savedAnswer;
}
```

The method checks whether the question exists and returns a 404 HTTP status code if it doesn't. The answer is then passed to the data repository to insert into the database. The saved answer is returned from the data repository, which is returned in the response.

An alternative approach would be to put the questionId into the URL (api/question/{questionId}/answer) and not in the body of the request. This could be achieved by changing the decorator and method signature to the following:

```
[HttpPost("{questionId}/answer")]
public ActionResult<AnswerGetResponse>
    PostAnswer(int questionId, AnswerPostRequest
answerPostRequest)
```

The QuestionId property could also be removed from the AnswerPostRequest model.

2. Let's try this out by running the app and using Postman. Set the HTTP method to POST and enter the api/questions/answer path. Add a request body containing an answer for question 1 and then click the **Send** button to send the request:

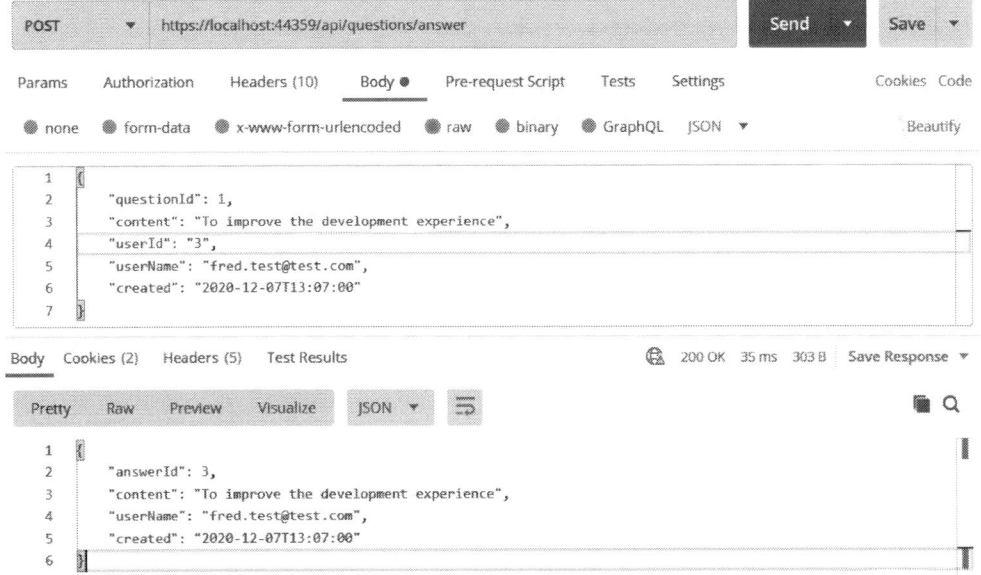

Figure 9.20 – Submitting an answer

The answer will be saved and returned in the response as expected.

3. Remove the `content` field from the request body and try sending the request again. An error occurs in the data repository when the request is sent:

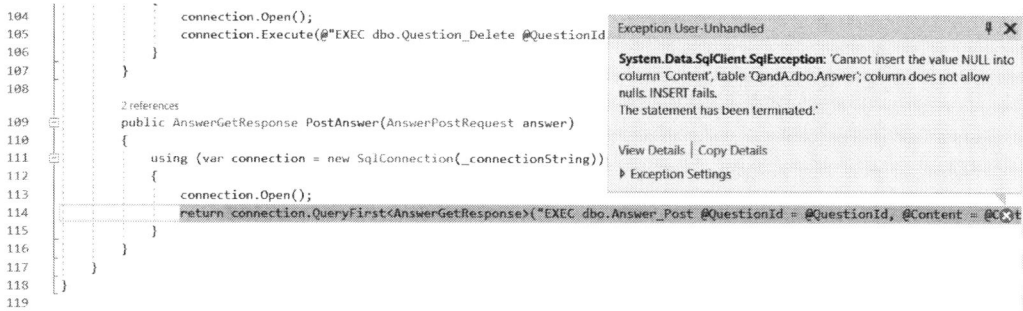

Figure 9.21 – SQL error when adding an answer with no content

This is because the stored procedure expects the content parameter to be passed into it and will protest if it is not.

4. Let's stop the app so that we're ready to resolve this issue in the next section.

An answer without any content is an invalid answer. Ideally, we should stop invalid requests being passed to the data repository and return HTTP status code `400` to the client with details about what is wrong with the request. How do we do this in ASP.NET? Let's find out in the next section.

Adding model validation

In this section, we are going to add some validation checks on the request models. ASP.NET will then automatically send HTTP status code `400` (bad request) with details of the problem.

Validation is critical to preventing bad data from getting in the database or unexpected database errors from happening, as we experienced in the previous section. Giving the client detailed information for bad requests also ensures the development experience is good because this will help to correct mistakes.

Adding validation to posting a question

We can add validation to a model by adding validation attributes to properties in the model that specify rules that should be adhered to. Let's add validation to the request for posting a question:

1. Open `QuestionPostRequest.cs` and add the following `using` statement underneath the existing `using` statements:

   ```
   using System.ComponentModel.DataAnnotations;
   ```

   This namespace gives us access to the validation attributes.

2. Add a `Required` attribute just above the `Title` property:

   ```
   [Required]
   public string Title { get; set; }
   ```

   The `Required` attribute will check that the `Title` property is not an empty string or `null`.

3. Before we try this out, put a breakpoint on the first statement within the `PostQuestion` action method in `QuestionsController.cs`.

4. Let's run the app and try to post a question without a title in Postman:

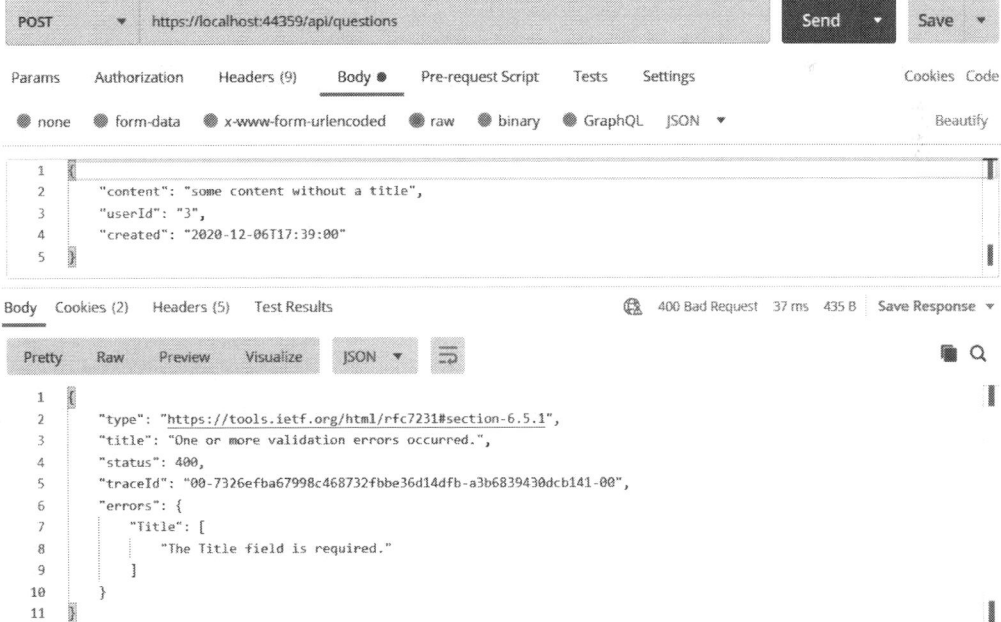

Figure 9.22 – Validation error when submitting a question with no title

We get a response with HTTP status code 400 as expected with great information about the problem in the response.

Notice also that the breakpoint wasn't reached. This is because ASP.NET checked the model, determined that it was invalid, and returned a bad request response before the action method was invoked.

5. Let's stop the app from running and implement another validation check on the `Title` property in the `QuestionPostRequest` class:

```
[Required]
[StringLength(100)]
public string Title { get; set; }
```

This check will ensure the title doesn't have more than 100 characters. A title containing more than 100 characters would cause a database error, so this is a valuable check.

6. A question must also have some content, so let's add a `Required` attribute to this:

```
[Required]
public string Content { get; set; }
```

7. We can add a custom error message to a validation attribute. Let's add an error message to the validation on the `Content` property:

```
[Required(ErrorMessage =
    "Please include some content for the question")]
public string Content { get; set; }
```

8. Let's run the app and try posting a new question without any content:

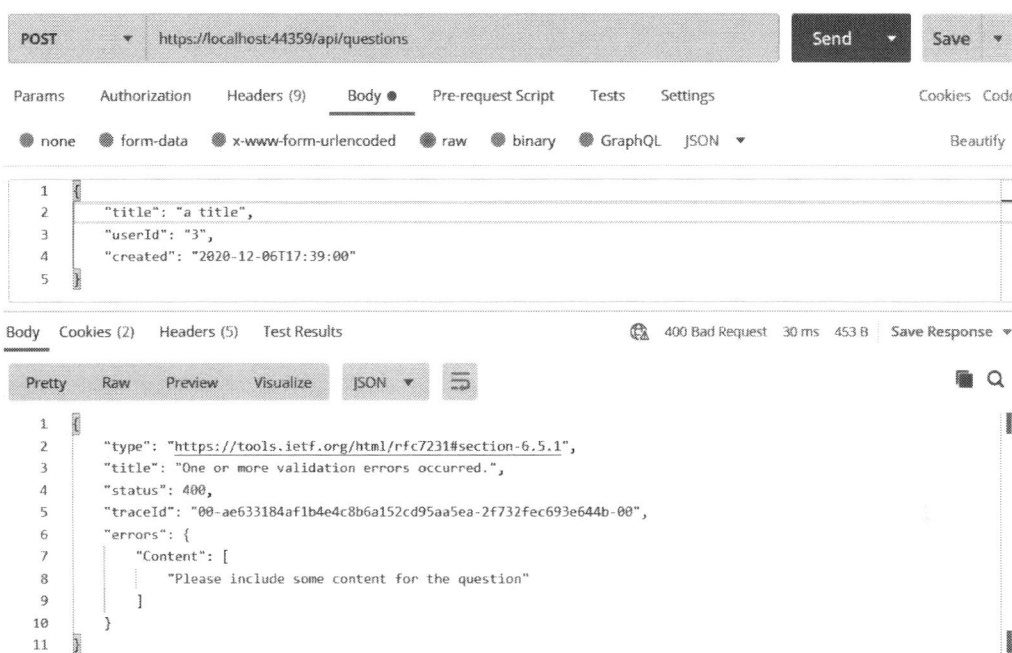

Figure 9.23 – Validation error when submitting a question with no content

We get our custom message in the response as expected.

9. Let's stop the app running.

The `UserId`, `UserName`, and `Created` properties should really be required properties as well. However, we aren't going to add validation attributes to them because we are going to work on them later in this chapter.

Adding validation to updating a question

Let's add validation to the request for updating a question:

1. Open `QuestionPutRequest.cs` and add the following using statement:

    ```
    using System.ComponentModel.DataAnnotations;
    ```

2. Add the following validation attribute to the `Title` property:

    ```
    public class QuestionPutRequest
    {
        [StringLength(100)]
        public string Title { get; set; }
    ```

```
public string Content { get; set; }
}
```

We are making sure that a new title doesn't exceed 100 characters.

3. Let's run the app and give this a try by updating a question to have a very long title:

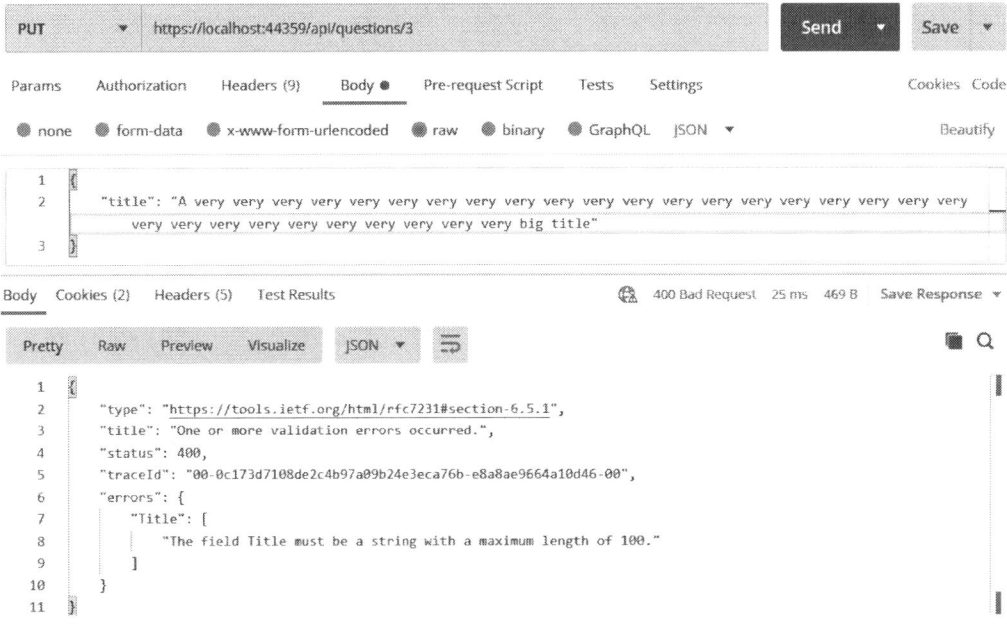

Figure 9.24 – Validation error when updating a question with a long title

A validation error is returned as expected.

4. Stop the app running so that we're ready to add the next piece of validation.

That completes the implementation of model validation for `PUT` requests to `api/questions`.

Adding validation to posting an answer

Let's add validation to the request for posting an answer:

1. Open `AnswerPostRequest.cs` and add the following `using` statement:

```
using System.ComponentModel.DataAnnotations;
```

2. Add the following validation attributes to make the `QuestionId` and `Content` properties mandatory:

   ```
   public class AnswerPostRequest
   {
       [Required]
       public int QuestionId { get; set; }
       [Required]
       public string Content { get; set; }
       ...
   }
   ```

3. Make the `QuestionId` property nullable by putting a question mark after the `int` type:

   ```
   public class AnswerPostRequest
   {
       [Required]
       public int? QuestionId { get; set; }
       [Required]
       public string Content { get; set; }
       ...
   }
   ```

   > **Important note**
   > The ? allows the property to have a `null` value as well as the declared type. `T?` is shortcut syntax for `Nullable<T>`.

   So, why does `QuestionId` need to be able to hold a `null` value? This is because an `int` type defaults to 0 and so if there is no `QuestionId` in the request body, `AnswerPostRequest` will come out of the model binding process with `QuestionId` set to 0, which will pass the required validation check. This means the `Required` attribute won't catch a request body with no `QuestionId`. If the `QuestionId` type is nullable, then it will come out of the model binding processing with a `null` value if it's not in the request body and will fail the required validation check, which is what we want.

4. We need to change the `PostAnswer` method in `QuestionsController.cs` so that it now references the `Value` property in `QuestionId`:

   ```
   [HttpPost("answer")]
   public ActionResult<AnswerGetResponse>
     PostAnswer(AnswerPostRequest answerPostRequest)
   {
   ```

```
        var questionExists =
          _dataRepository.QuestionExists(
            answerPostRequest.QuestionId.Value);
        if (!questionExists)
        {
            return NotFound();
        }
        var savedAnswer =
          _dataRepository.PostAnswer(answerPostRequest);
        return savedAnswer;

    }
```

That completes the implementation of model validation for `POST` requests to `api/questions/answer`.

We have experienced that model validation is super easy to implement in our request models. We simply decorate the property in the model that needs validating with the appropriate attribute. We used the `Required` and `StringLength` attributes in our implementation, but there are others available in ASP.NET, some of which are as follows:

- `[Range]`: Checks that the property value falls within the given range
- `[RegularExpression]`: Checks that the data matches the specified regular expression
- `[Compare]`: Checks that two properties in a model match
- `[CreditCard]`: Checks that the property has a credit card format
- `[EmailAddress]`: Checks that the property has an email format
- `[Phone]`: Checks that the property has a telephone format
- `[Url]`: Checks that the property has a URL format

We haven't added any validation to the `UserId`, `UserName`, or `Created` properties in our request models. In the next section, we are going to find out why and properly handle these properties.

Removing unnecessary request fields

At the moment, we are allowing the consumer to submit all the properties that our data repository requires, including `userId`, `userName`, and `created`. However, these properties can be set on the server. In fact, the client doesn't need to know or care about `userId`.

Exposing the client to more properties than it needs impacts the usability of the API and can also cause security issues. For example, a client can pretend to be any user submitting questions and answers with our current API.

In the following subsections, we are going to tighten up some requests so that they don't contain unnecessary information. We will start by removing the `userId`, `userName`, and `created` fields from posting questions before moving on to removing the `userId` and `created` fields from posting answers.

Removing unnecessary request fields from posting a question

Our `QuestionPostRequest` model is used both in the data repository to pass the data to the stored procedure as well as in the API controller to capture the information in the request body. This single model can't properly cater to both these cases, so we are going to create and use separate models. Implement the following steps:

1. In the `models` folder, create a new model called `QuestionPostFullRequest` as follows:

   ```
   public class QuestionPostFullRequest
   {
       public string Title { get; set; }
       public string Content { get; set; }
       public string UserId { get; set; }
       public string UserName { get; set; }
       public DateTime Created { get; set; }
   }
   ```

   This contains all the properties that are needed by the data repository to save a question.

2. We can then remove the `UserId`, `UserName`, and `Created` properties from the `QuestionPostRequest` class. So, the `QuestionPostRequest` class should now be as follows:

   ```
   public class QuestionPostRequest
   {
       [Required]
       [StringLength(100)]
       public string Title { get; set; }

       [Required(ErrorMessage =
         "Please include some content for the question")]
   ```

314   Creating REST API Endpoints

```
      public string Content { get; set; }
}
```

3. In the data repository interface, change the `PostQuestion` method to use the `QuestionPostFullRequest` model:

   ```
   QuestionGetSingleResponse
     PostQuestion(QuestionPostFullRequest question);
   ```

4. In the data repository, change the `PostQuestion` method to use the `QuestionPostFullRequest` model:

   ```
   public QuestionGetSingleResponse
     PostQuestion(QuestionPostFullRequest question)
   {
       ...
   }
   ```

5. We now need to map the `QuestionPostRequest` received in `QuestionsController` to the `QuestionFullPostRequest` that our data repository expects:

   ```
   [HttpPost]
   public ActionResult<QuestionGetSingleResponse>
     PostQuestion(QuestionPostRequest questionPostRequest)
   {
       var savedQuestion =
         _dataRepository.PostQuestion(new
         QuestionPostFullRequest
         {
           Title = questionPostRequest.Title,
           Content = questionPostRequest.Content,
           UserId = "1",
           UserName = "bob.test@test.com",
           Created = DateTime.UtcNow
         });
       return CreatedAtAction(nameof(GetQuestion),
         new { questionId = savedQuestion.QuestionId },
         savedQuestion);
   }
   ```

We've hardcoded the `UserId` and `UserName` values for now. In *Chapter 11, Securing the Backend*, we'll get them from our identity provider.

We've also set the Created property to the current date and time.

6. Let's run our app and give it a try:

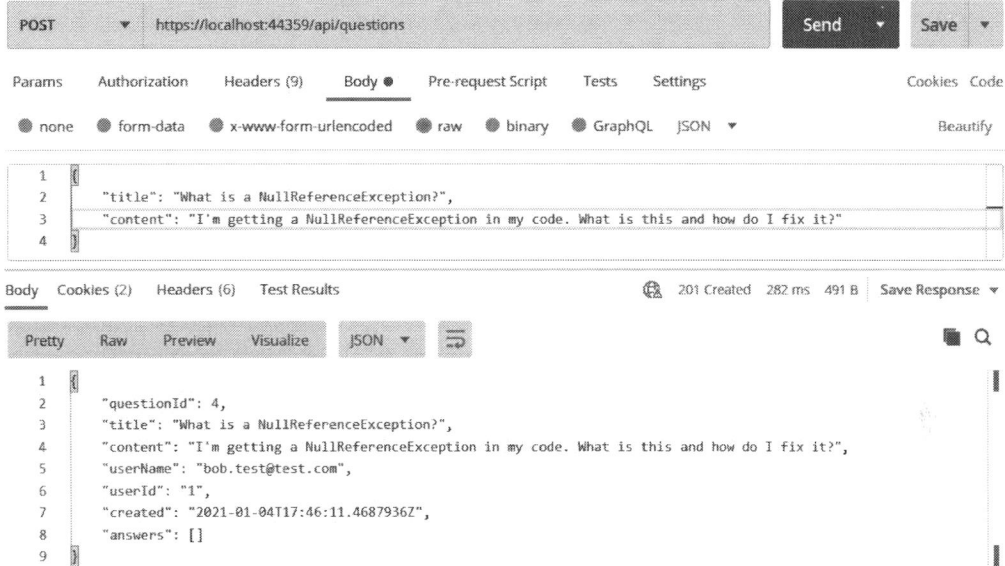

Figure 9.25 – Submitting a question

The user and created date are set and returned in the response as expected.

7. Finally, stop the app running.

That completes the separation of the models for the HTTP request and data repository for adding questions. This means we are only requesting the information that is necessary for POST requests to api/questions.

Removing unnecessary request fields from posting an answer

Let's tighten up posting an answer:

1. In the models folder, create a new model called AnswerPostFullRequest as follows:

```
public class AnswerPostFullRequest
{
    public int QuestionId { get; set; }
    public string Content { get; set; }
    public string UserId { get; set; }
    public string UserName { get; set; }
```

```
        public DateTime Created { get; set; }
}
```

This contains all the properties that are needed by the data repository to save an answer.

2. We can then remove the `UserId` and `Created` properties from the `AnswerPostRequest` class. So, the `AnswerPostRequest` class will now be as follows:

```
public class AnswerPostRequest
{
    [Required]
    public int? QuestionId { get; set; }
    [Required]
    public string Content { get; set; }
}
```

3. In the data repository interface, change the `PostAnswer` method to use the `AnswerPostFullRequest` model:

```
AnswerGetResponse PostAnswer(AnswerPostFullRequest answer);
```

4. In the data repository, change the `PostAnswer` method to use the `AnswerPostFullRequest` model:

```
public AnswerGetResponse
    PostAnswer(AnswerPostFullRequest answer)
{
    ...
}
```

5. We now need to map the `AnswerPostRequest` received in `QuestionsController` to the `AnswerPostFullRequest` that our data repository expects:

```
[HttpPost("answer")]
public ActionResult<AnswerGetResponse>
  PostAnswer(AnswerPostRequest answerPostRequest)
{
    var questionExists =
      _dataRepository.QuestionExists(
        answerPostRequest.QuestionId.Value);
    if (!questionExists)
    {
```

```
            return NotFound();
    }
    var savedAnswer =
      _dataRepository.PostAnswer(new
        AnswerPostFullRequest
          {
             QuestionId = answerPostRequest.
               QuestionId.Value,
             Content = answerPostRequest.Content,
             UserId = "1",
             UserName = "bob.test@test.com",
             Created = DateTime.UtcNow
          }
        );
      return savedAnswer;
}
```

6. Let's run our app and give it a try:

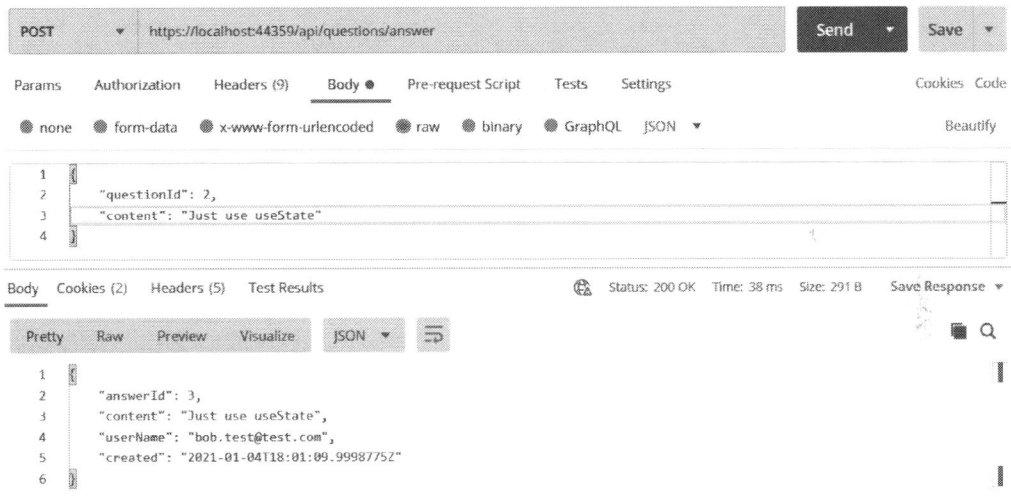

Figure 9.26 – Submitting an answer

The user and created date are set and returned in the response as expected.

So, that's our REST API tightened up a bit.

In this section, we manually mapped the request model to the model used in the data repository. For large models, it may be beneficial to use a mapping library such as `AutoMapper` to help us copy data from one object to another. More information on `AutoMapper` can be found at https://automapper.org/.

Summary

In this chapter, we learned how to implement an API controller to handle requests to a REST API endpoint. We discovered that inheriting from `ControllerBase` and decorating the controller class with the `ApiController` attribute gives us nice features such as automatic model validation handling and a nice set of methods for returning HTTP status codes.

We used `AddScoped` to register the data repository dependency so that ASP.NET uses a single instance of it in a request/response cycle. We were then able to inject a reference to the data repository in the API controller class in its constructor.

We learned about the powerful model binding process in ASP.NET and how it maps data from an HTTP request into action method parameters. We discovered that in some cases it is desirable to use separate models for the HTTP request and the data repository because some of the data can be set on the server, and requiring less data in the request helps usability and, sometimes, security.

We used ASP.NET validation attributes to validate models. This is a super simple way of ensuring that the database doesn't get infected with bad data.

We are now equipped to build robust and developer-friendly REST APIs that work with all the common HTTP methods and return responses with appropriate HTTP status codes.

In the next chapter, we are going to focus on the performance and scalability of our REST API.

Questions

Answer the following questions to test the knowledge that you have gained in this chapter:

1. We have a class that we want to register for dependency injection. During the handling of a request, the class will be referenced several times by other classes. We want a new instance of the class to be created when injected into a class rather than an existing instance to be used. What method in `IServiceCollection` should we use to register the dependency?

2. In a controller action method, if a resource can't be found, what method can we use in `ControllerBase` to return status code `404`?

3. In a controller action method to post a new building, we implement some validation that requires a database call to check whether the building already exists. If the building does already exist, we want to return HTTP status code 400:

   ```
   [HttpPost]
   public ActionResult<BuildingResponse>
   PostBuilding(BuildingPostRequest buildingPostRequest)
   {
       var buildingExists =
       _dataRepository.BuildingExists(buildingPostRequest.
          Code);
       if (buildingExists)
       {
           // TODO - return status code 400
       }
       ...
   }
   ```

   What method from `ControllerBase` can we use to return status code 400?

4. The model for the preceding action method is as follows:

   ```
   public class BuildingPostRequest
   {
       public string Code { get; set; }
       public string Name { get; set; }
       public string Description { get; set; }
   }
   ```

   We send an HTTP POST request to the resource with the following body:

   ```
   {
       "code": "BTOW",
       "name": "Blackpool Tower",
       "buildingDescription": "Blackpool Tower is a
          tourist attraction in Blackpool"
   }
   ```

   The `Description` property in the model isn't getting populated during the request. What is the problem?

5. In the preceding request model, we want to validate that the `code` and `name` fields are populated. How can we do this with validation attributes?

6. What validation attribute could we use to validate that a numerical property is between 1 and 10?

7. What `Http` attribute could we use to tell ASP.NET that an action method handles HTTP PATCH requests?

Answers

1. We can use the `AddTransient` method.
2. We can use the `NotFound` method.
3. We can use the `BadRequest` method.
4. The problem is that `buildingDescription` in the request doesn't match the name of the `Description` property in the model. If the request is changed to have a `description` field, then this will resolve the problem.
5. We can add `Required` attributes to `Code` and `Name` as follows:

   ```
   public class BuildingPostRequest
   {
       [Required]
       public string Code { get; set; }
       [Required]
       public string Name { get; set; }
       public string Description { get; set; }
   }
   ```

6. We can use a `Range` attribute as follows:

   ```
   [Range(1, 10)]
   ```

7. The `HttpPatch` attribute can be used to handle HTTP `PATCH` requests.

Further reading

Here are some useful links for learning more about the topics covered in this chapter:

- **Create web APIs with ASP.NET**: https://docs.microsoft.com/en-us/aspnet/core/web-api
- **Dependency injection**: https://docs.microsoft.com/en-us/aspnet/core/fundamentals/dependency-injection
- **Model binding**: https://docs.microsoft.com/en-us/aspnet/core/mvc/models/model-binding
- **Model validation**: https://docs.microsoft.com/en-us/aspnet/core/mvc/models/validation
- **Postman**: https://learning.getpostman.com/docs/postman/launching_postman/installation_and_updates/

10
Improving Performance and Scalability

In this chapter, we are going to improve the performance and scalability of our REST API. When we make each improvement, we'll use a load testing tool to verify that there has been an improvement.

We'll start by focusing on database calls and how we can reduce the number of calls to improve performance. We'll then move on to requesting less data with data paging. We'll also look at the impact that caching data in memory has on performance.

Then, we'll learn how to make our API controllers and data repository asynchronous. We'll eventually understand whether this makes our REST API more performant or perhaps more scalable.

In this chapter, we'll cover the following topics:

- Reducing database round trips
- Paging data
- Making API controllers asynchronous
- Caching data

At the end of this chapter, we'll have the knowledge to implement fast REST APIs that perform well under load.

Technical requirements

We'll use the following tools in this chapter:

- **Visual Studio 2019**: We'll use this to edit our ASP.NET code. This can be downloaded and installed from `https://visualstudio.microsoft.com/vs/`.
- **.NET 5**: This can be downloaded from `https://dotnet.microsoft.com/download/dotnet/5.0`.
- **SQL Server Management Studio**: We'll use this to execute a stored procedure in our database. This can be downloaded and installed from `https://docs.microsoft.com/en-us/sql/ssms/download-sql-server-management-studio-ssms?view=sql-server-2017`.
- **Postman**: We'll use this to try out changes we make to our REST API endpoints. This can be downloaded from `https://www.getpostman.com/downloads/`.
- **WebSurge**: This is a load testing tool that we can download from `https://websurge.west-wind.com/`.
- **Q&A**: We'll start with the Q&A backend project we finished in the previous chapter. This is available on GitHub at `https://github.com/PacktPublishing/ASP.NET-Core-5-and-React-Second-Edition` in the `chapter-10/start` folder.

All of the code snippets in this chapter can be found online at `https://github.com/PacktPublishing/ASP.NET-Core-5-and-React-Second-Edition`. To restore code from a chapter, the source code repository can be downloaded, and the relevant folder opened in the relevant editor. If the code is frontend code, then `npm install` can be entered in the terminal to restore the dependencies.

Check out the following video to see the Code in Action: `https://bit.ly/3piyUEx`.

Reducing database round trips

A database round trip is a request from the web API to the database. Database round trips are expensive. The greater the distance between the web API and the database, the more expensive the round trip is. So, we want to keep the trips from the web API to the database to a minimum in order to gain maximum performance.

We will start this section by understanding the N+1 problem and experiencing how it negatively impacts performance. We will then learn how to execute multiple queries in a single database round trip.

Understanding the N+1 problem

The N+1 problem is a classic query problem where there is a parent-child data model relationship. When data is retrieved for this model, the parent items are fetched in a query and then separate queries are executed to fetch the data for each child. So, there are *N* queries for the children and 1 additional query for the parent, hence the term N+1.

We are going to add the ability to return answers as well as questions in a GET request to the questions REST API endpoint. We are going to fall into the N+1 trap with our first implementation. Let's open our backend project in Visual Studio and carry out the following steps:

1. First, let's add an Answers property at the bottom of the QuestionGetManyResponse model:

   ```
   public class QuestionGetManyResponse
   {
     public int QuestionId { get; set; }
     public string Title { get; set; }
     public string Content { get; set; }
     public string UserName { get; set; }
     public DateTime Created { get; set; }
     public List<AnswerGetResponse> Answers { get; set; }
   }
   ```

2. Add a new method to our data repository interface just below the GetQuestions method:

   ```
   public interface IDataRepository
   {
       IEnumerable<QuestionGetManyResponse>
         GetQuestions();
       IEnumerable<QuestionGetManyResponse>
         GetQuestionsWithAnswers();
   ```

```
    ...
}
```

This method will get all of the questions in the database, including the answers for each question.

3. Now, add the implementation for the `GetQuestionsWithAnswers` method in the data repository just below the `GetQuestions` method:

```
public IEnumerable<QuestionGetManyResponse>
GetQuestionsWithAnswers()
{
  using (var connection = new
    SqlConnection(_connectionString))
  {
    connection.Open();

    var questions =
      connection.Query<QuestionGetManyResponse>(
        "EXEC dbo.Question_GetMany");
    foreach (var question in questions)
    {
      question.Answers =
        connection.Query<AnswerGetResponse>(
          @"EXEC dbo.Answer_Get_ByQuestionId
            @QuestionId = @QuestionId",
          new { QuestionId = question.QuestionId })
        .ToList();
    }
    return questions;
  }
}
```

So, this makes a database call to get all of the questions and then additional calls to get the answer for each question. We have fallen into the classic N+1 trap!

4. Let's move on to `QuestionsController` now and add the ability to include answers with the questions:

```
[HttpGet]
public IEnumerable<QuestionGetManyResponse>
  GetQuestions(string search, bool includeAnswers)
{
  if (string.IsNullOrEmpty(search))
  {
    if (includeAnswers)
```

```
        {
            return
            _dataRepository.GetQuestionsWithAnswers();
        }
        else
        {
            return _dataRepository.GetQuestions();
        }
    }
    else
    {
        return
        _dataRepository.GetQuestionsBySearch(search);
    }
}
```

We've added the ability to have an `includeAnswers` query parameter that, if set, will call the `GetQuestionsWithAnswers` data repository method we just added. A fuller implementation would allow answers to be included if a `search` query parameter is defined, but this implementation will be enough for us to see the N+1 problem and how we can resolve it.

5. Now, run the REST API by pressing *F5*.

6. In Postman, let's try requesting questions with answers:

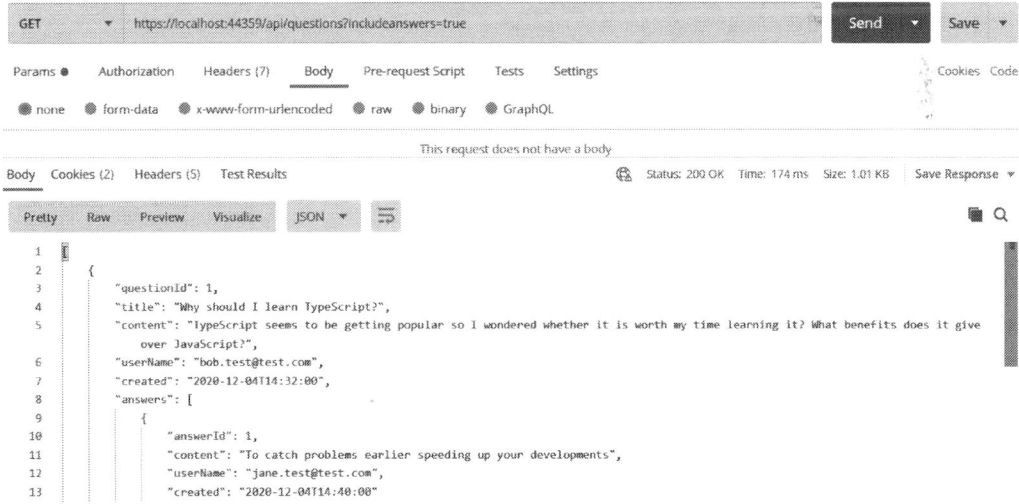

Figure 10.1 – Questions with answers in Postman

The answers are returned with each question, as we expected.

This doesn't seem like much of a problem though. The request took only **174 ms** to complete. Well, we only have a couple of answers in our database at the moment. If we had more questions, the request would slow down a fair bit. Also, the test we have just done is for a single user. What happens when multiple users make this request? We'll find out in the next section.

Using WebSurge to load test our endpoint

We must load test our API endpoints to verify that they perform appropriately under load. It is far better to find a performance issue in the development process before our users do. WebSurge is a simple load testing tool that we are going to use to test our `questions` endpoint with the N+1 problem. We are going to perform the load test in our development environment, which is fine for us to see the impact the N+1 problem has. Obviously, the load testing results we are going to see would be a lot faster in a production environment. To use WebSurge for load testing, implement the following steps:

1. Run the REST API by pressing *F5* if it's not already running.

2. Open WebSurge and click the **New Request** option on the **Session** tab:

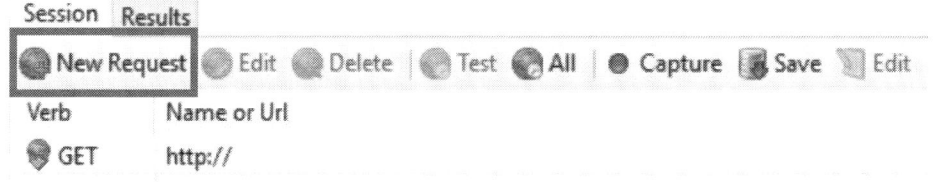

Figure 10.2 – New WebSurge request

3. Fill in the request details on the **Request** tab in the right-hand pane for a GET request to `api/questions/includeanswers=true`:

Reducing database round trips 327

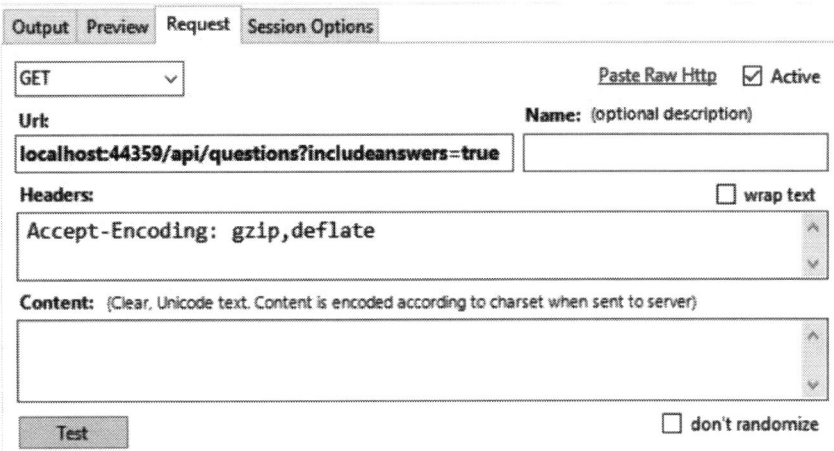

Figure 10.3 – Setting the WebSurge request path

4. To check that the request is correct, press the **Test** button at the bottom of the right-hand pane. We'll see the response we expect in the **Preview** tab:

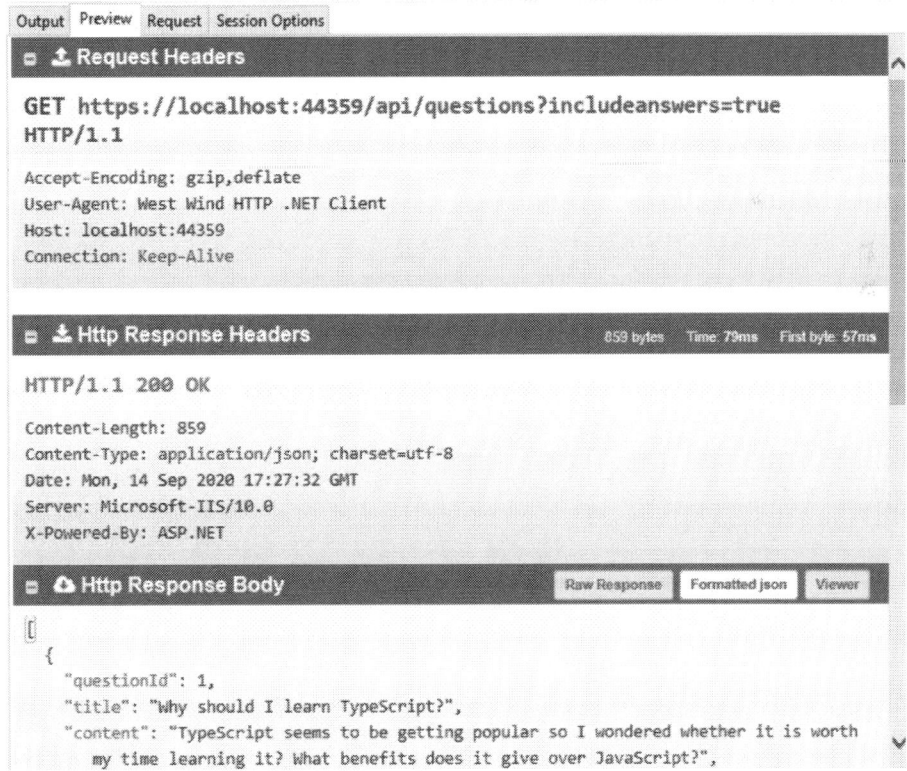

Figure 10.4 – WebSurge test response

328　Improving Performance and Scalability

5. We are nearly ready to do the load test now. Now specify that the test will run for 30 seconds with 5 threads by filling in the relevant boxes under the toolbar:

Figure 10.5 – Load test duration and threads

6. Run the load test by clicking the **Start** button. We'll immediately see requests being made in the **Output** tab in the right-hand pane:

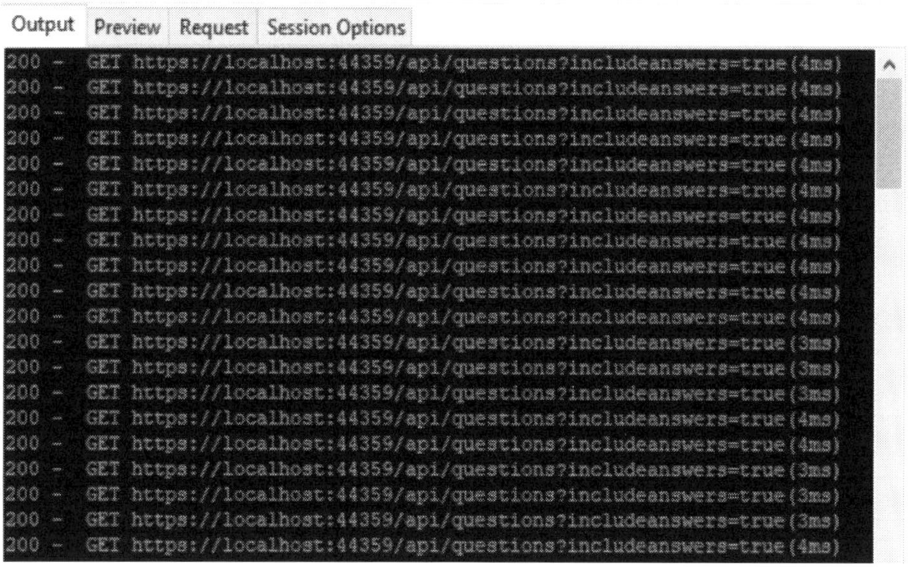

Figure 10.6 – Load test output

7. When the test has finished, we'll see the test results in the **Output** tab in the right-hand pane:

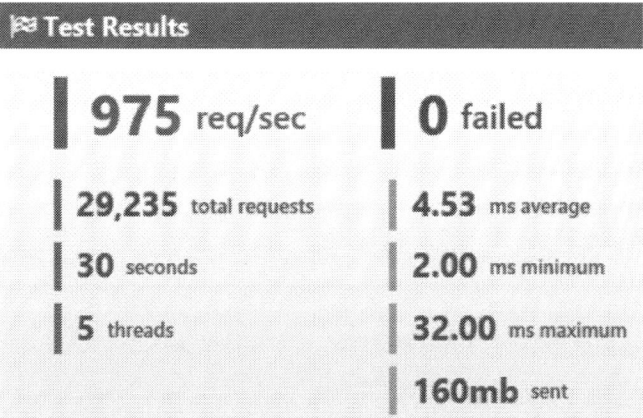

Figure 10.7 – Load test results

So, we managed to get **975** requests per second with this implementation of getting questions with answers. Obviously, the result you get will be different.

8. Stop the ASP.NET app from running by pressing *Shift* + *F5* so that you're ready to make the implementation more efficient.

Keep a note of the results—we'll use these in a comparison with an implementation that resolves the N+1 problem next.

Using Dapper multi-mapping to resolve the N+1 problem

Wouldn't it be great if we could get the questions and answers in a single database query and then map this data to the hierarchical structure that we require in our data repository? Well, this is exactly what we can do with a feature called **multi-mapping** in Dapper. Let's look at how we can use this. Follow these steps:

1. In the data repository, let's change the implementation of the GetQuestionsWithAnswers method to call a single stored procedure:

```
public IEnumerable<QuestionGetManyResponse>
    GetQuestionsWithAnswers()
{
  using (var connection = new
    SqlConnection(_connectionString))
  {
    connection.Open();

    return connection.Query<QuestionGetManyResponse>(
```

```
        "EXEC dbo.Question_GetMany_WithAnswers");
  }
}
```

This is a good start but the `Question_GetMany_WithAnswers` stored procedure returns tabular data and we require this to be mapped to the questions-and-answers hierarchical structure we have in our `QuestionGetManyResponse` model:

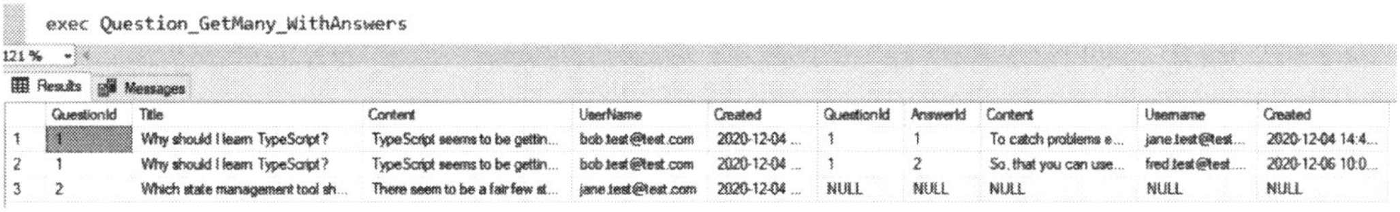

exec Question_GetMany_WithAnswers

	QuestionId	Title	Content	UserName	Created	QuestionId	AnswerId	Content	Username	Created
1	1	Why should I learn TypeScript?	TypeScript seems to be gettin...	bob.test@test.com	2020-12-04 ...	1	1	To catch problems e...	jane.test@test...	2020-12-04 14:4...
2	1	Why should I learn TypeScript?	TypeScript seems to be gettin...	bob.test@test.com	2020-12-04 ...	1	2	So, that you can use...	fred.test@test...	2020-12-06 10:0...
3	2	Which state management tool sh...	There seem to be a fair few st...	jane.test@test.com	2020-12-04 ...	NULL	NULL	NULL	NULL	NULL

Figure 10.8 – Tabular data from a stored procedure

This is where Dapper's multi-mapping feature comes in handy.

2. Change the implementation to the following:

```
public IEnumerable<QuestionGetManyResponse>
GetQuestionsWithAnswers()
{
  using (var connection = new
   SqlConnection(_connectionString))
  {
    connection.Open();

    var questionDictionary =
      new Dictionary<int, QuestionGetManyResponse>();
    return connection
      .Query<
        QuestionGetManyResponse,
        AnswerGetResponse,
        QuestionGetManyResponse>(
          "EXEC dbo.Question_GetMany_WithAnswers",
          map: (q, a) =>
          {
            QuestionGetManyResponse question;

            if (!questionDictionary.TryGetValue
              (q.QuestionId, out question))
            {
              question = q;
              question.Answers =
                new List<AnswerGetResponse>();
```

```
                questionDictionary.Add(question.
                    QuestionId, question);
            }
            question.Answers.Add(a);
            return question;
        },
        splitOn: "QuestionId"
        )
    .Distinct()
    .ToList();
    }
}
```

In the Dapper `Query` method, we provide a Lambda function that helps Dapper map each question. The function takes in the question and answers that Dapper has mapped from the stored procedure result and we map it to the structure we require. We use a `Dictionary` called `questionDictionary` to keep track of the questions we've already created so that we can create an instance of `new List<AnswerGetResponse>` for the answers for new questions.

We tell Dapper what models to map to with the first two generic parameters in the `Query` method, which are `QuestionGetManyResponse` and `AnswerGetResponse`, but how does Dapper know which fields have been returned from the stored procedure map to which properties in the models? The answer is that we tell Dapper using the `splitOn` parameter by saying everything before `QuestionId` goes into the `QuestionGetManyResponse` model, and everything after, including `QuestionId`, goes into the `AnswerGetResponse` model.

We tell Dapper what model the end result should map to with the last generic parameter in the `Query` method, which is `QuestionGetManyResponse` in this case.

We use the `Distinct` method on the results we get from Dapper to remove duplicate questions and then the `ToList` method to turn the results into a list.

3. With our revised implementation complete, let's run the app by pressing *F5*.

4. In WebSurge, run the same load test as we did before by clicking the **Start** button. After 30 seconds, we'll see the results:

Test Results

1,035 req/sec	0 failed
31,035 total requests	4.26 ms average
30 seconds	2.00 ms minimum
5 threads	29.00 ms maximum
	246mb sent

Figure 10.9 – Load test results

This time, our REST API managed to take **1,035** requests per second, which is a bit better than before.

So, Dapper's multi-mapping feature can be used to resolve the N+1 problem and generally achieve better performance. We do need to be careful with this approach, though, as we are requesting a lot of data from the database because of the duplicate parent records. Processing large amounts of data in the web server can be inefficient and lead to a slowdown in the garbage collection process.

Using Dapper's multi-results feature

There is another feature in Dapper that helps us reduce the amount of database round trips called **multi-results**. We are going to use this feature to improve the performance of the endpoint that gets a single question, which, at the moment, is making two database calls. To do that, follow these steps:

1. First, let's load test the current implementation by using WebSurge. Select the **Session** tab, highlight the first request in the list, and click the **Edit** option:

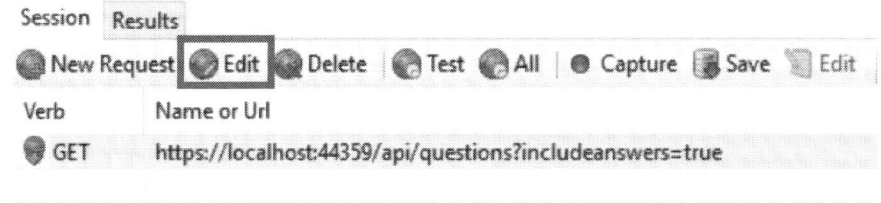

Figure 10.10 – Option to edit a request

2. Enter a path to a single question in the **Request** tab as in the following screenshot:

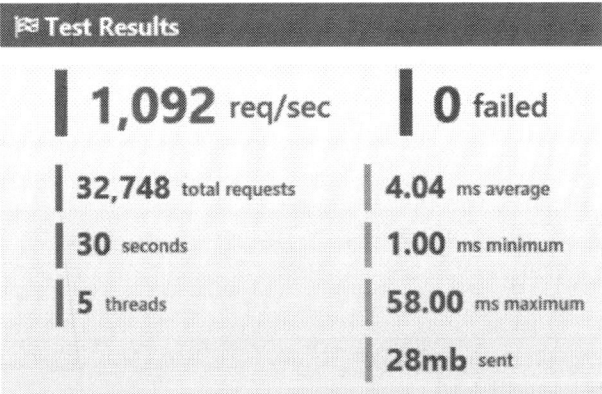

Figure 10.11 – Path to a single question

3. We'll leave the duration of the test at **30** seconds with **5** threads. Press the **Start** option to run the load test. When the test has finished, we'll get our results:

```
Test Results

1,092 req/sec        0 failed

32,748 total requests    4.04 ms average
30 seconds               1.00 ms minimum
5 threads                58.00 ms maximum
                         28mb sent
```

Figure 10.12 – Results of load testing getting a question

So, the current implementation can take **1,092** requests per second.

4. Now, stop the app from running and start to revise the implementation by adding the following `using` statement after the other `using` statements in `DataRepository.cs`:

```
using static Dapper.SqlMapper;
```

5. Now, we can change the implementation of `QuestionGetSingleResponse` to the following:

```
public QuestionGetSingleResponse GetQuestion(int 
questionId)
{
    using (var connection = new 
      SqlConnection(_connectionString))
    {
        connection.Open();
```

```
using (GridReader results =
  connection.QueryMultiple(
    @"EXEC dbo.Question_GetSingle
      @QuestionId = @QuestionId;
    EXEC dbo.Answer_Get_ByQuestionId
      @QuestionId = @QuestionId",
    new { QuestionId = questionId }
  )
)
{
  var question = results.Read<
   QuestionGetSingleResponse>().FirstOrDefault();
  if (question != null)
  {
    question.Answers =
      results.Read<AnswerGetResponse>().ToList();
  }
  return question;
 }
 }
}
```

We use the `QueryMultiple` method in Dapper to execute our two stored procedures in a single database round trip. The results are added into a `results` variable and can be retrieved using the `Read` method by passing the appropriate type in the generic parameter.

6. Let's start the app again in Visual Studio and carry out the same load test:

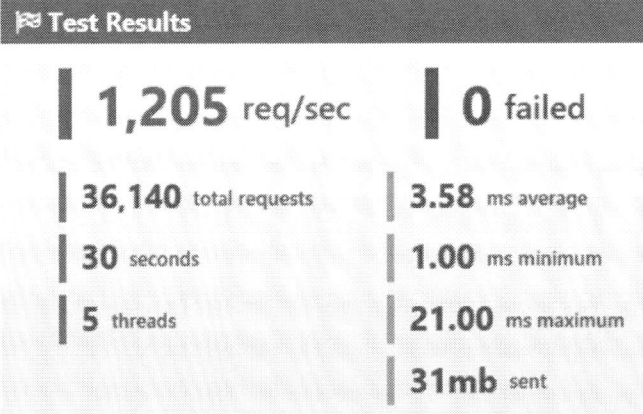

Figure 10.13 – Getting a question load test – improved results

Our improved API can now take **1,205** requests per second.

In this section, we learned how to fetch parent-child data in a single round trip using the multi-mapping feature in Dapper. We've also learned how to execute multiple queries in a single round trip using the multi-results feature in Dapper. We've also learned how to load test REST API endpoints using WebSurge.

As we mentioned in the multi-mapping example, processing large amounts of data can be problematic. How can we reduce the amount of data we read from the database and process on the web server? We'll find out in the next section.

Paging data

In this section, we are going to force the consumers of our `questions` endpoint to specify the *page* of data when executing the request with the `search` query parameter. So, we'll only be returning a portion of the data rather than all of it.

Paging helps with performance and scalability in the following ways:

- The number of page read I/Os is reduced when SQL Server grabs the data.
- The amount of data that's transferred from the database server to the web server is reduced.
- The amount of memory that's used to store the data on the web server in our model is reduced.
- The amount of data that's transferred from the web server to the client is reduced.

This all adds up to a potentially significant positive impact—particularly for large collections of data.

We will start this section by load testing the current implementation of the `questions` endpoint. We will then implement paging and see the impact this has on a load test.

Adding test questions for the load test

Let's carry out the following steps to add lots of questions to our database. This will allow us to see the impact of data paging:

1. Let's open SQL Server Management Studio, right-click on the **QandA** database in **Object Explorer**, and choose **New Query**.

2. In the query window that opens, add the following command:

   ```
   EXEC Question_AddForLoadTest
   ```

   This will execute a stored procedure that will add 10,000 questions to our database.

3. Press *F5* to run the stored procedure, which will take a few seconds to complete.

Now that we have our questions in place, let's test out the current implementation.

Load testing the current implementation

Before we implement data paging, let's see how the current implementation performs under load. To check and verify that, implement the following steps:

1. Let's start our REST API by pressing *F5* in Visual Studio, if it's not already running.

2. Now, we can load test the current implementation using WebSurge. Let's set the request URL path to `/api/questions?search=question` and stick to a duration of 30 seconds with 5 threads.

3. Before running the load test, check that the request works okay by clicking the **Test** option. We may get an error in the response body like the following one:

```
Http Response Body                                    Raw Response  Formatted json  Viewer

Invalid or partial JSON data cannot be formatted (try setting MaxResponseSize option to 0).
[{"questionId":1,"title":"Why should I learn TypeScript?","content":"TypeScript seems to be
getting popular so I wondered whether it is worth my time learning it? What benefits does it give
over JavaScript?","userName":"bob.test@test.com","created":"2019-05-18T14:32:00","answers":null}
,{"questionId":2,"title":"Which state management tool should I use?","content":"There seem to be
fair few state management tools around for React - React, Unstated, ... Which one should I use?"
,"userName":"jane.test@test.com","created":"2019-05-18T14:48:00","answers":null},{"questionId"
:36753,"title":"Question 1","content":"Content 1","userName":"bob.test@test.com","created":"2019
-03-06T18:08:01.7833333","answers":null},{"questionId":36754,"title":"Question 2","content"
```

Figure 10.14 – Response body error

This error can be resolved by changing the **MaxResponseSize** setting to 0 on the **Session Options** tab:

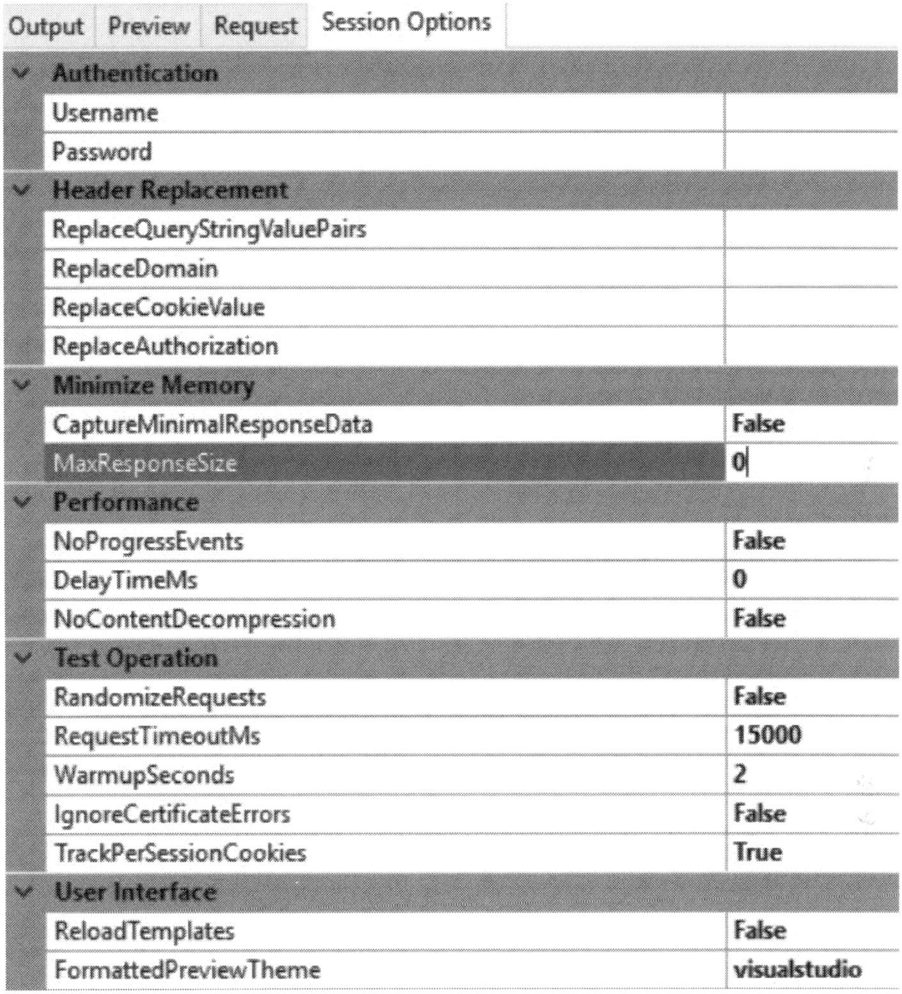

Figure 10.15 – Removing the maximum response size

4. Start the test. When the test has finished, we'll get our results as follows:

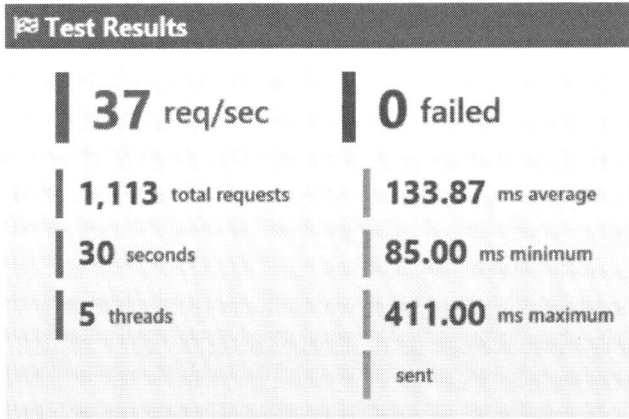

Figure 10.16 – Searching questions load test result

5. Stop the REST API running.

So, the requests-per-second value to beat is **37**.

Implementing data paging

Now, let's revise the implementation of the `questions` endpoint with the `search` query parameter so that we can use data paging. To implement that, let's work through the following steps:

1. Let's start by adding a new method that will search using paging in our data repository interface. Add the highlighted method interface after `GetQuestionsBySearch` in `IDataRepository.cs`:

   ```
   public interface IDataRepository
   {
     ...
     IEnumerable<QuestionGetManyResponse>
       GetQuestionsBySearch(string search);
     IEnumerable<QuestionGetManyResponse>
       GetQuestionsBySearchWithPaging(
         string search,
         int pageNumber,
         int pageSize);
     ...
   }
   ```

So, the method will take in the page number and size as parameters.

2. Now, we can add the following method implementation in the `DataRepository.cs` file after `GetQuestionsBySearch`:

```
public IEnumerable<QuestionGetManyResponse>
  GetQuestionsBySearchWithPaging(
    string search,
    int pageNumber,
    int pageSize
  )
{
  using (var connection = new SqlConnection(_
    connectionString))
  {
    connection.Open();
    var parameters = new
      {
        Search = search,
        PageNumber = pageNumber,
        PageSize = pageSize
      };
    return connection.Query<QuestionGetManyResponse>(
      @"EXEC dbo.Question_GetMany_BySearch_WithPaging
        @Search = @Search,
        @PageNumber = @PageNumber,
        @PageSize = @PageSize", parameters
    );
  }
}
```

So, we are calling a stored procedure named `Question_GetMany_BySearch_WithPaging` to get the page of data, and passing in the search criteria, page number, and page size as parameters.

3. Let's change the implementation of the `GetQuestions` action method in `QuestionsController.cs` so that we can call the new repository method:

```
[HttpGet]
public IEnumerable<QuestionGetManyResponse>
  GetQuestions(
    string search,
    bool includeAnswers,
    int page = 1,
    int pageSize = 20
  )
{
  if (string.IsNullOrEmpty(search))
```

```
{
    if (includeAnswers)
    {
        return
          _dataRepository.GetQuestionsWithAnswers();
    }
    else
    {
        return _dataRepository.GetQuestions();
    }
}
else
{
    return
      _dataRepository.GetQuestionsBySearchWithPaging(
        search,
        page,
        pageSize
      );
}
}
```

Notice that we also accept query parameters for the page number and page size, which default to 1 and 20, respectively.

4. Let's start our REST API by pressing *F5* in Visual Studio.

5. Now, we can load test the new implementation using WebSurge. Stick to a duration of **30** seconds with **5** threads and start the test. When the test has finished, we'll get our results:

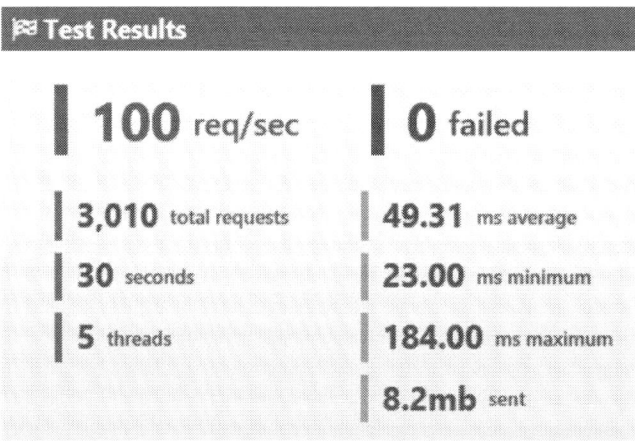

Figure 10.17 – Improved searching questions load test result

We get the performance improvement we hoped for, with the endpoint now able to take **100** requests per second.

In summary, we implemented data paging by accepting query parameters on the endpoint for the page number and the page size. These parameters are passed to the database query so that it only fetches the relevant page of data. Data paging is well worth considering for APIs that return collections of data, particularly if the collection is large.

In the next section, we are going to tackle the subject of asynchronous code and how this can help with scalability.

Making API controllers asynchronous

In this section, we are going to make the unanswered questions endpoint asynchronous to make it more scalable.

At the moment, all of our API code has been synchronous. For synchronous API code, when a request is made to the API, a thread from the thread pool will handle the request. If the code makes an I/O call (such as a database call) synchronously, the thread will block until the I/O call has finished. The blocked thread can't be used for any other work—it simply does nothing and waits for the I/O task to finish. If other requests are made to our API while the other thread is blocked, different threads in the thread pool will be used for the other requests. The following diagram is a visualization of synchronous requests in ASP.NET:

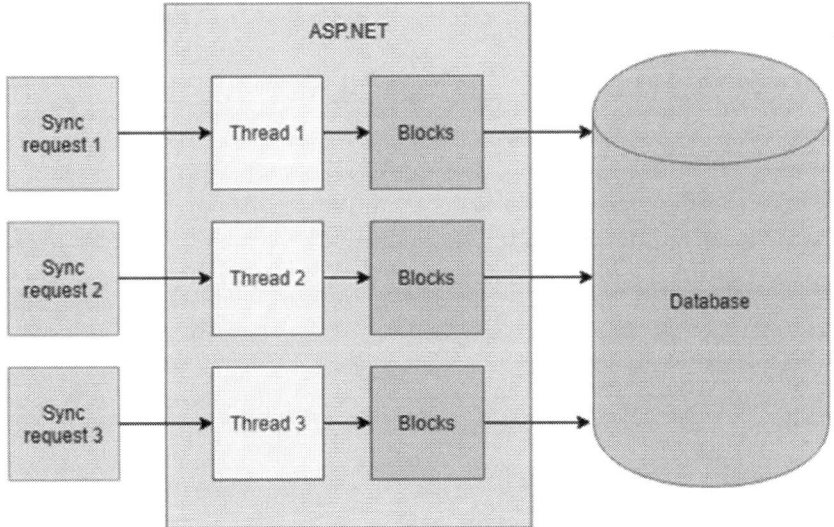

Figure 10.18 – Synchronous requests

There is some overhead in using a thread—a thread consumes memory and it takes time to spin a new thread up. So, really, we want our API to use as few threads as possible.

If the API was to work in an asynchronous manner, when a request is made to our API, a thread from the thread pool would handle the request (as in the synchronous case). If the code makes an asynchronous I/O call, the thread will be returned to the thread pool at the start of the I/O call and can be used for other requests. The following diagram is a visualization of asynchronous requests in ASP.NET:

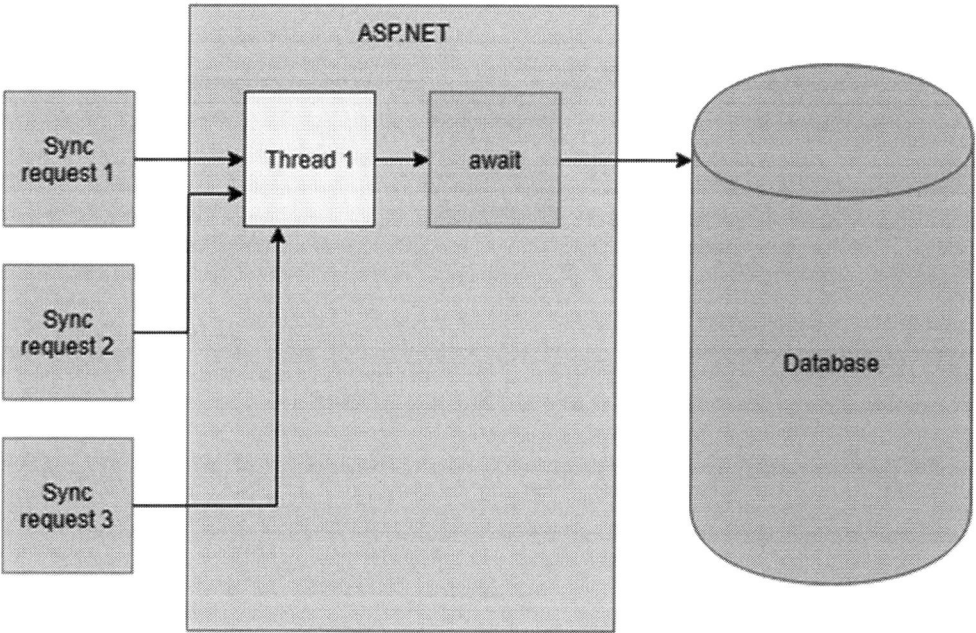

Figure 10.19 – Asynchronous requests

So, if we make our API asynchronous, it will be able to handle requests more efficiently and increase scalability. It is important to note that making an API asynchronous won't make it more performant because a single request will take roughly the same amount of time. The improvement we are about to make is so that our API can use the server's resources more efficiently.

In this section, we will convert the action method for unanswered questions to be asynchronous. We will profile the performance before and after this conversion to discover the impact. We will also discover what happens when asynchronous code makes I/O calls synchronously.

Testing the current implementation

Before we change the unanswered questions endpoint, let's test on the current implementation and gather some data to compare against the asynchronous implementation. We will use the performance profiler in Visual Studio along with WebSurge. Carry out the following steps:

1. Start by switching to the **Release** configuration. This can be done by choosing **Release** from the **Solution Configurations** option on the toolbar:

Figure 10.20 – Release configuration

This will make the test a little more realistic.

2. Press *Alt + F2* to open the Performance Profiler and tick the **.NET Async** tool:

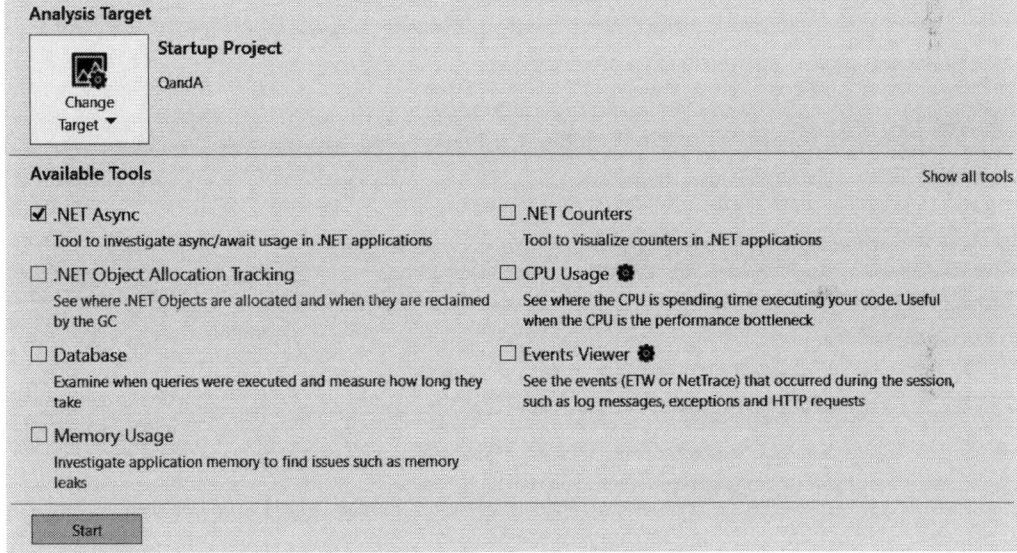

Figure 10.21 – Performance profiler

3. Click the **Start** button.

4. Now, we can simulate some load using WebSurge. Set the request URL path to `/api/questions/unanswered` and set the duration to `10` seconds with 5 threads:

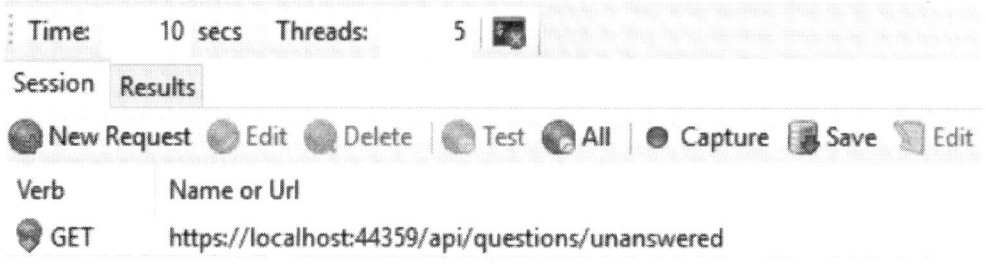

Figure 10.22 – Configuration for load testing unanswered questions

5. Start the load test.
6. After 10 seconds, switch to Visual Studio and click the **Stop Collection** option in **Performance Profiler**.
7. After a few seconds, data is presented in a hierarchical grid. Open up the details under the unanswered questions requests. We can see the average time it took to execute this code. Note this down:

Name	Count	Start Time (ms)	End Time (ms)	Total Time (ms)
▷ Microsoft.Extensions.DependencyInjection.ServiceLookup.DynamicServiceProviderEngine...	4	4478.07	4805.86	87.87 (avg.)
▷ Microsoft.Extensions.Hosting.HostingAbstractionsHostExtensions.RunAsync()	1	4845.13	[Incomplete]	[Incomplete]
▷ GET /api/questions	1	4925.96	6416.3	1490.34
▲ GET /api/questions/unanswered	581	9445.79	21579.79	98.48 (avg.)
▷ Microsoft.AspNetCore.Routing.Matching.ILEmitTrieJumpTable.InitializeILDelegateAsyn...	1	9447.22	9447.66	0.45 (avg.)
▷ Microsoft.Extensions.DependencyInjection.ServiceLookup.DynamicServiceProviderEngi...	5	9450.26	9591.74	4.62 (avg.)
▷ Microsoft.AspNetCore.Server.IIS.Core.IISHttpContext.HandleRequest()	581	9590.39	21579.84	32.76 (avg.)
▷ [Details]	581	9445.79	21579.79	98.48 (avg.)

Figure 10.23 – Performance on the synchronous version of unanswered questions

8. Close the report by clicking on the close icon on the tab.
9. Switch back to WebSurge and note down the results there as well:

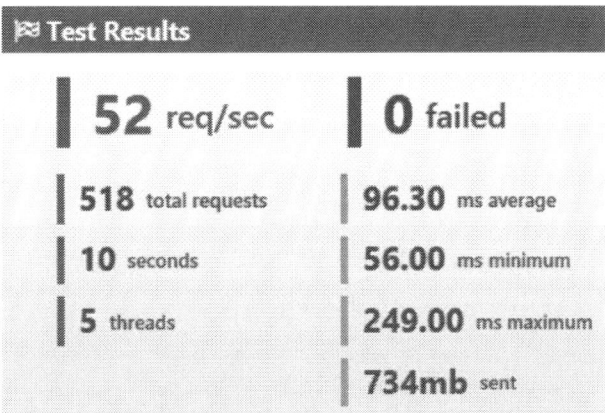

Figure 10.24 – Load test results on the synchronous version of unanswered questions

So, we now have some performance metrics from the synchronous implementation of unanswered questions.

Next, we are going discover how changing this code to be asynchronous impacts performance.

Implementing an asynchronous controller action method

Now, we are going to change the implementation of the unanswered questions endpoint so that it's asynchronous:

1. We are going to start by creating an asynchronous version of the data repository method that gets unanswered questions. So, let's create a new method in the data repository interface underneath `GetUnansweredQuestions` in `IDataRepository.cs`:

   ```
   public interface IDataRepository
   {
       ...
       IEnumerable<QuestionGetManyResponse>
         GetUnansweredQuestions();
       Task<IEnumerable<QuestionGetManyResponse>>
         GetUnansweredQuestionsAsync();
       ...
   }
   ```

   The key difference with an asynchronous method is that it returns a `Task` of the type that will eventually be returned.

2. Let's create the data repository method implementation in `DataRepository.cs` underneath `GetUnansweredQuestions`:

```
public async Task<IEnumerable<QuestionGetManyResponse>>
  GetUnansweredQuestionsAsync()
{
  using (var connection = new
    SqlConnection(_connectionString))
  {
    await connection.OpenAsync();
    return await
      connection.QueryAsync<QuestionGetManyResponse>(
        "EXEC dbo.Question_GetUnanswered");
  }
}
```

The `async` keyword before the return type signifies that the method is asynchronous. The implementation is very similar to the synchronous version, except that we use the asynchronous Dapper version of opening the connection and executing the query with the `await` keyword.

> **Important note**
> When making code asynchronous, all the I/O calls in the calling stack must be asynchronous. If any I/O call is synchronous, then the thread will be blocked rather than returning to the thread pool and so threads won't be managed efficiently.

3. Let's change the `GetUnansweredQuestions` method in `QuestionsController.cs` to call the method in the data repository we have just added:

```
[HttpGet("unanswered")]
public async Task<IEnumerable<QuestionGetManyResponse>>
  GetUnansweredQuestions()
{
  return await _dataRepository.
    GetUnansweredQuestionsAsync();
}
```

We mark the method as asynchronous with the `async` keyword and return a `Task` of the type we eventually want to return. We also call the asynchronous version of the data repository method with the `await` keyword.

Our unanswered questions endpoint is now asynchronous.

4. Press *Alt + F2* to open the **Performance Profiler** and make sure the **.NET Async** tool is still ticked. Click the **Start** button.

5. Switch to WebSurge and check the request URL path is still `/api/questions/unanswered` with the duration set to `10` seconds and `5` threads.

6. Start the load test.

7. After 10 seconds, switch to Visual Studio and click the **Stop Collection** option in **Performance Profiler**.

8. After a few seconds, the results will appear:

Name	Count	Start Time (ms)	End Time (ms)	Total Time (ms)
▷ Microsoft.Extensions.DependencyInjection.ServiceLookup.DynamicServiceProviderEngine...	5	4571.93	9070.73	79.81 (avg.)
▷ Microsoft.Extensions.Hosting.HostingAbstractionsHostExtensions.RunAsync()	1	4981.59	[Incomplete]	[Incomplete]
▷ GET /api/questions	1	5072.3	6629.44	1557.14
▲ GET /api/questions/unanswered	627	8840.65	20949.38	90.88 (avg.)
▷ Microsoft.AspNetCore.Routing.Matching.ILEmitTrieJumpTable.InitializeILDelegateAsyn...	1	8842.53	8842.88	0.35 (avg.)
▷ Microsoft.Extensions.DependencyInjection.ServiceLookup.DynamicServiceProviderEngi...	4	8845.08	8896.93	5.61 (avg.)
▷ Task.Unwrap	623	8903.17	20885.51	2.86 (avg.)
▷ Microsoft.AspNetCore.Server.IIS.Core.IISHttpContext.HandleRequest()	627	8903.89	20949.45	89.28 (avg.)
▷ Microsoft.Data.SqlClient.SqlCommand.BeginExecuteReaderAsyncCallback (Parameter,...	625	8906.7	20885.39	2.63 (avg.)
▷ Microsoft.Data.SqlClient.SqlCommand.BeginExecuteReaderInternal.AnonymousMetho...	612	8921.9	20885.42	0.09 (avg.)
▷ [Details]	627	8840.65	20949.38	90.88 (avg.)
▷ Task.Unwrap	1	8903.19	8932.49	29.3
▷ Task.Unwrap	1	8903.19	8932.54	29.35
Microsoft.Data.SqlClient.SqlCommand.BeginExecuteReaderAsyncCallback (Parameter, Pa...	1	8906.69	8927.87	21.18
Microsoft.Data.SqlClient.SqlCommand.BeginExecuteReaderAsyncCallback (Parameter, Pa...	1	8906.69	8927.9	21.21

Figure 10.25 – Performance on the asynchronous version of unanswered questions

Compare the results to the synchronous implementation results. The asynchronous one is slightly faster in my test. Notice the extra activities that happen in order to handle asynchronous code, which take up a bit of execution time.

9. Close the report by clicking on the close icon on the tab.

10. Switch back to WebSurge and note down the results there as well:

Test Results

56 req/sec | 0 failed
560 total requests | 89.03 ms average
10 seconds | 61.00 ms minimum
5 threads | 250.00 ms maximum
 | 794mb sent

Figure 10.26 – Load test results on the asynchronous version of unanswered questions

The results show a marginal performance improvement. In fact, your results may show a marginal decrease in performance. Asynchronous code can be slower than synchronous because of the overhead required to handle asynchronous code.

The benefit of asynchronous code is that it uses the web server's resources more efficiently under load. So, an asynchronous REST API will scale better than a synchronous REST API.

What happens when we use a synchronous database call in an asynchronous API controller method? We'll find out next.

Mixing asynchronous and synchronous code

An easy mistake to make is to mix asynchronous code with synchronous code. Let's find out what happens when this happens by changing the `GetUnansweredQuestions` action method:

1. Change this method to call the synchronous version of `GetUnansweredQuestions` in the data repository:

    ```
    [HttpGet("unanswered")]
    public async Task<IEnumerable<QuestionGetManyResponse>>
    GetUnansweredQuestions()
    {
        return _dataRepository.GetUnansweredQuestions();
    }
    ```

2. Press *Alt + F2* to open the **Performance Profiler** and make sure the **.NET Async** tool is still ticked. Click the **Start** button.

3. Switch to WebSurge and check the request URL path is still `/api/questions/unanswered` with the duration set to `10` seconds and `5` threads.
4. Start the load test.
5. After 10 seconds, switch to Visual Studio and click the **Stop Collection** option in **Performance Profiler**.
6. After a few seconds, the results will appear:

Name	Count	Start Time (ms) ▲	End Time (ms)	Total Time (ms)
▷ Microsoft.Extensions.DependencyInjection.ServiceLookup.DynamicServiceProviderEngine...	4	4697.91	5092.91	104.47 (avg.)
▷ 0x007ff7e73a777d	1	5141.73	[Incomplete]	[Incomplete]
▷ GET /api/questions	1	5255.54	7004.47	1748.93
▲ GET /api/questions/unanswered	579	11859.58	24056.57	97.64 (avg.)
▷ 0x007ff7e775ab04	1	11861.25	11861.6	0.35 (avg.)
▷ Microsoft.Extensions.DependencyInjection.ServiceLookup.DynamicServiceProviderEngi...	5	11863.36	12041.15	4.77 (avg.)
▷ 0x007ff7e75be7b1	50	12066.75	13486.93	47.14 (avg.)
▷ 0x007ff7e7a3ab59	529	13430.01	24056.61	28.8 (avg.)
▷ [Details]	579	11859.58	24056.57	97.64 (avg.)

Figure 10.27 – Results when sync and async code is mixed

The code functions as though it is synchronous code even though the action method is asynchronous.

7. Close the report by clicking on the close icon on the tab.
8. Revert this change so that the `GetUnansweredQuestions` method is as follows:

```
[HttpGet("unanswered")]
public async Task<IEnumerable<QuestionGetManyResponse>>
GetUnansweredQuestions()
{
    return await
    _dataRepository.GetUnansweredQuestionsAsync();
}
```

9. Switch back to the **Debug** configuration. This can be done by choosing `Debug` from the **Solution Configurations** option on the toolbar:

Figure 10.28 – Debug configuration

So, when synchronous and asynchronous code is mixed, it will behave like synchronous code and use the thread pool inefficiently. In asynchronous methods, it is important to check that all I/O calls are asynchronous, and that includes any I/O calls in child methods.

In the next section, we are going to look at how we can optimize requests for data by caching data.

Caching data

In this section, we are going to cache requests for getting a question. At the moment, the database is queried for each request to get a question. If we cache a question and can get subsequent requests for the question from the cache, this should be faster and reduce the load on the database. We will prove this with load tests.

Load testing the current implementation

Before we implement caching, we are going to load test the current implementation of getting a single question using the following steps:

1. Let's start our REST API by pressing *F5* in Visual Studio.

2. Now, we can load test the current implementation using WebSurge. Let's set the request URL path to `/api/questions/1` and change the duration to `30` seconds with 5 threads.

3. Start the test. When the test has finished, we'll get our results:

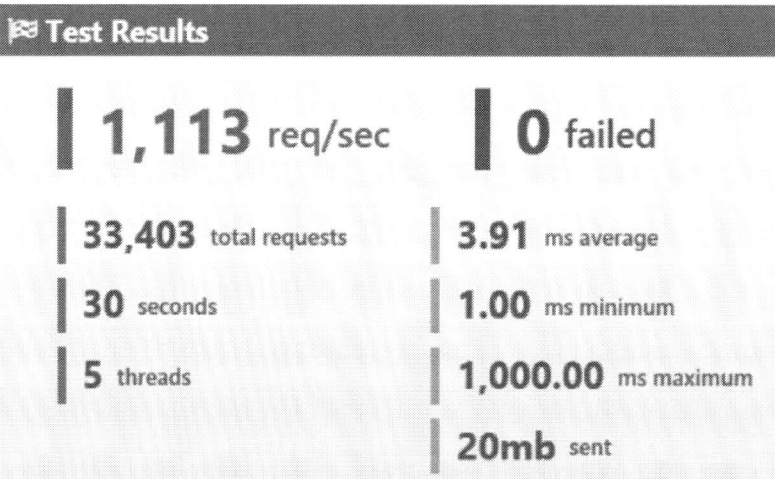

Figure 10.29 – Getting a question without cache – load test results

So, we get **1,113** requests per second without caching.

Stop the REST API from running so that we can implement and use a data cache.

Implementing a data cache

We are going to implement a cache for the questions using the memory cache in ASP.NET:

1. First, let's create an interface in the `Data` folder called `IQuestionCache`:

   ```
   using QandA.Data.Models;

   namespace QandA.Data
   {
     public interface IQuestionCache
     {
       QuestionGetSingleResponse Get(int questionId);
       void Remove(int questionId);
       void Set(QuestionGetSingleResponse question);
     }
   }
   ```

   So, we need the cache implementation to have methods for getting, removing, and updating an item in the cache.

2. Now, we can create a class in the `Data` folder called `QuestionCache`:

   ```
   using Microsoft.Extensions.Caching.Memory;
   using QandA.Data.Models;

   namespace QandA.Data
   {
     public class QuestionCache: IQuestionCache
     {
       // TODO - create a memory cache
       // TODO - method to get a cached question
       // TODO - method to add a cached question
       // TODO - method to remove a cached question
     }
   }
   ```

   Notice that we have referenced `Microsoft.Extensions.Caching.Memory` so that we can use the standard ASP.NET memory cache.

3. Let's create a constructor that creates an instance of the memory cache:

   ```
   public class QuestionCache: IQuestionCache
   {
     private MemoryCache _cache { get; set; }
     public QuestionCache()
     {
       _cache = new MemoryCache(new MemoryCacheOptions
   ```

```
        {
            SizeLimit = 100
        });
    }

    // TODO - method to get a cached question
    // TODO - method to add a cached question
    // TODO - method to remove a cached question
}
```

Notice that we have set the cache limit to be `100` items. This is to limit the amount of memory the cache takes up on our web server.

4. Let's implement a method to get a question from the cache:

```
public class QuestionCache: IQuestionCache
{
    ...

    private string GetCacheKey(int questionId) =>
      $"Question-{questionId}";

    public QuestionGetSingleResponse Get(int questionId)
    {
      QuestionGetSingleResponse question;
      _cache.TryGetValue(
        GetCacheKey(questionId),
        out question);
      return question;
    }

    // TODO - method to add a cached question
    // TODO - method to remove a cached question
}
```

We have created an expression to give us a key for a cache item, which is the word `Question` with a hyphen, followed by the question ID.

We use the `TryGetValue` method within the memory cache to retrieve the cached question. So, `null` will be returned from our method if the question doesn't exist in the cache.

5. Now, we can implement a method to add a question to the cache. We can add an item to the cache using the Set method in the ASP.NET memory cache:

```
public class QuestionCache: IQuestionCache
{
    ...

    public void Set(QuestionGetSingleResponse question)
    {
      var cacheEntryOptions =
        new MemoryCacheEntryOptions().SetSize(1);
      _cache.Set(
        GetCacheKey(question.QuestionId),
        question,
        cacheEntryOptions);
    }

    // TODO - method to remove a cached question
}
```

Notice that we specify the size of the question in the options when setting the cache value. This ties in with the size limit we set on the cache so that the cache will start to remove questions from the cache when there are 100 questions in it.

6. The last method we need to implement is a method to remove questions from the cache:

```
public class QuestionCache: IQuestionCache
{
    ...

    public void Remove(int questionId)
    {
      _cache.Remove(GetCacheKey(questionId));
    }
}
```

Note that if the question doesn't exist in the cache, nothing will happen and no exception will be thrown.

That completes the implementation of our question cache.

Using the data cache in an API controller action method

Now, we are going to make use of the questions cache in the `GetQuestion` method of our API controller. Work through the following steps:

1. First, we need to make the cache available for dependency injection so that we can inject it into `QuestionsController`. So, let's register `QuestionCache` for dependency injection in the `Startup` class after enabling the ASP.NET memory cache:

   ```
   public void ConfigureServices(IServiceCollection
   services)
   {
     ...

     services.AddMemoryCache();
     services.AddSingleton<IQuestionCache,
       QuestionCache>();
   }
   ```

   We register our cache as a singleton in the dependency injection system. This means that a single instance of our class will be created for the lifetime of the app. So, separate HTTP requests will access the same class instance and, therefore, the same cached data. This is exactly what we want for a cache.

2. In `QuestionsController.cs`, let's inject the cache into `QuestionsController`:

   ```
   ...
   private readonly IQuestionCache _cache;

   public QuestionsController(..., IQuestionCache
   questionCache)
   {
     ...
     _cache = questionCache;
   }
   ```

3. Let's change the implementation of `GetQuestion` to the following:

   ```
   [HttpGet("{questionId}")]
   public ActionResult<QuestionGetSingleResponse>
     GetQuestion(int questionId)
   {
     var question = _cache.Get(questionId);
   ```

```
      if (question == null)
      {
        question =
         _dataRepository.GetQuestion(questionId);
        if (question == null)
        {
            return NotFound();
        }
        _cache.Set(question);
      }
      return question;
    }
```

If the question isn't in the cache, then we get it from the data repository and put it in the cache.

4. When a question changes, we need to remove the item from the cache if it exists in the cache. This is so that subsequent requests for the question get the updated question from the database. Add the highlighted line of code to `PutQuestion` just before the `return` statement:

```
[HttpPut("{questionId}")]
public ActionResult<QuestionGetSingleResponse>
   PutQuestion(int questionId, QuestionPutRequest
     questionPutRequest)
{
    ...

    _cache.Remove(savedQuestion.QuestionId);

    return savedQuestion;
}
```

5. Similarly, when a question is deleted, we need to remove it from the cache if it exists in the cache. Add the highlighted line of code to `DeleteQuestion` just before the `return` statement:

```
HttpDelete("{questionId}")]
public ActionResult DeleteQuestion(int questionId)
{
    ...

    _cache.Remove(questionId);

    return NoContent();
}
```

6. We also need to remove the question from the cache when an answer is being posted. Add the highlighted line of code to `PostAnswer` just before the `return` statement:

    ```
    [HttpPost("answer")]
    public ActionResult<AnswerGetResponse>
      PostAnswer(AnswerPostRequest answerPostRequest)
    {
    ...

      _cache.Remove(answerPostRequest.QuestionId.Value);
      return savedAnswer;
    }
    ```

7. Let's start our REST API by pressing *F5* in Visual Studio.

8. Let's load test the `/api/questions/1` endpoint again with our improved implementation, keeping the duration to 30 seconds and number of threads to 5.

9. When the test has finished, we'll get our results, confirming the improvement:

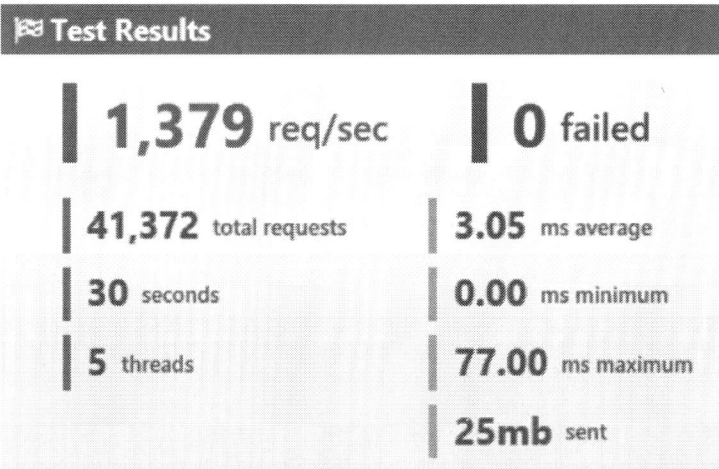

Figure 10.30 – Getting a question with cache load test results

10. Stop the REST API in Visual Studio by pressing *Shift* + *F5*.

This completes our implementation of the question endpoint with data caching.

It is important to remember to invalidate the cache when the data changes. In our example, this was straightforward, but it can be more complex, particularly if there are other processes outside of the REST API that change the data. So, if we don't have full control of the data changes in the REST API, a cache may not be worth implementing.

Another consideration for whether to use a cache is if the data changes very frequently. In this case, the caching process can actually negatively impact performance because lots of the requests will result in database calls anyway and we have all of the overhead of managing the cache.

However, if the data behind an endpoint changes infrequently and we have control over these changes, then caching is a great way to positively impact performance.

What if the REST API is distributed across several servers? Well, because the memory cache is local to each web server, this could result in database calls where the data is cached on a different server. A solution to this is to implement a distributed cache with `IDistributedCache` in ASP.NET, which would have a very similar implementation to our memory cache. The complexity is that this needs to connect to a third-party cache such as Redis, which adds financial costs and complexity to the solution. For high-traffic REST APIs, a distributed cache is well worth considering, though.

Summary

In this chapter, we learned that we can use Dapper's multi-mapping and multi-result features to reduce database round trips to positively impact performance and allow our REST API to accept more requests per second. We learned also that forcing the client to page through the data they need to consume helps with performance as well.

We learned how to make controller action methods asynchronous and how this positively impacts the scalability of a REST API built in ASP.NET. We also understood that all of the I/O calls in a method and its child methods need to be asynchronous to achieve scalability benefits.

We also learned how to cache data in memory to reduce the number of expensive database calls. We understand that data that is read often and rarely changed is a great case for using a cache.

We will continue to focus on the REST API in the next chapter and turn our attention to the topic of security. We will require users to be authenticated in order to access some endpoints with the REST API.

Questions

Try to answer the following questions to check the knowledge that you have gained in this chapter:

1. We have the following code in a data repository that uses Dapper's multi-results feature to return a single order with the many related detail lines in a single database call:

   ```
   using (var connection = new SqlConnection(_
   connectionString))
   {
     connection.Open();

     using (GridReader results = connection.QueryMultiple(
       @"EXEC dbo.Order_GetHeader @OrderId = @OrderId;
       EXEC dbo.OrderDetails_Get_ByOrderId @OrderId =
       @OrderId",
       new { OrderId = orderId }))
     {

       // TODO - Read the order and details from the
         // query result

       return order;
     }
   }
   ```

   What are the missing statements that will read the order and its details from the results, putting the details in the order model? The order model is of the `OrderGetSingleResponse` type and contains a `Details` property of the `IEnumerable<OrderDetailGetResponse>` type.

2. What is the downside of using Dapper's multi-mapping feature when reading data from a many-to-one related table in a single database call?

3. How does data paging help performance?

4. Does making code asynchronous make it faster?

5. What is the problem with the following asynchronous method?

```
public async AnswerGetResponse GetAnswer(int answerId)
{
  using (var connection = new SqlConnection(_
connectionString))
  {
    connection.Open();
    return await connection
      .QueryFirstOrDefaultAsync<AnswerGetResponse>(
        "EXEC dbo.Answer_Get_ByAnswerId @AnswerId =
        @AnswerId",
        new { AnswerId = answerId });
  }
}
```

6. Why it is a good idea to have a size limit on a memory cache?

7. In our `QuestionCache` implementation, when adding a question to the cache, how can we invalidate that item in the cache after 30 minutes?

8. When we registered our `QuestionCache` class for dependency injection, why did we use the `AddSingleton` method and not the `AddScoped` method like in the following code?

```
services.AddScoped<QuestionCache>();
```

Answers

1. We can add the following highlighted lines of code to read the order and its details from the results:

```
using (var connection = new SqlConnection(_
connectionString))
{
  connection.Open();

  using (GridReader results = connection.QueryMultiple(
    @"EXEC dbo.Order_GetHeader @OrderId = @OrderId;
    EXEC dbo.OrderDetails_Get_ByOrderId @OrderId = @
OrderId",
    new { OrderId = orderId }))
  {
    var order = results.Read<
      OrderGetSingleResponse>().FirstOrDefault();
    if (order != null)
```

```
        {
            order.Details = results.Read<
              OrderDetailGetResponse>().ToList();
        }
        return order;
    }
}
```

2. The trade-off of using Dapper's multi-mapping feature is that more data is transferred between the database and web server and is then processed on the web server, which can hurt performance.

3. Paging increases performance in the following ways:

    a) The number of page read I/Os is reduced when SQL Server grabs the data.

    b) The amount of data transferred from the database server to the web server is reduced.

    c) The amount of memory used to store the data on the web server in our model is reduced.

    d) The amount of data transferred from the web server to the client is reduced.

4. Asynchronous code isn't faster than synchronous code. Instead, it makes it more scalable by using the thread pool more efficiently.

5. The problem with the asynchronous method implementation is that opening the connection is synchronous. This means the thread is blocked and not returned to the thread pool until the connection is opened. So, the whole code will have the same thread pool inefficiency as synchronous code but will have the overhead of asynchronous code as well.

    Here is the corrected implementation:

```
public async AnswerGetResponse GetAnswer(int answerId)
{
    using (var connection = new SqlConnection(_
  connectionString))
    {
        await connection.OpenAsync();
        return await connection
            .QueryFirstOrDefaultAsync<AnswerGetResponse>(
               "EXEC dbo.Answer_Get_ByAnswerId @AnswerId = @
  AnswerId",
               new { AnswerId = answerId });
    }
}
```

6. It is a good idea to set a size limit on a memory cache to prevent the cache from taking up too much memory on the web server.

7. We can do the following to invalidate the item in the cache after 30 minutes:

```
public void Set(QuestionGetSingleResponse question)
{
  var cacheEntryOptions =
    new MemoryCacheEntryOptions()
    .SetSize(1)
    .SetSlidingExpiration(TimeSpan.FromMinutes(30));
  _cache.Set(GetCacheKey(question.QuestionId),
    question, cacheEntryOptions);
}
```

8. We registered our `QuestionCache` class for dependency injection with `AddSingleton` so that the cache lasts for the lifetime of the app. Using `AddScoped` would create a new instance of the cache for every request, which means the cache would be lost after each request.

Further reading

Here are some useful links if you want to learn more about the topics that were covered in this chapter:

- **Dapper multi-mapping**: `https://dapper-tutorial.net/result-multi-mapping`

- **Dapper multi-results**: `https://dapper-tutorial.net/result-multi-result`

- **Asynchronous programming with** `async` **and** `await`: `https://docs.microsoft.com/en-us/dotnet/csharp/programming-guide/concepts/async/`

- **ASP.NET memory cache**: `https://docs.microsoft.com/en-us/aspnet/core/performance/caching/memory`

- **ASP.NET distributed cache**: `https://docs.microsoft.com/en-us/aspnet/core/performance/caching/distributed`

# 11
Securing the Backend

In this chapter, we'll implement authentication and authorization in our Q&A app. We will use a popular service called Auth0, which implements **OpenID Connect** (**OIDC**), to help us to do this. We will start by understanding what OIDC is and why it is a good choice, before getting our app to interact with Auth0.

At the moment, our web API is accessible by unauthenticated users, which is a security vulnerability. We will resolve this vulnerability by protecting the necessary endpoints with simple authorization. This will mean that only authenticated users can access protected resources.

Authenticated users shouldn't have access to everything, though. We will learn how to ensure authenticated users only get access to what they are allowed to by using custom authorization policies.

We'll also learn how to get details about authenticated users so that we can include them when questions and answers are saved to the database.

We will end the chapter by enabling cross-origin requests in preparation for allowing our frontend to access the REST API.

In this chapter, we'll cover the following topics:

- Understanding OIDC
- Setting up Auth0 with our ASP.NET backend
- Protecting endpoints
- Using the authenticated user when posting questions and answers
- Adding CORS

Technical requirements

We'll use the following tools and services in this chapter:

- **Visual Studio 2019**: We'll use this to edit our ASP.NET code. This can be downloaded and installed from `https://visualstudio.microsoft.com/vs/`.
- **.NET 5**: This can be downloaded from `https://dotnet.microsoft.com/download/dotnet/5.0`.
- **Auth0**: We will use this to authenticate and manage users. The service is free to try and do some testing with, and an account can be created at `https://auth0.com/signup`.
- **Postman**: We'll use this to try out the changes to our REST API in this chapter. This can be downloaded from `https://www.getpostman.com/downloads/`.
- **Q&A**: We'll start with the Q&A starter project for this chapter. This is the backend project we finished in the previous chapter with all the controller methods asynchronous. This is available on GitHub at `https://github.com/PacktPublishing/ASP.NET-Core-5-and-React-Second-Edition` in the `chapter-11/start` folder.

All of the code snippets in this chapter can be found online at `https://github.com/PacktPublishing/ASP.NET-Core-5-and-React-Second-Edition`. To restore code from a chapter, the source code repository can be downloaded and the relevant folder opened in the relevant editor. If the code is frontend code, then `npm install` can be entered in the terminal to restore the dependencies.

Check out the following video to see the Code in Action: `http://bit.ly/2EPQ8DY`

Understanding OIDC

Before we cover OIDC, let's make sure we understand authentication and authorization. Authentication verifies that the user is who they say they are. In our app, the user will enter their email and password to prove who they are. Authorization decides whether a user has permission to access a resource. In our app, some of the REST API endpoints, such as posting a question, will eventually be protected by authorization checks.

OIDC is an industry-standard way of handling both authentication and authorization as well as other user-related operations. This works well for a wide variety of architectures, including **single-page applications** (**SPAs**) such as ours where there is a JavaScript client and a server-side REST API that need to be secured.

The following diagram shows the high-level flow of a user of our app being authenticated and then gaining access to protected resources in the REST API:

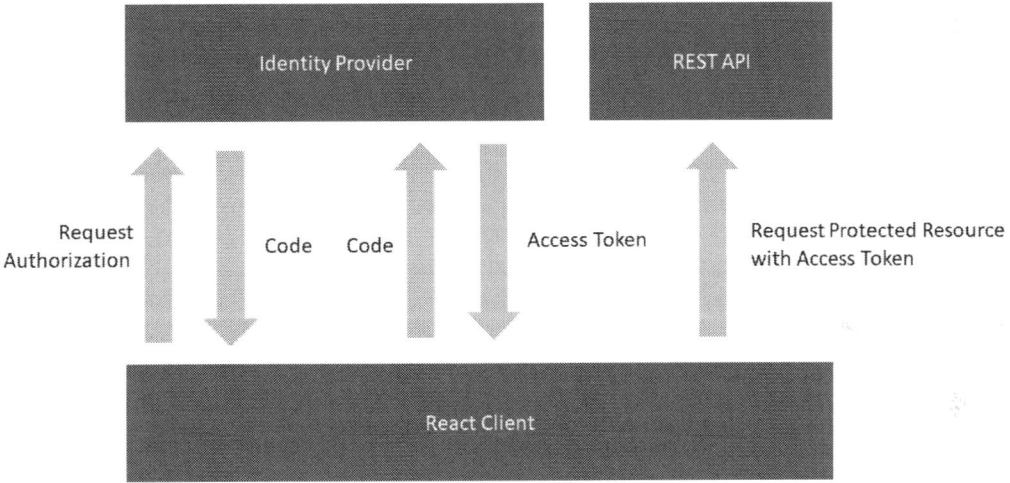

Figure 11.1 – OIDC authentication flow

Here are some more details of the steps that take place:

1. The client makes an authorization request to an identity provider because it wants to get access to a protected resource in the REST API.

2. The client is redirected to the identity provider so that the user can enter their credentials to prove who they are.

3. The identity provider then generates a code and redirects back to the client with the code.

4. The client then makes a web API request containing the generated code to get an access code. The identity provider validates the code and responds with an access token.

5. The client can then access protected resources in the REST API by including the access token in the requests.

Notice that our app never handles user credentials. When user authentication is required, the user will be redirected to the identity provider to carry out this process. Our app only ever deals with a secure token, which is referred to as an **access token**, which is a long-encoded string. This token is in **JSON Web Token (JWT)** format, which again is industry-standard.

The content of a JWT can be inspected using the `https://jwt.io/` website. We can paste a JWT into the **Encoded** box and then the site puts the decoded JWT in the **Decoded** box, as shown in the following screenshot:

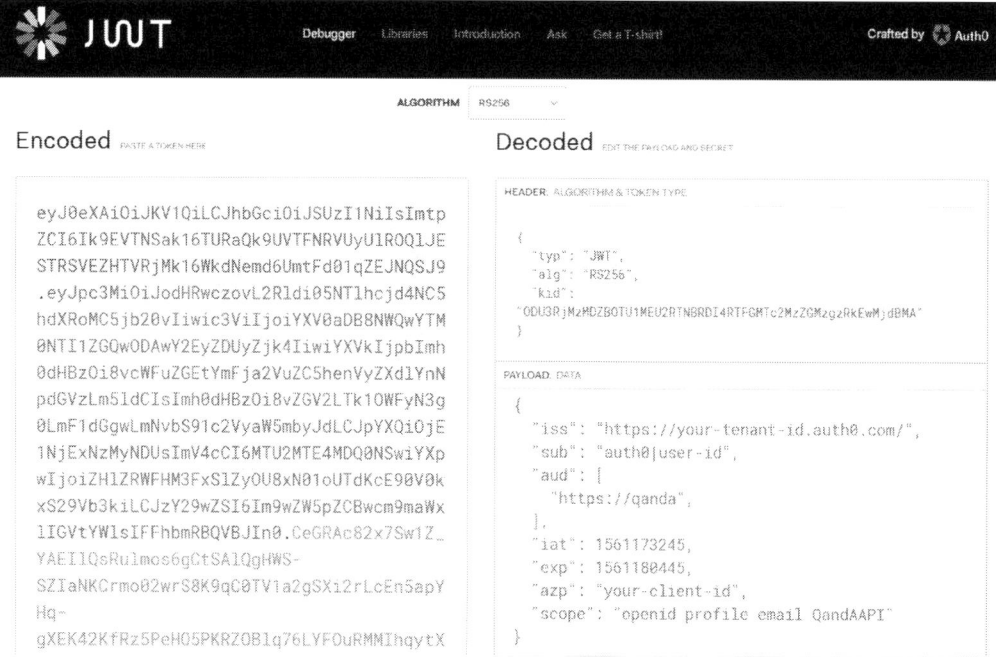

Figure 11.2 – JWT in jwt.io

There are three parts to a JWT, separated by dots, and they appear as different colors in `jwt.io`:

- **HEADER**
- **PAYLOAD**
- **SIGNATURE**

The header usually contains the type of the token in a `typ` field and the signing algorithm being used in an `alg` field. So, the preceding token is a JWT that uses an RSA signature with the SHA-256 asymmetric algorithm. There is also a `kid` field in the header, which is an opaque identifier that can be used to identify the key that was used to sign the JWT.

The payload of JWTs vary but the following fields are often included:

- `iss`: This is the identity provider that issued the token.
- `sub`: This is short for `subject` and is the user's identifier. This will be `UserId` for our app.
- `aud`: This is the intended audience. For our app, this will contain the name of our REST API.
- `iat`: This is when the JWT was issued. This is in Unix epoch time format, which is the seconds that have passed since January 1, 1970.
- `exp`: This is when the token expires and again is in Unix epoch time format.
- `azp`: This is the party to which the token was issued, which is a unique identifier for the client using the JWT. This will be the client ID of our React app in our case.
- `scope`: This is what the client can get access to. For our app, this is the REST API, as well as user profile information and their email address.
- The `openid` scope allows the client to verify a user's identity.

OIDC deals with securely storing passwords, authenticating users, generating access tokens, and much more. Being able to leverage an industry-standard technology such as OIDC not only saves us lots of time but also gives us the peace of mind that the implementation is very secure and will receive updates as attackers get smarter.

What we have just learned is implemented by Auth0. We'll start to use Auth0 in the next section.

Setting up Auth0 with our ASP.NET backend

We are going to use a ready-made identity service called **Auth0** in our app. Auth0 implements OIDC and is also free for a low number of users. Using Auth0 will allow us to focus on integrating with an identity service rather than spending time building our own.

In this section, we are going to set up Auth0 and integrate it into our ASP.NET backend.

Setting up Auth0

Let's carry out the following steps to set up Auth0 as our identity provider:

1. If you haven't already got an Auth0 account, sign up at `https://auth0.com/signup`.

2. Once we have an Auth0 account and have logged in, we need to change the default audience in our tenant settings. To get to your tenant settings, click on the user avatar and choose **Settings**:

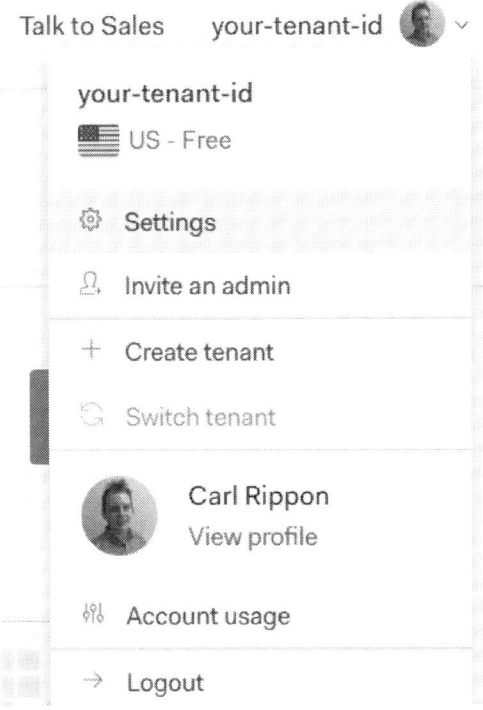

Figure 11.3 – Auth0 tenant settings option

The **Default Audience** option is in the **API Authorization Settings** section. Change this to `https://qanda:`

Setting up Auth0 with our ASP.NET backend 369

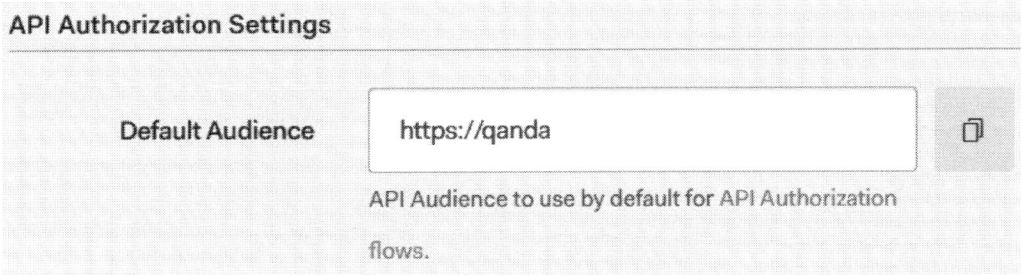

Figure 11.4 – Auth0 Default Audience setting

This tells Auth0 to add `https://qanda` to the `aud` payload field in the JWT it generates. This setting triggers Auth0 to generate access tokens in JWT format. Our ASP.NET backend will also check that access tokens contain this data before granting access to protected resources.

3. Next, we are going to tell Auth0 about our React frontend. On the left-hand navigation menu, click **Applications** and then click the **Create Application** button.
4. Select the **Single Page Web Applications** application type and click the **CREATE** button:

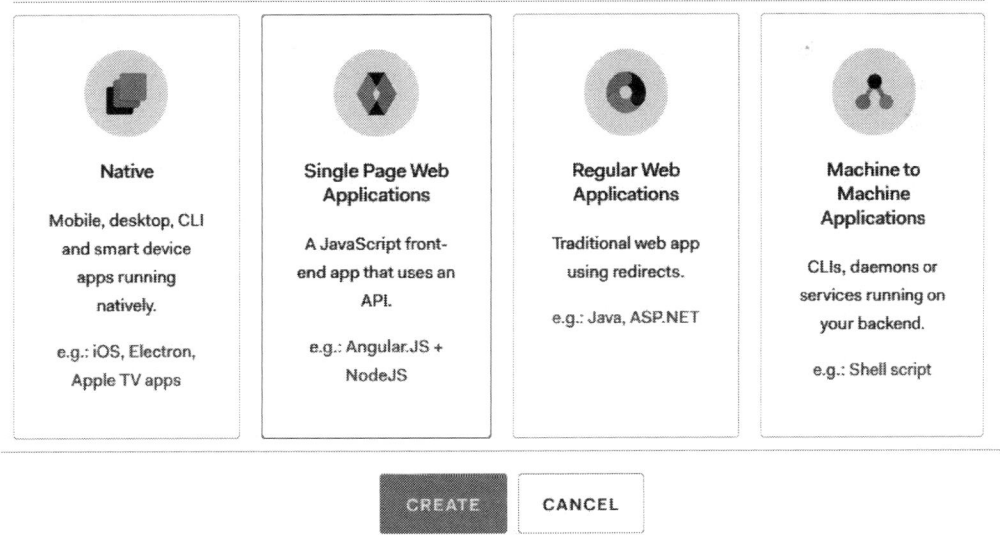

Figure 11.5 – Creating a SPA Auth0 client

Our SPA client configuration will then be created.

5. We need to change a few settings in the SPA client configuration, so select the **Settings** tab and set the following settings.

6. The name will appear on the login screen, so change it to `QandA`.

7. Specify the origin of the frontend in the **Allowed Web Origins** setting. So, let's set this to `http://localhost:3000`.

8. We need to specify the page Auth0 will redirect back to after a successful login in the **Allowed Callback URLs** setting. So, set this to `http://localhost:3000/signin-callback`. We will implement the `signin-callback` page in our frontend in *Chapter 12, Interacting with RESTful APIs*.

9. Similarly, we need to specify the page Auth0 will redirect back to after a successful logout in the **Allowed Logout URLs** setting. So, set this to `http://localhost:3000/signout-callback`. We will implement the `signout-callback` page in our frontend in *Chapter 12, Interacting with RESTful APIs*.

10. Don't forget to scroll to the bottom of the page and click the **Save Changes** button after entering these settings.

11. We now need to tell Auth0 about our ASP.NET backend. On the left-hand navigation menu, click **APIs** and then click the **Create API** button:

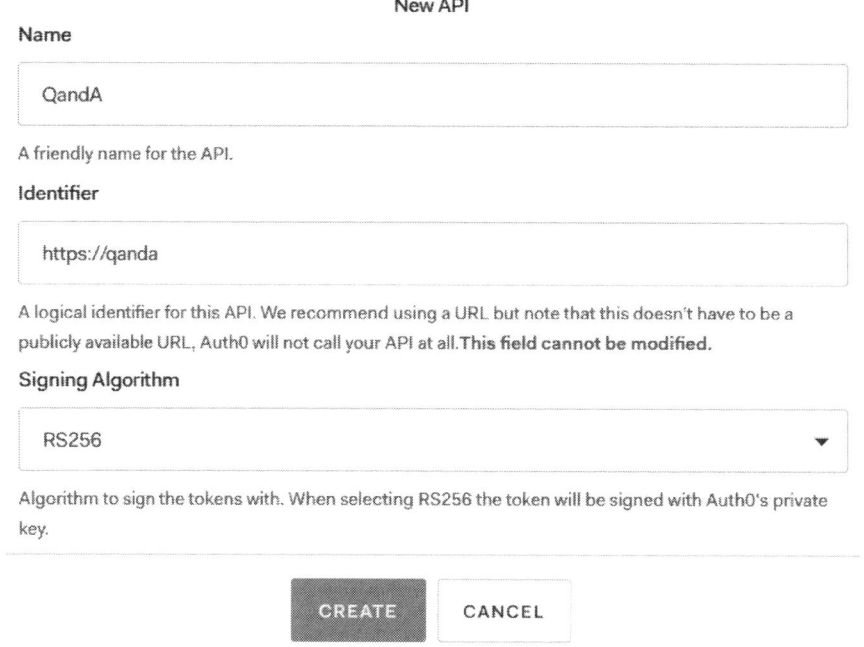

Figure 11.6 – Creating an API Auth0 client

The name can be anything we choose, but the **Identifier** setting must match the default audience we set on the tenant. Make sure **Signing Algorithm** is set to **RS256** and then click the **CREATE** button.

That completes the setup of Auth0.

Next, we will integrate our ASP.NET backend with Auth0.

Configuring our ASP.NET backend to authenticate with Auth0

We can now change our ASP.NET backend to authenticate with Auth0. Let's open the backend project in Visual Studio and carry out the following steps:

1. Install the following NuGet package:

   ```
   Microsoft.AspNetCore.Authentication.JwtBearer
   ```

   > **Important Note**
   > Make sure the version of the package you select is supported by the version of .NET you are using. So, for example, if you are targeting .NET 5.0, then select package version 5.0.*.

2. Add the following `using` statement to the `Startup` class:

   ```
   using Microsoft.AspNetCore.Authentication.JwtBearer;
   ```

   Add the following lines to the `ConfigureServices` method in the `Startup` class:

   ```
   public void ConfigureServices(IServiceCollection 
   services)
   {
     ...
     services.AddAuthentication(options =>
     {
       options.DefaultAuthenticateScheme = 
         JwtBearerDefaults.AuthenticationScheme;
       options.DefaultChallengeScheme = 
         JwtBearerDefaults.AuthenticationScheme;
     }).AddJwtBearer(options =>
     {
       options.Authority = 
         Configuration["Auth0:Authority"];
   ```

```
        options.Audience =
            Configuration["Auth0:Audience"];
    });
}
```

This adds JWT-based authentication specifying the authority and expected audience as the `appsettings.json` settings.

3. Let's add the authentication middleware to the `Configure` method. It needs to be placed between the routing and authorization middleware:

```
public void Configure(IApplicationBuilder app,
IWebHostEnvironment env)
{
    ...
    app.UseRouting();
    app.UseAuthentication();
    app.UseAuthorization();
    ...
}
```

This will validate the access token in each request if one exists. If the check succeeds, the user on the request context will be set.

4. The final step is to add the settings in `appsettings.json`, which we have referenced:

```
{
    ...,
    "Auth0": {
        "Authority": "https://your-tentant-id.auth0.com/",
        "Audience": "https://qanda"
    }
}
```

We will need to substitute our Auth0 tenant ID into the `Authority` field. The tenant ID can be found in Auth0 to the left of the user avatar:

Figure 11.7 – Auth0 user avatar

So, `Authority` for the preceding tenant is `https://your-tenant-id.auth0.com/`. The `Audience` field needs to match the audience we specified in Auth0.

Our web API is now validating access tokens in the requests.

Let's quickly recap what we have done in this section. We told our identity provider the path to our frontend and the paths for signing in and out. Identity providers often provide an administration page for us to supply this information. We also told ASP.NET to validate the bearer token in a request using the `UseAuthentication` method in the `Configure` method in the `Startup` class. The validation is configured using the `AddAuthentication` method in `ConfigureServices`.

We are going to start protecting some endpoints in the next section.

Protecting endpoints

We are going to start this section by protecting the `questions` endpoint for adding, updating, and deleting questions as well as posting answers so that only authenticated users can do these operations. We will then move on to implement and use a custom authorization policy so that only the author of the question can update or delete it.

Protecting endpoints with simple authorization

Let's protect the `questions` endpoint for the `POST`, `PUT`, and `DELETE` HTTP methods by carrying out these steps:

1. Open `QuestionsController` and add the following `using` statement:

   ```
   using Microsoft.AspNetCore.Authorization;
   ```

2. To secure the actions, we decorate them with an `Authorize` attribute. Add this attribute to the `PostQuestion`, `PutQuestion`, `DeleteQuestion`, and `PostAnswer` methods:

   ```
   [Authorize]
   [HttpPost]
   public async ... PostQuestion(QuestionPostRequest
   questionPostRequest)
   ...

   [Authorize]
   [HttpPut("{questionId}")]
   public async ... PutQuestion(int questionId,
   QuestionPutRequest questionPutRequest)
   ...

   [Authorize]
   [HttpDelete("{questionId}")]
   public async ... DeleteQuestion(int questionId)
   ```

```
...
[Authorize]
[HttpPost("answer")]
public async ... PostAnswer(AnswerPostRequest
answerPostRequest)
...
```

3. Run the Visual Studio project by pressing *F5*. We'll notice, as the browser opens with the `api/questions` path, that the data is successfully returned. This means that the `GetQuestions` action method is unprotected, as we expected.

4. Open Postman now and try to post a question:

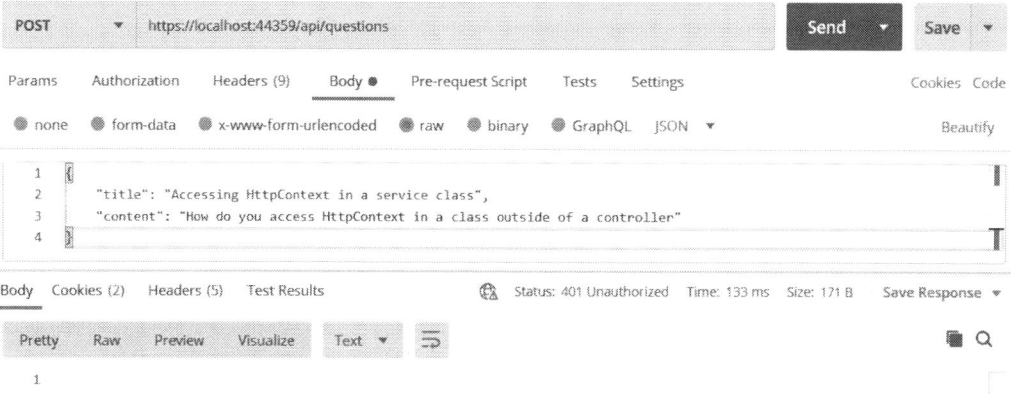

Figure 11.8 – Accessing a protected endpoint in Postman without being authenticated

We receive a response with status code **401 Unauthorized**. This shows that this action method is now protected.

5. We can obtain a test access token from Auth0 to check that we can post a question with a valid token. In Auth0, click on **APIs** in the left-hand navigation menu and then our **QandA** API.

6. Click on the **Test** tab and we will see a token that we can use for testing purposes.

7. Click the **COPY TOKEN** option to copy the access token to the clipboard:

Protecting endpoints 375

Figure 11.9 – Getting a test token from Auth0

8. Back in Postman, we need to add this token to an `Authorization` HTTP header after the `bearer` word and a space:

Figure 11.10 – Adding the Auth0 bearer token to an Authorization HTTP header in Postman

9. If we send the request, it will now be successful:

Figure 11.11 – Successfully accessing a protected endpoint in Postman

10. Press *Shift* + *F5* to stop the Visual Studio project from running so that we can add more code.

So, once the authentication middleware is in place, the `Authorize` attribute protects action methods. If a whole controller needs to be protected, the `Authorize` attribute can decorate the `controller` class:

```
[Authorize]
[Route("api/[controller]")]
[ApiController]
public class QuestionsController : ControllerBase
```

All of the action methods in the controller will then be protected without having to specify the `Authorize` attribute. We can also unprotect action methods in a protected controller by using the `AllowAnonymous` attribute:

```
[AllowAnonymous]
[HttpGet]
public IEnumerable<QuestionGetManyResponse> GetQuestions(string search, bool includeAnswers, int page = 1, int pageSize = 20)
```

So, in our example, we could have protected the whole controller using the `Authorize` attribute and unprotected the `GetQuestions`, `GetUnansweredQuestions`, and `GetQuestion` action methods with the `AllowAnonymous` attribute to achieve the behavior we want.

Next, we are going to learn how to implement a policy check with endpoint authorization.

Protecting endpoints with a custom authorization policy

At the moment, any authenticated user can update or delete questions. We are going to implement and use a custom authorization policy and use it to enforce that only the author of the question can do these operations. Let's carry out the following steps:

1. In the `Startup` class, let's add the following `using` statements:

    ```
    using Microsoft.AspNetCore.Http;
    using Microsoft.AspNetCore.Authorization;
    using QandA.Authorization;
    ```

    Note that the reference to the `QandA.Authorization` namespace doesn't exist yet. We'll implement this in a later step.

2. We'll need to eventually call an Auth0 web service, so let's make the HTTP client available in the `ConfigureServices` method:

   ```
   public void ConfigureServices(IServiceCollection
   services)
   {
     ...
     services.AddHttpClient();
   }
   ```

   The authorization policy has its requirements defined in a class called `MustBeQuestionAuthorRequirement`, which we'll implement in a later step.

3. Let's also add an authorization policy called `MustBeQuestionAuthor`:

   ```
   public void ConfigureServices(IServiceCollection
   services)
   {
     ...
     services.AddHttpClient();
     services.AddAuthorization(options =>
       options.AddPolicy("MustBeQuestionAuthor", policy
         =>
         policy.Requirements
           .Add(new MustBeQuestionAuthorRequirement())));
   }
   ```

   The authorization policy has its requirements defined in a class called `MustBeQuestionAuthorRequirement`, which we'll implement in a later step.

4. We also need to have a handler for the requirement, so let's register this for dependency injection:

   ```
   public void ConfigureServices(IServiceCollection
   services)
   {
     ...
     services.AddHttpClient();
     services.AddAuthorization(...);
     services.AddScoped<
       IAuthorizationHandler,
       MustBeQuestionAuthorHandler>();
   }
   ```

So, the handler for `MustBeQuestionAuthorRequirement` will be implemented in a class called `MustBeQuestionAuthorHandler`.

5. Our `MustBeQuestionAuthorHandler` class will need access to the HTTP requests to find out the question that is being requested. We need to register `HttpContextAccessor` for dependency injection to get access to the HTTP request information in a class. Let's do this now:

```
public void ConfigureServices(IServiceCollection 
services)
{
  ...
  services.AddHttpClient();
  services.AddAuthorization(...);
  services.AddScoped<
    IAuthorizationHandler,
    MustBeQuestionAuthorHandler>();
  services.AddHttpContextAccessor();
}
```

Note that `AddHttpContextAccessor` is a convenience method for `AddSingleton<IHttpContextAccessor,HttpContextAccessor>`.

6. We are going to create the `MustBeQuestionAuthorRequirement` class now. Let's create a folder called `Authorization` in the root of the project and then create a class called `MustBeQuestionAuthorRequirement` containing the following:

```
using Microsoft.AspNetCore.Authorization;

namespace QandA.Authorization
{
  public class MustBeQuestionAuthorRequirement:
    IAuthorizationRequirement
  {
    public MustBeQuestionAuthorRequirement()
    {
    }
  }
}
```

7. Next, we'll create the handler class for this requirement. Create a class called `MustBeQuestionAuthorHandler` with the following content in the `Authorization` folder:

```csharp
using System;
using System.Security.Claims;
using System.Threading.Tasks;
using Microsoft.AspNetCore.Authorization;
using Microsoft.AspNetCore.Http;
using QandA.Data;

namespace QandA.Authorization
{
    public class MustBeQuestionAuthorHandler :
        AuthorizationHandler<MustBeQuestionAuthorRequirement>
    {
        private readonly IDataRepository _dataRepository;
        private readonly IHttpContextAccessor
          _httpContextAccessor;

        public MustBeQuestionAuthorHandler(
            IDataRepository dataRepository,
            IHttpContextAccessor httpContextAccessor)
        {
            _dataRepository = dataRepository;
            _httpContextAccessor = httpContextAccessor;
        }

        protected async override Task
          HandleRequirementAsync(
              AuthorizationHandlerContext context,
              MustBeQuestionAuthorRequirement requirement)
        {
            // TODO - check that the user is authenticated
            // TODO - get the question id from the request
            // TODO - get the user id from the name
              // identifier claim
            // TODO - get the question from the data
              // repository
            // TODO - if the question can't be found go to
              // the next piece of middleware
            // TODO - return failure if the user id in the
              // question from the data repository is
                // different to the user id in the request
            // TODO - return success if we manage to get
```

```
                // here
            }
        }
    }
}
```

This inherits from the `AuthorizationHandler` class, which takes in the requirement it is handling as a generic parameter. We have injected the data repository and the HTTP context into the class.

8. We now need to implement the `HandleRequirementAsync` method. The first task is to check that the user is authenticated:

```
protected async override Task
    HandleRequirementAsync(
      AuthorizationHandlerContext context,
      MustBeQuestionAuthorRequirement requirement)
{
    if (!context.User.Identity.IsAuthenticated)
    {
        context.Fail();
        return;
    }

    // TODO - get the question id from the request
    // TODO - get the user id from the name identifier
    //   claim
    // TODO - get the question from the data repository
    // TODO - if the question can't be found go to the
    //   next piece of middleware
    // TODO - return failure if the user id in the
    //   question from the data repository is different
    //   to the user id in the request
    // TODO - return success if we manage to get here
}
```

The `context` parameter in the method contains information about the user's identity in an `Identity` property. We use the `IsAuthenticated` property within the `Identity` object to determine whether the user is authenticated or not. We call the `Fail` method on the `context` argument to tell it that the requirement failed.

9. Next, we need to get `questionId` from the request path:

```
protected async override Task
  HandleRequirementAsync(
    AuthorizationHandlerContext context,
    MustBeQuestionAuthorRequirement requirement)
{
  if (!context.User.Identity.IsAuthenticated)
  {
    context.Fail();
    return;
  }

  var questionId =
    _httpContextAccessor.HttpContext.Request
      .RouteValues["questionId"];
  int questionIdAsInt = Convert.ToInt32(questionId);

  // TODO - get the user id from the name identifier
  //   claim
  // TODO - get the question from the data repository
  // TODO - if the question can't be found go to the
    //next piece of middleware
  // TODO - return failure if the user id in the
    //question from the data repository is different
    // to the user id in the request
  // TODO - return success if we manage to get here
}
```

We use the `RouteValues` dictionary within the HTTP context request to get access to get the question ID. The `RoutesValues` dictionary contains the controller name, the action method name, as well as the parameters for the action method.

10. Next, we need to get `userId` from the user's identity claims:

```
protected async override Task
  HandleRequirementAsync(
    AuthorizationHandlerContext context,
    MustBeQuestionAuthorRequirement requirement)
{
  ...
  var questionId =
    _httpContextAccessor.HttpContext.Request
      .RouteValues["questionId"];
  int questionIdAsInt = Convert.ToInt32(questionId);
```

```
    var userId =
      context.User.FindFirst(ClaimTypes.NameIdentifier).
      Value;

    // TODO - get the question from the data repository
    // TODO - if the question can't be found go to the
    // next piece of middleware
    // TODO - return failure if the user id in the
    //question from the data repository is different
    // to the user id in the request
    // TODO - return success if we manage to get here
}
```

`userId` is stored in the name identifier claim.

> **Important Note**
>
> A claim is information about a user from a trusted source. A claim represents what the subject is, not what the subject can do. The ASP.NET authentication middleware automatically puts `userId` in a name identifier claim for us.

We have used the `FindFirst` method on the `User` object from the `context` parameter to get the value of the name identifier claim. The `User` object is populated with the claims by the authentication middleware earlier in the request pipeline after it has read the access token.

11. We can now get the question from the data repository. If the question isn't found, we want to pass the requirement because we want to return HTTP status code 404 (not found) rather than 401 (unauthorized). The action method in the controller will then be able to execute and return the HTTP 404 status code:

```
protected async override Task
  HandleRequirementAsync(
    AuthorizationHandlerContext context,
    MustBeQuestionAuthorRequirement requirement)
{
  ...
  var userId =
    context.User.FindFirst(ClaimTypes.NameIdentifier).
Value;

  var question =
    await _dataRepository.GetQuestion(questionIdAsInt);
  if (question == null)
  {
```

```
      // let it through so the controller can return a 404
      context.Succeed(requirement);
      return;
    }

    // TODO - return failure if the user id in the
      //question from the data repository is different
      // to the user id in the request
    // TODO - return success if we manage to get here
}
```

12. Now, check that `userId` in the request matches the question in the database and return `Fail` if not:

```
protected async override Task
  HandleRequirementAsync(
    AuthorizationHandlerContext context,
    MustBeQuestionAuthorRequirement requirement)
{
  ...

  var question =
    await _dataRepository.GetQuestion(questionIdAsInt);
  if (question == null)
  {
    // let it through so the controller can return
    // a 404
    context.Succeed(requirement);
    return;
  }

  if (question.UserId != userId)
  {
    context.Fail();
    return;
  }

  context.Succeed(requirement);
}
```

13. The final task is to add the policy we have just created to the `Authorize` attribute on the relevant action methods in `QuestionsController`:

    ```
    [Authorize(Policy = "MustBeQuestionAuthor")]
    [HttpPut("{questionId}")]
    public ... PutQuestion(int questionId, QuestionPutRequest
    questionPutRequest)
    ...

    [Authorize(Policy = "MustBeQuestionAuthor")]
    [HttpDelete("{questionId}")]
    public ... DeleteQuestion(int questionId)
    ...
    ```

    We have now applied our authorization policy to updating and deleting a question.

    Unfortunately, we can't use the test access token that Auth0 gives us to try this out but we will circle back to this and confirm that it works in *Chapter 12, Interacting with RESTful APIs*.

Custom authorization policies give us lots of flexibility and power to implement complex authorization rules. As we have just experienced in our example, a single policy can be implemented centrally and used on different action methods.

Let's quickly recap what we have learned in this section:

- We protect endpoints or particular HTTP methods within an endpoint by decorating the controller class or the action methods with the `Authorize` attribute.

- We can reference a custom authorization policy in the `Authorize` attribute and implement its logic by extending the `AuthorizationHandler` class.

In the next section, we will learn how to reference information about the authenticated user in an API controller.

Using the authenticated user when posting questions and answers

Now that our REST API knows about the user interacting with it, we can use this to post the correct user against questions and answers. Let's carry out the following steps:

1. We'll start by adding the following `using` statements in `QuestionsController.cs`:

    ```
    using System.Security.Claims;
    using Microsoft.Extensions.Configuration;
    using System.Net.Http;
    using System.Text.Json;
    ```

2. Let's focus on posting a question first by posting it with the authenticated user's ID:

    ```
    public async ...
      PostQuestion(QuestionPostRequest
        questionPostRequest)
    {
      var savedQuestion =
        await _dataRepository.PostQuestion(new
          QuestionPostFullRequest
          {
            Title = questionPostRequest.Title,
            Content = questionPostRequest.Content,
            UserId =
            User.FindFirst(ClaimTypes.NameIdentifier).Value,
            UserName = "bob.test@test.com",
            Created = DateTime.UtcNow
          });
      ...
    }
    ```

`ControllerBase` contains a `User` property that gives us information about the authenticated user, including the claims. So, we use the `FindFirst` method to get the value of the name identifier claim.

3. Unfortunately, the username isn't in the JWT, so we are going to need to get this from Auth0. Let's create a model that will represent an Auth0 user. Create a new class called User in the Models folder with the following content:

```
namespace QandA.Data.Models
{
    public class User
    {
        public string Name { get; set; }
    }
}
```

Note that there is more user information that we can get from Auth0 but we are only interested in the username in our app.

4. Now, inject the HTTP client as well as the path to get information about the user from Auth0 into QuestionsController:

```
...
private readonly IHttpClientFactory _clientFactory;
private readonly string _auth0UserInfo;

public QuestionsController(
    ...,
    IHttpClientFactory clientFactory,
    IConfiguration configuration)
{
    ...
    _clientFactory = clientFactory;
    _auth0UserInfo =
        $"{configuration["Auth0:Authority"]}userinfo";
}
```

5. Let's create a method that will call Auth0 to get the username. So, add the following method at the bottom of QuestionsController:

```
private async Task<string> GetUserName()
{
    var request = new HttpRequestMessage(
        HttpMethod.Get,
        _auth0UserInfo);
    request.Headers.Add(
        "Authorization",
        Request.Headers["Authorization"].First());

    var client = _clientFactory.CreateClient();
```

```
            var response = await client.SendAsync(request);

            if (response.IsSuccessStatusCode)
            {
                var jsonContent =
                    await response.Content.ReadAsStringAsync();
                var user =
                    JsonSerializer.Deserialize<User>(
                        jsonContent,
                        new JsonSerializerOptions
                        {
                            PropertyNameCaseInsensitive = true
                        });
                return user.Name;
            }
            else
            {
                return "";
            }
}
```

We make a GET HTTP request to the Auth0 user information endpoint with the `Authorization` HTTP header from the current request to the ASP.NET backend. This HTTP header will contain the access token that will give us access to the Auth0 endpoint.

If the request is successful, we parse the response body into our `User` model. Notice that we use the new JSON serializer in .NET. Notice also that we specify case-insensitive property mapping so that the camel case fields in the response map correctly to the title case properties in the class.

6. Use the username in the `PostQuestion` method now:

```
public async ... PostQuestion(QuestionPostRequest
questionPostRequest)
{
   var savedQuestion = await
     _dataRepository.PostQuestion(new
   QuestionPostFullRequest
     {
       Title = questionPostRequest.Title,
       Content = questionPostRequest.Content,
       UserId =
       User.FindFirst(ClaimTypes.NameIdentifier).Value,
```

```
        UserName = await GetUserName(),
        Created = DateTime.UtcNow
    });
    ...
}
```

7. Do the same in the `PostAnswer` action method:

```
[Authorize]
[HttpPost("answer")]
public ActionResult<AnswerGetResponse>
PostAnswer(AnswerPostRequest answerPostRequest)
{
    ...
    var savedAnswer = _dataRepository.PostAnswer(new
      AnswerPostFullRequest
      {
        QuestionId = answerPostRequest.QuestionId.Value,
        Content = answerPostRequest.Content,
        UserId =
        User.FindFirst(ClaimTypes.NameIdentifier).Value,
        UserName = await GetUserName(),
        Created = DateTime.UtcNow
    });
    ...
}
```

Unfortunately, we can't use the test access token that Auth0 gives us to try this out because it doesn't have a user associated with it. However, we will circle back to this and confirm that it works in *Chapter 12, Interacting with RESTful APIs*.

Our question controller is interacting with the authenticated user nicely now.

To recap, information about the authenticated user is available in a `User` property within an API controller. The information in the `User` property is limited to the information contained in the JWT. Additional information can be obtained by requesting it from the relevant endpoint in the identity service provider.

Adding CORS

CORS stands for **Cross-Origin Resource Sharing** and is a mechanism that uses HTTP headers to tell a browser to let a web application run at certain origins (domains) so that it has permission to access certain resources on a server at a different origin.

Adding CORS   389

In this section, we will start by trying to access our REST API from a browser application and discover that it isn't accessible. We will then add and configure CORS in the REST API and verify that it is accessible from a browser application.

Let's carry out the following steps:

1. Run the backend project by pressing *F5* in Visual Studio.
2. In a browser, browse to `https://resttesttest.com/` address. This is a browser application that we can use to check whether our REST API is accessible from a browser.
3. Enter the path to the `questions` endpoint and press the **Ajax request** button. We see that the request is unsuccessful:

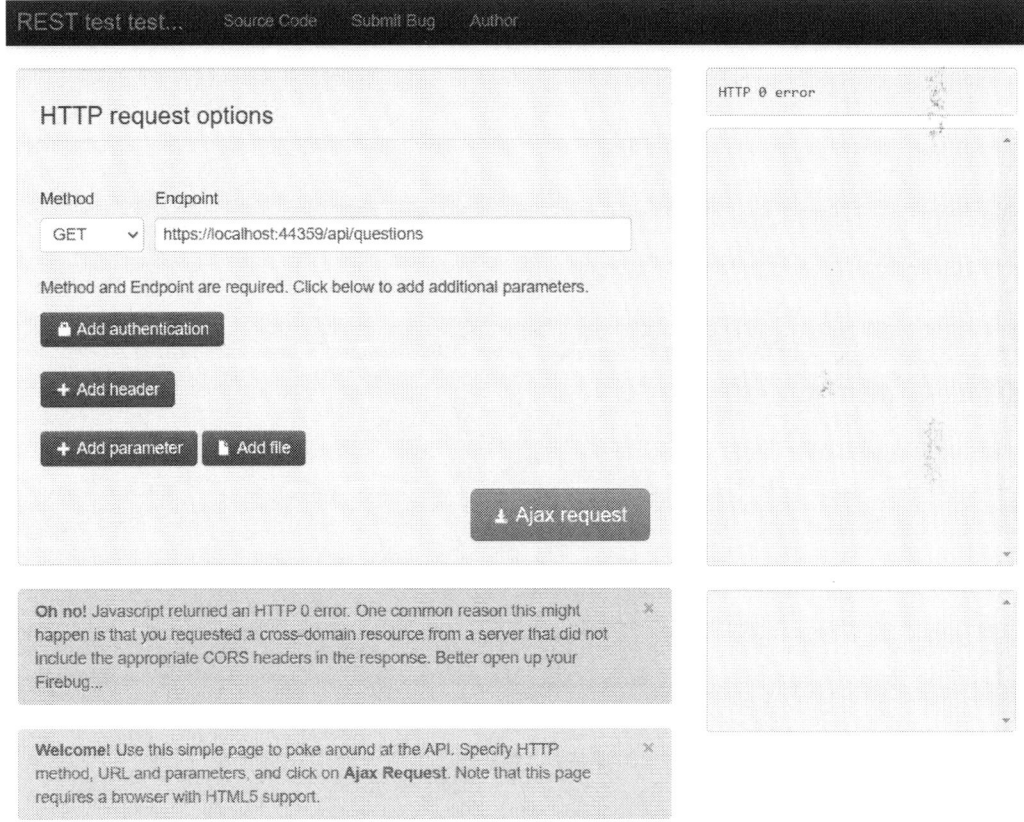

Figure 11.12 – CORS error when accessing the REST API from the browser

4. Stop the backend from running by pressing *Shift + F5* in Visual Studio and enter the following statement at the bottom of the `ConfigureServices` method in `Startup.cs`:

```
public void ConfigureServices(IServiceCollection
services)
{
   ...
   services.AddCors(options =>
     options.AddPolicy("CorsPolicy", builder =>
       builder
         .AllowAnyMethod()
         .AllowAnyHeader()
         .WithOrigins(Configuration["Frontend"])));
}
```

This has defined a CORS policy that allows origins specified in `appsettings.json` to access the REST API. It also allows requests with any HTTP method and any HTTP header.

5. Now, we can enable the use of this policy in the `Configure` method. Let's add the following statement between the routing and authentication in the `Configure` method:

```
public void Configure(IApplicationBuilder app,
IHostingEnvironment env)
{
   ...
   app.Routing();
   app.UseCors("CorsPolicy");
   app.UseAuthentication();
   ...
}
```

6. In `appsettings.json`, add the following setting to allow the browser app access to the REST API:

```
{
   ...,
   "Frontend": "https://resttesttest.com"
}
```

7. Run the backend project again by pressing *F5*.

8. In the browser app, press the **Ajax request** button again. We see that the request is successful this time:

```
HTTP 200 success
```

```
[{"questionId":1,"title":"Why should I learn TypeScript?","content":"TypeScript s
eems to be getting popular so I wondered whether it is worth my time learning it?
 What benefits does it give over JavaScript?","userName":"bob.test@test.com","crea
```

Figure 11.13 – Successful cross-origin request

9. Stop the backend from running by pressing *Shift* + *F5* in Visual Studio. In `appsettings.json`, change the `Frontend` setting to the local address of our frontend:

```
{
    ...,
    "Frontend": "http://localhost:3000"
}
```

CORS is straightforward to add in ASP.NET. First, we create a policy and use this in the request pipeline. It is important that the `UseCors` method is placed between the `UseRouting` and `UseEndpoint` methods in the `Configure` method for it to function correctly.

Summary

Auth0 is an OIDC identity provider that we can leverage to authenticate and authorize clients. An access token in JWT format is available from an identity provider when a successful sign-in has been made. An access token can be used in requests to access protected resources.

ASP.NET can validate JWTs by first using the `AddAuthentication` method in the `ConfigureServices` method in the `Startup` class and then `UseAuthentication` in the `Configure` method.

Once authentication has been added to the request pipeline, REST API resources can be protected by decorating the controller and action methods using the `Authorize` attribute. Protected action methods can then be unprotected by using the `AllowAnonymous` attribute. We can access information about a user, such as their claims, via a controller's `User` property.

Custom policies are a powerful way to allow a certain set of users to get access to protected resources. Requirement and handler classes must be implemented that define the policy logic. The policy can be applied to an endpoint using the `Authorize` attribute by passing in the policy name as a parameter.

ASP.NET disallows cross-origin requests out of the box. We are required to add and enable a CORS policy for the web clients that require access to the REST API.

Our backend is close to completion now. In the next chapter, we'll turn our attention back to the frontend and start to interact with the backend we have built.

Questions

Let's answer the following questions to practice what we have learned in this chapter:

1. In the `Configure` method in the `Startup` class, what is wrong with the following?

   ```
   public void Configure(...)
   {
       ...

       app.UseEndpoints(...);
       app.UseAuthentication();
   }
   ```

2. What attribute can be added to a protected action method to allow unauthenticated users to access it?

3. We are building an app with an ASP.NET backend and using an identity provider to authenticate users. The default audience has been set to `http://my-app` in the identity provider, and we have configured the authentication service in our ASP.NET backend as follows:

   ```
   services.AddAuthentication(options =>
   {
       options.DefaultAuthenticateScheme =
         JwtBearerDefaults.AuthenticationScheme;
       options.DefaultChallengeScheme =
         JwtBearerDefaults.AuthenticationScheme;
   }).AddJwtBearer(options =>
   {
       ...
       options.Audience = "https://myapp";
   });
   ```

When we try to access protected resources in our ASP.NET backend, we receive an HTTP 401 status code. What is the problem here?

4. A JWT has the following decoded payload data. On what date and time does it expire?

```
{
    "nbf": 1609671475,
    "auth_time": 1609671475,
    "exp": 1609757875,
    ...
}
```

Tip: You can decode the Unix dates using this website: https://www.unixtimestamp.com/index.php.

5. We have a valid access token from an identity provider and are using it to access a protected resource. We have set the following HTTP header in the request:

```
Authorisation: bearer some-access-token
```

We receive an HTTP 401 status code from the request, though. What is the problem?

6. How can we access HTTP request information in a class outside of an API controller?

7. In an API controller, how can we access an authenticated user ID?

Answers

1. The problem is that authentication comes after the endpoints are handled in the request pipeline, which means that the user will always be unauthenticated in controller action methods even if the request has a valid access token. This means that protected resources will never be able to be accessed. `UseAuthentication` should come before `UseEndpoints` in the `Configure` method.

2. An `AllowAnonymous` attribute can be added to a protected action method to allow unauthenticated users to access it.

3. The problem is that the ASP.NET Core backend validates that the audience in the JWT is https://myapp, but the identity provider has been configured to set the audience to http://my-app. This results in the request being unauthorized.

4. The `exp` field gives the expiry date, which is 1609757875 seconds after January 1, 1970, which, in turn, is January 4, 2021, 10:57:55 (GMT).

5. The problem is that the HTTP header name needs to be `Authorization` – that is, we have spelled it with an *s* rather than a *z*.
6. Request information can be accessed by injecting `IHttpContextAccessor` into a class as follows:

   ```
   private readonly IHttpContextAccessor _
   httpContextAccessor;

   public MyClass(IHttpContextAccessor httpContextAccessor)
   {
     _httpContextAccessor = httpContextAccessor;
   }

   public SomeMethod()
   {
     var request = _httpContextAccessor.HttpContext.Request;
   }
   ```

   The `HttpContextAccessor` service must be added to the `ConfigureServices` method in the `Startup` class, as follows:

   ```
   services.AddSingleton<IHttpContextAccessor, HttpContextAccessor>();
   ```

7. We can access the user ID in the controller's `User` property as follows:

   ```
   User.FindFirst(ClaimTypes.NameIdentifier).Value
   ```

Further reading

Here are some useful links to learn more about the topics covered in this chapter:

- **Open ID ConnectOIDC**: https://openid.net/connect/
- **ASP.NET Security and Identity**: https://docs.microsoft.com/en-us/aspnet/core/security
- **JSON Web Tokens**: https://jwt.io/introduction/
- **Auth0**: https://auth0.com/docs

12
Interacting with RESTful APIs

Having completed our REST API, it's now time to interact with it in our React frontend app. We will start by interacting with the unauthenticated endpoints to get questions by using the browser's `fetch` function. We will deal with the situation when a user navigates away from a page before data is fetched, preventing state errors.

We will leverage the Auth0 tenant that we set up in the last chapter to securely sign users in and out of our app. We will then use the access token from Auth0 to access protected endpoints. We will also make sure that authenticated users are only able to see options that they have permission to perform.

By the end of this chapter, our frontend will be interacting fully with the backend, securely and robustly.

In this chapter, we'll cover the following topics:

- Using `fetch` to interact with unauthenticated REST API endpoints
- Interacting with Auth0 from the frontend
- Controlling authenticated options
- Using `fetch` to interact with authenticated REST API endpoints
- Aborting data fetching

Technical requirements

We'll use the following tools and services in this chapter:

- **Visual Studio Code**: We'll use this to edit our React code. This can be downloaded and installed from `https://code.visualstudio.com/`.

- **Node.js and npm**: These can be downloaded from `https://nodejs.org/`. If you already have these installed, make sure that Node.js is at least version 8.2 and that `npm` is at least version 5.2.

- **Visual Studio 2019**: We'll use this to run our ASP.NET Core code backend. This can be downloaded and installed from `https://visualstudio.microsoft.com/vs/`.

- **.NET 5**: This can be downloaded from `https://dotnet.microsoft.com/download/dotnet/5.0`.

- **Auth0**: We will use the tenant we set up in the last chapter to authenticate and manage users.

- **Q and A**: We'll start with the Q and A frontend project that is available on GitHub at `https://github.com/PacktPublishing/ASP.NET-Core-5-and-React-Second-Edition` in the `chapter-12/start` folder. It is important to start from this project for all of the code to work correctly in this chapter.

All of the code snippets in this chapter can be found online at `https://github.com/PacktPublishing/ASP.NET-Core-5-and-React-Second-Edition`. To restore code from a chapter, the source code repository can be downloaded and the relevant folder opened in the relevant editor. If the code is frontend code, then `npm install` can be entered in the Terminal to restore the dependencies.

Check out the following video to see the code in action: `https://bit.ly/37CQqNx`

Using fetch to interact with unauthenticated REST API endpoints

In this section, we are going to use the native `fetch` function to get unanswered questions from our real REST API. We are then going to use a wrapper function over `fetch` to make interacting with our backend a little easier. This approach will also centralize the code that interacts with the REST API, which is beneficial when we want to make improvements to it. We'll then move on to using the real REST API to get a single question and search for questions.

Getting unanswered questions from the REST API

We are going to start interacting with the REST API on the home page when displaying the list of unanswered questions. The `HomePage` component won't actually change, but the `getUnansweredQuestions` function in `QuestionsData.ts` will. In `getUnansweredQuestions`, we'll leverage the native browser `fetch` function to interact with our REST API. If you haven't already, let's open Visual Studio Code and carry out the following steps.

Open `QuestionsData.ts`, find the `getUnansweredQuestions` function, and replace the implementation with the following content:

```
export const getUnansweredQuestions = async (): Promise<
  QuestionData[]
> => {
  let unansweredQuestions: QuestionData[] = [];

  // TODO - call api/questions/unanswered
  // TODO - put response body in unansweredQuestions

  return unansweredQuestions;
};
```

The function takes exactly the same parameters and returns the same type as before, so the components that consume this function shouldn't be impacted by the changes we are about to make. Follow the steps given here:

1. Let's call `fetch` to request unanswered questions from our backend:

   ```
   export const getUnansweredQuestions = async (): Promise<
     QuestionData[]
   > => {
     let unansweredQuestions: QuestionData[] = [];
     const response = await fetch(
       'http://localhost:17525/api/questions/unanswered'
     )

     // TODO - put response body in unansweredQuestions

     return unansweredQuestions;
   };
   ```

So, for a `GET` request, we simply put the path we are requesting in the `fetch` argument. If your REST API is running on a different port, then don't forget to change the path so that it calls your REST API.

Notice the `await` keyword before the `fetch` call. This is because it is an asynchronous function and we want to wait for its promises to be resolved before the next statement is executed.

We have assigned a `response` variable to the HTTP response object that is returned from the `fetch` function. Here are some useful properties on the `response` object that we could interact with:

- `ok`: Whether the response was successful (in other words, whether the HTTP status code is in the range 200-299)
- `status`: The HTTP status code for the response
- `headers`: An object that gives access to the headers in the HTTP response

2. There is also a method called `json` on the response object. This can be used to request the parsed JSON body. Add the highlighted line underneath the call to the `fetch` function:

```
export const getUnansweredQuestions = async (): Promise<
  QuestionData[]
> => {
  let unansweredQuestions: QuestionData[] = [];
  const response = await fetch(
    "http://localhost:17525/api/questions/unanswered"
  );
  unansweredQuestions = await response.json();
  return unansweredQuestions;
};
```

3. Before we give this a try, open the backend project in Visual Studio and substitute the Auth0 tenant ID into the `Authority` setting in `appsettings.json`.

We have already discovered where to find our Auth0 tenant in the last chapter but, as a reminder, it is to the left of our user avatar:

Figure 12.1 – Auth0 tenant ID

4. Press *F5* to start the backend running. We'll leave this running for the whole of this chapter.

5. Back in Visual Studio Code, start our frontend by typing `npm start` in the Terminal. When the app runs, we get the following error:

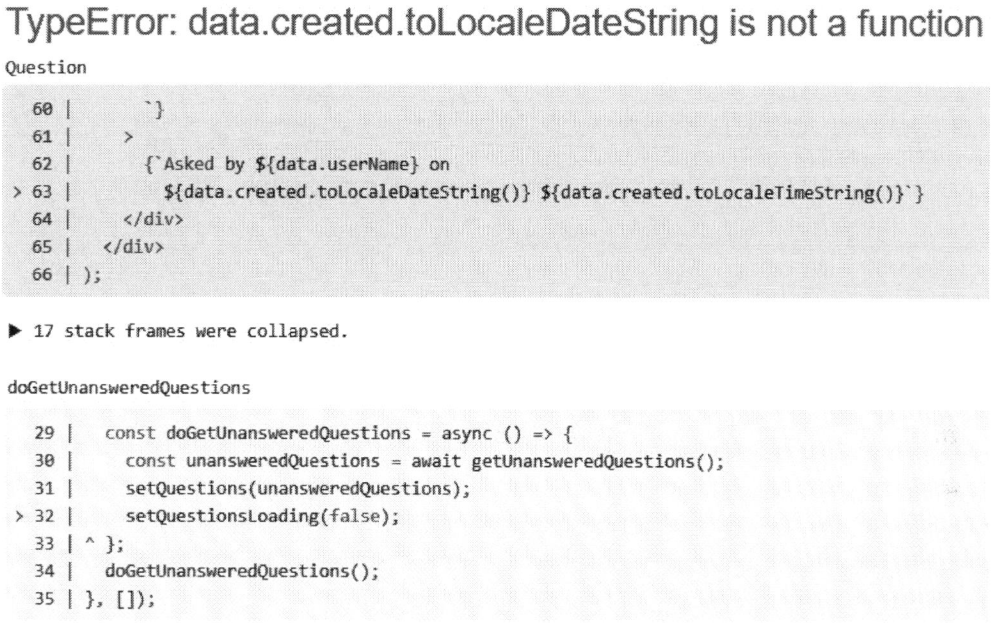

TypeError: data.created.toLocaleDateString is not a function

Question

```
60 |       `}
61 |     >
62 |       {`Asked by ${data.userName} on
> 63 |         ${data.created.toLocaleDateString()} ${data.created.toLocaleTimeString()}`}
64 |     </div>
65 |   </div>
66 | );
```

▶ 17 stack frames were collapsed.

doGetUnansweredQuestions

```
29 |   const doGetUnansweredQuestions = async () => {
30 |     const unansweredQuestions = await getUnansweredQuestions();
31 |     setQuestions(unansweredQuestions);
> 32 |     setQuestionsLoading(false);
33 |   ^ };
34 |   doGetUnansweredQuestions();
35 | }, []);
```

Figure 12.2 – Error on question created date

The problem here is that the `created` property is deserialized as a string and not a `Date` object like the `Question` component expects.

6. Let's resolve this by mapping the `created` property to a `Date` object in the `return` statement:

```
export const getUnansweredQuestions = async (): Promise<
  QuestionData[]
> => {
  let unansweredQuestions: QuestionData[] = [];
  const response = await fetch(
    'http://localhost:17525/api/questions/unanswered',
  );
  unansweredQuestions = await response.json();
  return unansweredQuestions.map((question) => ({
    ...question,
    created: new Date(question.created),
  }));
};
```

We use the array `map` function to iterate through all of the questions, returning a copy of the original question (using the spread syntax) and then overwriting the `created` property with a `Date` object from the `string` date.

7. If we save the file and look at the running app, we'll see the unanswered questions output correctly:

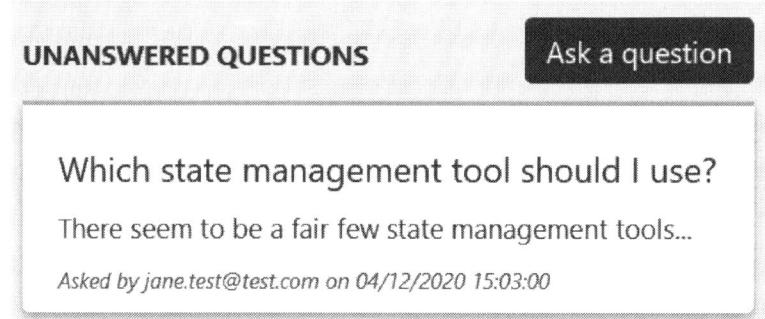

Figure 12.3: Unanswered questions output correctly

Great stuff! Our React app is now interacting with our REST API!

Extracting out a generic HTTP http function

We'll need to use the `fetch` function in every function that needs to interact with the REST API. So, we are going to create a generic `http` function that we'll use to make all of our HTTP requests. This will nicely centralize the code that calls the REST API. Let's carry out the following steps:

1. Create a new file called `http.ts` with the following content:

   ```
   import { webAPIUrl } from './AppSettings';

   export interface HttpRequest<REQB> {
     path: string;
   }
   export interface HttpResponse<RESB> {
     ok: boolean;
     body?: RESB;
   }
   ```

   We've started by importing the root path to our REST API from `AppSettings.ts`, which was set up in our starter project. The `AppSettings.ts` file is where we will build all of the different paths that will vary between development and production. Make sure `webAPIUrl` contains the correct path for your REST API.

We have also defined interfaces for the request and response. Notice that the interfaces contain a generic parameter for the type of the body in the request and response.

2. Let's use these interfaces to implement a generic `http` function that we'll use to make HTTP requests:

```
export const http = async <
  RESB,
  REQB = undefined
>(
  config: HttpRequest<REQB>,
): Promise<HttpResponse<RESB>> => {
};
```

We have defaulted the type for the request body to `undefined` so that the consumer of the function doesn't need to pass it.

3. Use `fetch` to invoke the request:

```
export const http = async <
  RESB,
  REQB = undefined
>(
  config: HttpRequest<REQB>,
): Promise<HttpResponse<RESB>> => {
  const request = new Request(
    `${webAPIUrl}${config.path}`
  );
  const response = await fetch(request);
};
```

Notice that we create a new instance of a `Request` object and pass that into `fetch` rather than just passing the request path into `fetch`. This will be useful later in this chapter as we expand this function for different HTTP methods and authentication.

4. Let's check whether the request was successful by checking the `ok` property in the `response` object:

```
export const http = async <
  RESB,
  REQB = undefined
>(
  config: HttpRequest<REQB>,
): Promise<HttpResponse<RESB>> => {
  const request = new Request(
```

```
    `${webAPIUrl}${config.path}`,
  );
  const response = await fetch(request);
  if (response.ok) {
  } else {
  }
};
```

5. If the request is successful, we can get the body using the json method in the response object:

```
export const http = async <
  RESB,
  REQB = undefined
>(
  config: HttpRequest<REQB>,
): Promise<HttpResponse<RESB>> => {
  const request = new Request(
    `${webAPIUrl}${config.path}`,
  );
  const response = await fetch(request);
  if (response.ok) {
    const body = await response.json();
  } else {
  }
};
```

6. Return the response object with its parsed body for a successful request and just the response object for an unsuccessful request:

```
export const http = async <
  RESB,
  REQB = undefined
>(
  config: HttpRequest<REQB>,
): Promise<HttpResponse<RESB>> => {
  const request = new Request(
    `${webAPIUrl}${config.path}`,
  );
  const response = await fetch(request);
  if (response.ok) {
    const body = await response.json();
    return { ok: response.ok, body };
  } else {
    return { ok: response.ok };
```

```
    }
  };
```

If the response isn't successful, we are going to log the HTTP error.

7. Let's invoke a function called `logError` to do this, which we will implement in the next step. Place the function call just before the unsuccessful response is returned and pass both the `request` and `response` objects to it:

```
export const http = async <
  RESB,
  REQB = undefined
>(
  config: HttpRequest<REQB>,
): Promise<HttpResponse<RESB>> => {
  const request = new Request(
    `${webAPIUrl}${config.path}`,
  );
  const response = await fetch(request);
  if (response.ok) {
    const body = await response.json();
    return { ok: response.ok, body };
  } else {
    logError(request, response);
    return { ok: response.ok };
  }
};
```

8. Add the following `logError` function below the `http` function:

```
const logError = async (
  request: Request,
  response: Response,
) => {
  const contentType = response.headers.get(
    'content-type',
  );
  let body: any;
  if (
    contentType &&
    contentType.indexOf('application/json') !== -1
  ) {
    body = await response.json();
  } else {
    body = await response.text();
  }
```

```
      console.error(
        `Error requesting ${request.method}
        ${request.url}`,
        body,
      );
    };
```

The function checks whether the response is in JSON format and if so calls the `json` method on the response object to get the JSON body. If the response isn't in JSON format, then the body is retrieved using the `text` method on the response object. The body of the response is then output to the console along with the HTTP request method and path.

9. Go back to `QuestionData.ts` and leverage the `http` function we have just implemented in `getUnansweredQuestions`. First, we need to import it:

```
import { http } from './http';
```

10. We can now refactor `getUnansweredQuestions`:

```
export const getUnansweredQuestions = async (): Promise<
  QuestionData[]
> => {
  const result = await http<
    QuestionDataFromServer[]
  >({
    path: '/questions/unanswered',
  });
  if (result.ok && result.body) {
    return result.body.map(mapQuestionFromServer);
  } else {
    return [];
  }
};
```

We pass `QuestionDataFromServer[]` as the expected `response` into the `http` function as the expected response body type. `QuestionDataFromServer` is an interface that was added to our starter project for this chapter that has the `created` date as a string—exactly how it arrives from the REST API.

We use a mapping function to return the parsed response body with the `created` property set as a proper date if there is a response body. Otherwise, we return an empty array. The `mapQuestionFromServer` mapping function was added to our starter project for this chapter.

This renders the unanswered questions when we save these changes, as it did before:

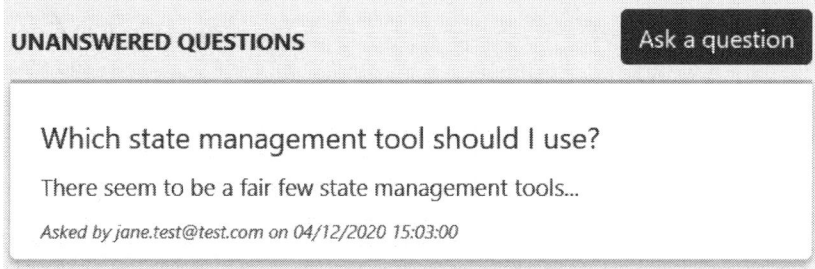

Figure 12.4 – Unanswered questions output correctly

Our revised implementation of `getUnansweredQuestions` is a little better because the root path to our REST API isn't hardcoded within it and we are handling HTTP errors better. We'll continue to use and expand our generic `http` function throughout this chapter.

Getting a question from the REST API

In this sub-section, we are going to refactor our existing `getQuestion` function to use our `http` function to get a single question from our REST API. Carry out the following steps in `QuestionsData.ts`:

1. We'll start by clearing out the current implementation, like so:

   ```
   export const getQuestion = async (
     questionId: number,
   ): Promise<QuestionData | null> => {

   };
   ```

2. Let's make the HTTP request to get the question:

   ```
   export const getQuestion = async (
     questionId: number,
   ): Promise<QuestionData | null> => {
     const result = await http<
       QuestionDataFromServer
     >({
       path: `/questions/${questionId}`,
     });
   };
   ```

3. Return the response body with correctly typed dates if the request is successful or return `null` if the response isn't successful:

    ```
    export const getQuestion = async (
      questionId: number,
    ): Promise<QuestionData | null> => {
      const result = await http<
        QuestionDataFromServer
      >({
        path: `/questions/${questionId}`,
      });
      if (result.ok && result.body) {
        return mapQuestionFromServer(result.body);
      } else {
        return null;
      }
    };
    ```

4. When we save the changes and go to the question page in the running app, we will see the question correctly rendered on the screen:

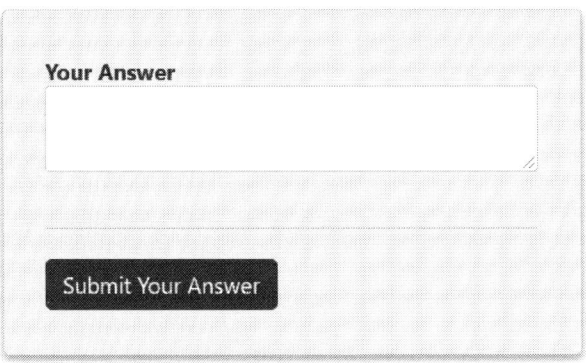

Figure 12.5 – Question page

We didn't have to make any changes to any of the frontend components. Nice!

Searching questions with the REST API

In this sub-section, we are going to refactor our existing `searchQuestion` function to use our `http` function to use our REST API to search questions. This is very similar to what we have just done, so we'll do this in one go:

```
export const searchQuestions = async (
  criteria: string,
): Promise<QuestionData[]> => {
  const result = await http<
    QuestionDataFromServer[]
  >({
    path: `/questions?search=${criteria}`,
  });
  if (result.ok && result.body) {
    return result.body.map(mapQuestionFromServer);
  } else {
    return [];
  }
};
```

We make a request to the `questions` endpoint with the `search` query parameter containing the criteria. We return the response body with created `Date` objects if the request is successful or an empty array if the request fails.

The `searchQuestions` parameter and return type haven't changed. So, when we save the changes and search for a question in the running app, the matched questions will render correctly:

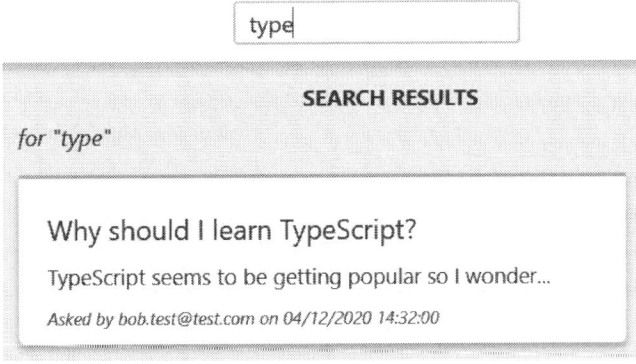

Figure 12.6 – Search page

In the next section, we will take a break from implementing our generic `http` function and implement code to sign users in to our app via our Auth0.

Interacting with Auth0 from the frontend

In this section, we will fully implement the sign-in and sign-out processes from our React frontend. We are going to interact with Auth0 as a part of these processes.

We will start by installing the Auth0 JavaScript client before creating React Router routes and logic to handle the Auth0 sign-in and sign-out processes.

We will also learn about React context in this section. We will use this React feature to centralize information and functions for authentication that components can easily access.

Installing the Auth0 JavaScript client

There is a standard Auth0 JavaScript library for single-page applications that we can leverage that will interact nicely with Auth0. The npm package for the library is called @auth0/auth0-spa-js. Let's install this by running the following command in the Visual Studio Code Terminal:

```
> npm install @auth0/auth0-spa-js
```

TypeScript types are included in this library, so the Auth0 client library for single-page applications is now installed in our project.

Recapping the sign-in and sign-out flows

Let's quickly recap the sign-in flow between our app and Auth0:

1. Our app redirects to Auth0 to allow the user to enter their credentials.
2. After the user has successfully signed in, Auth0 redirects back to our app with a code.
3. Our app can then request an access token from Auth0 with the code.

The sign-out flow is as follows:

1. Our app redirects to Auth0 to perform the logout.
2. A redirect then occurs back to our app.

So, we will have the following routes in our frontend app:

- `/signin`: Our app will navigate to this page to start the sign-in process. This page will call a method in the Auth0 client, which will redirect to a page in Auth0.
- `/signin-callback`: This is the page in our app that Auth0 will redirect back to with the code.
- `/signout`: Our app will navigate to this page to start the sign-out process. This page will call a method in the Auth0 client, which will redirect to a page in Auth0.
- `/signout-callback`: This is the page in our app that Auth0 will redirect back to after the logout has completed.

Creating the sign-in and sign-out routes

We now understand that we need four routes in our app to handle the sign-in and sign-out processes. The `SignInPage` component will handle both of the `signin` and `signin-callback` routes. The `SignOutPage` component will handle both of the `signout` and `signout-callback` routes.

Our app already knows about the `SignInPage` component with the route we have declared in `App.tsx`. However, it is not handling the sign-in callback from the Auth0. Our app also isn't handling signing out. Let's implement all of this in `App.tsx` by following these steps:

1. We'll start by importing the `SignOutPage` component into `App.tsx`. Add the following `import` statement under the `import` statement for `SignInPage`:

   ```
   import { SignOutPage } from './SignOutPage';
   ```

2. We will start with the sign-in route. Instead of just referencing the `SignInPage` component, we need to render it and pass `'signin'` in the `action` prop:

   ```
   <Route
     path="signin"
     element={<SignInPage action="signin" />}
   />
   ```

   The `action` prop doesn't exist yet on the `SignInPage` component; hence, our app will not compile at the moment. We'll implement the `action` prop later.

3. Next, let's add a sign-in callback route under the sign-in route:

```
<Route
  path="/signin-callback"
  element={<SignInPage action="signin-callback" />}
/>
```

4. Lastly, we'll implement the routes for the sign-out process:

```
<Route
  path="signout"
  element={
    <SignOutPage action="signout" />
  }
/>
<Route
  path="/signout-callback"
  element={
    <SignOutPage action="signout-callback" />
  }
/>
```

All of the routes are in place now for the sign-in, sign-up, and sign-out processes.

Implementing a central authentication context

We are going to put state and functions for authentication in a central place in our code. We could use Redux for this, but we are going to take this opportunity to use a **context** in React.

> **Important Note**
>
> React **context** is a standard feature in React that allows components to share data without having to pass it through component properties. More information on React context can be found at `https://reactjs.org/docs/context.html`.

We are going to put our authentication state and functions in a React context that we'll provide to all of the components in our app. Let's carry out the following steps:

1. Create a new file in the `src` folder called `Auth.tsx` with the following import statements:

   ```
   import React from 'react';
   import createAuth0Client from '@auth0/auth0-spa-js';
   import Auth0Client from '@auth0/auth0-spa-js/dist/typings/Auth0Client';
   import { authSettings } from './AppSettings';
   ```

2. We'll start the implementation by creating a strongly typed context. Add the following code under the `import` statements in `Auth.tsx`:

   ```
   interface Auth0User {
     name: string;
     email: string;
   }
   interface IAuth0Context {
     isAuthenticated: boolean;
     user?: Auth0User;
     signIn: () => void;
     signOut: () => void;
     loading: boolean;
   }
   export const Auth0Context = React.createContext<IAuth0Context>({
     isAuthenticated: false,
     signIn: () => {},
     signOut: () => {},
     loading: true
   });
   ```

   So, our context provides properties for whether the user is authenticated, the user's profile information, functions for signing in and out, and whether the context is loading.

   The `createContext` function requires a default value for the context, so we've passed in an object with appropriate initial property values and empty functions for signing in and out.

3. Let's provide a function that components can use to get access to the state and functions in the authentication context:

```
export const useAuth = () => React.
  useContext(Auth0Context);
```

This is a **custom hook** in React.

> **Important Note**
> Custom hooks are a mechanism for sharing logic in components. They allow the use of React components features such as `useState`, `useEffect`, and `useContext` outside a component. More information on custom hooks can be found at https://reactjs.org/docs/hooks-custom.html.

A common naming convention for custom hooks is to have a prefix of `use`. So, we've called our custom hook `useAuth`.

4. Next, implement a provider component for the context:

```
export const AuthProvider: React.FC = ({
  children,
}) => {
  const [
    isAuthenticated,
    setIsAuthenticated,
  ] = React.useState<boolean>(false);
  const [user, setUser] = React.useState<
    Auth0User | undefined
  >(undefined);
  const [
    auth0Client,
    setAuth0Client,
  ] = React.useState<Auth0Client>();
  const [loading, setLoading] = React.useState<
    boolean
  >(true);
};
```

We have used a standard type, `FC`, from the React types to type the component props. This contains a type for the `children` prop that we are using.

We have declared a state to hold whether the user is authenticated, the user's profile information, a client object from Auth0, and whether the context is loading.

5. Add the following JSX to the `Provider` component:

```
export const AuthProvider: React.FC = ({
  children,
}) => {
  ...
  return (
    <Auth0Context.Provider
      value={{
        isAuthenticated,
        user,
        signIn: () =>
          getAuth0ClientFromState().loginWithRedirect(),
        signOut: () =>
          getAuth0ClientFromState().logout({
            client_id: authSettings.client_id,
            returnTo:
              window.location.origin +
              '/signout-callback',
          }),
        loading,
      }}
    >
      {children}
    </Auth0Context.Provider>
  );
};
```

This returns the context's `Provider` component from React. The object we pass in the `value` property will be available to consumers of the context we are creating. So, we are giving consumers of the context access to whether the user is authenticated, the user's profile, and functions for signing in and out.

6. The functions for signing in and out reference a function called `getAuth0ClientFromState`, which isn't implemented yet. So, let's add this inside our provider component:

```
export const AuthProvider: FC = ({ children }) => {
  ...
  const getAuth0ClientFromState = () => {
    if (auth0Client === undefined) {
      throw new Error('Auth0 client not set');
    }
    return auth0Client;
  };
```

```
  return (
    <Auth0Context.Provider
      ...
    </Auth0Context.Provider>
  );
};
```

So, this function returns the Auth0 client from the state but throws an error if it is `undefined`.

7. When the provider is loaded, we want to create the instance of the Auth0 client and set the state values. Let's implement this using a `useEffect` Hook:

```
export const AuthProvider: FC = ({ children }) => {
  ...

  React.useEffect(() => {
    const initAuth0 = async () => {
      setLoading(true);
      const auth0FromHook = await
        createAuth0Client(authSettings);
      setAuth0Client(auth0FromHook);

      const isAuthenticatedFromHook = await
        auth0FromHook.isAuthenticated();
      if (isAuthenticatedFromHook) {
        const user = await auth0FromHook.getUser();
        setUser(user);
      }
      setIsAuthenticated(isAuthenticatedFromHook);
      setLoading(false);
    };
    initAuth0();
  }, []);

  ...

  return (
    <Auth0Context.Provider
      ...
    </Auth0Context.Provider>
  );
};
```

We've put the logic in a nested `initAuth0` function and invoked this because the logic is asynchronous.

We use the `createAuth0Client` function from Auth0 to create the Auth0 client instance. We pass in some settings using an `authSettings` variable, which is located in a file called `AppSettings.ts`. We'll change these settings later in this chapter to reference our specific Auth0 instance.

We call the `isAuthenticated` function in the Auth0 client to determine whether the user is authenticated and set our `isAuthenticated` state value. If the user is authenticated, we call the `getUser` function in the Auth0 client to get the user profile and set our `user` state.

8. We want to handle the sign-in callback when the provider loads, so let's add a branch of code to do that:

```
const initAuth0 = async () => {
  setLoading(true);
  const auth0FromHook = await
createAuth0Client(authSettings);
  setAuth0Client(auth0FromHook);

  if (
    window.location.pathname === '/signin-callback' &&
    window.location.search.indexOf('code=') > -1
  ) {
    await auth0FromHook.handleRedirectCallback();
    window.location.replace(window.location.origin);
  }

  const isAuthenticatedFromHook = await auth0FromHook.
   isAuthenticated();
  if (isAuthenticatedFromHook) {
    const user = await auth0FromHook.getUser();
    setUser(user);
  }
  setIsAuthenticated(isAuthenticatedFromHook);
  setLoading(false);
};
```

We call the Auth0 client `handleRedirectCallback` function, which will parse the URL, extract the code, and store it in a variable internally. We also redirect the user to the home page after this has been completed.

That's our authentication provider component complete.

9. The last item we are going to implement in Auth.tsx is a function that gets the access token:

```
export const getAccessToken = async () => {
  const auth0FromHook = await createAuth0Client(authSettings);
  const accessToken = await auth0FromHook.getTokenSilently();
  return accessToken;
};
```

This calls the Auth0 client `getTokenSilently` function, which will, in turn, make a request to the Auth0 `token` endpoint to get the access token securely.

We will use our `getAccessToken` function later in this chapter to make REST API requests to protected resources.

10. Let's move to App.tsx and import our authentication provider component:

```
import { AuthProvider } from './Auth';
```

11. Now, we'll provide the authentication context to all of the components in our app:

```
function App() {
  return (
    <AuthProvider>
      <BrowserRouter>
        ...
      </BrowserRouter>
    </AuthProvider>
  );
};
```

That's our central authentication context complete. We'll use this extensively throughout this chapter.

The `App` component still isn't compiling because of the missing `action` prop on the `SignInPage` and `SignOutPage` components. We'll resolve these issues next.

Implementing the sign-in process

Let's implement the sign-in page in `SignInPage.tsx` as follows:

1. We'll start by adding the following `import` statements:

   ```
   import { StatusText } from './Styles';
   import { useAuth } from './Auth';
   ```

   `StatusText` is a shared style we are going to use when we inform the user that we are redirecting to and from Auth0. `useAuth` is the custom Hook we implemented earlier that will give us access to the authentication context.

2. Let's define the `Props` type for the page component:

   ```
   type SigninAction = 'signin' | 'signin-callback';

   interface Props {
     action: SigninAction;
   }
   ```

   The component takes in an `action` prop that gives the current stage of the sign-in process.

3. We can start to implement the component now. Replace the current `SignInPage` component with the following:

   ```
   export const SignInPage = ({ action }: Props) => {
   };
   ```

4. Let's get the `signIn` function from the authentication context:

   ```
   export const SignInPage = ({ action }: Props) => {
     const { signIn } = useAuth();
   };
   ```

5. We can now call the `signIn` function if we are in the process of signing in:

   ```
   export const SignInPage = ({ action }: Props) => {
     const { signIn } = useAuth();
     if (action === 'signin') {
       signIn();
     }
   };
   ```

Our final task is to return the JSX:

```
export const SignInPage = ({ action }: Props) => {
  const { signIn } = useAuth();
  if (action === 'signin') {
    signIn();
  }
  return (
    <Page title="Sign In">
      <StatusText>Signing in ...</StatusText>
    </Page>
  );
};
```

We render the page informing the user that the sign-in process is taking place.

Implementing the sign-out process

Let's implement the sign-out page in `SignOutPage.tsx`, which is similar in structure to the `SignInPage` component. Replace the current content in `SignOutPage.tsx` with the following code:

```
import React from 'react';
import { Page } from './Page';
import { StatusText } from './Styles';
import { useAuth } from './Auth';

type SignoutAction = 'signout' | 'signout-callback';

interface Props {
  action: SignoutAction;
}

export const SignOutPage = ({ action }: Props) => {
  let message = 'Signing out ...';

  const { signOut } = useAuth();

  switch (action) {
    case 'signout':
      signOut();
      break;
    case 'signout-callback':
      message = 'You successfully signed out!';
      break;
  }
```

```
  return (
    <Page title="Sign out">
      <StatusText>{message}</StatusText>
    </Page>
  );
};
```

A slight difference is that when the component receives the callback, this component will stay in view with a message informing them that they have been successfully signed out.

Configuring Auth0 settings in our frontend

We are nearly ready to give the sign-in and sign-out processes a try. First, we need to configure our frontend to interact with the correct Auth0 tenant. These are configured in `AppSettings.ts`:

```
export const authSettings = {
  domain: 'your-domain',
  client_id: 'your-clientid',
  redirect_uri: window.location.origin + '/signin-
    callback',
  scope: 'openid profile QandAAPI email',
  audience: 'https://qanda',
};
```

We need to substitute our specific Auth0 domain and client ID in this settings file. We discovered where to find these details from Auth0 in the last chapter but, as a reminder, here are the steps:

1. On the Auth0 website, go to the **Applications** section. The client ID is against our Q and A single-page application:

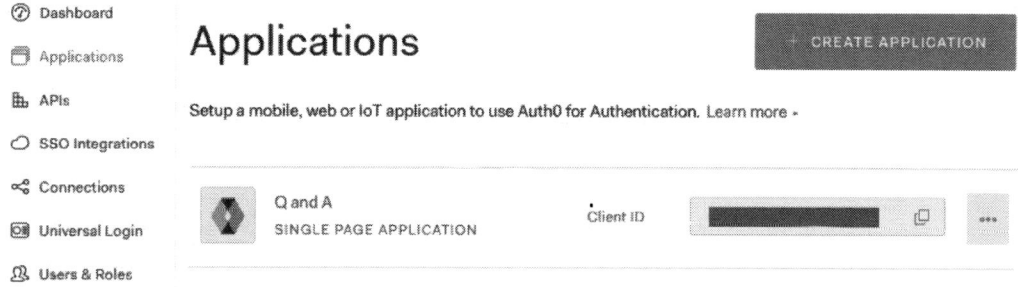

Figure 12.7 – Auth0 client ID

2. Click on the Q and A single-page application list item and go to the **Settings** tab. The domain is available in one of the fields in this tab:

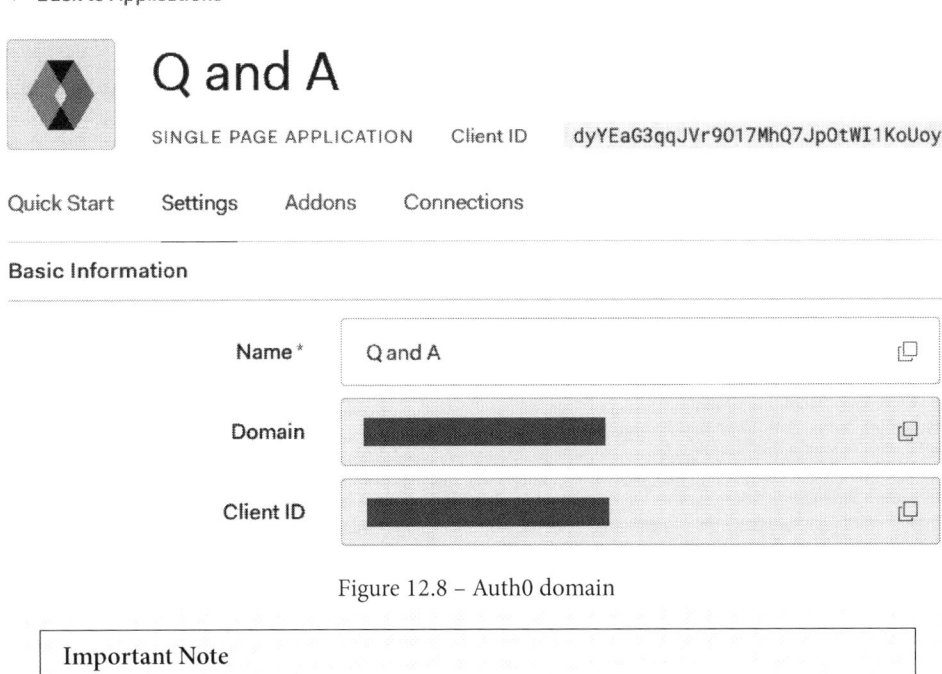

Figure 12.8 – Auth0 domain

> **Important Note**
> The `domain` setting doesn't include `https://` at the front.

3. Go to the **APIs** section in the left panel. The audience is visible against the Q and A API:

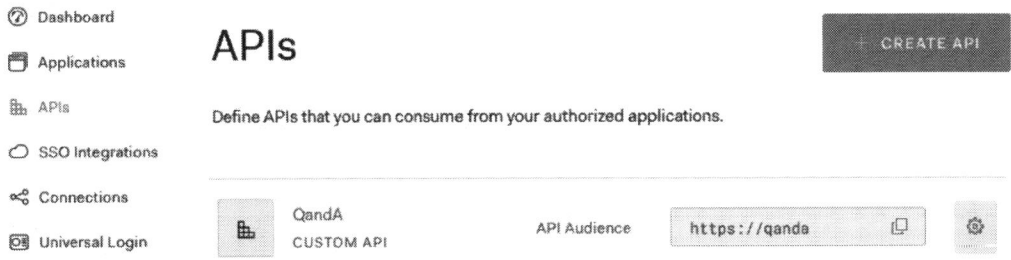

Figure 12.9 – Auth0 API audience

We are now ready to try the sign-in and sign-out processes.

Testing the sign-in and sign-out processes

All of the pieces are in place now to give the sign-in and sign-out processes a try. Let's carry out the following steps:

1. First, we need to create an Auth0 user to sign in with. In Auth0, on the left-hand navigation menu, choose **Users & Roles | Users** and then click the **Create User** button. Fill in the form with the user we want to create and click the **CREATE** button:

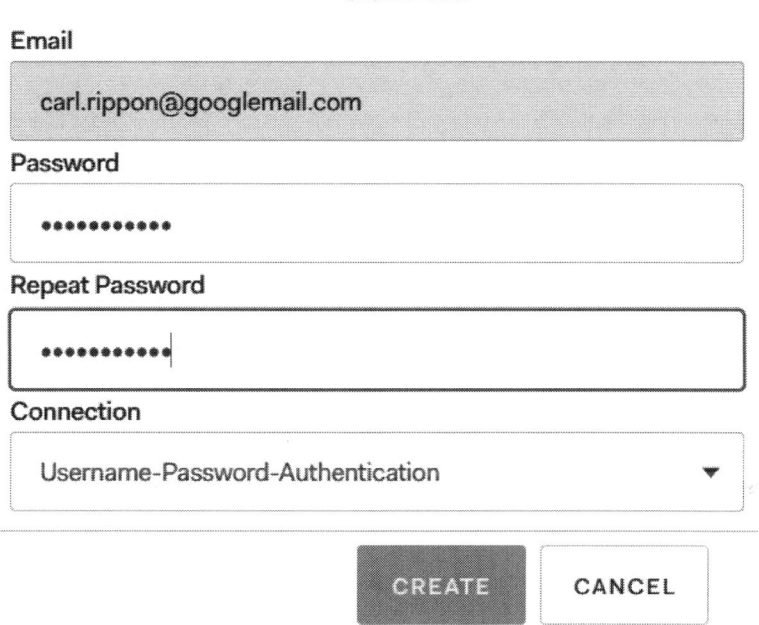

Figure 12.10 – Adding a new user in Auth0

2. Let's make sure both the backend and frontend are running. Then, we can click the **Sign In** button in the header of the frontend. We are redirected to Auth0 to log in:

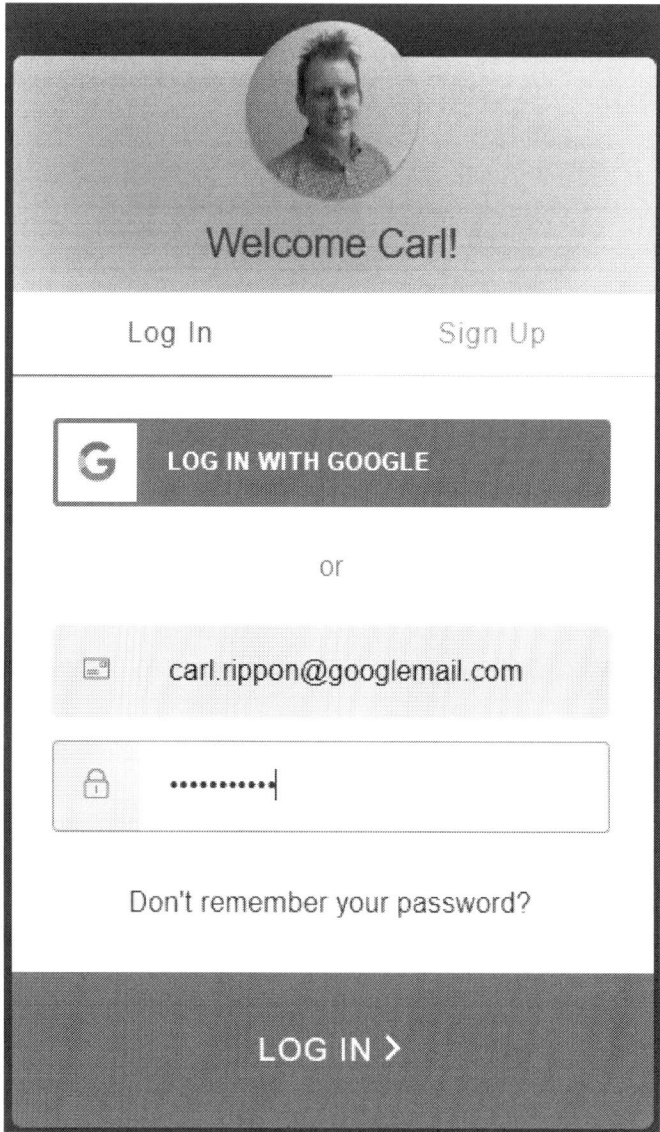

Figure 12.11 – Auth0 login form

3. After entering the user's credentials, click the **LOG IN** button. We are then asked to authorize the **Q and A** app to access the profile and email data:

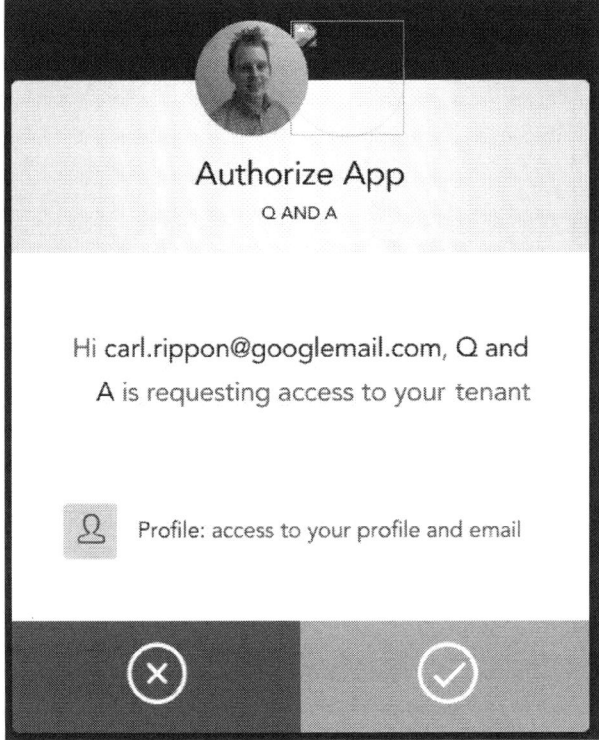

Figure 12.12 – App authorization in Auth0

This authorization process happens because this is the first login for this user.

4. After clicking on the tick icon, we will be successfully logged in and redirected back to our frontend.

5. Now, let's click the **Sign Out** button. The browser briefly navigates to Auth0 to log the user out and then redirects to our sign-out callback page:

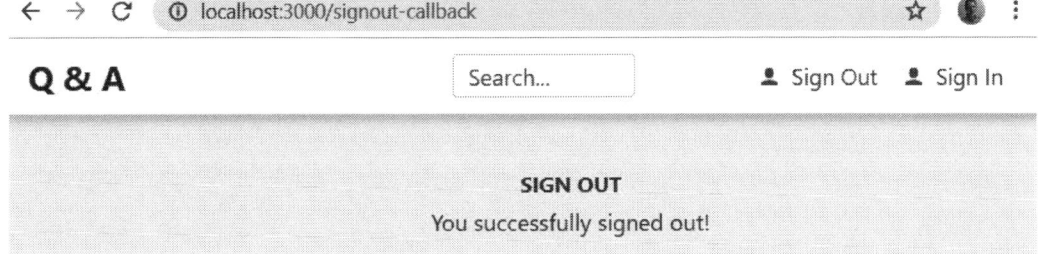

Figure 12.13: Sign-out confirmation message

That completes the sign-in and sign-out process implementations.

At the moment, all of the options in our app are visible regardless of whether the user is authenticated. However, certain options will only function correctly if the user is signed in. For example, if we try submitting a question while not signed in, it will fail. We'll clean this up in the next section.

Controlling authenticated options

In this section, we are going to only make relevant options visible for authenticated users. We will do this using the `isAuthenticated` flag from the `useAuth` Hook we created in the last section.

We will start by showing either the **Sign In** option or the **Sign Out** option in the `Header` component. We will then only allow authenticated users to ask questions in the `HomePage` component and answer a question in the `QuestionPage` component. As part of this work, we will create a reusable `AuthorizedPage` component that can be used on page components to ensure that they are only accessed by authenticated users.

Displaying the relevant options in the header

At the moment, the `Header` component shows the **Sign In** and **Sign Out** options, but the **Sign In** option is only relevant if the user hasn't signed in. The **Sign Out** option is only relevant if the user is authenticated. Let's clean this up in `Header.tsx` in the following steps:

1. We'll start by importing the authentication context Hook:

   ```
   import { useAuth } from './Auth';
   ```

2. Let's Hook into the authentication context and return the `user` object, whether the user is authenticated, and whether the context has loaded just before the JSX is returned:

   ```
   export const Header = () => {
     ...
     const { isAuthenticated, user, loading } =
       useAuth();

     return (
       ...
     );
   };
   ```

3. We can use the `loading` and `isAuthenticated` properties to show the relevant options in the JSX:

```
<div ...>
  <Link ...>
    Q & A
  </Link>
  <form onSubmit={handleSearchSubmit}>
    ...
  </form>
  <div>
    {!loading &&
      (isAuthenticated ? (
        <div>
          <span>{user!.name}</span>
          <Link to="/signout" css={buttonStyle}>
            <UserIcon />
            <span>Sign Out</span>
          </Link>
        </div>
      ) : (
        <Link to="/signin" css={buttonStyle}>
          <UserIcon />
          <span>Sign In</span>
        </Link>
      ))}
  </div>
</div>
```

We use a short circuit expression to ensure that the **Sign In** and **Sign Out** buttons can't be accessed while the context is loading. We use a ternary expression to show the username and the **Sign Out** button if the user is authenticated and the **Sign In** button if not.

4. Let's give this a try by first making sure the frontend and backend are running. We should see the **Sign In** button before the user has signed in:

Figure 12.14 – Header for an unauthenticated user

5. Click the **Sign In** button and authenticate as a user. We should see the username and a **Sign Out** button after the user has been authenticated:

Figure 12.15 – Header for an authenticated user

That completes the changes needed in the `Header` component.

Next, we will use our `useAuth` Hook again to control whether users can ask questions.

Only allowing authenticated users to ask a question

Let's move to the `HomePage` component and only show the **Ask a question** button if the user is authenticated:

1. We'll start by importing the authentication Hook:

   ```
   import { useAuth } from './Auth';
   ```

2. Let's Hook into the authentication context and return whether the user is authenticated just before the JSX is returned:

   ```
   export const HomePage = () => {
     ...

     const { isAuthenticated } = useAuth();

     return (
       ...
     );
   };
   ```

3. We can then use the `isAuthenticated` property and a short-circuit operator to only render the **Ask a question** button if the user is signed in:

   ```
   <Page>
     <div
       ...
     >
       <PageTitle>Unanswered Questions</PageTitle>
       {isAuthenticated && (
         <PrimaryButton onClick={handleAskQuestionClick}>
           Ask a question
         </PrimaryButton>
   ```

```
    )}
    </div>
    ...
</Page>
```

That completes the changes to the home page. However, the user could still get to the ask page by manually putting the relevant path in the browser.

4. Let's stop unauthenticated users from manually navigating to the ask page and asking a question in `AskPage.tsx`. We are going to create an `AuthorizedPage` component to help us to do this that will only render its child components if the user is authenticated. Let's create a file called `AuthorizedPage.tsx` in the `src` folder with the following content:

```
import React from 'react';
import { Page } from './Page';
import { useAuth } from './Auth';

export const AuthorizedPage: React.FC = ({ children }) =>
{
  const { isAuthenticated } = useAuth();
  if (isAuthenticated) {
    return <>{children}</>;
  } else {
    return (
      <Page title="You do not have access to this
        page">
        {null}
      </Page>
    );
  }
};
```

We use our `useAuth` Hook and render the child components if the user is authenticated. If the user isn't authenticated, we inform them that they don't have access to the page.

5. Let's move to `App.tsx` and import `AuthorizedPage`:

```
import { AuthorizedPage } from './AuthorizedPage';
```

6. We can then wrap the `AuthorizedPage` component around the `AskPage` component in the `App` component JSX:

```
<Route
  path="ask"
  element={
    <React.Suspense
      ...
    >
      <AuthorizedPage>
        <AskPage />
      </AuthorizedPage>
    </React.Suspense>
  }
/>
```

7. Let's give all this a try in the running app. Make sure the user is signed out and go to the home page:

Figure 12.16 – No Ask button for the unauthenticated user

We'll see that there is no button to ask a question, as we expected.

8. Try to go to the ask page by manually putting the `/ask` path into the browser:

Figure 12.17 – Protected page for the unauthenticated user

We are informed that we don't have permission to view the page, as we expected.

9. Let's sign in now:

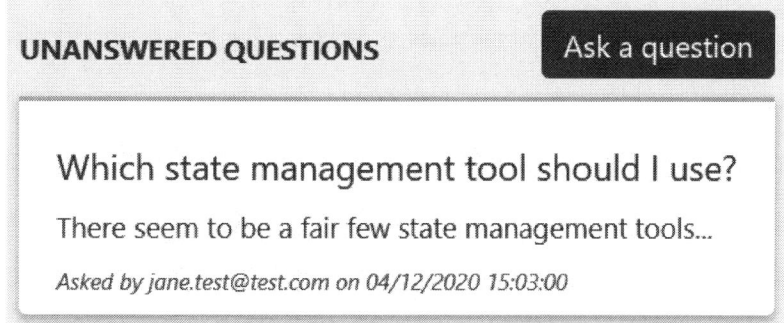

Figure 12.18 – Ask button for the authenticated user

The **Ask a question** button is now available, as we expected.

That concludes the changes we need to make for asking a question.

Only allowing authenticated users to answer a question

Let's focus on the `QuestionPage` component now and only allow an answer to be submitted if the user is authenticated:

1. We'll start by importing the authentication Hook in `QuestionPage.tsx`:

   ```
   import { useAuth } from './Auth';
   ```

2. Let's Hook into the authentication context and return whether the user is authenticated just before the JSX is returned:

   ```
   export const QuestionPage: ... = ( ... ) => {
     ...

     const { isAuthenticated } = useAuth();

     return (
       ...
     );
   };
   ```

3. We can then use the `isAuthenticated` property and a short-circuit operator to only render the answer form if the user is signed in:

```
<AnswerList data={question.answers} />
{isAuthenticated && (
  <form
      ...
    >
      ...
  </form>
)}
```

4. Let's give all this a try in the running app. Make sure the user is signed out and go to the question page:

Which state management tool should I use?

There seem to be a fair few state management tools around for React - React, Unstated, ... Which one should I use?

Asked by jane.test@test.com on 04/12/2020 15:03:00

Figure 12.19 – No answer form for the unauthenticated user

There is no answer form, as we expected.

5. Let's sign in and go to the question page again:

Which state management tool should I use?

There seem to be a fair few state management tools around for React - React, Unstated, ... Which one should I use?

Asked by jane.test@test.com on 04/12/2020 15:03:00

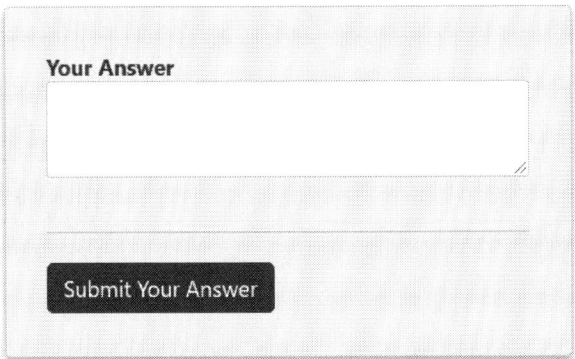

Figure 12.20 – Answer form for the authenticated user

The answer form is available, as we expected.

That completes the changes to the question page.

In the next section, we are going to interact with the REST API endpoints that require an authenticated user to perform tasks such as submitting a question.

Using fetch to interact with authenticated REST API endpoints

In this section, we'll properly wire up posting questions and answers to our REST API. As part of this work, we will enhance our `http` function to use a bearer token from Auth0 in the HTTP request. This is because the endpoints for posting questions and answers are protected in the REST API and require a valid bearer token.

All of our changes will be in `QuestionsData.ts`—our user interface components will be unchanged.

Posting a question to the REST API

We are going to change the implementation for posting a question to use an access token from Auth0:

1. Let's start by importing the function that gets the access token from Auth0 into `QuestionsData.ts`:

   ```
   import { getAccessToken } from './Auth';
   ```

2. Let's change the implementation of the `postQuestion` function to the following:

   ```
   export const postQuestion = async (
     question: PostQuestionData,
   ): Promise<QuestionData | undefined> => {
     const accessToken = await getAccessToken();
     const result = await http<
       QuestionDataFromServer,
       PostQuestionData
     >({
       path: '/questions',
       method: 'post',
       body: question,
       accessToken,
     });
     if (result.ok && result.body) {
       return mapQuestionFromServer(
         result.body,
   ```

```
      );
    } else {
      return undefined;
    }
  };
```

We get the access token from Auth0 and pass it into the generic `http` function. If the request was successful, we return the question from the response body with the correct type for the created dates; otherwise, we return `undefined`.

3. The ability to do `POST` requests in our `http` function is not supported yet. Access tokens aren't supported as well. So, let's move to `http.ts` and start to implement these features:

```
export interface HttpRequest<REQB> {
  path: string;
  method?: string;
  body?: REQB;
  accessToken?: string;
}
```

We've started by adding the HTTP method, body, and access token to the request interface.

4. Let's move on to the changes we need to make in the `http` function:

```
export const http = async <
  RESB,
  REQB = undefined
>(
  config: HttpRequest<REQB>,
): Promise<HttpResponse<RESB>> => {
  const request = new Request(
    `${webAPIUrl}${config.path}`,
    {
      method: config.method || 'get',
      headers: {
        'Content-Type': 'application/json',
      },
      body: config.body
        ? JSON.stringify(config.body)
        : undefined,
    }
  );
  ...
};
```

We are providing a second argument to the Request constructor that defines the HTTP request method, headers, and body.

Notice that we convert the request body into a string using JSON.stringify. This is because the fetch function doesn't convert the request body into a string for us.

5. Now, let's add support for the access token:

```
export const http = async <
  RESB,
  REQB = undefined
>(
  config: HttpRequest<REQB>,
): Promise<HttpResponse<RESB>> => {
  const request = new Request(
    ...
  );
  if (config.accessToken) {
    request.headers.set(
      'authorization',
      `bearer ${config.accessToken}`,
    );
  }
  ...
};
```

If the access token is provided, we add it to an HTTP request header called authorization after the word bearer and the space.

> **Important Note**
>
> authorization is a standard HTTP header that contains credentials to authenticate a user. The value is set to the type of authentication followed by a space, followed by the credentials. So, the word bearer in our case denotes the type of authentication.

6. Let's give this a try by first making sure the frontend and backend are running. Let's sign in as a user, open up the browser's DevTools, and go to the **Network** panel. Let's submit a new question:

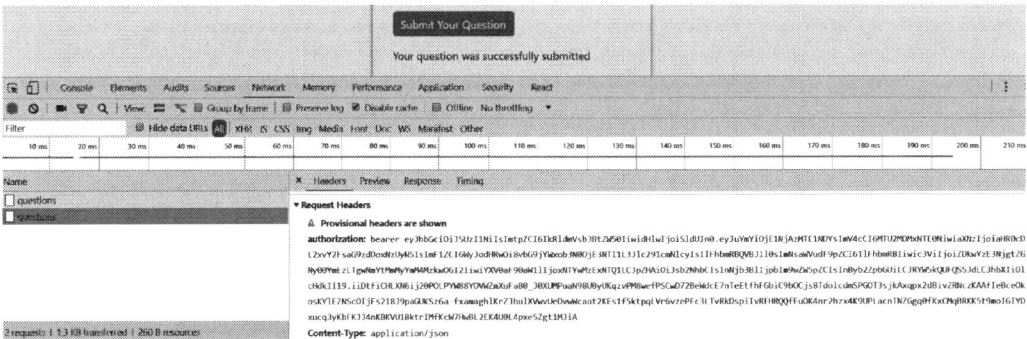

Figure 12.21 – Bearer token included in the HTTP request

The question is saved successfully, as we expected. We can also see the access token sent in the HTTP `authorization` header with the request.

One of the things we couldn't check in the last chapter was whether the correct user was being saved against the question. If we have a look at the question in the database, we'll see the correct user ID and user name stored against the question:

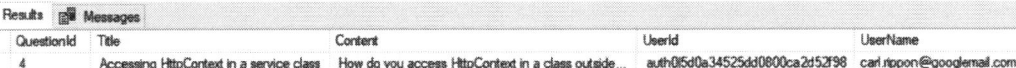

Figure 12.22 – Correct user ID and username stored with the question

That completes posting a question. No changes are required to the `AskPage` component.

Posting an answer to the REST API

We are going to change the implementation for posting an answer to use the access token and our generic `http` function. Let's revise the implementation of the `postAnswer` function to the following:

```
export const postAnswer = async (
  answer: PostAnswerData,
): Promise<AnswerData | undefined> => {
  const accessToken = await getAccessToken();
  const result = await http<
    AnswerData,
    PostAnswerData
  >({
    path: '/questions/answer',
```

```
    method: 'post',
    body: answer,
    accessToken,
  });
  if (result.ok) {
    return result.body;
  } else {
    return undefined;
  }
};
```

This follows the same pattern as the `postQuestion` function, getting the access token from Auth0 and making the HTTP POST request with the JWT using the `http` function.

That completes the changes needed for posting an answer.

We can now remove the `questions` array mock data from `QuestionsData.ts` as this is no longer used. The `wait` function can also be removed.

This completes this section on interacting with protected REST API endpoints.

Aborting data fetching

There is a slight problem in the page components at the moment when they request data and set it in the state. The problem is that if the user navigates away from the page while the data is still being fetched, the state will attempt to be set on a component that no longer exists. We are going to resolve this issue on the `HomePage`, `QuestionPage`, and `SearchPage` components by using a `cancelled` flag that is set when the components are unmounted. We will check this flag after the data is returned and the state is about to be set.

Let's carry out the following steps:

1. In `HomePage.tsx`, let's change the `useEffect` call to the following:

    ```
    React.useEffect(() => {
      let cancelled = false;
      const doGetUnansweredQuestions = async () => {
        const unansweredQuestions = await
        getUnansweredQuestions();
        if (!cancelled) {
          setQuestions(unansweredQuestions);
          setQuestionsLoading(false);
        }
      };
    ```

```
    doGetUnansweredQuestions();
    return () => {
      cancelled = true;
    };
  }, []);
```

We use a `cancelled` variable to track whether the user has navigated away from the page and, we don't set any state if this is `true`. We will know whether the user has navigated away from the page because the `return` function will be called, which sets the `cancelled` flag.

2. Let's follow the same pattern for the `QuestionPage` component:

```
React.useEffect(() => {
  let cancelled = false;
  const doGetQuestion = async (questionId: number) =>
  {
    const foundQuestion = await
    getQuestion(questionId);
    if (!cancelled) {
      setQuestion(foundQuestion);
    }
  };
  ...
  return () => {
    cancelled = true;
  };
}, [questionId]);
```

3. Lastly, let's follow the same pattern for the `SearchPage` component:

```
React.useEffect(() => {
  let cancelled = false;
  const doSearch = async (criteria: string) => {
    const foundResults = await
    searchQuestions(criteria);
    if (!cancelled) {
      setQuestions(foundResults);
    }
  };
  doSearch(search);
  return () => {
    cancelled = true;
  };
}, [search]);
```

This completes the changes to the page components. The data fetching process within the page components is now a little more robust.

Summary

In this chapter, we learned that the browser has a handy `fetch` function that allows us to interact with REST APIs. This allows us to specify HTTP headers such as `authorization`, which we use to supply the user's access token in order to access the protected endpoints.

Leveraging the standard Auth0 JavaScript library allows single-page applications to interact with the Auth0 identity provider. It makes all of the required requests and redirects to Auth0 in a secure manner.

Using the React context to share information about the user to components allows them to render information and options that are only relevant to the user.

The `AuthProvider` and `AuthorizedPage` components we built in this chapter are generic components that could be used in other apps to help to implement frontend authorization logic.

Our app is very nearly complete now. In the next chapter, we are going to put the frontend and backend through their paces with some automated tests.

Questions

The following questions will test our knowledge of what we have just learned:

1. What is wrong with the following HTTP POST request using the `fetch` function?

   ```
   fetch('http://localhost:17525/api/person', {
     method: 'post',
     headers: {
       'Content-Type': 'application/json',
     },
     body: {
       firstName: 'Fred'
       surname: 'Smith'
     }
   })
   ```

2. What is wrong with the following request using the `fetch` function?

   ```
   const res = await fetch('http://localhost:17525/api/person/1');
   console.log('firstName', res.body.firstName);
   ```

3. What is wrong with the following request using the `fetch` function?

   ```
   fetch('http://localhost:17525/api/person/21312')
     .then(res => res.json())
     .catch(res => {
       if (res.status === 404) {
         console.log('person not found')
       }
     });
   ```

4. We have an endpoint for deleting users that only administrators have access to use. We have the user's access token in a variable called `jwt`. What is wrong with the following request?

   ```
   fetch('http://localhost:17525/api/person/1', {
     method: 'delete',
     headers: {
       'Content-Type': 'application/json',
       'authorization': jwt
     }
   });
   ```

5. In this chapter, we implemented an `AuthorizedPage` component that we could wrap around a page component so that it is only rendered for authenticated users. We could implement a similar component to wrap around components within a page so that they are only rendered for authenticated users. Have a go at implementing this.

Answers

1. The problem is that the `fetch` function expects the body to be in `string` format. The corrected call is as follows:

   ```
   fetch('http://localhost:17525/api/person', {
     method: 'post',
     headers: {
       'Content-Type': 'application/json',
     },
     body: JSON.stringify({
       firstName: 'Fred'
   ```

```
      surname: 'Smith'
    })
  })
```

2. The problem is that the response body cannot be accessed directly in the response like this. Instead, the response's json asynchronous method should be used:

```
const res = await fetch('http://localhost:17525/api/person/1');
const body = await res.json();
console.log('firstName', body.firstName);
```

3. The problem is that the catch method is for network errors and not HTTP request errors. HTTP request errors can be dealt with in the then method:

```
fetch('http://localhost:17525/api/person/21312')
  .then(res => {
    if (res.status === 404) {
      console.log('person not found')
    } else {
      return res.json();
    }
  });
```

4. The problem is that the word bearer followed by a space is missing from the authorization HTTP header. The corrected call is as follows:

```
fetch('http://localhost:17525/api/person/1', {
  method: 'delete',
  headers: {
    'Content-Type': 'application/json',
    'authorization': `bearer ${jwt}`
  });
```

5. The component implementation is as follows:

```
import React from 'react';
import { useAuth } from './Auth';

export const AuthorizedElement: React.FC = ({ children }) => {
  const auth = useAuth();
  if (auth.isAuthenticated) {
    return < >{children}</ >;
  } else {
    return null;
```

```
    }
};
```

The component would be consumed as follows:

```
<AuthorizedElement>
  <PrimaryButton ...>
    Ask a question
  </PrimaryButton>
</AuthorizedElement>
```

Further reading

Here are some useful links to learn more about the topics covered in this chapter:

- **The Fetch API**: https://developer.mozilla.org/en-US/docs/Web/API/Fetch_API
- **Auth0**: https://auth0.com/docs

Section 4: Moving into Production

In this last section, we will add automated tests to both the ASP.NET Core and React apps. We will deploy the app to Azure using Visual Studio and Visual Studio Code before fully automating the deployment by implementing build and release pipelines in Azure DevOps.

This section comprises the following chapters:

- *Chapter 13, Adding Automated Tests*
- *Chapter 14, Configuring and Deploying to Azure*
- *Chapter 15, Implementing CI and CD with Azure DevOps*

13
Adding Automated Tests

Now, it's time to get our *QandA* app ready for production. In this chapter, we are going to add automated tests to the frontend and backend of our app, which will give us the confidence to take the next step: moving our app into production.

First, we will focus on the backend and use xUnit to implement unit tests on pure functions with no dependencies. Then, we'll move on to testing our `QuestionsController`, which does have dependencies. We will also learn how to use Moq to replace our real implementation of dependencies with a fake implementation.

Next, we will turn our attention to testing the frontend of our app with the popular Jest tool. We will learn how to implement unit tests on pure functions and integration tests on React components by leveraging the fantastic React Testing Library.

Then, we will learn how to implement end-to-end tests with Cypress. We'll use this to test a key path through the app where the frontend and backend will be working together.

By the end of this chapter, our tests will give us more confidence that we are not breaking existing functionality when developing and shipping new versions of our app.

In this chapter, we'll cover the following topics:

- Understanding the different types of automated test
- Implementing .NET tests with xUnit
- Implementing React tests with Jest
- Testing React components
- Implementing end-to-end tests with Cypress

Let's get started!

Technical requirements

We will need the following tools and services in this chapter:

- **Visual Studio 2019**: We'll use this to write tests for our ASP.NET Core code backend. This can be downloaded and installed from `https://visualstudio.microsoft.com/vs/`.
- **.NET 5**: This can be downloaded from `https://dotnet.microsoft.com/download/dotnet/5.0`.
- **Visual Studio Code**: We'll use this to implement tests on our React code. This can be downloaded and installed from `https://code.visualstudio.com/`.
- **Node.js and npm**: These can be downloaded from `https://nodejs.org/`. If you already have these installed, make sure that Node.js is at least version 8.2 and that npm is at least version 5.2.
- **Q and A**: We'll start with the QandA frontend project that is available on GitHub at `https://github.com/PacktPublishing/ASP.NET-Core-5-and-React-Second-Edition` in the `chapter-13/start` folder.

All the code snippets in this chapter can be found online at `https://github.com/PacktPublishing/ASP.NET-Core-5-and-React-Second-Edition`. In order to restore code from a chapter, you can download the source code repository and open the relevant folder in the relevant editor. If the code is frontend code, then `npm install` can be entered into the Terminal to restore the dependencies. You will also need to substitute your Auth0 tenant ID and client ID in the `appsettings.json` file in the backend project, as well as the `AppSettings.ts` file in the frontend project.

Check out the following video to see the code in action: `https://bit.ly/3h3Aib6`.

Understanding the different types of automated test

A robust suite of automated tests helps us deliver software faster without sacrificing its quality. There are various types of test, though each type has its own benefits and challenges. In this section, we are going to understand the different types of test and the benefits they bring to a single-page application.

The following diagram shows the three different types of test:

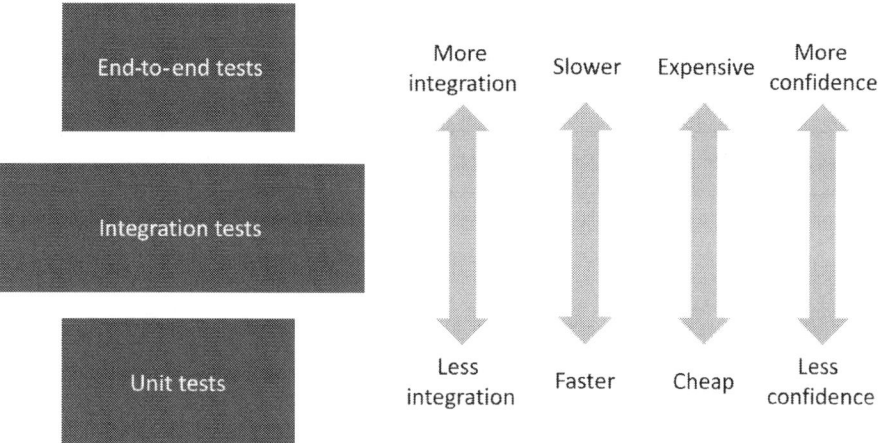

Figure 13.1 – Types of test

In the following subsections, we will examine each type of test, along with their pros and cons.

Unit tests

Unit tests verify that individual and isolated parts of an app work as expected. These tests generally execute very fast, thus giving us a very tight feedback loop so that we know the part of the app that we are developing is working correctly.

These tests can be quick to implement, but this is not necessarily the case if we need to mock out the dependencies of the unit we are testing. This is often the case when unit testing a React frontend, since a true unit test on a component needs to mock out any child components that are referenced in its JSX.

Perhaps the biggest downside of these tests is that they give us the least amount of confidence that the app as a whole is working correctly. We can have a large unit test suite that covers all the different parts of our app, but this is no guarantee that all the parts work together as expected.

The following is an example of a unit test being performed on the `increment` method of a `Counter` class:

```
[Fact]
public void Increment_WhenCurrentCountIs1_ShouldReturn2()
{
    var counter = new Counter(1);
    var result = counter.increment();
    Assert.Equal(2, result);
}
```

There are no external dependencies on the `Counter` class or the `increment` method, so this is a great candidate for a unit test.

End-to-end tests

End-to-end tests verify that key paths work together as expected. No parts of the app are isolated and mocked away. These tests run a fully functioning app just like a user would, so this gives us the maximum amount of confidence that our app is functioning correctly.

These tests are slow to execute, though, which can delay the feedback loop during development; they're also the most expensive to write and maintain. This is because everything that the tests rely on, such as the data in the database, needs to be consistent each time the tests are executed, which is a challenge when we implement multiple tests that have different data requirements.

The following is a code snippet from an end-to-end test for capturing a subscription email address:

```
cy.findByLabelText('Email')
  .type('carl.rippon@googlemail.com')
  .should('have.value', 'carl.rippon@googlemail.com');
cy.get('form').submit();
cy.contains('Thanks for subscribing!');
```

The statements drive interactions on the web page and check the content of the elements on the page, which are updated along the way.

Integration tests

Integration tests verify that several parts of an app work together correctly. They give us more confidence than unit tests in terms of ensuring that the app as a whole is working as expected. These tests provide the most scope in terms of what is tested because of the many app part combinations that we can choose to test.

These tests are generally quick to execute because slow components such as database and network requests are often mocked out. The time it takes to write and maintain these tests is also short.

For single-page applications, the **Return on Investment** (**ROI**) of integration tests is arguably greater than the other two testing types if we choose our tests wisely. This is why the relevant box in the preceding diagram is bigger than other testing types.

The following is an example of an integration test being performed on a React `Card` component:

```
test('When the Card component is rendered with a title
  prop, it should contain the correct title', () => {
    const { queryByText } = render(
      <Card title="Title test" />
    );
    const titleText = queryByText('Title test');
    expect(titleText).not.toBeNull();
});
```

The test verifies that passing the `title` prop results in the correct text being rendered. The `Card` component may contain child components, which will be executed and rendered in the test. This is why this is classed as an integration test rather than a unit test.

Now that we understand the different types of test, we are going to start implementing them on our *QandA* app. We'll start by unit testing the .NET backend.

Implementing .NET tests with xUnit

In this section, we are going to implement some backend unit tests on our question controller using a library called **xUnit**. Before we do this, we are going to become familiar with xUnit by implementing some unit tests on a class with no dependencies.

Getting started with xUnit

In this section, we are going to create a new project in our backend Visual Studio solution and start to implement simple unit tests to get comfortable with xUnit, which is the tool we are going to use to run our backend tests. So, let's open our backend project and carry out the following steps:

1. Open up the **Solution Explorer** window, right-click on **Solution**, choose **Add**, and then choose **New Project...**.

2. Select **xUnit Test Project** from the dialog box that opens and click on the **Next** button:

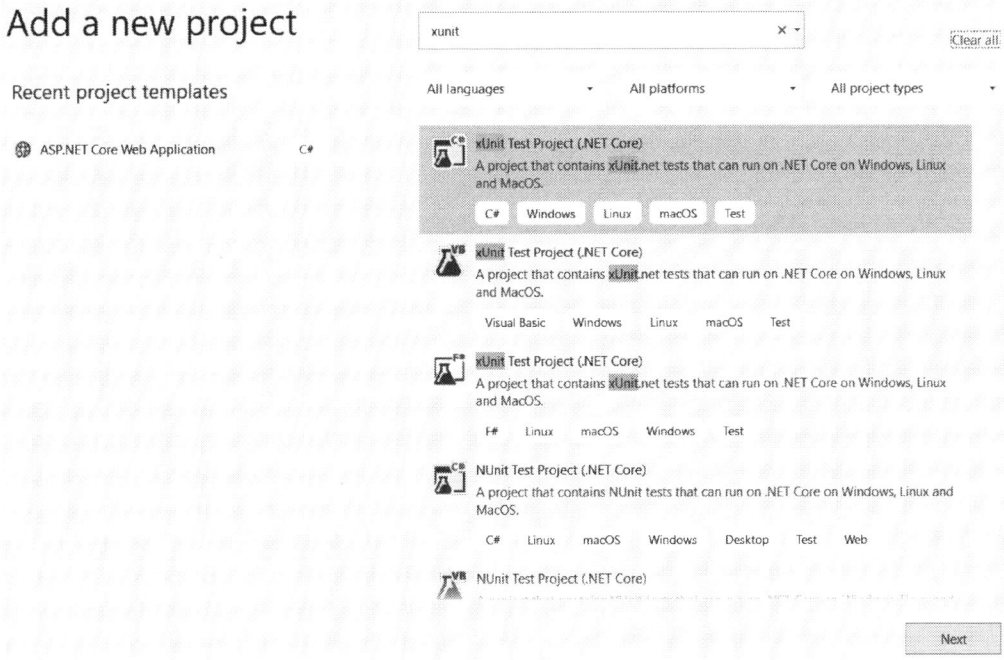

Figure 13.2 – Creating a new xUnit project

3. Enter **BackendTests** as the project name and set **Location** to the folder that the solution is in. Click **Create** to create the project.

4. In **Solution Explorer**, right-click on the **BackendTests** project and choose **Edit Project File**. Make sure the `TargetFramework` node in the XML is set to at least `net5.0`:

   ```
   <Project Sdk="Microsoft.NET.Sdk">
     <PropertyGroup>
       <TargetFramework>net5.0</TargetFramework>
       ...
     </PropertyGroup>
     ...
   </Project>
   ```

5. We are going to create a simple class so that we can write some unit tests for it. This will get us comfortable with xUnit. Create a static class in our unit test project called `Calc` with the following content:

   ```
   using System;

   namespace BackendTests
   {
     public static class Calc
     {
       public static decimal Add(decimal a, decimal b)
       {
         return a + b;
       }
     }
   }
   ```

   The class contains a method called `Add`, which simply adds two numbers together that are passed in its parameters. `Add` is a pure function, which means the return value is always consistent for a given set of parameters and it doesn't give off any side effects. Pure functions are super easy to test, as we'll see next.

6. We are going to create some unit tests for the `Add` method in the `Calc` class. Let's create a new class in the unit test project called `CalcTests` with the following content:

   ```
   using Xunit;

   namespace BackendTests
   {
     public class CalcTests
     {
       [Fact]
       public void
   ```

```
        Add_When2Integers_ShouldReturnCorrectInteger()
        {
            // TODO - call the Calc.Add method with 2
            // integers
            // TODO - check the result is as expected
        }
    }
}
```

We have named our test method `Add_When2Integers_ShouldReturnCorrectInteger`.

> **Important Information**
>
> It is useful to have a good naming convention for tests. When we look at a failed test report, we can start to get an understanding of the problem immediately if the name of the test describes what is being tested. In this case, the name starts with the method we are testing, followed by a brief description of the conditions for the test and what we expect to happen.

Note that the test method is decorated with the `Fact` attribute.

> **Important Information**
>
> The `Fact` attribute denotes that the method is a unit test for xUnit. Another attribute that denotes a unit test is called `Theory`. This can be used to feed the method a range of parameter values.

7. Let's implement the unit test:

```
[Fact]
public void Add_When2Integers_ShouldReturnCorrectInteger()
{
    var result = Calc.Add(1, 1);
    Assert.Equal(2, result);
}
```

We call the method we are testing and put the return value in a `result` variable. Then, we use the `Assert` class from xUnit and its `Equal` method to check that the result is equal to 2.

8. Let's run our test by right-clicking inside the test method and choosing **Debug Test(s)** from the menu:

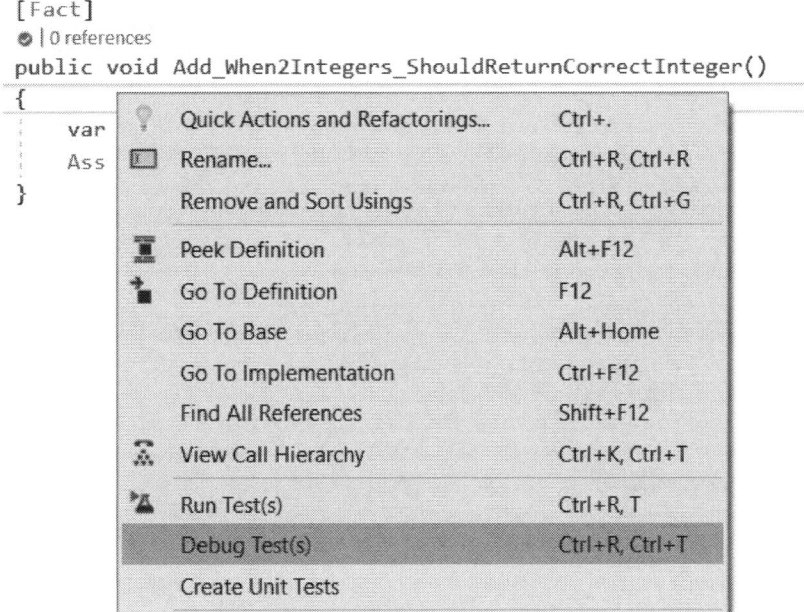

Figure 13.3 – Debugging a test

9. After a few seconds, the test will run, and the result will appear in the **Test Explorer** window:

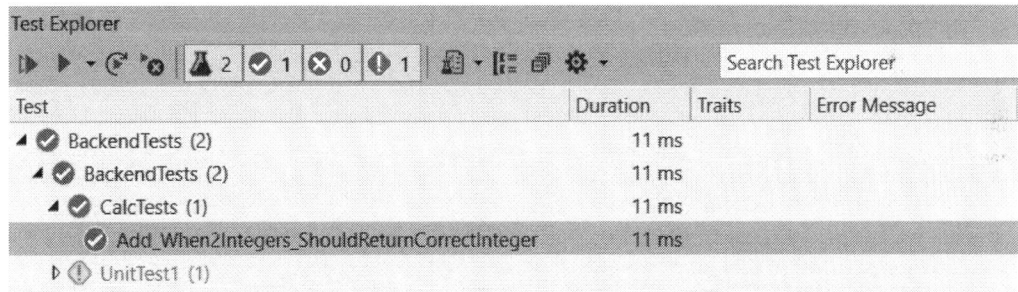

Figure 13.4 – Test result

As we expected, the test passes. Congratulations – you have just created your first unit test!

452   Adding Automated Tests

We used the `Equal` method in the `Assert` class in this test. The following are some other useful methods we can use in this class:

- `True`: Checks that a value is `true`
- `NotNull`: Checks that a value isn't `null`
- `Contains`: Checks that the value is in a `string`
- `InRange`: Checks that the value is within a range
- `Throws`: Checks that an exception has been raised

Now, we are starting to understand how to write unit tests. We haven't written any tests on our Q and A app yet, but we will do so next.

Testing controller action methods

In this section, we are going to create tests for some question controller actions.

Our API controller has dependencies for a cache and a data repository. We don't want our tests to execute the real cache and data repository because we require the data in the cache and data repository to be predicable. This helps us get predicable results that we can check. In addition, if the tests are running on the real database, the test execution will be much slower. So, we are going to use a library called Moq to help us replace the real cache and data repository with fake implementations that give predicable results.

Let's get started:

1. First, we need to reference the `QandA` project from the `BackendTests` project. We can do this by right-clicking on the **Dependencies** node in **Solution Explorer** in the `BackendTests` project and choosing **Add Project Reference…**:

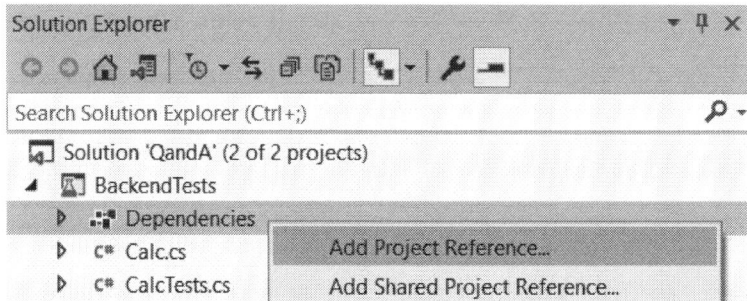

Figure 13.5 – Adding a project reference

2. Then, we need to tick the **QandA** project and click the **OK** button:

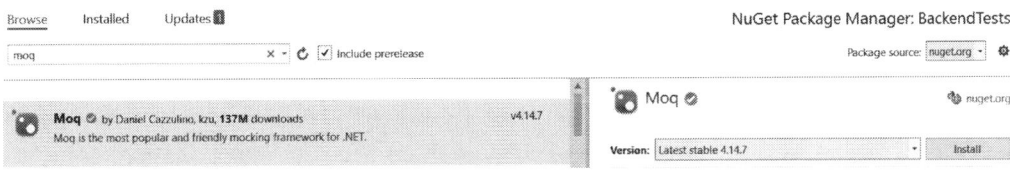

Figure 13.6 – Adding a reference to the QandA project

3. Let's install **Moq** into our test project using **NuGet Package Manager**:

Figure 13.7 – Installing Moq

The `BackendTests` project is now set up, ready for our first test to be implemented.

Testing the action method for getting questions

Follow these steps to implement a couple of tests on the `GetQuestions` method:

1. We'll start by creating a new class called `QuestionsControllerTests` in the `BackendTests` project with the following content:

```
using System.Collections.Generic;
using System.Linq;
using System.Threading.Tasks;
using Microsoft.AspNetCore.Mvc;
using Microsoft.Extensions.Configuration;
using Xunit;
```

Adding Automated Tests

```csharp
using Moq;
using QandA.Controllers;
using QandA.Data;
using QandA.Data.Models;

namespace BackendTests
{
  public class QuestionsControllerTests
  {

  }
}
```

2. We are going to verify that calling `GetQuestions` with no parameters returns all the questions. Let's create the test method for this and 10 mock questions:

```csharp
[Fact]
public async void GetQuestions_WhenNoParameters_ReturnsAllQuestions()
{
  var mockQuestions = new
    List<QuestionGetManyResponse>();
  for (int i = 1; i <= 10; i++)
  {
    mockQuestions.Add(new QuestionGetManyResponse
    {
      QuestionId = 1,
      Title = $"Test title {i}",
      Content = $"Test content {i}",
      UserName = "User1",
      Answers = new List<AnswerGetResponse>()
    });
  }
}
```

Notice that the method is flagged as asynchronous with the `async` keyword because the action method we are testing is asynchronous.

3. Let's create a mock data repository definition using Moq:

```csharp
[Fact]
public async void GetQuestions_WhenNoParameters_ReturnsAllQuestions()
{
  ...
  var mockDataRepository = new
    Mock<IDataRepository>();
```

```
      mockDataRepository
        .Setup(repo => repo.GetQuestions())
        .Returns(() => Task.FromResult(mockQuestions.
          AsEnumerable()));
    }
```

We can create a mock object from the `IDataRepository` interface using the `Mock` class from Moq. We can then use the `Setup` and `Returns` methods on the mock object to define that the `GetQuestions` method should return our mock questions. The method we are testing is asynchronous, so we need to wrap the mock questions with `Task.FromResult` in the mock result.

4. We need to mock the configuration object that reads `appsettings.json`. This is what the controller depends on:

```
    [Fact]
    public async void GetQuestions_WhenNoParameters_
    ReturnsAllQuestions()
    {
      ...
      var mockConfigurationRoot = new
        Mock<IConfigurationRoot>();
      mockConfigurationRoot.SetupGet(config =>
        config[It.IsAny<string>()]).Returns("some
          setting");
    }
```

The preceding code will return any string when `appsettings.json` is read, which is fine for our test.

5. Next, we need to create an instance of the API controller by passing in an instance of the mock data repository and mock configuration settings:

```
    [Fact]
    public async void GetQuestions_WhenNoParameters_
    ReturnsAllQuestions()
    {
      ...
      var questionsController = new QuestionsController(
        mockDataRepository.Object,
        null,
        null,
        mockConfigurationRoot.Object
      );
    }
```

The `Object` property on the mock data repository definition gives us an instance of the mock data repository to use.

Notice that we can pass in `null` for cache and HTTP client factory dependencies. This is because they are not used in the action method implementation we are testing.

6. Now, we can call the action method we are testing:

```
[Fact]
public async void GetQuestions_WhenNoParameters_
ReturnsAllQuestions()
{
  ...
  var result = await
    questionsController.GetQuestions(null, false);
}
```

We pass `null` in as the `search` parameter and `false` as the `includeAnswers` parameter. The other parameters are optional, so we don't pass these in.

7. Now, we can check the result is as expected:

```
[Fact]
public async void GetQuestions_WhenNoParameters_
ReturnsAllQuestions()
{
  ...
  Assert.Equal(10, result.Count());
  mockDataRepository.Verify(
    mock => mock.GetQuestions(),
    Times.Once()
  );
}
```

Here, we have checked that the 10 items are returned.

We have also checked that the `GetQuestions` method in the data repository is called once.

8. Let's give this a try by right-clicking the test in **Test Explorer** and selecting **Run Selected Tests**:

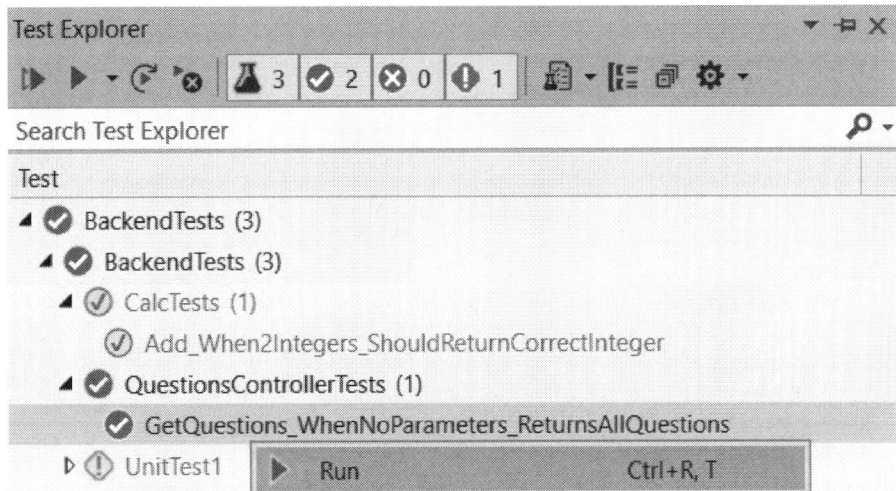

Figure 13.8 – Running a test in Test Explorer

The test passes, as we expected.

9. Now, we are going to create a second test to verify that calling `GetQuestions` with a `search` parameter calls the `GetQuestionsBySearchWithPaging` method in the data repository. Add the following method to our `QuestionsControllerTests` class:

```
[Fact]
public async void GetQuestions_WhenHaveSearchParameter_
ReturnsCorrectQue stions()
{
  var mockQuestions = new List<QuestionGetManyResponse>();
  mockQuestions.Add(new QuestionGetManyResponse
  {
    QuestionId = 1,
    Title = "Test",
    Content = "Test content",
    UserName = "User1",
    Answers = new List<AnswerGetResponse>()
  });

  var mockDataRepository = new
    Mock<IDataRepository>();
  mockDataRepository
    .Setup(repo =>
```

```
          repo.GetQuestionsBySearchWithPaging("Test", 1,
            20))
        .Returns(() =>
          Task.FromResult(mockQuestions.AsEnumerable()));

    var mockConfigurationRoot = new
      Mock<IConfigurationRoot>();
    mockConfigurationRoot.SetupGet(config =>
        config[It.IsAny<string>()]).Returns("some
         setting");

    var questionsController = new QuestionsController(
      mockDataRepository.Object,
      null,
      null,
      mockConfigurationRoot.Object
    );

    var result = await questionsController.
  GetQuestions("Test", false);

    Assert.Single(result);
    mockDataRepository.Verify(mock =>
      mock.GetQuestionsBySearchWithPaging("Test", 1,
        20),
      Times.Once());
}
```

This follows the same pattern as the previous test, but this time, we're mocking the `GetQuestionsBySearchWithPaging` method in the data repository and checking that this is called. If we run the test, it will pass as expected.

That completes the tests on the `GetQuestions` method.

Testing the action method to get a single question

Follow these steps to implement a couple of tests on the `GetQuestion` method:

1. Let's add the following test to the `QuestionsControllerTests` class to verify that we get the correct result when the question isn't found:

    ```
    [Fact]
    public async void GetQuestion_WhenQuestionNotFound_
    Returns404()
    {
      var mockDataRepository = new
    ```

```
      Mock<IDataRepository>();
   mockDataRepository
      .Setup(repo => repo.GetQuestion(1))
      .Returns(() => Task.
 FromResult(default(QuestionGetSingleResponse)));

   var mockQuestionCache = new Mock<IQuestionCache>();
   mockQuestionCache
      .Setup(cache => cache.Get(1))
      .Returns(() => null);

   var mockConfigurationRoot = new
     Mock<IConfigurationRoot>();
   mockConfigurationRoot.SetupGet(config =>
      config[It.IsAny<string>()]).Returns("some
        setting");

   var questionsController = new QuestionsController(
     mockDataRepository.Object,
     mockQuestionCache.Object,
     null,
     mockConfigurationRoot.Object
   );

   var result = await
     questionsController.GetQuestion(1);

   var actionResult =
     Assert.IsType<
        ActionResult<QuestionGetSingleResponse>
     >(result);
   Assert.IsType<NotFoundResult>(actionResult.Result);
}
```

This follows the same pattern as the previous tests. A difference in this test is that we mock the cache in this test because this is used in the GetQuestion method. Our mock will return null from the fake cache, which is what we expect when the question isn't in the cache.

Here, we checked that the result is of the NotFoundResult type.

2. Let's add another test to verify a question is returned when the one that's requested does exist:

```
[Fact]
public async void GetQuestion_WhenQuestionIsFound_
ReturnsQuestion()
{
  var mockQuestion = new QuestionGetSingleResponse
  {
    QuestionId = 1,
    Title = "test"
  };

  var mockDataRepository = new
    Mock<IDataRepository>();
  mockDataRepository
    .Setup(repo => repo.GetQuestion(1))
    .Returns(() => Task.FromResult(mockQuestion));

  var mockQuestionCache = new Mock<IQuestionCache>();
  mockQuestionCache
    .Setup(cache => cache.Get(1))
    .Returns(() => mockQuestion);

  var mockConfigurationRoot = new
    Mock<IConfigurationRoot>();
  mockConfigurationRoot.SetupGet(config =>
    config[It.IsAny<string>()]).Returns("some
      setting");

  var questionsController = new QuestionsController(
    mockDataRepository.Object,
    mockQuestionCache.Object,
    null,
    mockConfigurationRoot.Object
  );

  var result = await
    questionsController.GetQuestion(1);

  var actionResult =
    Assert.IsType<
      ActionResult<QuestionGetSingleResponse>
    >(result);
  var questionResult =
    Assert.IsType<QuestionGetSingleResponse>(actionResult.
```

```
        Value);
    Assert.Equal(1, questionResult.QuestionId);
}
```

This time, we checked that the result is of the `QuestionGetSingleResponse` type and that the correct question is returned by checking the question ID.

That completes the tests we are going to perform on our `GetQuestion` action method.

The same approach and pattern can be used to add tests for controller logic we haven't covered yet. We can do this using Moq, which mocks out any dependencies that the method relies on. In the next section, we'll start to implement tests on the frontend.

Implementing React tests with Jest

In this section, we are going to turn our attention to creating automated tests for the frontend with Jest. Jest is the de facto testing tool in the React community and is maintained by Facebook. Jest is included in **Create React App** (**CRA**) projects, which means that it has already been installed and configured in our project.

We are going to start by testing a simple function so that we can get familiar with Jest before moving on to testing a React component.

Getting started with Jest

We'll start to get familiar with Jest by adding some unit tests to the `mapQuestionFromServer` function in `QuestionsData.ts`. So, let's open our frontend project in Visual Studio Code and carry out the following steps:

1. Remove the example test that was installed when the project was created with Create React App by removing the `App.test.tsx` file in the `src` folder.

2. Create a new file called `QuestionsData.test.ts` in the `src` folder that contains the following content:

    ```
    import { mapQuestionFromServer } from './QuestionsData';

    test('When mapQuestionFromServer is called with question,
    created should be turned into a Date', () => {
    });
    ```

Notice that the extension of the file is `test.ts`.

> **Important Information**
>
> The `test.ts` extension is important because Jest automatically looks for files with this extension when searching for tests to execute. Note that if our tests contained JSX, we would need to use the `test.tsx` extension.

The `test` function in Jest takes in two parameters:

- The first parameter is a description of the test that will be shown in the test output.
- The second parameter is an arrow function, which will contain our test.

The test is going to check that `mapQuestionFromServer` functions correctly and maps the `created` property to a `question` object.

3. Let's call the `mapQuestionFromServer` function with a question and assign the returned object to a `result` variable:

```
test('When mapQuestionFromServer is called with question,
created should be turned into a Date', () => {
  const result = mapQuestionFromServer({
    questionId: 1,
    title: "test",
    content: "test",
    userName: "test",
    created: "2021-01-01T00:00:00.000Z",
    answers: []
  });
});
```

4. Add the following highlighted code to test that the `result` variable is as we expect:

```
test('When mapQuestionFromServer is called with question,
created should be turned into a Date', () => {
  const result = mapQuestionFromServer({
    questionId: 1,
    title: "test",
    content: "test",
    userName: "test",
    created: "2021-01-01T00:00:00.000Z",
    answers: []
  });
  expect(result).toEqual({
    questionId: 1,
    title: "test",
    content: "test",
```

```
      userName: "test",
      created: new Date(Date.UTC(2021, 0, 1, 0, 0, 0,
        0)),
      answers: []
    });
  });
```

We pass the `result` variable we are checking into the Jest `expect` function. Then, we chain a `toEqual` matcher function onto this, which checks that the `result` object has the same property values as the object we passed into it.

`toEqual` is one of many Jest matcher functions we can use to check a variable's value. The full list of functions can be found at `https://jestjs.io/docs/en/expect`.

5. Let's create another test on the `mapQuestionFromServer` function to check that the `created` property in `answers` is mapped correctly:

```
test('When mapQuestionFromServer is called with
  question and answers, created should be turned into
    a Date', () => {
  const result = mapQuestionFromServer({
    questionId: 1,
    title: "test",
    content: "test",
    userName: "test",
    created: "2021-01-01T00:00:00.000Z",
    answers: [{
      answerId: 1,
      content: "test",
      userName: "test",
      created: "2021-01-01T00:00:00.000Z"
    }]
  });
  expect(result).toEqual({
    questionId: 1,
    title: "test",
    content: "test",
    userName: "test",
    created: new Date(Date.UTC(2021, 0, 1, 0, 0, 0,
      0)),
    answers: [{
      answerId: 1,
      content: "test",
      userName: "test",
      created: new Date(Date.UTC(2021, 0, 1, 0, 0, 0,
```

```
            0)),
    }]
  });
});
```

6. It's time to check that our tests pass. Enter the following command in the Terminal:

```
> npm test
```

Jest will run the tests that it finds in our project and output the results:

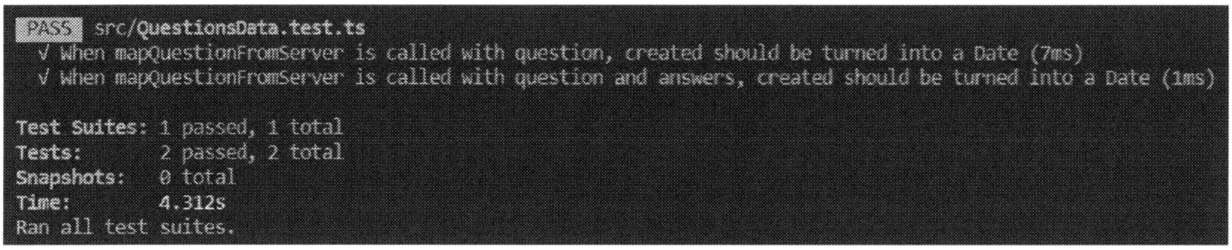

```
PASS  src/QuestionsData.test.ts
  √ When mapQuestionFromServer is called with question, created should be turned into a Date (7ms)
  √ When mapQuestionFromServer is called with question and answers, created should be turned into a Date (1ms)

Test Suites: 1 passed, 1 total
Tests:       2 passed, 2 total
Snapshots:   0 total
Time:        4.312s
Ran all test suites.
```

Figure 13.9 – Jest test results

So, Jest found our two tests and they both passed – that's great news!

The `mapQuestionFromServer` function is straightforward to test because it has no dependencies. But how do we test a React component that has lots of dependencies, such as the browser's DOM and React itself? We'll find out in the next section.

Testing React components

In this section, we are going to implement tests on the `Page`, `Question`, and `HomePage` components. React component tests can be challenging because they have dependencies, such as the browser's DOM and sometimes HTTP requests. Due to this, we are going to leverage the React Testing Library and Jest's mocking functionality to help us implement our tests.

Testing the Page component

Carry out the following steps to test that the `Page` component renders correctly:

1. Create a file for the tests called `Page.test.tsx` with the following content:

```
import React from 'react';
import { render, cleanup } from '@testing-library/react';
import { Page } from './Page';
```

```
test('When the Page component is rendered, it should
contain the correct title and content', () => {

});
```

We imported React with our `Page` component, along with some useful functions from the React Testing Library.

The React Testing Library was installed by Create React App when we created the frontend project. This library will help us select elements that we want to check, without using internal implementation details such as element IDs or CSS class names.

2. Let's render the `Page` component in the test by adding the following highlighted lines of code:

```
test('When the Page component is rendered, it should
contain the correct title and content', () => {
  const { queryByText } = render(
    <Page title="Title test">
      <span>Test content</span>
    </Page>,
  );
});
```

We use the `render` function from React Testing Library to render the `Page` component by passing in JSX.

The `render` function returns various useful items. One of these items is the `queryByText` function, which will help us select elements that we'll use and understand in the next step.

3. Now, we can check that the page title has been rendered:

```
test('When the Page component is rendered, it should
contain the correct title and content', () => {
  const { queryByText } = render(
    <Page title="Title test">
      <span>Test content</span>
    </Page>,
  );
  const title = queryByText('Title test');
  expect(title).not.toBeNull();
});
```

Here, we used the `queryByText` function from the React Testing Library, which was returned from the `render` function, to find the element that has `"Title test"` in the text's content. Notice how we are using something that the user can see (the element text) to locate the element rather than any implementation details. This means that our test won't break if implementation details such as the DOM structure or DOM IDs change.

Having located the title element, we then used Jest's `expect` function to check that the element was found by asserting that it is not `null`.

4. We can do a similar check on the page content:

```
test('When the Page component is rendered, it should
  contain the correct title and content', () => {
    const { queryByText } = render(
      <Page title="Title test">
        <span>Test content</span>
      </Page>,
    );
    const title = queryByText('Title test');
    expect(title).not.toBeNull();
    const content = queryByText('Test content');
    expect(content).not.toBeNull();
});
```

5. The last thing we need to do is clean up the DOM once the test has been executed. We can do this for all the tests in a file by using the `afterEach` function from Jest and the `cleanup` function from the React Testing Library. Let's add this after the `import` statements:

```
afterEach(cleanup);
```

6. If Jest is still running after we save the file, our new test will run. If we have killed Jest, then we can start it again by executing `npm test` in the Terminal:

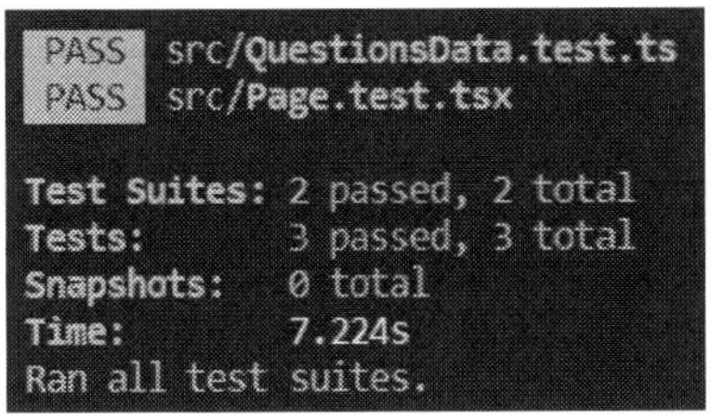

```
PASS  src/QuestionsData.test.ts
PASS  src/Page.test.tsx

Test Suites: 2 passed, 2 total
Tests:       3 passed, 3 total
Snapshots:   0 total
Time:        7.224s
Ran all test suites.
```

Figure 13.10 – Jest test results

Our tests pass as expected, which makes three passing tests in total.

Testing the Question component

Carry out the following steps to test that the `Question` component renders correctly:

1. Let's start by creating a new file called `Question.test.tsx` with the following content:

   ```
   import React from 'react';
   import { render, cleanup } from '@testing-library/react';
   import { QuestionData } from './QuestionsData';
   import { Question } from './Question';
   import { BrowserRouter } from 'react-router-dom';

   afterEach(cleanup);

   test('When the Question component is rendered, it should contain the correct data', () => {

   });
   ```

   This imports all the items we need for our test. We have also implemented the `cleanup` function, which will run after the test.

2. Now, let's try to render the component:

   ```
   test('When the Question component is rendered, it should contain the correct data', () => {
     const question: QuestionData = {
       questionId: 1,
       title: 'Title test',
       content: 'Content test',
       userName: 'User1',
       created: new Date(2019, 1, 1),
       answers: [],
     };
     const { queryByText } = render(
       <Question data={question} />,
     );
   });
   ```

   We render the `Question` component using the `render` function by passing in a mocked `data` prop value.

There's a problem, though. If we run the test, we will receive an error message stating `Error: useHref() may be used only in the context of a <Router> component`. The problem here is that the `Question` component uses a `Link` component, which expects the `Router` component to be higher up in the component tree. However, it isn't present in our test.

3. The solution is to include `BrowserRouter` in our test:

```
test('When the Question component is rendered, it should contain the correct data', () => {
  ...
  const { queryByText } = render(
    <BrowserRouter>
      <Question data={question} />
    </BrowserRouter>
  );
});
```

4. Now, we can assert that the correct data is being rendered by adding the following highlighted statements to our test:

```
test('When the Question component is rendered, it should contain the correct data', () => {
  ...
  const titleText = queryByText('Title test');
  expect(titleText).not.toBeNull();
  const contentText = queryByText('Content test');
  expect(contentText).not.toBeNull();
  const userText = queryByText(/User1/);
  expect(userText).not.toBeNull();
  const dateText = queryByText(/2019/);
  expect(dateText).not.toBeNull();
});
```

We are using the `queryByText` method again here to locate rendered elements and check that the element that's been found isn't `null`. Notice that, when finding the element that contains the username and date, we pass in a regular expression to do a partial match.

Testing the HomePage component

The final component we are going to implement tests for is the `HomePage` component. Carry out the following steps to do so:

1. Let's create a file called `HomePage.test.tsx` with the following content:

    ```
    import React from 'react';
    import { render, cleanup } from '@testing-library/react';
    import { HomePage } from './HomePage';
    import { BrowserRouter } from 'react-router-dom';

    afterEach(cleanup);

    test('When HomePage first rendered, loading indicator
    should show', async () => {
      const { findByText } = render(
        <BrowserRouter>
          <HomePage />
        </BrowserRouter>,
      );
      const loading = await findByText('Loading...');
      expect(loading).not.toBeNull();
    });
    ```

    The test verifies that a **Loading...** message appears in the `HomePage` component when it is first rendered. We use the `findByText` function to wait and find the element that contains the loading text.

2. Let's implement another test to check that unanswered questions are rendered okay:

    ```
    test('When HomePage data returned, it should render
    questions', async () => {
      const { findByText } = render(
        <BrowserRouter>
          <HomePage />
        </BrowserRouter>,
      );
      expect(await findByText('Title1
        test')).toBeInTheDocument();
      expect(await findByText('Title2
        test')).toBeInTheDocument();
    });
    ```

    We use the `findByText` function again to wait for the questions to be rendered. We then use the `toBeInTheDocument` function to check that the found elements are in the document.

However, the test fails. This is because the `HomePage` component is making an HTTP request to get the data but there is no REST API to handle the request.

3. We are going to mock the `getUnansweredQuestions` function with a Jest mock. Let's add the following code above our test:

```
jest.mock('./QuestionsData', () => ({
  getUnansweredQuestions: () => {
    return Promise.resolve([
      {
        questionId: 1,
        title: 'Title1 test',
        content: 'Content2 test',
        userName: 'User1',
        created: new Date(2019, 1, 1),
        answers: [],
      },
      {
        questionId: 2,
        title: 'Title2 test',
        content: 'Content2 test',
        userName: 'User2',
        created: new Date(2019, 1, 1),
        answers: [],
      },
    ]);
  },
}));

test('When HomePage first rendered, loading indicator should show', async () => ...
```

The mock function returns two questions that we use in the test assertions.

Now, the test will pass when it runs.

That completes our component tests.

As we've seen, tests on components are more challenging to write than tests on pure functions, but the React Testing Library and Jest mocks make life fairly straightforward.

In the next section, we are going to complete our test suite by implementing an end-to-end test.

Implementing end-to-end tests with Cypress

Cypress is an end-to-end testing tool that works really well for **single-page applications** (**SPAs**) like ours. Cypress can run the whole application, simulate a user interacting with it, and check the state of the user interface along the way. So, Cypress is ideal for producing end-to-end tests on a SPA.

In this section, we are going to implement an end-to-end test for signing in and asking a question.

Getting started with Cypress

Cypress executes in our frontend, so let's carry out the following steps to install and configure Cypress in our frontend project:

1. We'll start by installing `cypress` from the Terminal:

    ```
    > npm install cypress --save-dev
    ```

2. We are going to add an `npm` script to open Cypress by adding the following line to `package.json`:

    ```
    "scripts": {
      ...,
      "cy:open": "cypress open"
    },
    ```

3. Let's open Cypress by executing our `npm` script in the Terminal:

    ```
    > npm run cy:open
    ```

    After a few seconds, Cypress will open, showing a list of example test files that have just been installed:

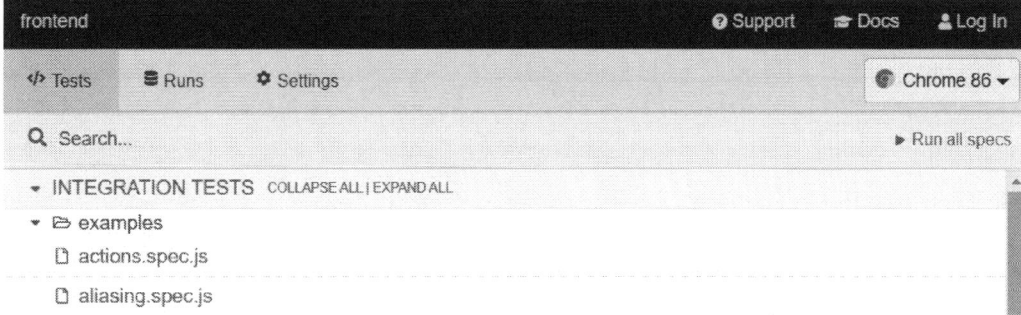

Figure 13.11 – Cypress example tests

These examples can be found in the `cypress/integration/examples` folder in our project. If we open one of these test files, we'll see that they are written in JavaScript. These examples are a great source of reference as we learn and get up to speed with Cypress.

4. In the Cypress browser window, click the `actions.spec.js` item. This will open this test and execute it:

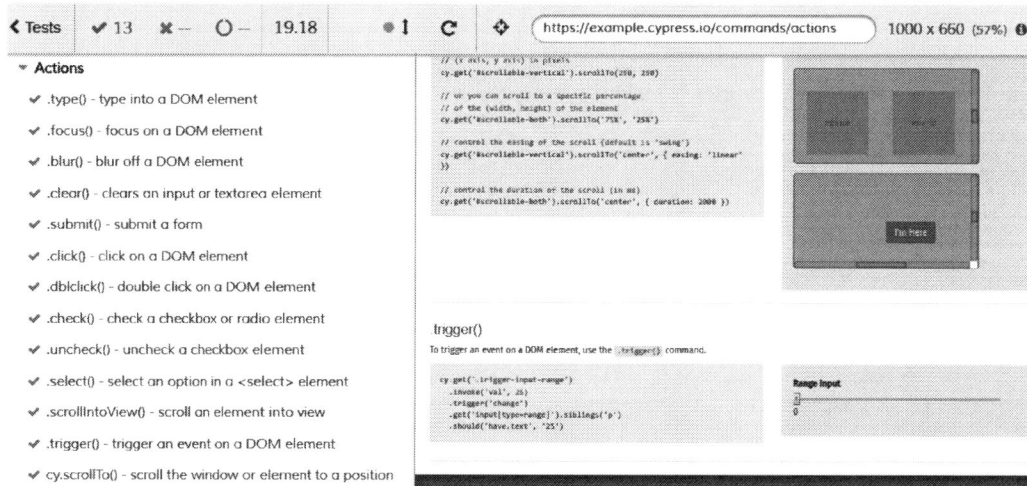

Figure 13.12 – Test output in Cypress

We can see the tests on the left and check whether they have passed or failed with the app that is being tested on the right.

5. If we click the **submit() - submit a form** test, we'll see all the steps in the test. If we click on a step, we'll see the app on the right in the state it was in at that juncture:

Implementing end-to-end tests with Cypress   473

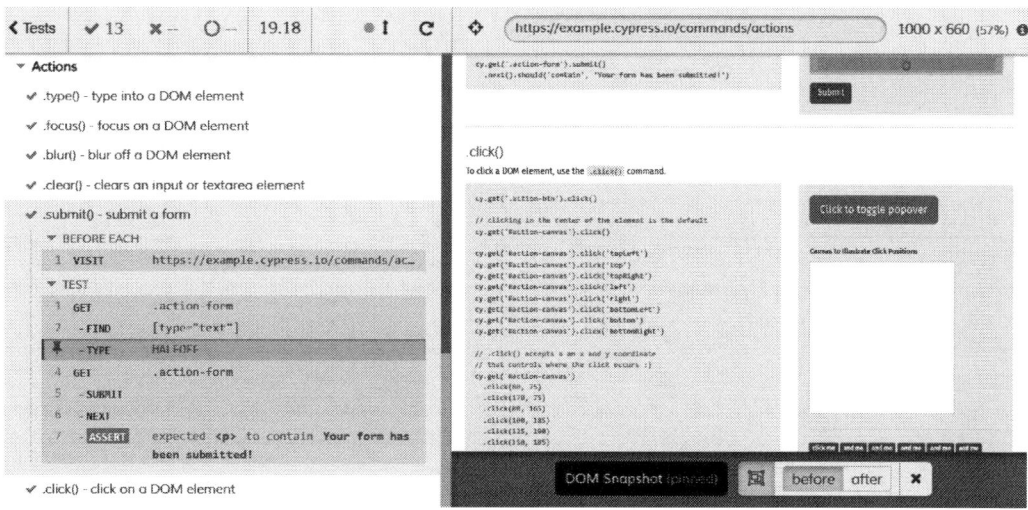

Figure 13.13 – Cypress test result step details

This is really useful when debugging test failures.

6. Let's close Cypress for now and return to the Terminal to install the Cypress Testing Library:

```
> npm install @testing-library/cypress --save-dev
```

The Cypress Testing Library is similar to the React Testing Library in that it helps us select elements to check without using internal implementation details.

7. To add Cypress Testing Library commands, we need to insert the following line at the top of the `commands.js` file, which can be found in the `support` folder of the `cypress` folder:

```
import '@testing-library/cypress/add-commands';
```

8. Let's add some Cypress configuration settings by opening the `cypress.json` file in the root of the project and adding the following settings:

```
{
    "baseUrl": "http://localhost:3000",
    "chromeWebSecurity": false
}
```

The `baseUrl` setting is the root URL of the app we are testing.

Our test will be using Auth0 and our app, so it will be working on two different origins. We need to disable Chrome security using the `chromeWebSecurity` setting to allow the test to work across different origins.

Cypress runs our app and Auth0 in an IFrame. To prevent clickjacking attacks, running in an IFrame is disabled by default in Auth0.

9. Disable clickjacking protection in Auth0 by selecting the **Settings** option under our user avatar menu and then selecting the **Advanced** tab. An option called **Disable clickjacking protection for Classic Universal Login** can be found toward the bottom of the **Advanced** tab. We need to turn this option on:

Figure 13.14 – Disable clickjacking protection option in Auth0

10. When we write our tests, we will be accessing a global `cy` object from Cypress. Let's tell ESLint that `cy` is okay by adding the following to the `.eslintrc.json` file:

```
{
  ...,
  "globals": {
    "cy": true
  }
}
```

Now, Cypress has been installed and configured so that we can implement a test on our Q and A app.

Testing asking a question

In this section, we are going to implement a test on our app using Cypress; the test signs in and then asks a question. Carry out the following steps to do so:

1. Let's create a new file called `qanda.js` in the `integration` folder, which can be found in the `cypress` folder, with the following content:

   ```
   describe('Ask question', () => {
     beforeEach(() => {
       cy.visit('/');
     });
     it('When signed in and ask a valid question, the
         question should successfully save', () => {

     });
   });
   ```

   The `describe` function allows us to group a collection of tests on a feature. The first parameter is the title for the group, while the second parameter is a function that contains the tests in the group.

   The `it` function allows us to define the actual test. The first parameter is the title for the test, while the second parameter is a function that contains the steps in the test.

   The `beforeEach` function allows us to define steps to be executed before each test runs. In our case, we are using the `visit` command to navigate to the root of the app. Remember that the root URL for the app is defined in the `baseUrl` setting in the `cypress.json` file.

2. Let's add the following step to our test:

   ```
   it('When signed in and ask a valid question, the
       question should successfully save', () => {
     cy.contains('Q & A');
   });
   ```

   Here, we are checking that the page contains the `Q & A` text using the `contains` Cypress command. We can access Cypress commands from the global `cy` object.

   Cypress commands are built to fail if they don't find what they expect to find. Due to this, we don't need to add an `assert` statement. Neat!

3. Let's give the test a try. We'll need to run our backend in our Visual Studio project. We'll also need to run our frontend by executing npm start in the Terminal. In an additional Terminal window, enter the following to open Cypress:

```
> npm run cy:open
```

4. Cypress will detect our test and list it underneath the example tests:

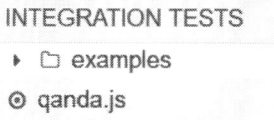

Figure 13.15 – QandA test in Cypress

5. Click on the test to execute it:

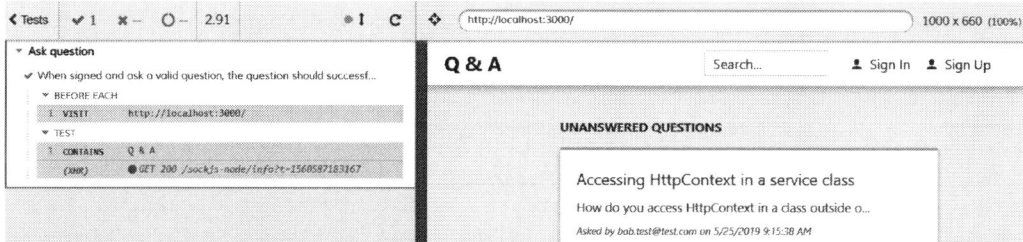

Figure 13.16 – Our test passing in Cypress

The test successfully executes and passes. We'll leave the test runner open because it will automatically rerun as we implement and save our test.

6. Let's add the following additional step to our test:

```
cy.contains('UNANSWERED QUESTIONS');
```

Here, we are checking that the page contains the correct title. If we save the test and look at the test runner, we'll see that the test has failed:

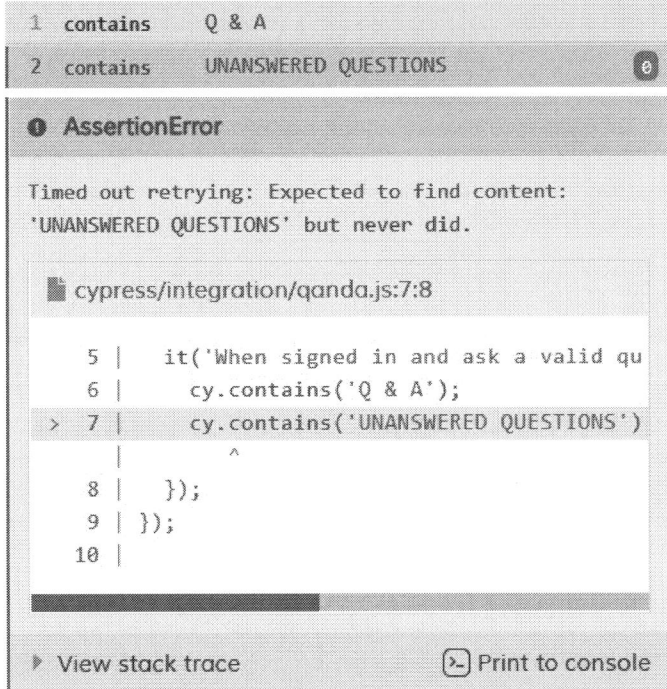

Figure 13.17 – Failing test in Cypress

This is because the title's text isn't actually in capitals – a CSS rule transformed the text into capitals.

Notice the message Cypress uses to inform us of the failing test: **Timed out retrying**. Cypress will keep trying commands until they pass or a timeout occurs. This behavior is really convenient for us because it allows us to write synchronous style code, even though the operations we are testing are asynchronous. Cypress abstracts this complexity from us.

7. Let's correct this problematic test statement by changing it to check for the title in the correct case:

```
cy.contains('Unanswered Questions');
```

8. Let's add some code for going to the sign-in page:

```
cy.contains('Sign In').click();
cy.url().should('include', 'auth0');
```

Here, we use the Cypress `contains` command to locate the **Sign In** button and chain a `click` command to this to click the button.

Then, we use the `url` command to get the browser's URL and chain a `should` command to this statement to verify that it contains the correct path.

If we look at the test runner, we'll see that the test managed to navigate to Auth0 correctly.

Let's think about these steps that Cypress is executing. The navigation to Auth0 is an asynchronous operation, but our test code doesn't appear to be asynchronous. We haven't added a special wait function to wait for the page navigation to complete. Cypress makes testing single-page apps that have asynchronous user interfaces a breeze because it deals with this complexity for us!

Next, we'll implement some steps so that we can fill in the sign-in form:

```
cy.findByLabelText('Email')
  .type('your username')
  .should('have.value', 'your username');

cy.findByLabelText('Password')
  .type('your password')
  .should('have.value', 'your password');
```

Here, we use the `findByLabelText` command from the Cypress Testing Library to locate our `input`. It does this by finding the label containing the text we specified and then finding the associated `input` (referenced in the label's `for` attribute). This is another neat function that frees the tests from implementation details such as element IDs and class names.

We chain the Cypress `type` command so that we can enter characters into `input` and the `should` command to verify that the input's `value` property has been set correctly.

> **Important Information**
> Substitute your test username and password appropriately.

9. Let's submit the sign-in form and check that we are taken back to the Q and A app:

```
cy.get('form').submit();

cy.contains('Unanswered Questions');
```

We use the Cypress `get` command to locate the form and then submit it. Then, we check that the page contains the `Unanswered Questions` text to verify we are back in the Q and A app. Cypress takes care of the asynchronicity of these steps for us.

10. Next, we'll click the **Ask a question** button to go to the ask page:

    ```
    cy.contains('Ask a question').click();
    cy.contains('Ask a question');
    ```

11. Then, we'll fill in the ask form:

    ```
    var title = 'title test';
    var content = 'Lots and lots and lots and lots and lots of content test';
    cy.findByLabelText('Title')
      .type(title)
      .should('have.value', title);
    cy.findByLabelText('Content')
      .type(content)
      .should('have.value', content);
    ```

    We fill in the title and content fields by using the same commands that we did on the sign-in form. The title must be at least 10 characters, and the content must be at least 50 characters, to satisfy the validation rules.

12. Next, we'll submit the question and check that the submission is okay:

    ```
    cy.contains('Submit Your Question').click();
    cy.contains('Your question was successfully submitted');
    ```

13. To complete the test, we are going to sign out and check we've been redirected to the correct page:

    ```
    cy.contains('Sign Out').click();
    cy.contains('You successfully signed out!');
    ```

If we look at the test runner, we'll discover that our test runs and passes successfully:

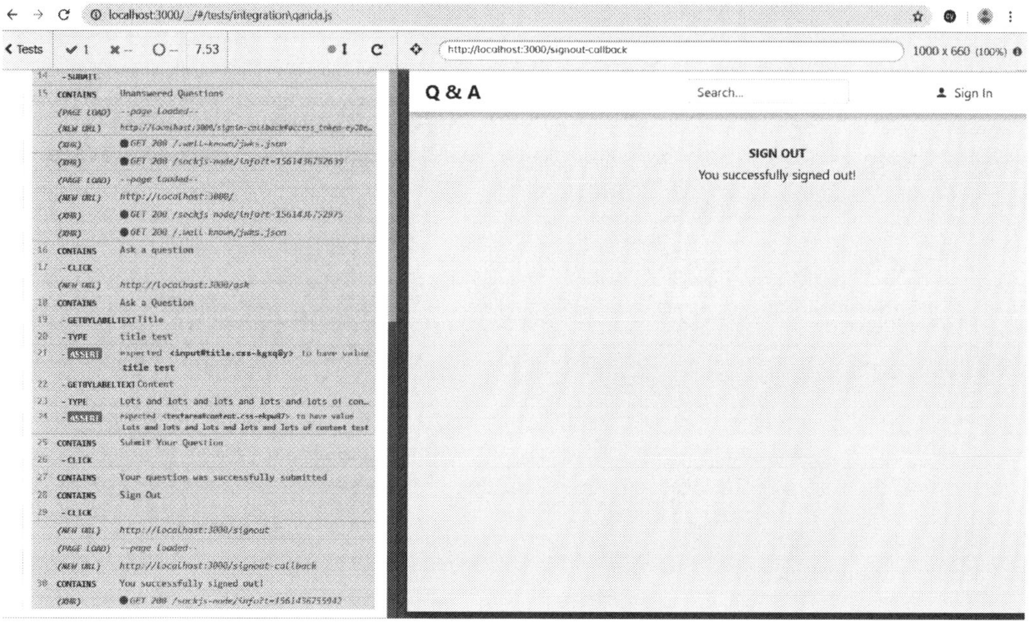

Figure 13.18 – Test run

If the test is failing, it may be because the user was signed into the browser session before the test started. If this is the case, click the **Sign Out** button and rerun the test.

That completes our end-to-end test and all the tests we are going to create in this chapter. Now that we've written the appropriate unit tests, integration tests, and end-to-end tests, we have a feel for the benefits and challenges of each type, as well as how to implement them.

Summary

End-to-end tests with Cypress allow us to quickly cover areas of our app. However, they require a fully operational frontend and backend, including a database. Cypress abstracts away the complexity of the asynchronous nature of single-page applications, making our tests nice and easy to write.

Unit tests can be written using xUnit in .NET and can be placed in a xUnit project, separate from the main app. xUnit test methods are decorated with the `Fact` attribute, and we can use the `Assert` class to carry out checks on the item that we are testing.

Unit tests can be written using Jest for React apps and are contained in files with `test.ts` or `test.tsx` extensions. Jest's `expect` function gives us many useful matcher functions, such as `toBe`, that we can use to make test assertions.

Unit tests often require dependencies to be mocked. Moq is a popular mocking tool in the .NET community and has a `Mock` class, which can be used to mock dependencies. On the frontend, Jest has a range of powerful mocking capabilities that we can use to mock out dependencies, such as REST API calls.

A page is often composed of several components and sometimes, it is convenient to just write integration tests on the page component without mocking the child components. We can implement these tests using Jest in exactly the same way as we can implement a unit test.

The React Testing Library and the Cypress Testing Library help us write robust tests by allowing us to locate elements in a way that doesn't depend on implementation details. This means that if the implementation changes while its features and the behavior remain the same, the test is unlikely to break. This approach reduces the maintenance cost of our test suite.

Now that our app has been built and we've covered automated tests, it's time to deploy it to Azure. We'll do this in the next chapter.

Questions

The following questions will test your knowledge of the topics that were covered in this chapter:

1. We have the following xUnit test method, but it isn't being picked up by the test runner. What's wrong?

    ```
    public void Minus_When2Integers_
    ShouldReturnCorrectInteger()
    {
      var result = Calc.Add(2, 1);
      Assert.Equal(1, result);
    }
    ```

2. We have a `string` variable called `successMessage` in a xUnit test and we need to check that it contains the word `"success"`. What method in the `Assert` class could we use?

3. We have created some Jest unit tests on a `List` component in a file called `ListTests.tsx`. However, when the Jest test runner runs, the tests aren't picked up. Why is this happening?

4. We are implementing a test in Jest and we have a variable called `result` that we want to check isn't `null`. Which Jest matcher function can we use?

5. Let's say we have a variable called `person` that is of the `Person` type:

   ```
   interface Person {
     id: number;
     firstName: string;
     surname: string
   }
   ```

   We want to check that the person variable is `{ id: 1, firstName: "Tom", surname: "Smith" }`. What Jest matcher function can we use?

6. We are writing an end-to-end test using Cypress for a page. The page has a heading called **Sign In**. What Cypress command can we use to check that this has rendered okay?

7. We are writing an end-to-end test using Cypress for a page that renders some text, **Loading...**, while data is being fetched. How can we assert that this text is being rendered and then disappears when the data has been fetched?

Answers

1. The `Fact` attribute is missing from the test method.
2. We would use the `Assert.Contains` method in the `Assert` class.
3. The test filename needs to end with `.test.tsx`. So, if we rename the file `List.test.tsx`, then the test will get picked up.
4. We can use the following code to check an object isn't `null`:

   ```
   expect(result).not.toBeNull();
   ```

5. We can use the `toEqual` Jest matcher function to compare objects:

   ```
   expect(person).toEqual({
     id: 1,
     firstName: "Tom",
     surname: "Smith"
   });
   ```

6. We can use the following Cypress command to check the page heading:

   ```
   cy.contains('Sign In');
   ```

7. We can use the following Cypress command to check that **Loading...** only appears while data is being fetched:

   ```
   cy.contains('Loading...');
   cy.contains('Loading...').should('not.exist');
   ```

   The first command will check that the page renders `Loading...` on the initial render. The second command will wait until `Loading...` disappears – that is, the data has been fetched.

Further reading

The following resources are useful if you want to find out more about testing with xUnit and Jest:

- **Unit testing in .NET Core**: `https://docs.microsoft.com/en-us/dotnet/core/testing/unit-testing-with-dotnet-test`
- **xUnit**: `https://xunit.net/`
- **Moq**: `https://github.com/moq/moq`
- **Jest**: `https://jestjs.io/`
- **React Testing Library**: `https://testing-library.com/docs/react-testing-library/intro`
- **Cypress**: `https://docs.cypress.io`
- **Cypress Testing Library**: `https://testing-library.com/docs/cypress-testing-library/intro`

14
Configuring and Deploying to Azure

In this chapter, we'll deploy our app into production in Microsoft Azure so that all of our users can start to use it. We will focus on the backend to start with, making the necessary changes to our code so that it can work in production and staging environments in Azure. We will then deploy our backend **application programming interfaces** (**APIs**), along with the **Structured Query Language** (**SQL**) database, to both staging and production from within Visual Studio. After the first deploy, subsequent deploys will be able to be done with the click of a button in Visual Studio.

We will then turn our attention to the frontend, again making changes to our code to support development, staging, and production environments. We will then deploy our frontend to Azure to both the staging and production environments.

In this chapter, we'll cover the following topics:

- Getting started with Azure
- Configuring the ASP.NET Core backend for staging and production
- Publishing our ASP.NET Core backend to Azure
- Configuring the React frontend for staging and production
- Publishing the React frontend to Azure

Technical requirements

We'll use the following tools and services in this chapter:

- **Visual Studio 2019**: We'll use this to edit our ASP.NET Core code. This can be downloaded and installed from `https://visualstudio.microsoft.com/vs/`.
- **.NET 5**: This can be downloaded from `https://dotnet.microsoft.com/download/dotnet/5.0`.
- **Visual Studio Code**: We'll use this to edit our React code. This can be downloaded and installed from `https://code.visualstudio.com/`.
- **Node.js and npm**: These can be downloaded from `https://nodejs.org/`. If you already have these installed, make sure that Node.js is at least version 8.2 and that `npm` is at least version 5.2.
- **Microsoft Azure**: We will use several Azure app services and SQL databases for our app. An account can be created at `https://azure.microsoft.com/en-us/free/`.
- **Q and A**: We'll start with the Q and A frontend and backend projects we finished in the last chapter, which are available at `https://github.com/PacktPublishing/ASP.NET-Core-5-and-React-Second-Edition` in the `chapter-14/start` folder.

All of the code snippets in this chapter can be found online at `https://github.com/PacktPublishing/ASP.NET-Core-5-and-React-Second-Edition`. To restore code from a chapter, the source code repository can be downloaded and the relevant folder opened in the relevant editor. If the code is frontend code, then `npm install` can be entered in the Terminal to restore the dependencies.

Check out the following video to see the Code in Action: `https://bit.ly/34u28bd`

Getting started with Azure

In this section, we are going to sign up for Azure if we haven't already got an account. We'll then have a quick look around the Azure portal and understand the services we are going to use to run our app.

Signing up to Azure

If you already have an Azure account, there's never been a better time to sign up and give Azure a try. At the time of writing this book, you can sign up to Azure and get 12 months of free services at the following link: `https://azure.microsoft.com/en-us/free/`.

We'll need a Microsoft account to sign up for Azure, which is free to create if you haven't already got one. You are then required to complete a sign-up form that contains the following personal information:

- Country of origin
- Name
- Email address
- Phone number

You then need to go through two different verification processes. The first is verification via a text message or a call on your phone. The second is to verify your credit card details.

> **Important Note**
> Note that your credit card won't be charged unless you upgrade from the free trial.

The last step in the sign-up process is to agree to the terms and conditions.

Understanding the Azure services we are going to use

After we have an Azure account, we can sign in to the Azure portal using our Microsoft account. The **Uniform Resource Locator** (**URL**) for the portal is `https://portal.azure.com`.

488   Configuring and Deploying to Azure

When we log in to the Azure portal, we'll see that it contains a wide variety of services, as illustrated in the following screenshot:

Figure 14.1 – Azure home page

We are going to use just a couple of these fantastic services, as follows:

- **App Services**: We will use this service to host our ASP.NET Core backend API as well as our React frontend.
- **SQL databases**: We will use this service to host our SQL Server database.

We are going to put all of these resources into what's called a **resource group**. Let's create the resource group now, as follows:

1. Click on the **Resource groups** option. A list of resource groups appears, which of course will be empty if we have just signed up to Azure. Click on the **Add** option, as illustrated in the following screenshot:

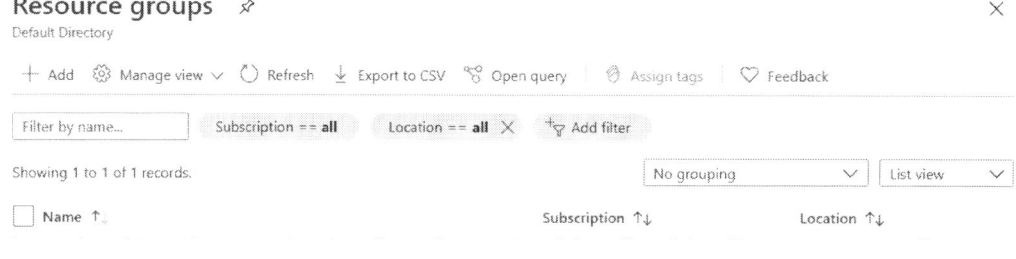

Figure 14.2 – Resource groups page

2. Fill in the form that opens. Choose an appropriate name for the resource group. We'll need to use this name later in this chapter, so make sure you remember it. Click the **Review + create** button, as illustrated in the following screenshot:

Home > Resource groups >

Create a resource group

Basics Tags Review + create

Resource group - A container that holds related resources for an Azure solution. The resource group can include all the resources for the solution, or only those resources that you want to manage as a group. You decide how you want to allocate resources to resource groups based on what makes the most sense for your organization. Learn more

Project details

Subscription * | Free Trial

Resource group * | QandAResources

Resource details

Region * | (US) East US

[Review + create] [< Previous] [Next : Tags >]

Figure 14.3 – Creating a resource group

3. Click on the **Create** button on the review screen that opens. Our resource group will eventually be shown in the resource group list, as can be seen in the following screenshot:

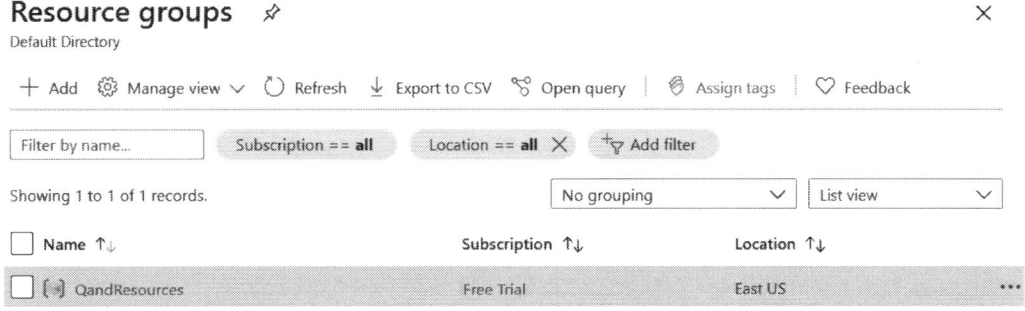

Figure 14.4 – Resource groups list with our new resource group

> **Important Note**
> If the resource group doesn't show after a few seconds, click the **Refresh** option to refresh the resource groups.

Our resource group is now ready for the other services to be provisioned. Before we provision any other services, we'll configure our backend for production in the next section.

Configuring the ASP.NET Core backend for staging and production

In this section, we are going to create separate `appsettings.json` files for staging and production as well as for working locally in development. Let's open our backend project in Visual Studio and carry out the following steps:

1. Let's now go to **Solution Explorer**, as illustrated in the following screenshot:

Figure 14.5 – The appsettings files in Solution Explorer

Notice that two settings files start with the word `appsettings`.

> **Important Note**
> We can have different settings files for different environments. The `appsettings.json` file is the default settings file and can contain settings common to all environments. `appsettings.Development.json` is used during development when we run the backend in Visual Studio and overrides any duplicate settings that are in the `appsettings.json` file. The middle part of the filename needs to match an environment variable called `ASPNETCORE_ENVIRONMENT`, which is set to `Development` in Visual Studio by default and `Production` by default in Azure. So, `appsettings.Production.json` can be used for settings specific to the production environment in Azure.

2. At the moment, all of our settings are in the default `appsettings.json` file. Let's add our `ConnectionStrings` setting and also a frontend setting to the `appsettings.Development.json` file, as follows:

```
{
  "ConnectionStrings": {
    "DefaultConnection":
      "Server=localhost\\SQLEXPRESS;Database=
        QandA;Trusted_Connection=True;"
  },
  "Frontend": "http://localhost:3000"
}
```

We will leave the Auth0 settings in the default `appsettings.json` file because these will apply to all environments.

3. Remove the `ConnectionStrings` setting from the default `appsettings.json` file.

4. Let's add an `appsettings.Production.json` file now by right-clicking the **QandA** project in **Solution Explorer**, choosing **Add | New Item...**, selecting the **App Settings File** item, naming the file `appsettings.Production.json`, and then clicking the **Add** button, as illustrated in the following screenshot:

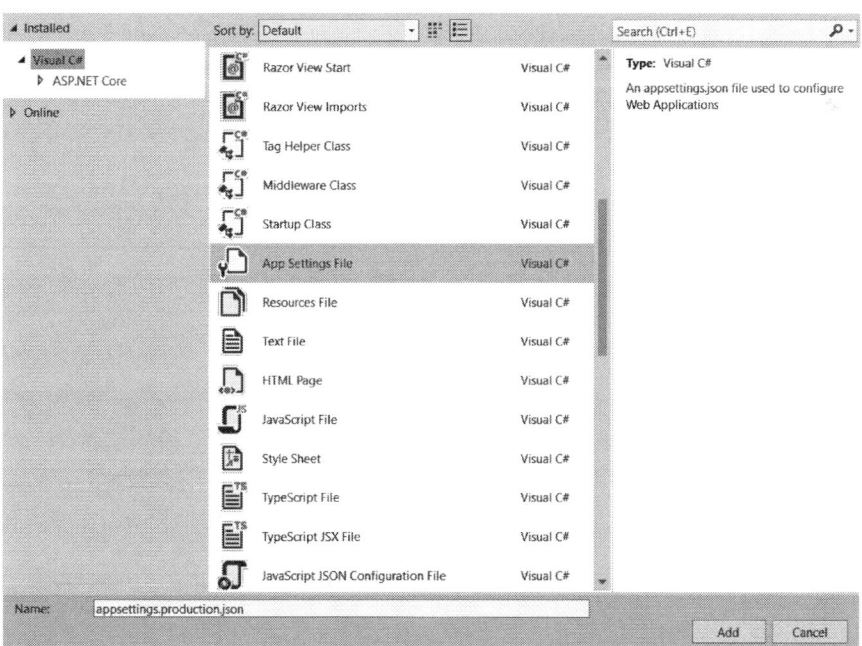

Figure 14.6 – Adding an appsettings file for production

5. Replace the content in the `appsettings.Production.json` file with the following:

```
{
  "Frontend": "https://your-
    frontend.azurewebsites.net"
}
```

So, this contains the production frontend URL that we will create in Azure. Take note of this setting because we will need it when we provision the frontend in Azure.

6. Similarly, let's add an `appsettings.Staging.json` file with the following content:

```
{
  "Frontend": "https://your-frontend-
    staging.azurewebsites.net"
}
```

We haven't specified the production or staging connection strings because we will store these in Azure. This is because these connection strings store secret usernames and passwords, which are more secure in Azure than our source code.

We are now ready to start to create Azure services and deploy our backend. We'll do this in the next section.

Publishing our ASP.NET Core backend to Azure

In this section, we are going to deploy our database and backend API to Azure using Visual Studio. We will create publish profiles for deployment to a production environment as well as a staging environment. During the process of creating the profiles, we will create the required Azure app services and SQL databases. At the end of this section, we will have two profiles that we can use to quickly deploy to our staging and production environments.

Publishing to production

Let's carry out the following steps to create a production deployment profile and use it to deploy our backend to production:

1. In **Solution Explorer**, right-click on the **QandA** project and select **Publish...**.
2. The **Publish** dialog opens, which asks us to choose a publish target. Choose **Azure** and click **Next**, as illustrated in the following screenshot:

Publishing our ASP.NET Core backend to Azure   493

Publish

Where are you publishing today?

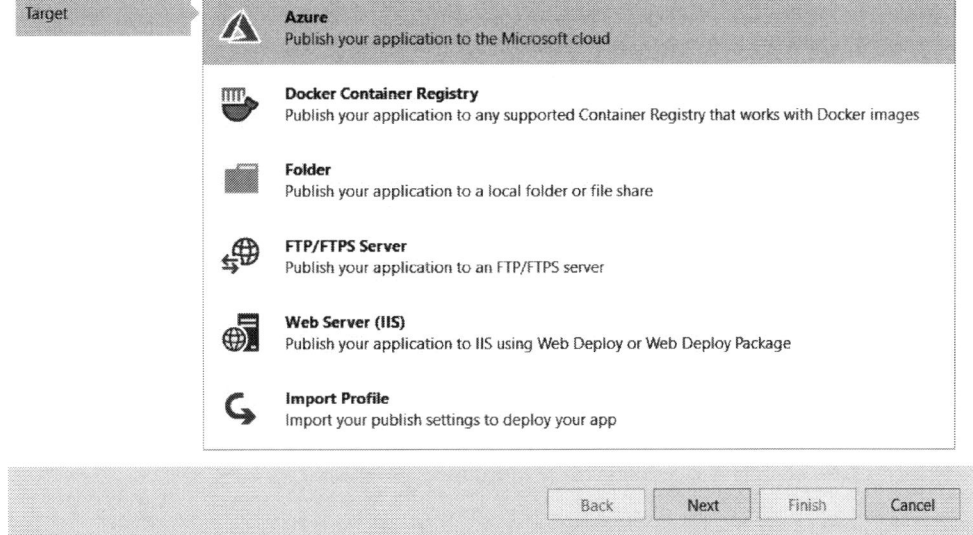

Figure 14.7 – Selecting Azure as the publish target

3. We are then asked which service we want to deploy to in Azure. Select the **Azure App Service (Windows)** option and click **Next**, as illustrated in the following screenshot:

Figure 14.8 – Selecting Azure App Service as the publish specific target

494   Configuring and Deploying to Azure

4. The next step is to specify our Microsoft account. We could then search for and select an existing app service to deploy to. However, we are going to create a new app service, so click the green plus icon, as illustrated in the following screenshot:

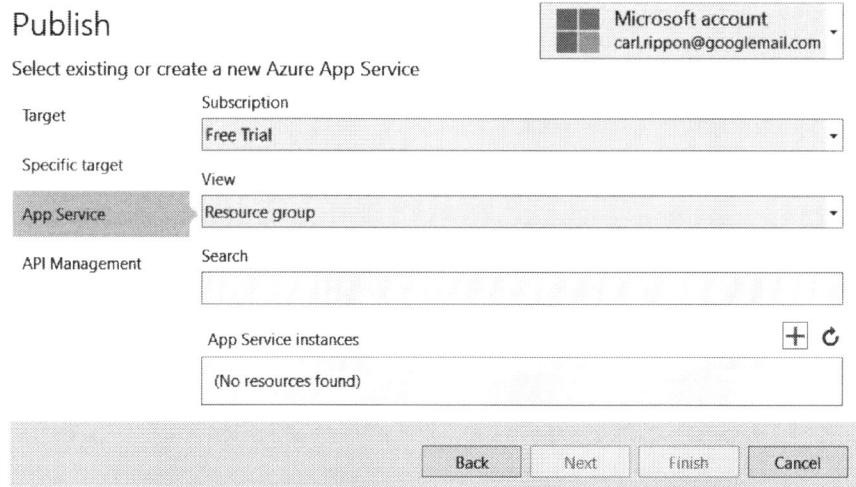

Figure 14.9 – Selecting or creating a new app service

5. Fill in the name for the production app service. This name will form part of the URL to the **REpresentational State Transfer** (**REST**) API, so the name will need to be globally unique. In the example in the following screenshot, the URL will be `https://qanda2021.azurewebsite.net`. Note down the name you choose, because we'll eventually reference this in the frontend project:

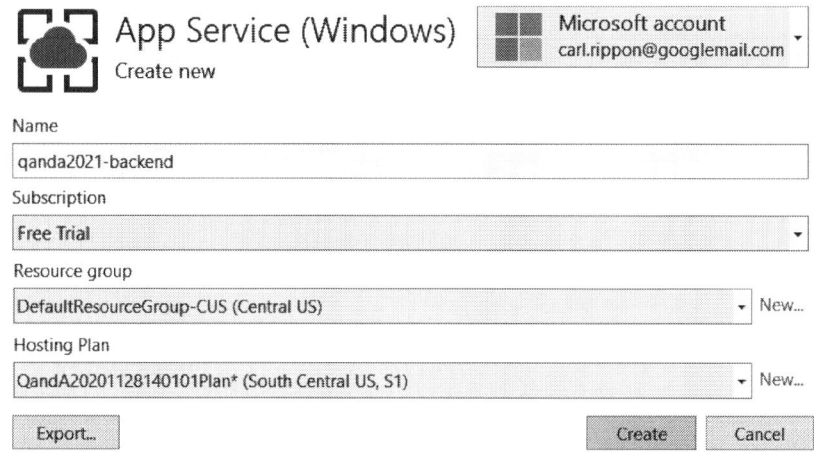

Figure 14.10 – Creating the app service

6. You can choose the default hosting plan for the app service. Alternatively, you can associate it with a new one by clicking the **New...** option.
7. Click **Create** to create the app service—this will take a few minutes to complete.
8. After the app service has been created, the **Create New App Service** dialog will close and we will see the app service in the **App Service instances** list on the **Publish** dialog. Select the new app service and click **Next**, as illustrated in the following screenshot:

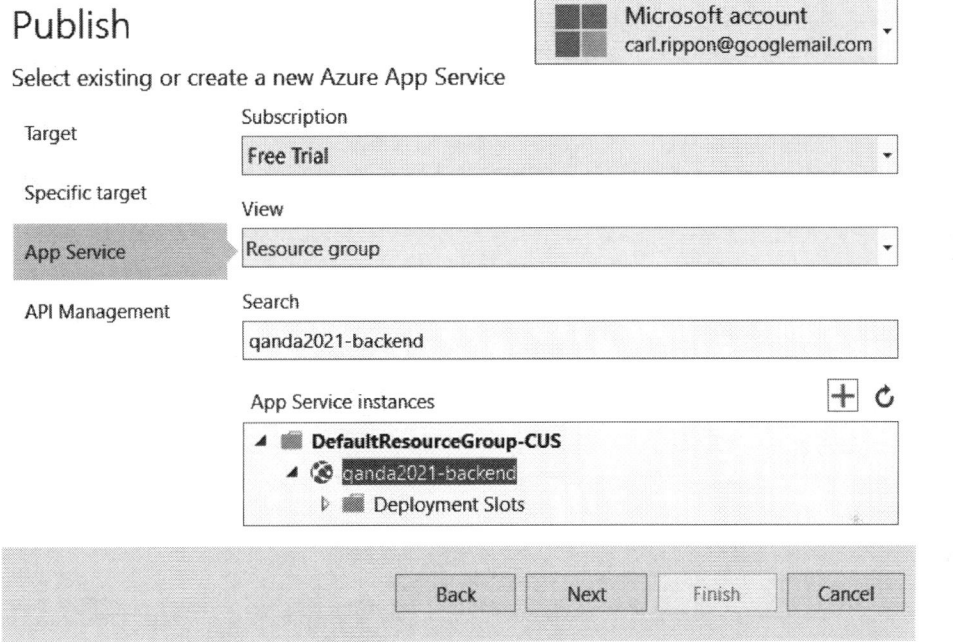

Figure 14.11 – Selecting the app service to deploy to

9. We will skip the next step for API Management. Check the **Skip this step** checkbox and click **Finish**. The profile for our production deployment is now saved and we are taken to a screen that summarizes it, as illustrated in the following screenshot:

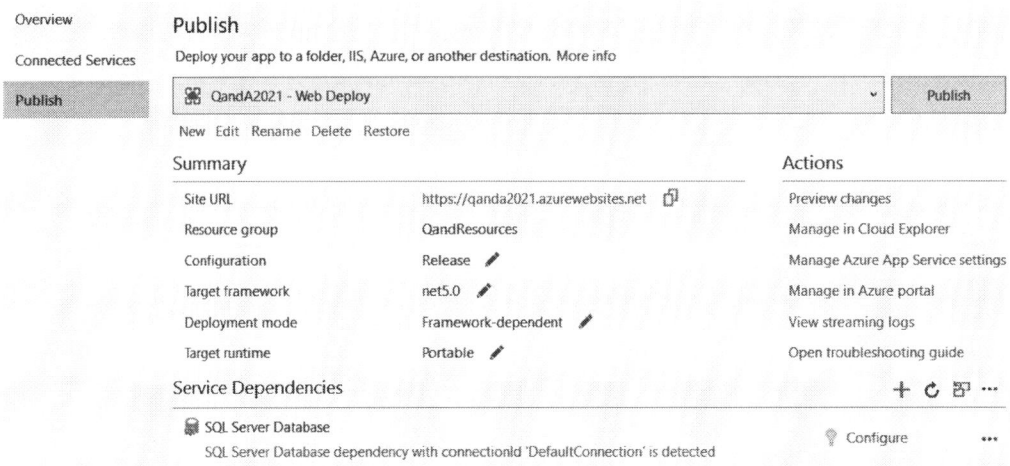

Figure 14.12 – Summary of publish configuration

10. Our app service is created but our backend still isn't deployed. We can confirm this by browsing to the link to the right of **Site URL**, which results in the following screen:

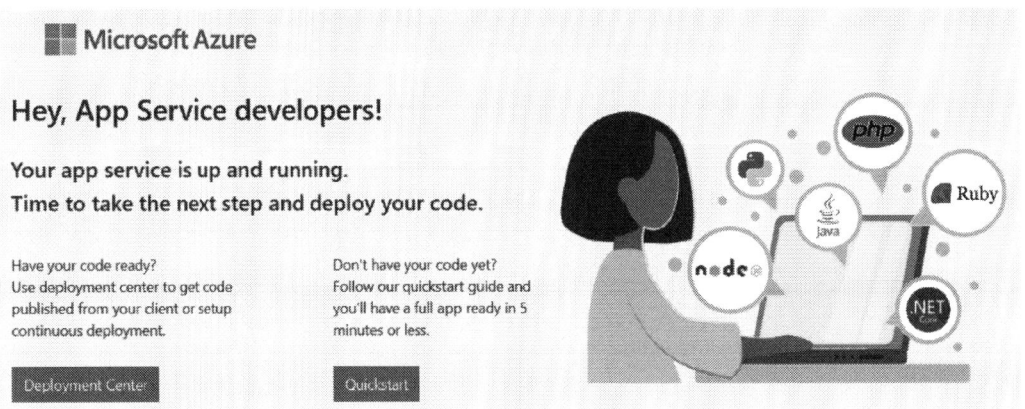

Figure 14.13 – App Service URL with a site that isn't deployed

11. We haven't provisioned anything to host our SQL database yet. We are going to do this now by clicking the **Add** option in the **Service Dependencies** section in the profile summary, back in Visual Studio.

12. The **Add dependency** dialog opens. Choose **Azure SQL Database** and click **Next**, as illustrated in the following screenshot:

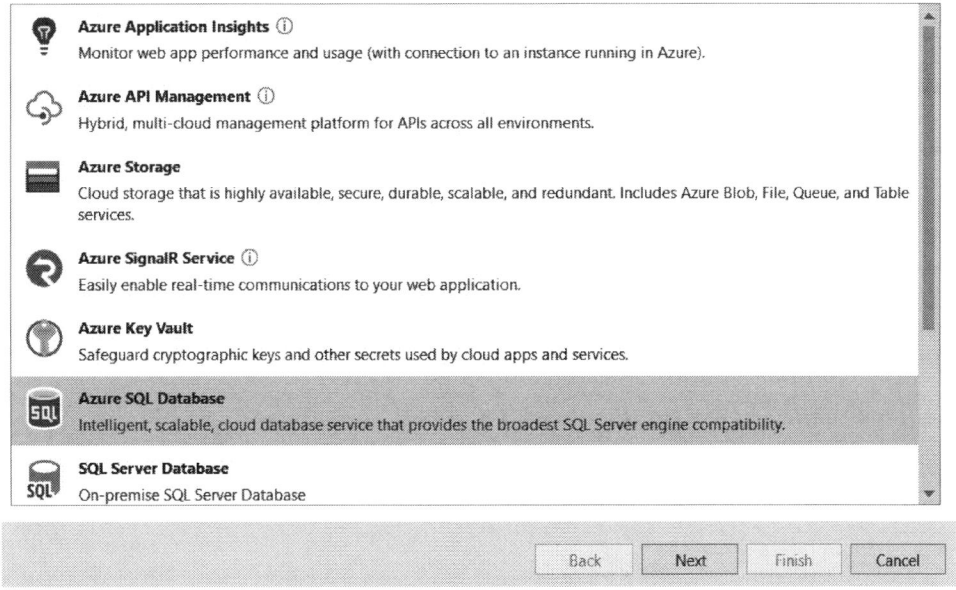

Figure 14.14 – Selecting Azure SQL Database

13. The dialog then shows the SQL databases in our Azure subscription. Click the green plus icon to create a new SQL database, as illustrated in the following screenshot:

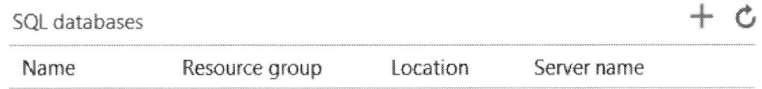

Figure 14.15 – Option to create a new SQL database

14. In the dialog that opens, enter your choice of database name. We will need this later, so keep a note of it.

15. We need to create a new database server, so click the **New...** option to the right of the **Database server** field.

16. Fill in the server details in the dialog that appears. Choose your own server name, username, and password. Take note of these details because we will need these again in a later step. Click the **OK** button to confirm the server details, as illustrated in the following screenshot:

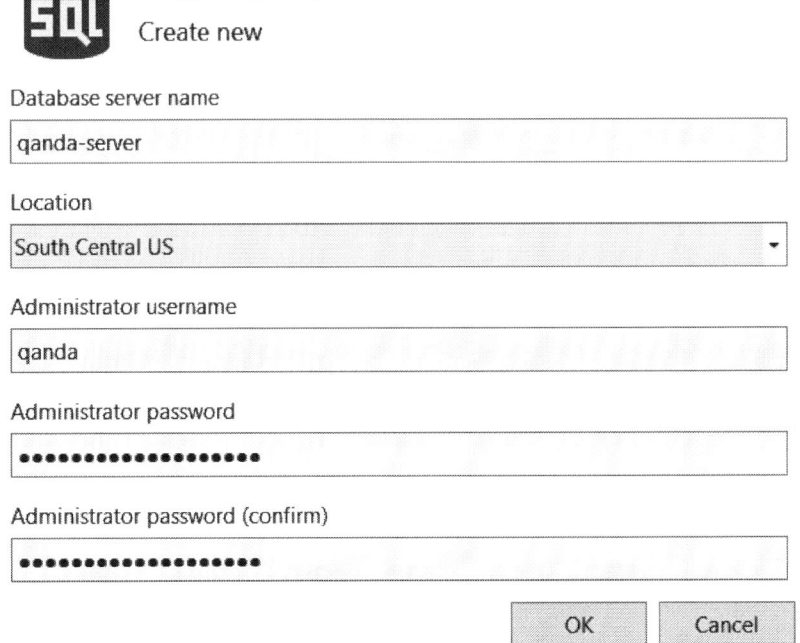

Figure 14.16 – New SQL Server dialog

17. Click the **Create** button on the **Azure SQL Database** dialog, as illustrated in the following screenshot. This will create the database in Azure, so it may take a few minutes to complete:

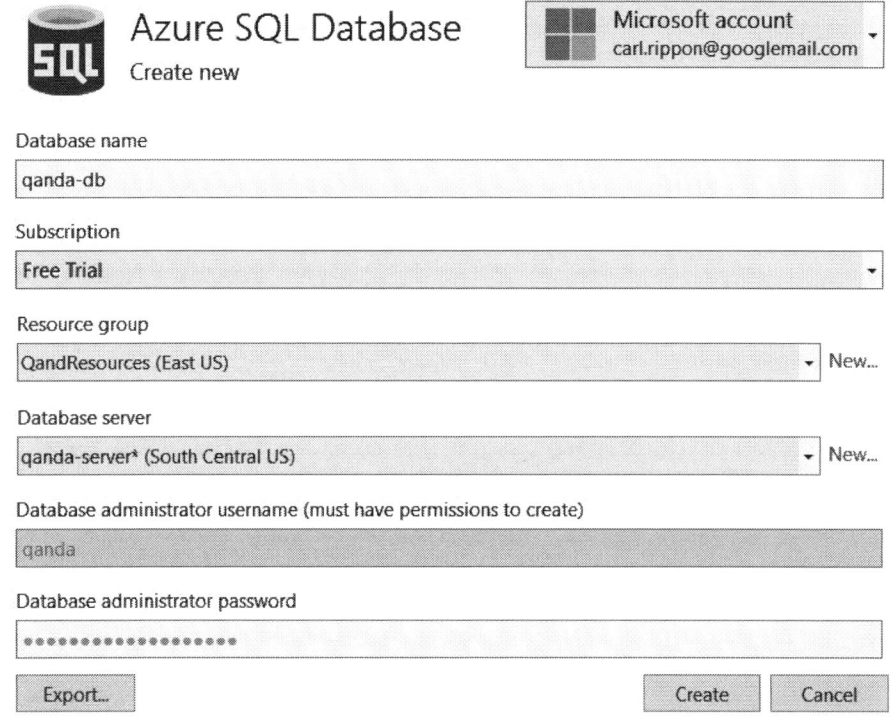

Figure 14.17 – New SQL Database dialog

18. After the database has been created, the **Azure SQL Database** dialog will close. The database will appear in the **SQL databases** list in the **Configure Azure SQL Database** dialog. Click on the database we have just created to select it, and click **Next**, as illustrated in the following screenshot:

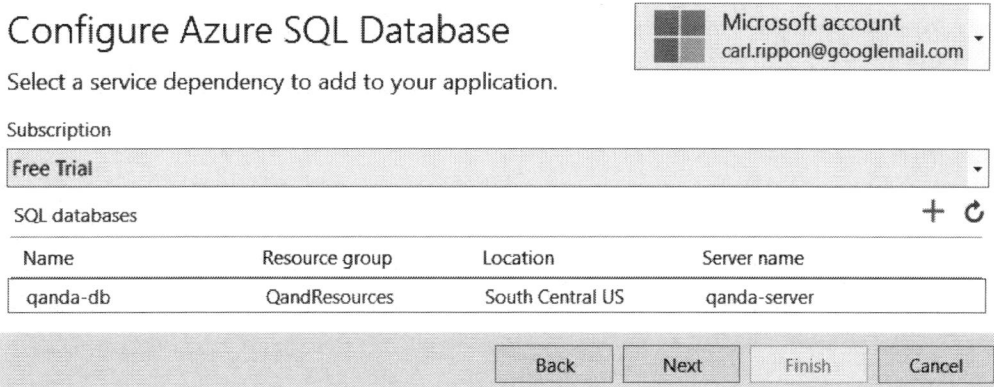

Figure 14.18 – SQL database list

19. Next, we are asked to define our database connection string. Make sure the connection name is `DefaultConnection`, and fill in the username and password we entered earlier when creating our database. Select **Azure App Settings** for where to save the connection string, and click **Next**, as illustrated in the following screenshot:

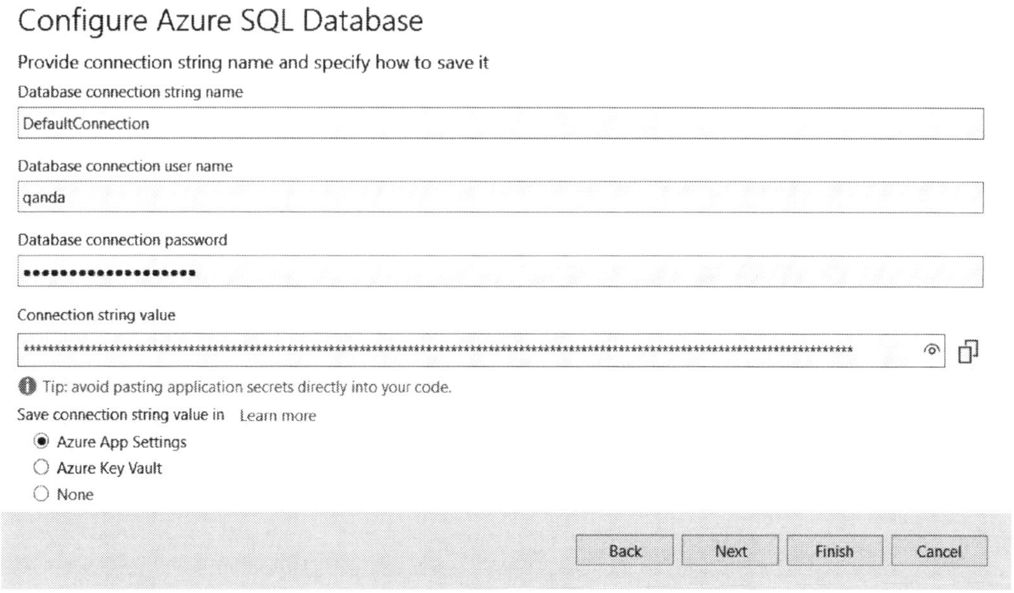

Figure 14.19 – Connection string configuration

This connection string will now be stored in the **Application Settings** section in our Azure App Service.

20. Press **Finish** on the summary dialog that appears, and then press **Close**.

21. We are taken back to the summary of the publish configuration, with confirmation that the SQL database has been configured, as illustrated in the following screenshot:

Publishing our ASP.NET Core backend to Azure

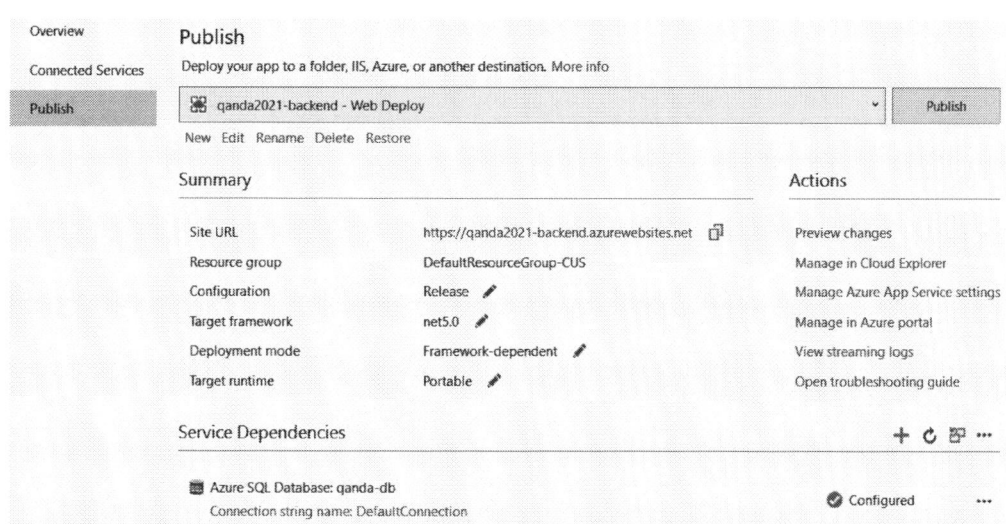

Figure 14.20 – Summary of publish configuration

22. The last thing to do before we deploy is to configure the deployment so that the .NET Core runtime and libraries are included in the deployment. We do this by clicking the pencil icon against **Deployment mode**, setting **Deployment Mode** to be **Self-Contained** in the dialog that appears, and clicking **Save**, as illustrated in the following screenshot:

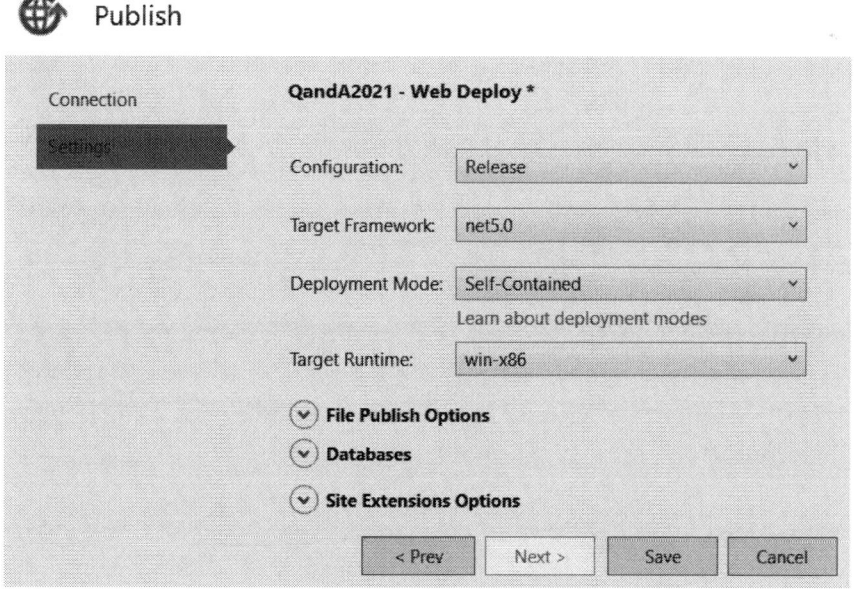

Figure 14.21 – Setting deployment mode to Self-Contained

23. Click the **Publish** button to deploy our code to Azure. This will take a few minutes to complete.

24. Eventually, a browser window will open, containing the path to our deployed backend. Add `/api/questions` to the path in the browser, as illustrated in the following screenshot:

[{"questionId":1,"title":"Why should I learn TypeScript?","content":"TypeScript seems to be getting popular so I wondered whether it is worth my time learning it? What benefits does it give over JavaScript?","userName":"bob.test@test.com","created":"2021-01-18T14:32:00","answers":null},{"questionId":2,"title":"Which state management tool should I use?","content":"There seem to be a fair few state management tools around for React - React, Unstated, ... Which one should I use?","userName":"jane.test@test.com","created":"2021-01-18T14:48:00","answers":null}]

Figure 14.22 – Our REST API in Azure

We will see the default questions from our database. Congratulations! We have just deployed our first SQL database and ASP.NET Core app in Azure!

Let's go to the Azure portal by navigating to `https://portal.azure.com`. Select the **All resources** option, which results in the following screen:

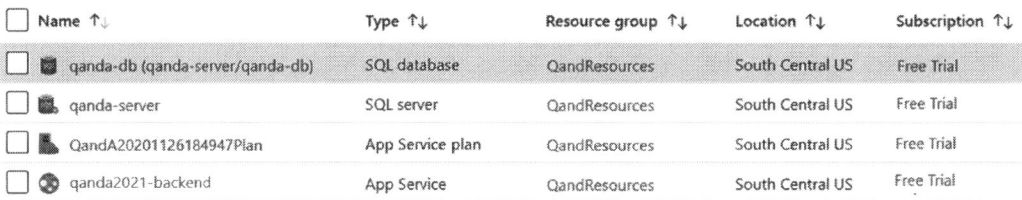

Figure 14.23 – Provisioned services in Azure

As expected, we see the services that we have just provisioned.

Excellent! We have just successfully deployed our backend in Azure!

As our backend is further developed, we can return to this profile and use the **Publish** button to quickly deploy our updated backend.

Next, let's follow a similar process to deploy to a staging environment.

Publishing to staging

Let's carry out the following steps to deploy our backend to a staging environment:

1. In **Solution Explorer**, right-click on the **QandA** project and select **Publish...**. This will open the publish screen, where we will see our production publish profile.

2. Select the **New** option to create a new publish profile.

3. Select **Azure** as the target and click **Next**.

4. Select **Azure App Service (Windows)** as the specific target and click **Next**.
5. Click the green plus icon to add a new Azure app service.
6. In the dialog that appears, enter the name for the new app service. This is going to be the service to host our backend in the staging environment. Note down the name you choose because we'll eventually reference this in the frontend project. Use the same resource group and hosting plan as we used for the production environment. Click **Create** to create the app service in Azure—this will take a few minutes.
7. When the **App Service** dialog has closed, we are taken back to the **Publish** dialog. Make sure our staging app service is selected in the **App Service Instances** list, and click **Next**.
8. Skip the **API Management** step by checking the **Skip this step** checkbox.
9. Press **Finish** to save the publish profile.
10. We want to create our staging database, so click on the **Configure** option in the **Service Dependencies** section.
11. Select **Azure SQL Database** in the dialog that appears, and click **Next**.
12. Click the green plus icon to create a database. The **Azure SQL Database** dialog opens.
13. Enter your choice of database name. We will need this later, so keep a note of it.
14. We will create a new database server for the staging environment, so click the **New...** option to the right of the **Database server** field.
15. Fill in the server details in the dialog that appears. Choose your own server name, username, and password. Take note of these details because we will need these again in a later step. Click the **OK** button to confirm these details.
16. Click the **Create** button on the **Azure SQL Database** dialog. This will create the database in Azure, so it may take a few minutes to complete.
17. When the **Azure SQL Database** dialog has closed, we are taken back to the **Configure Azure SQL Database** dialog. Make sure our staging database is selected, and click **Next**.
18. Next, we are asked to define our database connection string. Leave the connection name as `DefaultConnection`, and fill in the username and password we entered earlier when creating our staging database. Select **Azure App Settings** and click **Next**.
19. Press **Finish** on the summary dialog that appears, and then press **Close**.

20. In the publish summary, click the pencil icon against **Deployment mode**, and set **Deployment Mode** to be **Self-Contained** in the dialog that appears. Click **Save**.

21. We can then publish our code to the Azure services by clicking the **Publish** button. Again, this will take a few minutes to complete.

22. A browser window will eventually open, pointing to the new staging app service. If we add `/api/questions` to the path in the browser, we will see data returned from our staging database.

23. We need to tell our new app service that it is the staging environment rather than a production environment. This is so that it uses the `appsettings.Staging.json` file, which contains the `Frontend` setting for **Cross-Origin Resource Sharing** (**CORS**). By default, Azure assumes the environment is production, which means the `appsettings.Production.json` file is being used at the moment. Let's go to the Azure portal and select the staging app service in the **App Services** area.

24. In the **Settings** area, select **Configuration** and go to the **Application settings** tab.

25. Under **Application settings**, click the **New application setting** option and enter `ASPNETCORE_ENVIRONMENT` as the name and `Staging` as the value, and then click the **OK** button followed by the **Save** button. This creates an environment variable called `ASPNETCORE_ENVIRONMENT` with a `Staging` value. ASP.NET Core will look at this variable and then use the `appsettings.Staging.json` file for its configuration settings, as illustrated in the following screenshot:

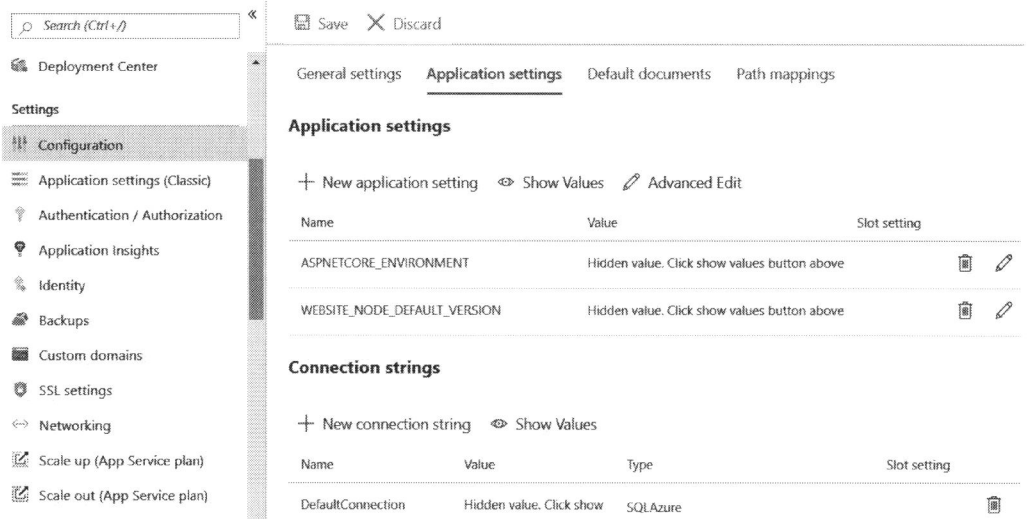

Figure 14.24 – Azure App Service application settings

That completes the deployment of our app to a staging environment.

That's great progress! Azure works beautifully with Visual Studio. In the next section, we are going to turn our attention to the frontend and make changes so that it will work in the Azure staging and production environments, as well as in development.

Configuring the React frontend for staging and production

In this section, we are going to change our frontend so that it makes requests to the correct backend APIs in staging and production. At the moment, the REST API has a hardcoded path set to the localhost. We are going to make use of environment variables as we did in our backend, to differentiate between the different environments. Let's open our frontend project in Visual Studio Code and carry out the following steps:

1. First, we are going to install a library called `cross-env` that will allow us to set environment variables. Let's execute the following command in the Terminal:

   ```
   > npm install cross-env --save-dev
   ```

2. Let's add the following scripts in `package.json` to execute staging and production builds:

   ```
   "scripts": {
     ...,
     "build": "react-scripts build",
     "build:production": "cross-env
       REACT_APP_ENV=production npm run build",
     "build:staging": "cross-env REACT_APP_ENV=staging
       npm run build",
     ...
   },
   ```

3. These scripts use the `cross-env` library to set an environment variable called `REACT_APP_ENV` to `staging` and `production` before doing an optimized build.

   So, `npm run build:staging` will execute a staging build and `npm run build:production` will execute a production build.

4. Let's make use of the `REACT_APP_ENV` environment variable when setting the `server` variable in the `AppSettings.ts` file. Open up `AppSettings.ts` and make the following changes:

```
export const server =
  process.env.REACT_APP_ENV === 'production'
    ? 'https://your-backend.azurewebsites.net'
    : process.env.REACT_APP_ENV === 'staging'
    ? 'https://your-backend-staging.azurewebsites.net'
    : 'http://localhost:17525';
```

We use a ternary expression to set the correct backend location, depending on the environment the app is running in. The production server is set to `https://your-backend.azurewebsites.net`, and the staging server is set to `https://your-backend-staging.azurewebsites.net`.

Make sure the staging and production locations you enter match the location of your deployed backends:

1. For deep links to work in Azure, we need to specify a URL rewrite rule to redirect all requests to the frontend to our `index.html` file. We can do this by adding a `web.config` file to the `public` folder with the following content:

```
<?xml version="1.0" encoding="utf-8"?>
<configuration>
  <system.webServer>
    <rewrite>
      <rules>
        <rule name="React Routes"
          stopProcessing="true">
          <match url=".*" />
          <conditions logicalGrouping="MatchAll">
            <add input="{REQUEST_FILENAME}"
              matchType="IsFile" negate="true" />
          </conditions>
          <action type="Rewrite" url="/"
            appendQueryString="true" />
        </rule>
      </rules>
    </rewrite>
  </system.webServer>
</configuration>
```

2. Now, let's do one final thing in preparation for deploying our frontend. Let's change the app to render the environment we are in. Let's open `Header.tsx` and add the environment name after the app name in the link to the home page, like this:

```
<Link
  to="/"
  css={ ... }
>
  Q & A
  <span
    css={css`
      margin-left: 5px;
      font-size: 14px;
      font-weight: normal;
    `}
  >
    {process.env.REACT_APP_ENV || 'dev'}
  </span>
</Link>
```

If the environment variable isn't populated, we assume we are in the development environment.

That completes the changes we need to make to our frontend. In the next section, we are going to deploy the frontend to Azure.

Publishing the React frontend to Azure

In this section, we are going to deploy our React frontend to Azure, to both staging and production environments.

Publishing to production

Let's carry out the following steps to publish our frontend to a production environment:

1. We'll start by provisioning an Azure app service. So, let's go to the Azure portal in a browser and go to the **App Services** area, and click the **Add** option.

2. Complete the form that opens by choosing the existing resource group, choosing an app name, and selecting `.NET 5` as the runtime stack and `Windows` as the operating system. Note that the app name we choose needs to be reflected in the `Frontend` setting in the `appsettings.Production.json` file in our backend project. Click the **Review + create** button and then the **Create** button to create the app service.

3. Let's move to Visual Studio Code now and create a production build by running the following command in the Terminal:

```
> npm run build:production
```

After the build has finished, the production build will consist of all of the files in the `build` folder.

4. We are going to use the **Azure App Service** extension to perform the Azure deployment. So, go to the **Extensions** area in Visual Studio Code (*Ctrl + Shift + X*), search `Azure App Service`, and install the extension shown in the following screenshot:

Figure 14.25 – Azure App Service extension in Visual Studio Code

5. Click the Azure icon in the left-hand navigation options to open the Azure App Service panel, as illustrated in the following screenshot:

Figure 14.26 – Azure App Service panel

6. Click on the **Sign in to Azure...** option. We are prompted to enter our Microsoft account credentials, so let's enter these.

7. We should see the frontend app service listed in the tree. Right-click on this and choose the **Deploy to Web App...** option, as illustrated in the following screenshot:

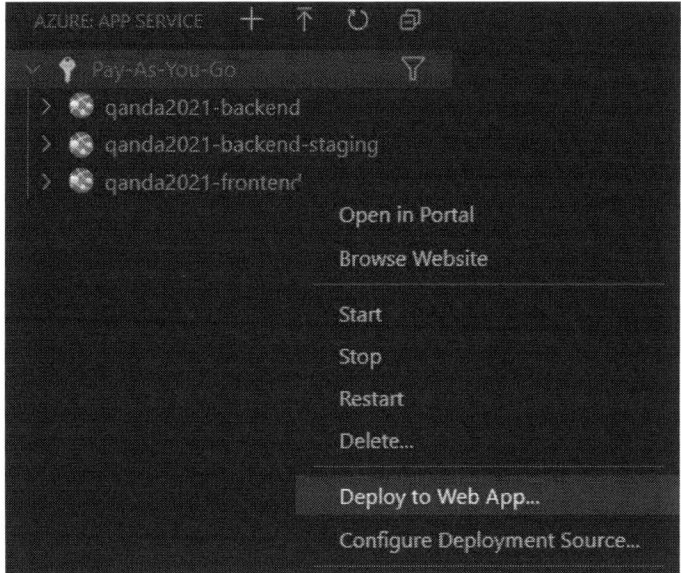

Figure 14.27 – Deploying an app to an Azure app service

8. We should select our build folder when prompted for the folder to deploy.

9. We are then asked to confirm the deployment, which we do by clicking the **Deploy** button, as illustrated in the following screenshot:

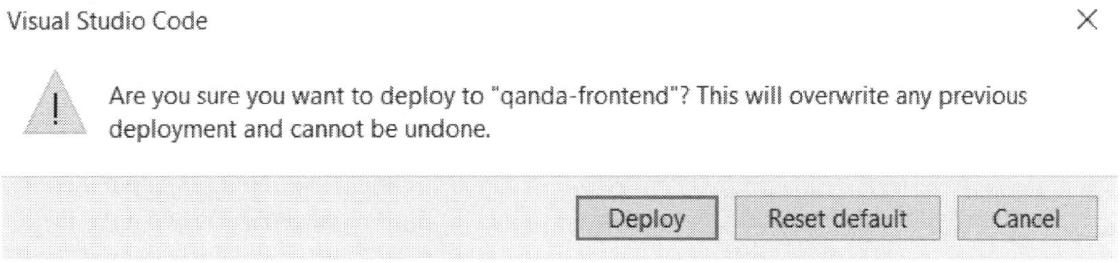

Figure 14.28 – Deployment confirmation

10. Deployment will take a minute or so before we get confirmation that it is complete, as illustrated in the following screenshot:

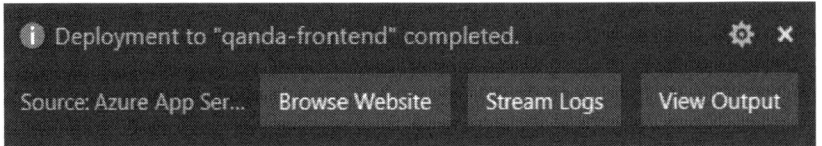

Figure 14.29 – Confirmation of deployment completion

11. If we click on the **Browse Website** option, our frontend in Azure will display in a browser, as illustrated in the following screenshot:

Figure 14.30 – Q&A app running in production

Our frontend is now deployed nicely to the production environment. We won't be able to sign in successfully yet—we'll resolve this after we have published our frontend to the staging environment.

Publishing to staging

Let's carry out the following steps to deploy our frontend to a staging environment:

1. We'll start by provisioning another Azure app service. So, let's go to the Azure portal in a browser and go to the **App Services** area, and click the **Add** option.

2. Enter an app name and choose the existing resource group. Remember that the app name we choose needs to be reflected in the `Frontend` setting of the `appsettings.Staging.json` file in our backend project. Remember also that the runtime stack should be `.NET 5` and that `Windows` should be the operating system. Click the **Review + create** button and then the **Create** button to create the app service.

3. Let's move to Visual Studio Code now and create a staging build by running the following command in the Terminal:

```
> npm run build:staging
```

Publishing the React frontend to Azure 511

After the build has finished, the staging build will consist of all of the files in the `build` folder overwriting the production build.

4. In the **Azure App Service** section in Visual Studio Code, we should see the frontend staging app service listed in the tree. Note that we might need to click the **Refresh** toolbar option for it to appear. Right-click on the frontend staging app service and choose the **Deploy to Web App...** option.

5. We should select our `build` folder when prompted for the folder to deploy, and then confirm the deployment when prompted.

6. After a minute or so, we'll get confirmation that the deployment is complete. If we click on the **Browse Website** option, our staging frontend in Azure will show in a browser, as illustrated in the following screenshot:

Figure 14.31 – Q&A app running in staging

7. Next, let's tell Auth0 about the Azure staging and production URLs it should trust. In Auth0, we need to update the following settings against our Q&A application. Refer to *Chapter 11*, *Securing the Backend*, if you can't remember how to do this.

    Allowed Callback URLs—This is shown in the following screenshot:

Figure 14.32 – Auth0 allowed callback URLs

Allowed Web Origins—This is shown in the following screenshot:

Allowed Web Origins

> http://localhost:3000, https://qanda2021-frontend.azurewebsites.net, https://qanda2021-frontend-staging.azurewebsites.net

Figure 14.33 – Auth0 allowed web origins

Allowed Logout URLs—This is shown in the following screenshot:

Allowed Logout URLs

> http://localhost:3000/signout-callback, https://qanda2021-frontend.azurewebsites.net/signout-callback, https://qanda2021-frontend-staging.azurewebsites.net/signout-callback

Figure 14.34 – Auth0 allowed logout URLs

We can find these settings by clicking on the **Applications** item in the left-hand navigation menu and then clicking on the **Q and A** application. We add the additional URLs for both the staging and production environments after the development environment URLs. The URLs for the different environments need to be separated by a comma.

We should now be able to sign in to our production and staging Q&A apps successfully.

That completes the deployment of our frontend to both production and staging environments.

Summary

Azure works beautifully with both React and ASP.NET Core apps. In ASP.NET Core, we can have different `appsettings.json` files to store the different settings for the different environments, such as the frontend location for CORS. In our React code, we can use an environment variable to make requests to the appropriate backend. We also need to include a `web.config` file in our React app so that deep links are redirected to the `index.html` page and then handled by React Router. The environment variable can be set in specific build `npm` scripts for each environment. We used three environments in this chapter, but both the frontend and backend could easily be configured to support more environments.

Azure has integration from both Visual Studio and Visual Studio Code that makes deploying React and ASP.NET Core apps a breeze. We use the built-in **Publish...** option in Visual Studio to provision the SQL database with app services and then perform the deployment. We can also provision app services in the Azure portal, which we did for our frontend. We can then use the **Azure App Service Visual Studio Code** extension to deploy the frontend to an app service.

Although deploying our app to Azure was super-easy, we can make it even easier by automating the deployment when we check code into source control. We'll do this in the next chapter.

Questions

The following questions will test what we have learned in this chapter:

1. In ASP.NET Core, what is the name of the file where we store any settings specific to the production environment?

2. What is the reason for our ASP.NET Core backend needing the `Frontend` setting?

3. Let's pretend we have introduced a QA environment and have created the following npm script to execute a build for this environment:

   ```
   "build:qa": "cross-env REACT_APP_ENV=qa npm run build"
   ```

   Which npm command would we use to produce a QA build?

4. What would be broken if we didn't include the `web.config` file with our React frontend?

5. Why didn't we store the production and staging connection strings in the `appsettings.Product.json` or `appsettings.Staging.json` files?

Answers

1. In ASP.NET Core, the name of the file where we store any settings specific to the production environment is called `appsettings.Production.json`.

2. The reason for our ASP.NET Core backend needing the `Frontend` setting is to set up the allowed origin in a CORS policy.

3. We would use `npm run build:qa` to produce a QA build.

4. If we didn't include the `web.config` file with our React frontend, we wouldn't be able to deep-link into our app—for example, putting the path to a question (such as `https://qandafrontend.z19.web.core.windows.net/questions/1`) directly in the browser's address bar and pressing *Enter* will result in a **Page not found** error being returned.

5. Connection strings contain a secret username and password. It is safer to store these in Azure rather than in our source code.

Further reading

The following resources are useful for finding more information on deploying ASP.NET Core and React apps to Azure:

- **Using multiple environments in ASP.NET Core**: `https://docs.microsoft.com/en-us/aspnet/core/fundamentals/environments`
- **Deploying ASP.NET Core apps to Azure App Service**: `https://docs.microsoft.com/en-us/aspnet/core/host-and-deploy/azure-apps`
- **Deploying a static website to Azure from VS Code**: `https://code.visualstudio.com/tutorials/static-website/getting-started`

15
Implementing CI and CD with Azure DevOps

In this chapter, we are going to implement **Continuous Integration** (**CI**) and **Continuous Delivery** (**CD**) for our Q&A app using Azure DevOps. We'll start by understanding exactly what CI and CD are before getting into Azure DevOps.

In Azure DevOps, we'll implement CI for the frontend and backend using a build pipeline. The CI process will be triggered when developers push code to our source code repository. Then, we'll implement CD for the frontend and backend using a release pipeline that will be automatically triggered when a CI build completes successfully. The release pipeline will do a deployment to the staging environment automatically, run our backend integration tests, and then promote the staging deployment to production.

By the end of this chapter, we'll have a robust process of delivering features to our users incredibly quickly with a great level of reliability, thus making our team very productive.

In this chapter, we'll cover the following topics:

- Getting started with CI and CD
- Implementing CI
- Implementing CD

Technical requirements

We'll use the following tools and services in this chapter:

- **GitHub**: This chapter assumes that the source code for our app is hosted on GitHub. An account and repository can be set up for free at `https://github.com`.
- **Azure DevOps**: We will use this to implement and host our CI and CD processes. This can be found at `https://dev.azure.com/`.
- **Microsoft Azure**: We will use the Azure app services and SQL databases that we set up in the previous chapter. The Azure portal can be found at `https://portal.azure.com`.
- **Visual Studio Code**: This can be downloaded and installed from `https://code.visualstudio.com/`.
- **Node.js and npm**: These can be downloaded from `https://nodejs.org/`. If you already have these installed, make sure that Node.js is at least version 8.2 and that npm is at least version 5.2.
- **Q and A**: We'll start with the Q and A frontend and backend projects we finished in the previous chapter, which are available at `https://github.com/PacktPublishing/ASP.NET-Core-5-and-React-Second-Edition` in the `chapter-15/start` folder.

All the code snippets in this chapter can be found online at `https://github.com/PacktPublishing/ASP.NET-Core-5-and-React-Second-Edition`. In order to restore code from a chapter, the source code repository can be downloaded and the relevant folder opened in the relevant editor. If the code is frontend code, then `npm install` can be entered in the Terminal to restore the dependencies.

Check out the following video to see the code in action: `https://bit.ly/3mE6Qta`.

Getting started with CI and CD

In this section, we'll start by understanding what CI and CD are before making a change in our frontend code to allow the frontend tests to work in CI. Then, we'll create our Azure DevOps project, which will host our build and release pipelines.

Understanding CI and CD

CI is the process of developer working copies being merged to a shared master branch of code in a source code system several times a day, automatically triggering what is called a **build**. A build is the process of automatically producing all the artifacts that are required to successfully deploy, test, and run our production software. The benefit of CI is that it automatically gives the team feedback on the quality of the changes that are being made.

CD is the process of getting changes that developers make to the software into production, regularly and safely, in a sustainable way. So, it is the process of taking the build from CI and getting that deployed to the production environment. The CI build may be deployed to a staging environment, where the end-to-end tests are executed and passed before deployment is made to the production environment. At its most extreme, the CD process is fully automated and triggered when a CI build finishes. Often, a member of the team has to approve the final step of deploying the software to production, which should have already passed a series of automated tests in staging. CD is also not always triggered automatically when a CI build finishes; sometimes, it is automatically triggered at a particular time of day. The benefit of CD is that the development team delivers value to users of the software faster and more reliably.

The following diagram shows the high-level CI and CD flow that we are going to set up:

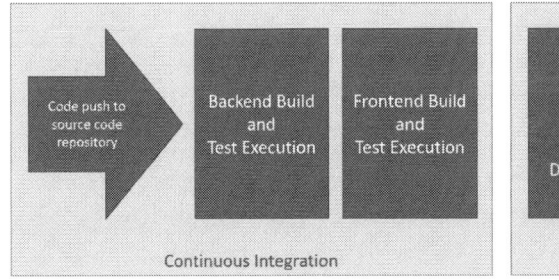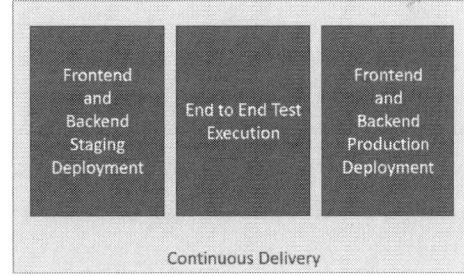

Figure 15.1 – High-level CI and CD flow

When code is pushed to our source code repository, we are going to build all the backend and frontend artifacts and execute the xUnit and Jest tests. If the builds and tests are successful, this will automatically kick off a staging deployment. The Cypress tests will execute on the staging deployment and, if they pass, a production deployment will be triggered.

Enabling our tests to run in CI and CD

We need to make some changes to the configuration of the frontend tests and end-to-end tests so that they execute correctly in the build and deployment pipelines. Let's open the frontend project in Visual Studio Code and make the following changes:

1. First, we'll add a script named `test:ci` in the `package.json` file, which will run the Jest tests in CI mode, as follows:

   ```
   ...
   "scripts": {
     ...
     "test": "react-scripts test",
     "test:ci": "cross-env CI=true react-scripts test",
     ...
   },
   ...
   ```

   This script sets an environment variable called `CI` to `true` before running the Jest tests.

2. Our Cypress tests are going to execute in the deployment pipeline on the staging app after it has been deployed. We need to do a few things to ensure that our Cypress tests run in the deployment pipeline. First, let's create a `cypress.json` file in the `cypress` folder with the following content:

   ```
   {
     "baseUrl": "https://your-frontend-
       staging.azurewebsites.net",
     "integrationFolder": "integration",
     "pluginsFile": "plugins/index.js",
     "supportFile": "support/index.js",
     "chromeWebSecurity": false
   }
   ```

   This is going to be the `cypress.json` file that runs the tests on the staging app after it has been deployed. Here's an explanation of the settings we have added:

   - `baseUrl`: This is the root path for the app, which should be the **Uniform Resource Locator** (**URL**) of our staging app. Change this appropriately for the staging app that you have deployed.
   - `integrationFolder`: This is the folder where our end-to-end tests are located, relative to the `cypress.json` file. In our case, this is a folder called `integration`.

- pluginsFile: This is a file that contains any plugins relative to the `cypress.json` file. In our case, this is a file called `index.js`, which can be found in the `plugins` folder.
- supportFile: This is a file relative to the `cypress.json` file that contains code to execute before the tests run. In our case, this is a file called `index.js`, which can be found in the `support` folder.
- chromeWebSecurity: Setting this to `false` allows the Q&A app to navigate to Auth0 to authenticate.

3. Next, let's create a `package.json` file in the `cypress` folder with the following content:

```
{
  "name": "cypress-app-tests",
  "version": "0.1.0",
  "private": true,
  "scripts": {
    "cy:run": "cypress run"
  },
  "devDependencies": {
    "@testing-library/cypress": "^7.0.1",
    "cypress": "^5.4.0"
  }
}
```

The key items in this file are declaring Cypress and the Cypress Testing Library as development dependencies and the `cy:run` script, which we'll use later to run the Cypress tests.

4. Next, we are going to remove all the example tests that Cypress originally installed for us. So, let's delete the `examples` folder from the `integration` folder, which can be found in the `cypress` folder. Now, the only file in the `integration` folder should be our `qanda.js` file.

Now, our Jest and Cypress tests will be able to execute during a build and deployment.

Creating an Azure DevOps project

Azure DevOps can be found at `https://dev.azure.com/`. We can create an account for free if we haven't got one already.

To create a new project, click the **New project** button on the home page and enter a name for the project in the panel that appears. We can choose to make our project public or private before clicking the **Create** button, as illustrated in the following screenshot:

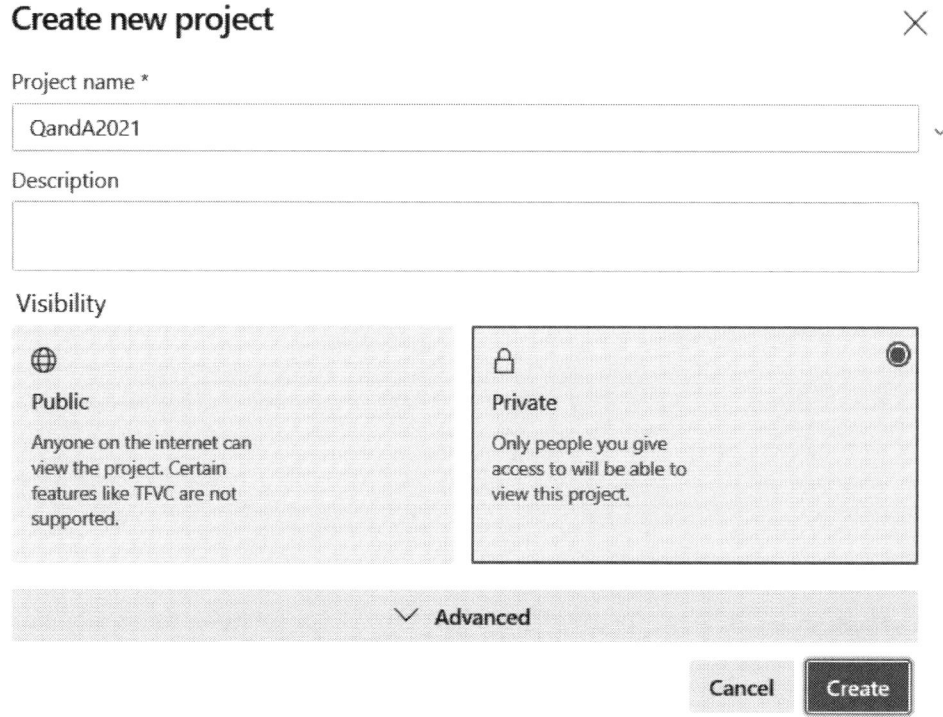

Figure 15.2 – Creating a new Azure DevOps project

That's our Azure DevOps project created. In the next section, we will create a build pipeline in our Azure DevOps project for our Q&A app.

Implementing CI

In this section, we are going to implement CI for our Q&A app using a build pipeline in Azure DevOps. We will start by creating a build pipeline from a template and add extra steps to build all the artifacts of the Q&A app. We'll also observe the build trigger when code is pushed to our source code repository.

Creating a build pipeline

Let's carry out the following steps to create a build pipeline from a template:

1. Click on **Pipelines** in the left-hand navigation menu and then click on **Create pipeline.**

2. We will be asked to specify where our code repository is hosted, as illustrated in the following screenshot:

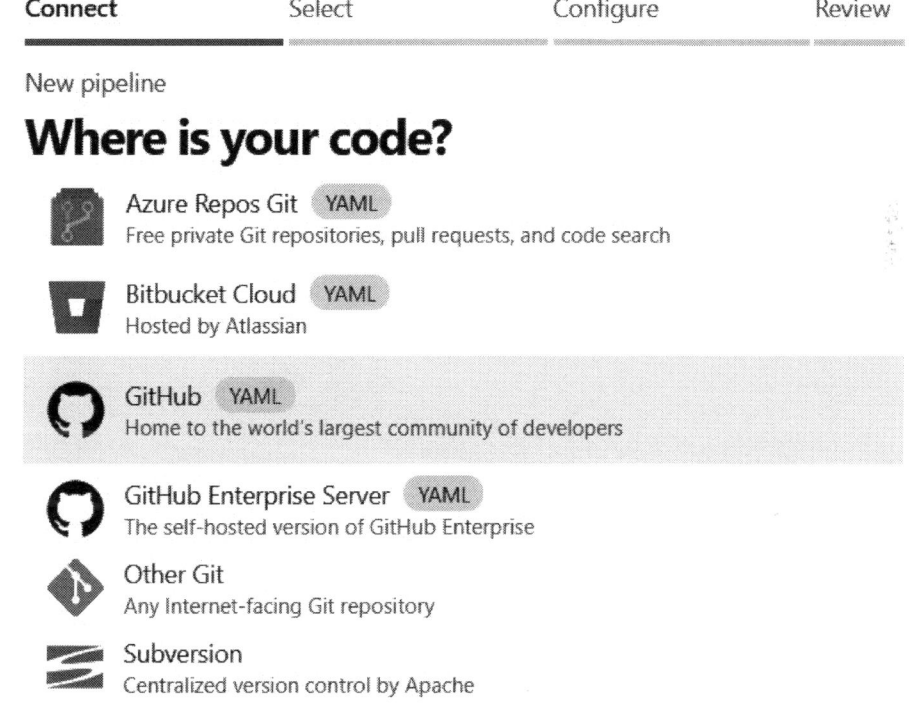

Figure 15.3 – Selecting the code repository host for the new build pipeline

3. Click on the appropriate option. Azure DevOps will go through an authorization process to allow Azure DevOps to access our repositories.

4. Then, we will be prompted to choose a specific repository for our code and authorize access to it, as illustrated in the following screenshot:

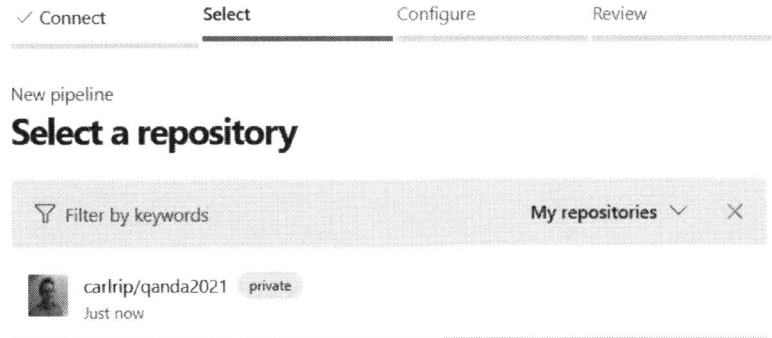

Figure 15.4 – Selecting code repository for the new build pipeline

5. Azure DevOps will inspect the code in the repository so that it can suggest an appropriate CI template for the technology in play. Select the **ASP.NET Core** template. Don't choose the **ASP.NET Core (.NET Framework)** template. You may need to click the **Show more** button to find the **ASP.NET Core** template.

6. Then, a build pipeline is created for us from the template. The steps in the pipeline are defined in an `azure-pipelines.yml` file, which will be added to our source code repository. We will make changes to this file in the next section, *Implementing CD*, but for now, let's click the **Save and run** button, as illustrated in the following screenshot:

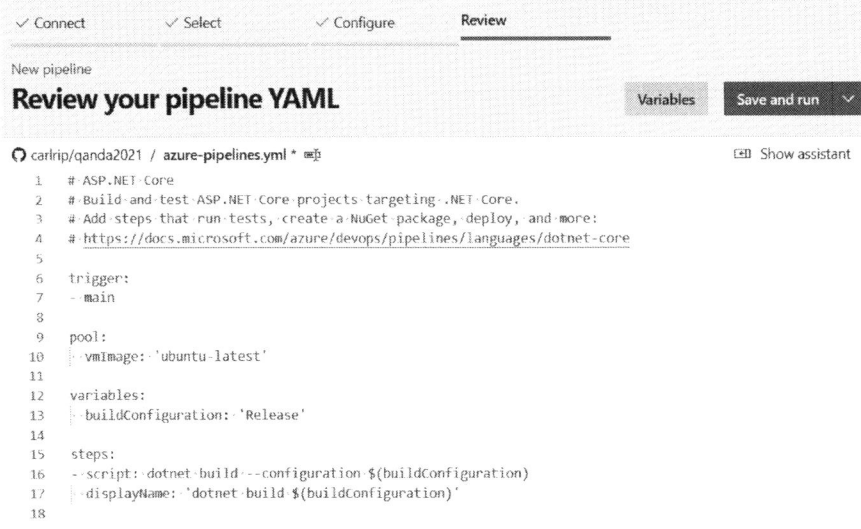

Figure 15.5 – Build pipeline code review step

7. Click on the **Save and run** button in the confirmation panel that appears. The pipeline will be saved, and a build will be triggered. The build will fail, but don't worry about that—we'll resolve this in the next section, *Implementing CD*.

8. After a minute or so, click on the **Pipelines** option in the **Pipelines** section. This lists the build pipelines in our project as well as useful information about when it was last run. We'll see confirmation that the pipeline failed, as illustrated in the following screenshot:

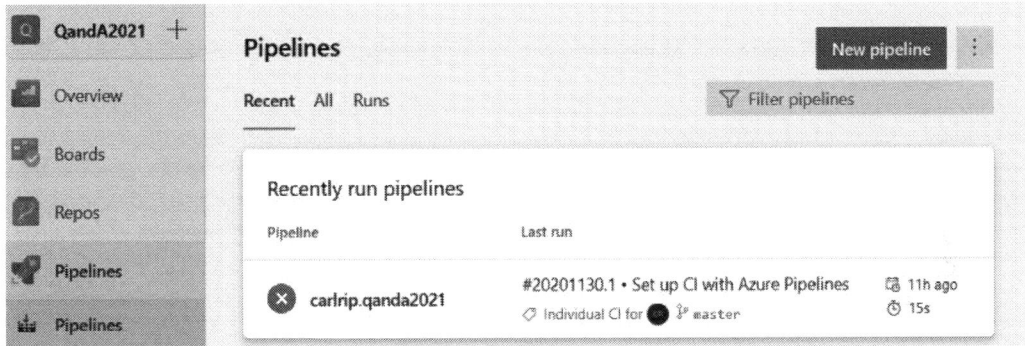

Figure 15.6 – Build pipeline list

9. Click on this build pipeline in the list. We are then taken to the build pipeline page, which shows its run history. The **Edit** option allows us to change the build pipeline. The **Run pipeline** option allows us to manually run the build pipeline. These options are illustrated in the following screenshot:

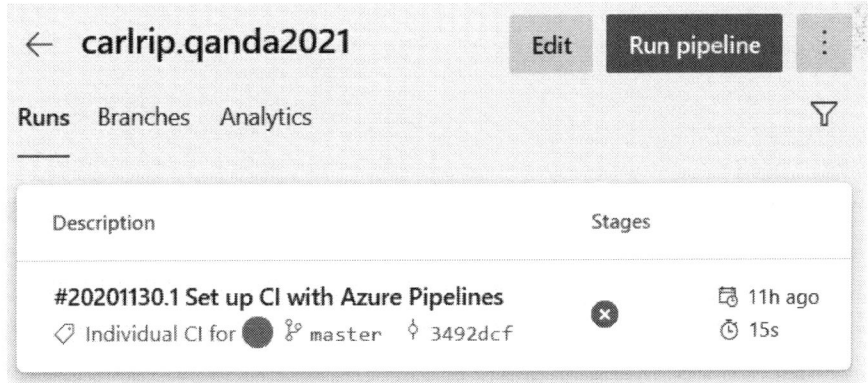

Figure 15.7 – Build pipeline page

That's our basic build pipeline created. In the next section, we'll fully implement the build pipeline for our Q&A app.

Implementing a build pipeline for our Q&A app

We are now going to change the build pipeline so that it builds and publishes all the artifacts in our Q&A app. The published artifacts that we require are as follows:

- `backend`: This will contain our .NET Core backend, which will be used for the staging and production environments.
- `frontend-production`: This contains our React frontend for the production environment.
- `frontend-staging`: This contains our React frontend for the staging environment.

Let's carry out the following steps:

1. In our Azure DevOps project, on our build pipeline, click the **Edit** button to edit the pipeline. The build pipeline is defined in a **YAML Ain't Markup Language** (**YAML**) file called `azure-pipelines`. Azure DevOps lets us edit this file in its YAML editor.

   > **Important Note**
   > YAML is commonly used for configuration files because it is a little more compact than **JavaScript Object Notation** (**JSON**) and can contain comments.

   The following YAML file was generated by the ASP.NET Core build pipeline template:

   ```
   # ASP.NET Core
   # Build and test ASP.NET Core projects targeting .NET Core.
   # Add steps that run tests, create a NuGet package, deploy, and more:
   # https://docs.microsoft.com/azure/devops/pipelines/languages/dotnet-core

   trigger:
   - main

   pool:
     vmImage: 'ubuntu-latest'

   variables:
     buildConfiguration: 'Release'

   steps:
   ```

```
- script: dotnet build --configuration
$(buildConfiguration)
    displayName: 'dotnet build $(buildConfiguration)'
```

> **Important Note**
>
> The steps in a build are defined after the `steps:` keyword. Each step is defined after a hyphen (`-`). The `script:` keyword allows a command to be executed, while the `displayName:` keyword is the description of the step that we'll see in the log file. The variables that are used in the steps are declared after the `variables:` keyword. The `trigger:` keyword determines when a build should be started.

So, the build contains a single step, which executes the `dotnet build` command with `Release` passed into the `--configuration` parameter.

2. The reason our build failed was that the agent couldn't find a .NET solution to build because it isn't in the root directory in our source code repository—it is in a folder called `backend`. So, let's change this step to the following:

```
steps:
- script: dotnet build --configuration
$(buildConfiguration)
    workingDirectory: backend
    displayName: 'backend build'
```

We have specified that the working directory is the `backend` folder and changed the step name slightly.

3. We are also going to make sure the build is using the correct version of .NET Core. Add the following highlighted lines as the first step, before the build step:

```
steps:
- task: UseDotNet@2
  inputs:
    packageType: 'sdk'
    version: '5.0.100'
- script: dotnet build --configuration
$(buildConfiguration)
    workingDirectory: backend
    displayName: 'backend build'
```

If you are using a different version of .NET Core, then change the version as required.

4. The trigger for the build pipeline is set to a branch called `main` at the moment. Change this to `master`, as follows:

```
trigger:
- master
```

5. Let's click the **Save** button to save the build configuration.

6. A confirmation dialog appears that allows us to change the Git commit message and branch. Commit this to the master branch and click **Save**, as illustrated in the following screenshot:

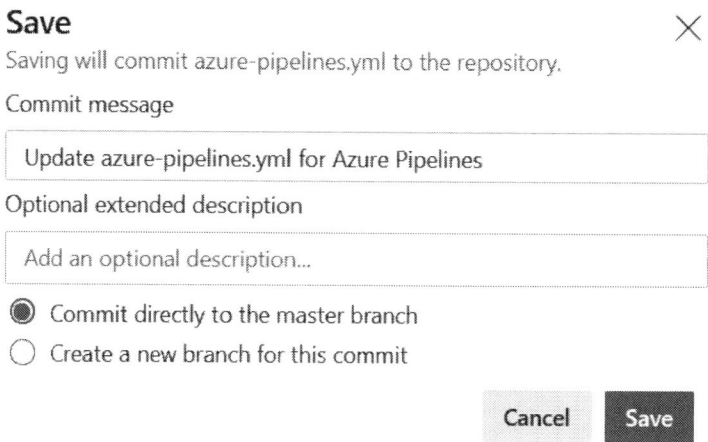

Figure 15.8 – Build pipeline save confirmation

7. A build will automatically be triggered because the `azure-pipelines.yml` file has changed in our repository. After a few minutes, go to the build pipeline page again. We'll see that the pipeline has succeeded this time, as illustrated in the following screenshot:

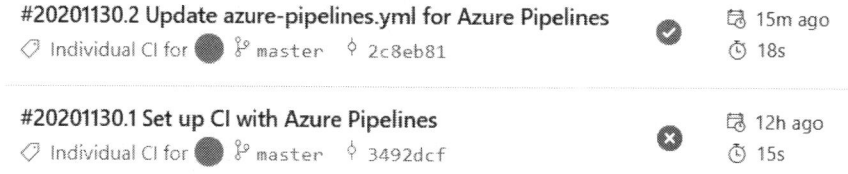

Figure 15.9 – Successful build pipeline execution

8. We need to do more work in our build configuration before it is complete. So, let's edit the build pipeline again and add a step to run the .NET tests, as follows:

```
steps:
- task: UseDotNet@2
  inputs:
    packageType: 'sdk'
    version: '5.0.100'
- script: dotnet build --configuration $(buildConfiguration)
  workingDirectory: backend
  displayName: 'backend build'
- script: dotnet test
  workingDirectory: backend
  displayName: 'backend tests'
```

Here, we use the `dotnet test` command to run the automated tests.

9. Next, let's add a step so that we can publish the .NET backend, as follows:

```
steps:
...

- script: dotnet publish -c $(buildConfiguration) --self-contained true -r win-x86
  workingDirectory: backend
  displayName: 'backend publish'
```

Here, we use the `dotnet publish` command in order to publish the code. What's the difference between `dotnet build` and `dotnet publish`? Well, the `dotnet build` command just outputs the artifacts from the code we have written and not any third-party libraries such as Dapper.

We are deploying the backend in self-contained mode under the win-86 architecture, like we did in the last chapter with Visual Studio.

10. Now, we need to zip up the published files using the `ArchiveFile@2` task, as follows:

```
steps:
...

- task: ArchiveFiles@2
  inputs:
    rootFolderOrFile: 'backend/bin/Release/net5.0/win-x86/publish'
    includeRootFolder: false
    archiveType: zip
```

```
        archiveFile: '$(Build.ArtifactStagingDirectory)/
          backend/$(Build.BuildId).zip'
        replaceExistingArchive: true
      displayName: 'backend zip files'
```

11. The last step for our backend build is to publish the ZIP file we have just created to the build pipeline so that it can be picked up by the release pipeline, which we'll configure in the next section. The code for this is illustrated in the following snippet:

```
steps:
...

- task: PublishBuildArtifacts@1
  inputs:
    pathtoPublish: '$(Build.ArtifactStagingDirectory)/
      backend'
    artifactName: 'backend'
  displayName: 'backend publish to pipeline'
```

Here, we use the `PublishBuildArtifacts@1` task to publish the ZIP file to the pipeline. We named it `backend`.

This completes the build configuration for the backend. Let's move on to the frontend now.

12. In the same YAML file, add the following command to install the frontend dependencies:

```
steps:
...

- script: npm install
  workingDirectory: frontend
  displayName: 'frontend install dependencies'
```

Here, we use the `npm install` command to install the dependencies. Notice that we have set the working directory to `frontend`, which is where our frontend code is located.

13. The next step is to run the frontend tests, as follows:

```
steps:
...

- script: npm run test:ci
  workingDirectory: frontend
  displayName: 'frontend tests'
```

Here, we use the `npm run test:ci` command to run the tests rather than `npm run test`, because the CI environment variable is set to `true`, meaning that the tests will run correctly in our build.

14. In the next block of steps, we will produce a frontend build for the staging environment, zip up the files in this build, zip up the Cypress tests, and then publish this to the pipeline, like this:

```yaml
steps:
...

- script: npm run build:staging
  workingDirectory: frontend
  displayName: 'frontend staging build'

- task: ArchiveFiles@2
  inputs:
    rootFolderOrFile: 'frontend/build'
    includeRootFolder: false
    archiveType: zip
    archiveFile: '$(Build.ArtifactStagingDirectory)/
      frontend-staging/build.zip'
    replaceExistingArchive: true
  displayName: 'frontend staging zip files'

- task: ArchiveFiles@2
  inputs:
    rootFolderOrFile: 'frontend/cypress'
    includeRootFolder: false
    archiveType: zip
    archiveFile: '$(Build.ArtifactStagingDirectory)/
      frontend-staging/tests.zip'
    replaceExistingArchive: true
  displayName: 'frontend cypress zip files'

- task: PublishBuildArtifacts@1
  inputs:
    pathtoPublish: '$(Build.ArtifactStagingDirectory)/
      frontend-staging'
    artifactName: 'frontend-staging'
  displayName: 'frontend staging publish to pipeline'
```

Here, we use the `npm run build:staging` command to produce the staging build, which sets the `REACT_APP_ENV` environment variable to `staging`. We use the `ArchiveFiles@2` task we used previously to zip up the frontend build and Cypress tests, and then the `PublishBuildArtifacts@1` task to publish the ZIP file to the pipeline.

15. Next, we'll produce a build for the production environment, zip it up, and then publish this to the pipeline, as follows:

```yaml
steps:
...

- script: npm run build:production
  workingDirectory: frontend
  displayName: 'frontend production build'

- task: ArchiveFiles@2
  inputs:
    rootFolderOrFile: 'frontend/build'
    includeRootFolder: false
    archiveType: zip
    archiveFile: '$(Build.ArtifactStagingDirectory)/
      frontend-production/build.zip'
    replaceExistingArchive: true
  displayName: 'frontend production zip files'

- task: PublishBuildArtifacts@1
  inputs:
    pathtoPublish: '$(Build.ArtifactStagingDirectory)/
      frontend-production'
    artifactName: 'frontend-production'
  displayName: 'frontend production publish to pipeline'
```

Here, we use the `npm run build:production` command to produce the build, which sets the `REACT_APP_ENV` environment variable to `production`. We use the `ArchiveFiles@2` task we used previously to zip up the build and the `PublishBuildArtifacts@1` task to publish the ZIP file to the pipeline.

16. That completes the build configuration. So, let's save the build pipeline by clicking the **Save** button and then confirming this. The build will trigger and succeed, as illustrated in the following screenshot:

Figure 15.10 – Another successful pipeline execution

17. Let's click on the most recent pipeline run to view details of the execution. Click on the successful job and we can see information about each step that ran, including how long it took, as illustrated in the following screenshot:

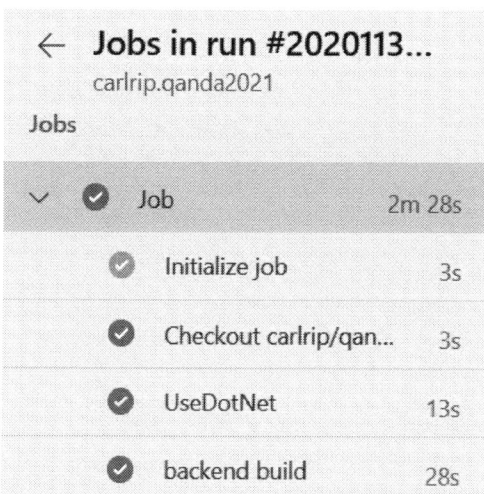

Figure 15.11 – Pipeline step execution details

That is our build pipeline complete. We will use the published build artifacts in the next section when we deploy these to Azure using a release pipeline.

Implementing CD

In this section, we are going to implement a release pipeline in Azure DevOps by implementing a CD process for our app. This process will consist of deploying to the staging environment, followed by the Cypress end-to-end tests being executed before the deployment is promoted to production.

Deploying to staging

Carry out the following steps in the Azure DevOps portal to deploy a build to the staging environment:

1. In the **Pipelines** section in the left-hand bar, select **Releases**, as illustrated in the following screenshot:

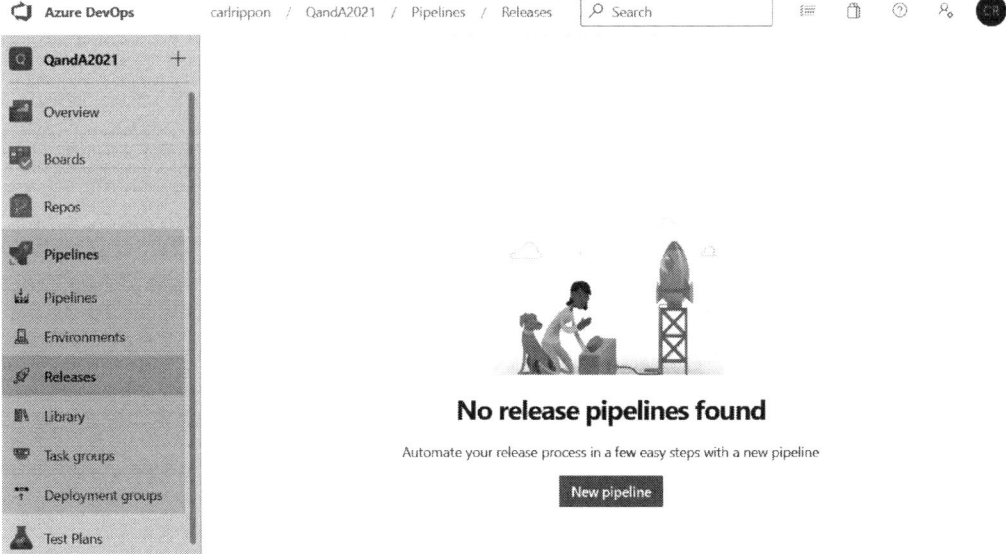

Figure 15.12 – Release pipelines

2. Click on the **New pipeline** button.
3. We will be prompted to select a template for the release pipeline. Let's choose the **Azure App Service deployment** template and click **Apply**, as illustrated in the following screenshot:

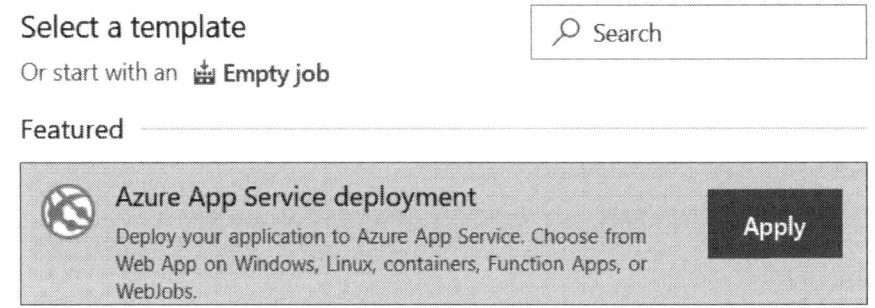

Figure 15.13 – Release pipeline template selection

4. A nice visual representation of the release pipeline will appear, along with a panel to the right, where we can set some properties of the first stage. Let's call the stage `Staging` since this is where we will deploy our app to the staging environment and execute the automated integration tests. We can close the right-hand panel by clicking the cross icon at the top right of the panel. The process is illustrated in the following screenshot:

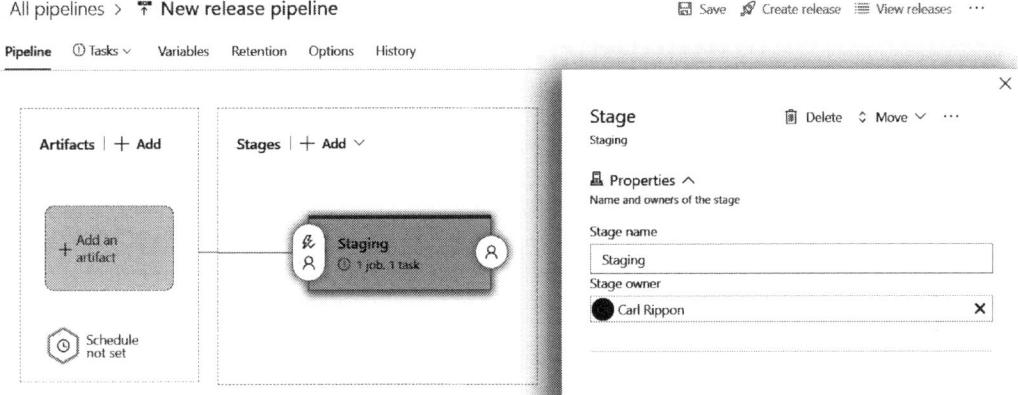

Figure 15.14 – Visual representation of release pipeline

5. We can change the pipeline name by clicking on it in the breadcrumb section and changing **New release pipeline** to the name of our choice, as illustrated in the following screenshot:

Figure 15.15 – QandA pipeline

6. We need to specify the artifacts that the pipeline will use. Click on the **Add** option in the **Artifacts** section.

7. In the dialog that appears, make sure our Azure DevOps project is selected. Set the source to our build pipeline and click **Add**, as illustrated in the following screenshot:

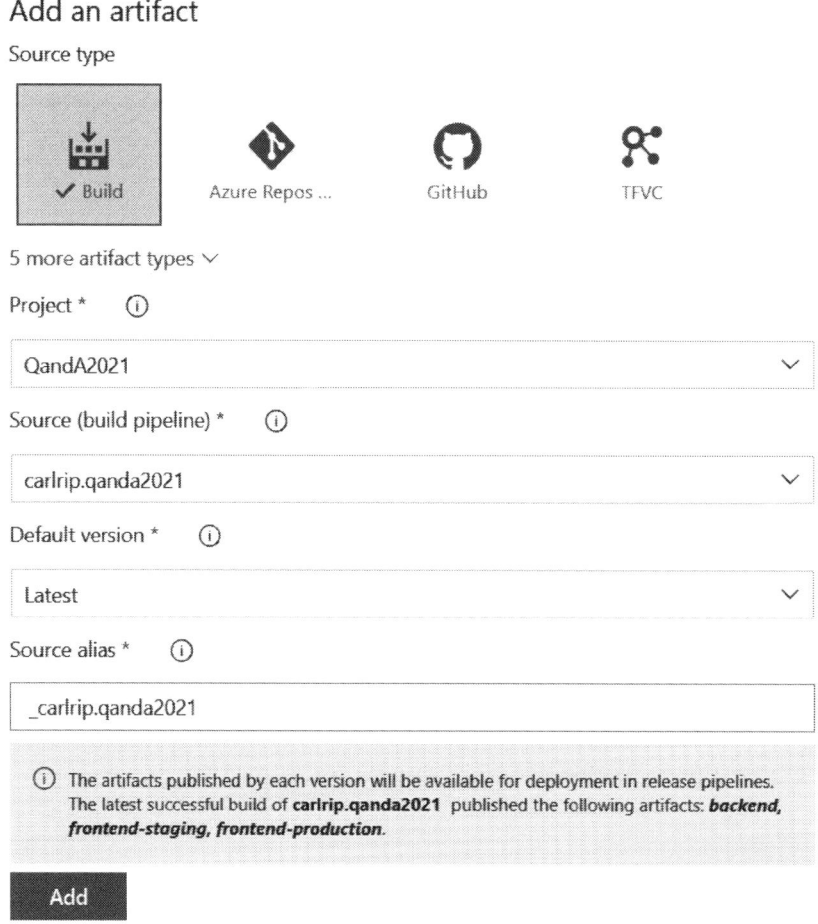

Figure 15.16 – Adding an artifact

8. We are now going to specify the tasks required to deploy the artifacts to the staging environment. Let's click on the **Tasks** tab. We need to deploy to two different app services for the frontend and backend. So, we are going to remove the parameters by clicking the **Unlink all** option, as illustrated in the following screenshot:

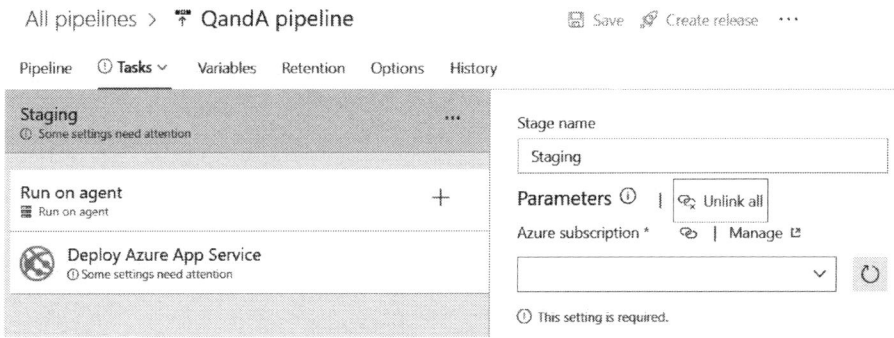

Figure 15.17 – Unlinking parameters

9. We already have a task from the template to deploy to Azure App Service, but we need to specify some additional information. We are going to use this task to deploy the backend, so let's change the display name to `Backend App Service`. We'll need to specify our Azure subscription and then authorize it. We also need to specify the service name, which is the backend staging service we created in the last chapter. Lastly, we need to specify where the build ZIP file is, which is `$(System.DefaultWorkingDirectory)/**/backend/*.zip`. The process is illustrated in the following screenshot:

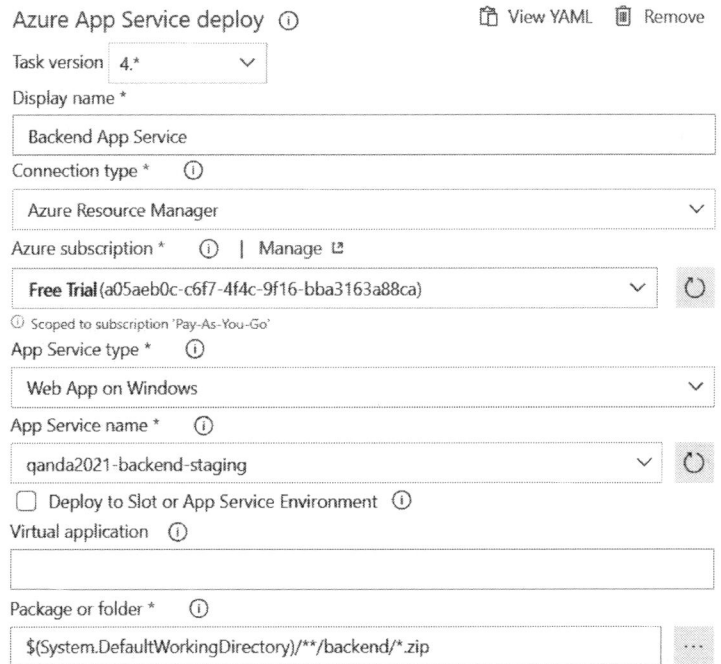

Figure 15.18 – Backend staging release

10. Click the **Save** option to save the changes to the task.

11. Click the **+** icon at the top of the task list to add a new task. Select the **Azure App Service deploy** task and click **Add**, as illustrated in the following screenshot:

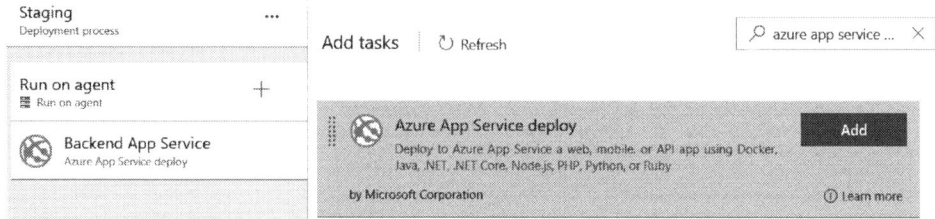

Figure 15.19 – Adding the Azure App Service deploy task

12. Now, we need to set the different properties of the task, just like we did in the backend service. This time, we'll call the task `Frontend App Service` and set the app service and the build ZIP file to the frontend staging ones, as illustrated in the following screenshot:

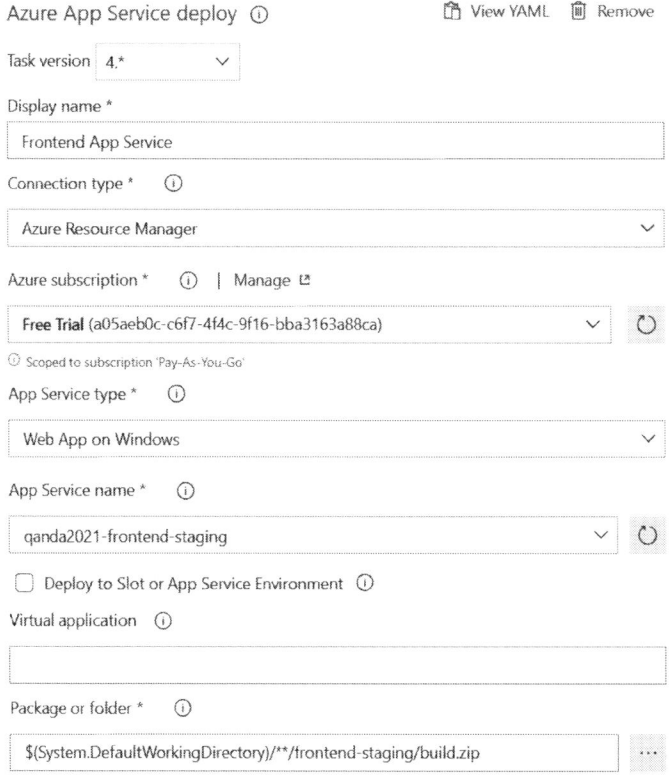

Figure 15.20 – Frontend staging release

13. Click the **Save** option to save the changes to the task.

14. Click the + icon at the top of the task list to add a new task. Select the **Extract files** task and click **Add**, as illustrated in the following screenshot:

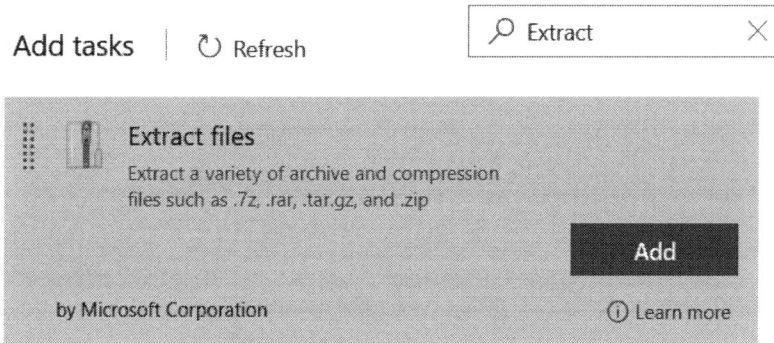

Figure 15.21 – Adding the Extract files task

15. This task is going to extract the Cypress test files so that they're ready for when the tests are executed in the next task. So, let's call the task `Extract Cypress test files`, set the ZIP file patterns to `$(System.DefaultWorkingDirectory)/**/frontend-staging/tests.zip`, and set the destination folder to `$(System.DefaultWorkingDirectory)/cypress`, as illustrated in the following screenshot:

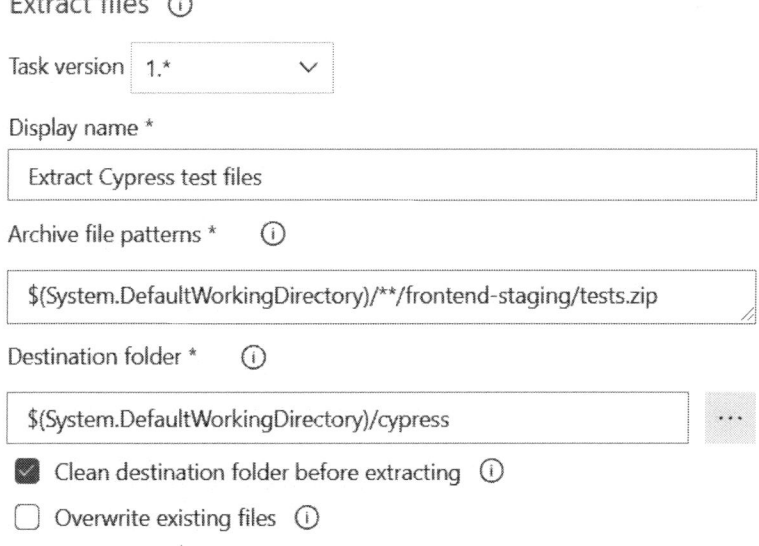

Figure 15.22 – Extracting Cypress tests

16. Click the **Save** option to save the changes to the task.

17. Click the + icon at the top of the task list to add a new task. Select the **Command line** task and click **Add**, as illustrated in the following screenshot:

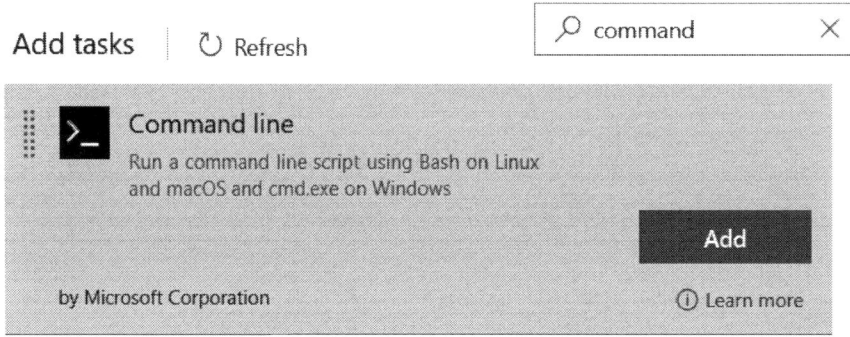

Figure 15.23 – Adding the Command line task

18. This task is going to install the Cypress tests, so let's call it `Install Cypress tests`. The script to execute is shown here:

```
> npm install
```

We need to set the working directory to be `$(System.DefaultWorkingDirectory)/cypress`, as illustrated in the following screenshot:

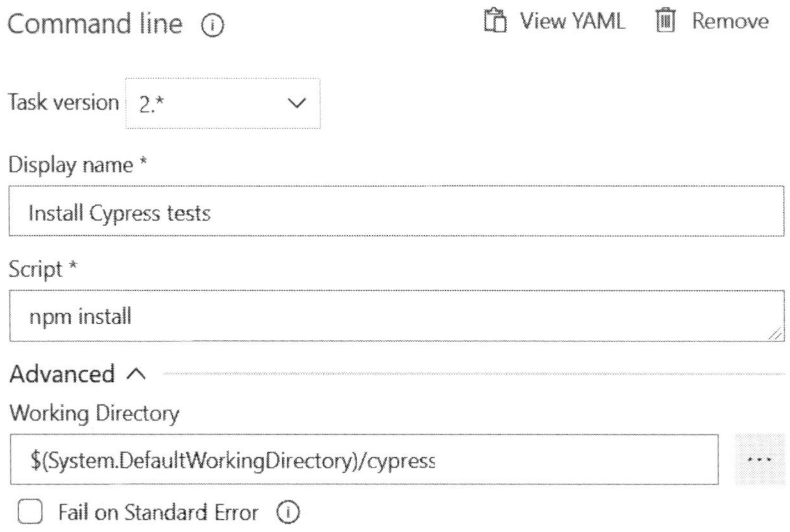

Figure 15.24 – Task for installing the Cypress tests

19. Click the **Save** option to save these changes to the task.
20. Click the + icon at the top of the task list to add a new task. Select the **Command line** task and click **Add**.
21. This task is going to execute the Cypress tests, so let's call it Run Cypress tests. The script to execute is shown here:

```
> npm run cy:run
```

We need to set the working directory to be $(System.DefaultWorkingDirectory)/cypress, as illustrated in the following screenshot:

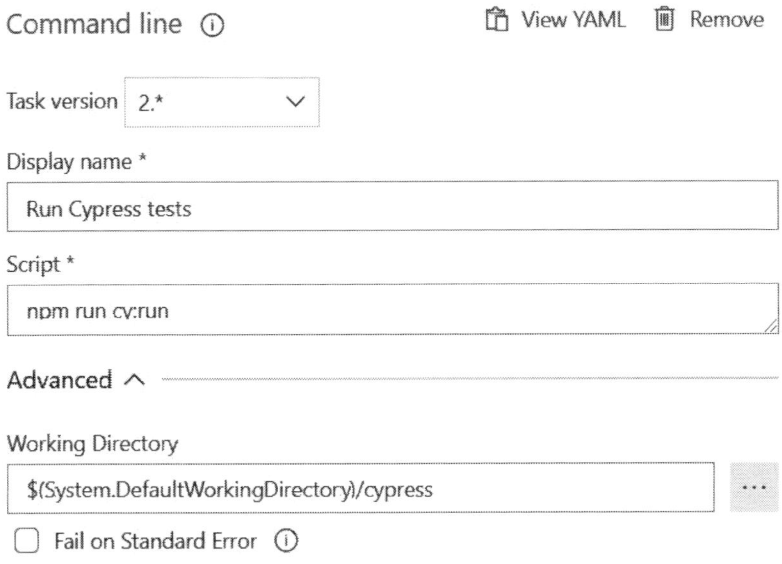

Figure 15.25 – Task for running the Cypress tests

22. Click the **Save** option to save these changes to the task.

That completes the staging deployment configuration and execution of the end-to-end tests. Next, we will add tasks to carry out the production deployment.

Deploying to production

Carry out the following steps in the release pipeline to deploy build artifacts to the production environment:

1. If it's not open already, open the release pipeline with the **Pipeline** tab selected, with a visual diagram showing.

2. Here, we are going to add a stage for the production deployment. Hover over the **Staging** card, and click on the **Clone** option, as illustrated in the following screenshot:

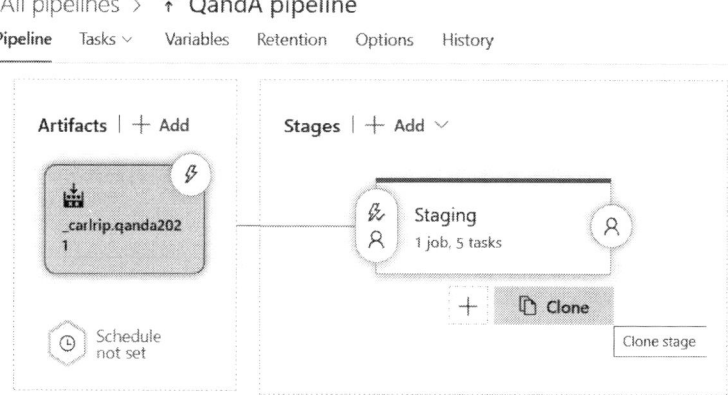

Figure 15.26 – Cloning a release pipeline stage

3. Let's click on the stage we have just created and call it `Production`, as illustrated in the following screenshot:

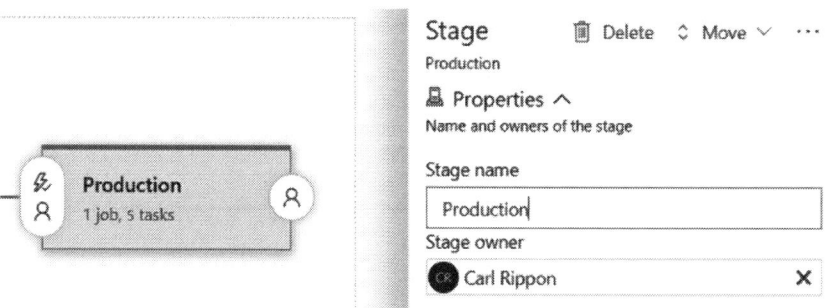

Figure 15.27 – Naming the production stage

4. Select the **Tasks** tab so that we can change the tasks for the **Production** stage, as illustrated in the following screenshot:

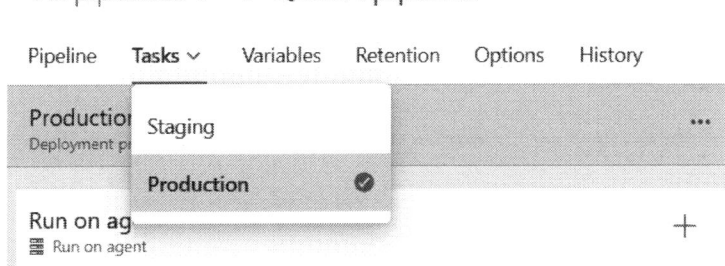

Figure 15.28 – Selecting the production tasks

5. The last two tasks can be removed because we don't need to run any tests. To remove a task, click on it and click the **Remove** option, as illustrated in the following screenshot:

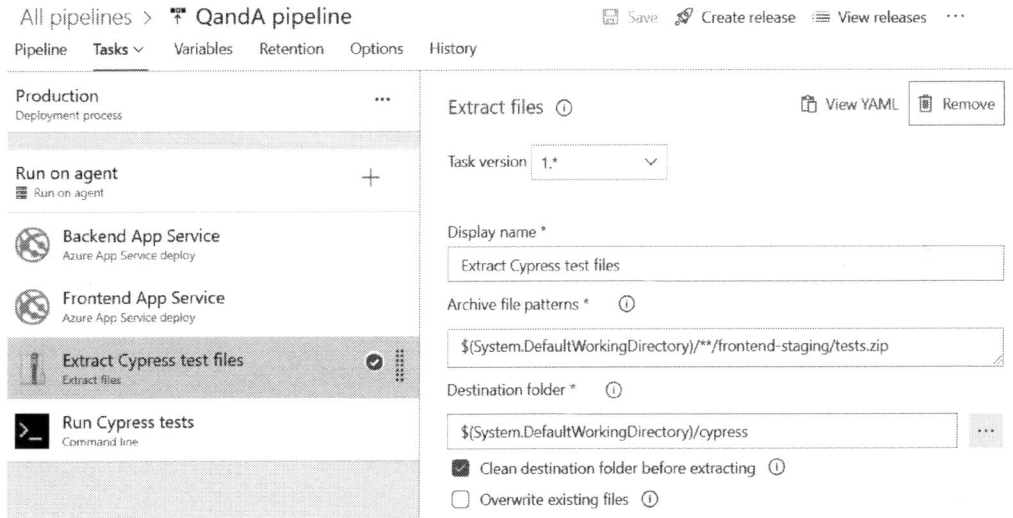

Figure 15.29 – Removing a task

6. We need to change the **Backend App Service** task so that it deploys the backend to the production app service, as illustrated in the following screenshot:

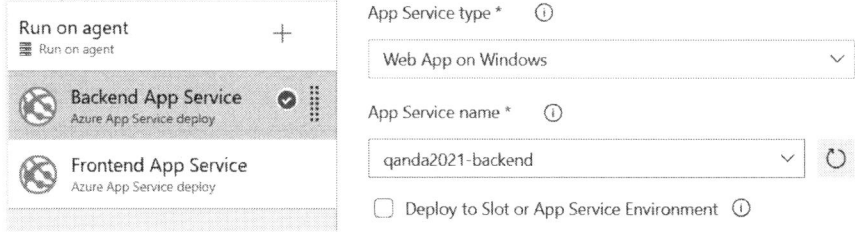

Figure 15.30 – Changing the production backend app service

7. We also need to change the **Frontend App Service** task so that it deploys to the production frontend app service from the production ZIP file, as illustrated in the following screenshot:

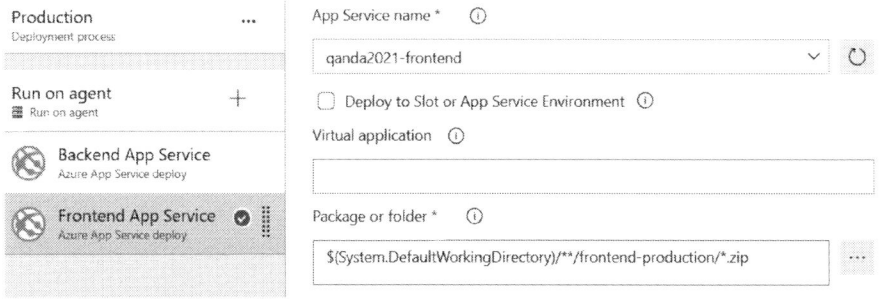

Figure 15.31 – Changing the production frontend app service and package

8. We want a release to be triggered when a new build has been completed. Click on the lightning icon in the **Artifacts** card and turn the **Enabled** switch on, as illustrated in the following screenshot:

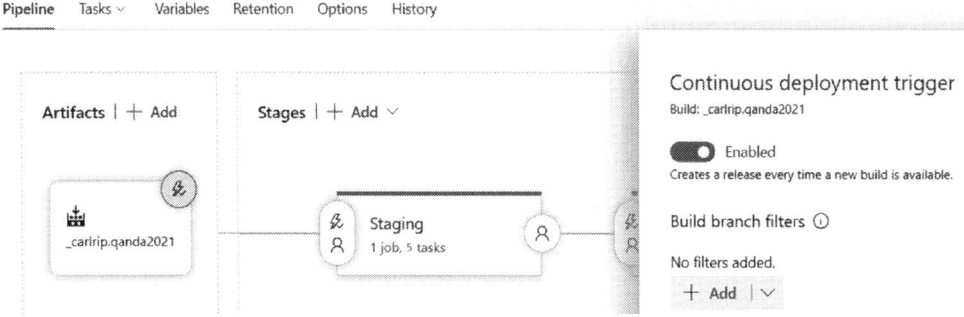

Figure 15.32 – Enabling continuous deployment

9. Click on **Save** to save all the changes.

That completes the production deployment configuration. Next, we will test our automated deployment.

Testing the automated deployment

We are now going to make a code change and push it to our source code repository. This should trigger a build and deployment. Let's give this a try, as follows:

1. Open up the frontend code and open `Header.tsx`. Add an exclamation mark after the app name, as illustrated in the following code snippet:

    ```
    <Link ... >
      Q & A!
      ...
    </Link>
    ```

2. Commit and push the change to the source code repository.
3. In Azure DevOps, if we go to the build pipelines, we'll see that a build has been triggered, as illustrated in the following screenshot:

Figure 15.33 – Build in progress

4. When the build has successfully completed, go to the **Releases** section. We will see the release in progress, as illustrated in the following screenshot:

Figure 15.34 – Release in progress

5. Finally, when the staging deployment completes successfully, the production deployment is triggered. The successful release will appear in the release history, as illustrated in the following screenshot:

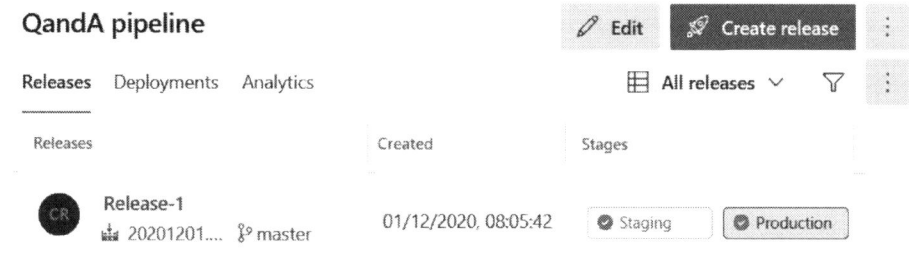

Figure 15.35 – Successfully completed release

That completes our CD pipeline.

Summary

In this final chapter, we learned that CI and CD are automated processes that get code changes that developers make into production. Implementing these processes improves the quality of our software and helps us deliver value to users of the software extremely quickly.

Implementing CI and CD processes in Azure DevOps is ridiculously easy. CI is implemented using a build pipeline, and Azure DevOps has loads of great templates for different technologies to get us started. The CI process is scripted in a YAML file where we execute a series of steps, including command-line commands and other tasks such as zipping up files. The steps in the YAML file must include tasks that publish the build artifacts to the build pipeline so that they can be used in the CD process.

The CD process is implemented using a release pipeline and a visual editor. Again, there are lots of great templates to get us started. We define stages in the pipeline, which execute tasks on the artifacts that are published from the build pipeline. We can have multiple stages deploying to our different environments. We can make each stage automatically execute, or execute only when a trusted member of the team approves it. There are many task types that can be executed, including deploying to an Azure service such as an app service and running .NET tests.

So, we have reached the end of this book. We've created a performant and secure **REpresentational State Transfer (REST) application programming interface (API)** that interacts with a SQL Server database using Dapper. Our React frontend interacts beautifully with this API and has been structured so that it scales in complexity by using TypeScript throughout.

We've learned how to manage simple as well as complex frontend state requirements and learned how to build reusable components to help speed up the process of building frontends. We completed the development of our app by adding automated tests, and deployed it to Azure with CI and CD processes using Azure DevOps.

Questions

The following questions will test your knowledge of the topics that were covered in this chapter:

1. Which environment variable needs to be set for Jest tests to work well in a CI environment?
2. When we change the `azure-pipelines.yml` file, why does this trigger a build?
3. Which YAML step task can be used to execute npm commands?
4. Which YAML step task can be used to publish artifacts to the pipeline?
5. Why do we have several builds of a React frontend for different environments?
6. Which task type in a release pipeline stage can be used to deploy build artifacts to Azure App Service?

Answers

1. An environment variable called `CI` needs to be set to `true` for Jest tests to work well in a CI environment.
2. When we change the `azure-pipelines.yml` file, it is automatically committed and pushed to our master branch in our source code repository. The `trigger` option in the file specifies that a build should trigger when code is pushed to the master branch. So, a build is triggered when this happens.
3. The `-script` task can be used to execute npm commands.
4. The `PublishBuildArtifacts@1` task can be used to publish artifacts to the pipeline.
5. The frontend build sets an environment variable called `REACT_APP_ENV`, which the code uses to determine which environment it is in. This is the reason we have different frontend builds.
6. The `Azure App Service Deploy` task type in a release pipeline stage can be used to deploy build artifacts to Azure App Service.

Further reading

The following resource is useful if you want to find out more about implementing CI and CD with Azure DevOps: `https://docs.microsoft.com/en-us/azure/devops/pipelines/?view=azure-devops`.

Other Books You May Enjoy

If you enjoyed this book, you may be interested in these other books by Packt:

An Atypical ASP.NET Core 5 Design Patterns Guide
Carl-Hugo Marcotte

ISBN: 978-1-78934-609-1

- Apply the SOLID principles for building flexible and maintainable software
- Get to grips with .NET 5 dependency injection
- Work with GoF design patterns such as strategy, decorator, and composite
- Explore the MVC patterns for designing web APIs and web applications using Razor
- Discover layering techniques and tenets of clean architecture
- Become familiar with CQRS and vertical slice architecture as an alternative to layering
- Understand microservices, what they are, and what they are not
- Build ASP.NET UI from server-side to client-side Blazor

C# 9 and .NET 5 – Modern Cross-Platform Development - Fifth Edition
Mark J. Price

ISBN: 978-1-80056-810-5

- Build your own types with object-oriented programming
- Query and manipulate data using LINQ
- Build websites and services using ASP.NET Core 5
- Create intelligent apps using machine learning
- Use Entity Framework Core and work with relational databases
- Discover Windows app development using the Universal Windows Platform and XAML
- Build rich web experiences using the Blazor framework
- Build mobile applications for iOS and Android using Xamarin.Forms

Leave a review - let other readers know what you think

Please share your thoughts on this book with others by leaving a review on the site that you bought it from. If you purchased the book from Amazon, please leave us an honest review on this book's Amazon page. This is vital so that other potential readers can see and use your unbiased opinion to make purchasing decisions, we can understand what our customers think about our products, and our authors can see your feedback on the title that they have worked with Packt to create. It will only take a few minutes of your time, but is valuable to other potential customers, our authors, and Packt. Thank you!

Index

Symbols

.NET tests
  implementing, with xUnit 447

A

access token 366
action method 31
  creating, for deleting question 303
  creating, for obtaining
    questions 287-289
  creating, for obtaining single
    question 293-295
  creating, for obtaining unanswered
    questions 292, 293
  creating, for posting answer 304-306
  creating, for posting question 296-299
  creating, for updating question 299-303
actions
  about 215, 216
  creating 220
  creating, to interact with store 220
  creating, to search questions 223
  creating, to view questions 222
    creating, to obtain unanswered
      questions 221, 222

answer form
  form submission,
    implementing 207-210
  implementing 194-196
  validation, implementing on 199-201
AnswerList component
  creating 166-169
API controller
  creating 282
  creating, for questions 283, 284
  data repository, injecting into 284-286
API controller action method
  data cache, using 354-357
App component
  styling, with CSS 123, 124
  styling, with Emotion 130-133
ask form
  form submission,
    implementing 203-206
  implementing 191-193
  validation, implementing on 196-199
ASP.NET backend
  Auth0, setting up with 368
  configuring, to authenticate
    with Auth0 371, 372
ASP.NET Core app

Index

backend entry point 25, 26
  creating 22-24
ASP.NET Core backend
  about 22
  configuring, for staging and
    production 490-492
  publishing, to Azure 492
  publishing, to production 492-502
  publishing, to staging 502-504
ASP.NET Core Web API project
  creating 59-62
asynchronous API controller
  action method, implementing 345-348
  asynchronous and synchronous
    code, mixing 348, 349
  creating 341, 342
  current implementation, testing 343-345
Auth0
  ASP.NET backend, configuring to
    authenticate with 371, 372
  central authentication context,
    implementing 410-416
  interacting, from frontend 408
  setting up, as identity provider 368-371
  setting up, with ASP.NET backend 368
  sign-in and sign-out flows,
    recapping 408, 409
  sign-in and sign-out processes,
    testing 421-424
  sign-in and sign-out routes,
    creating 409, 410
  sign-in process, implementing 417
  sign-out process, implementing 418, 419
Auth0 JavaScript client
  installing 408
Auth0 settings
  configuring, in frontend 419, 420

authenticated options
  authenticated users, are allowed
    to answer question 429-431
  authenticated users, are allowed
    to ask question 426-429
  controlling 424
  relevant options, displaying
    in header 424-426
authenticated REST API endpoints
  fetch, used for interacting with 431
authenticated user
  information, referencing 385-388
AutoMapper
  URL 317
automated test, types
  about 445
  end-to-end tests 446
  integration tests 447
  unit test 445, 446
await keyword 50
Azure
  ASP.NET Core backend,
    publishing to 492
  React frontend, publishing to 507
  services, using 487-489
  signing up to 487
  starting with 487
  URL 487
Azure DevOps project
  creating 519, 520

B

Babel 46
blank pages
  creating 152, 153
Block, Element, Modifier (BEM)
  reference link 127

boilerplate code, reducing with
   React Hook Form
   about 185
   answer form, implementing 194-196
   ask form, implementing 191-193
   form styled components,
      creating 188-190
   Header component, refactoring to
      use React Hook Form 186-188
   React Hook Form, installing 186
Bootstrap 4.1 42
build 517
build pipeline
   creating 521-523
   implementing, for Q&A app 524-531
button click event
   handling 116, 117

C

central authentication context
   implementing 410-416
children prop 102, 103
CI and CD
   about 517
   Azure DevOps project, creating 519, 520
   tests, enabling to run in 518, 519
   working with 517
code autoformat, adding to
   React and TypeScript
   errors, resolving 72
   Prettier, adding 70, 71
component containing routes
   creating 153, 154
component props
   implementing 93

components
   styling, with CSS 122
   styling, with CSS modules 127-129
   styling, with Emotion 129
   wiring up 96-98
components, connecting to store
   about 229
   home page, connecting 230-233
   question page, connecting 234, 235
   search page, connecting 236, 237
   store provider, adding 229, 230
component state
   implementing 106
   implementing, with useState 110-115
const assertion 221
container 115
context 410
Continuous Delivery (CD)
   automated deployment, testing 543, 544
   implementing 531
   production, deploying 540-543
   staging, deploying 532-539
Continuous Integration (CI)
   about 65
   build pipeline, creating 521-523
   build pipeline, implementing
      for Q&A app 524-531
   implementing 520
controlled components 182-185
controller action methods
   creating 287
   testing 452, 453
   testing, to get questions 453-458
   testing, to get single question 458-461
controllers 31

Create React App (CRA)
  about 62, 461
  React app, creating with 64, 65
  tool 34
  TypeScript app, creating with 64, 65
Cross-Origin Resource Sharing (CORS)
  about 388, 504
  adding 389-391
CSS
  App component, styling 123, 124
  document body, styling 122, 123
  Header component, styling 125, 126
  used, for styling components 122
CSS modules
  used, for styling components 127-129
custom hook 412
custom middleware
  adding, to ASP.NET Core
    request/response pipeline 28-31
Cypress
  end-to-end tests, implementing
    with 471
  Q and A app, testing 475-480
  working with 471-474

D

Dapper
  about 250
  advantages 250
  configuring 250-252
  installing 250-252
  used, for reading data 252
  used, for writing data 265
Dapper multi-mapping
  using, to resolve N+1 problem 329-332
Dapper multi-results feature
  using 332-334

database
  creating 245-247
  implementing 245
  migration, performing 274-277
  stored procedures, creating 248, 249
  tables, creating 247, 248
database round trip
  Dapper multi-mapping, using to
    resolve N+1 problem 329-332
  Dapper multi-results feature,
    using 332-334
  N+1 problem 323-325
  reducing 323
  WebSurge, using to load test
    endpoint 326-329
data cache
  about 350
  current implementation,
    performance in load test 350
  implementing 351, 353
  using, in API controller action
    method 354-357
data fetching
  aborting 435, 436
data paging
  about 335
  current implementation, performance
    in load test 336-338
  implementation 338-341
  test questions, adding for load test 336
data, reading with Dapper
  about 252
  repository class, creating 253-256
  repository method, creating to check
    whether question exists 263
  repository method, creating
    to get answer 264

repository method, creating to
get questions 256-258
repository method, creating to get
questions by search 259, 260
repository method, creating to get
single question 261-263
repository method, creating to get
unanswered questions 260
data repository
injecting, into API controller 284-286
data, writing with Dapper
about 265
methods, adding to write data to
repository interface 265
repository method, creating
to add answer 268
repository method, creating to
add new question 265, 266
repository method, creating to
change question 266, 267
repository method, creating to
delete question 267, 268
DbUp
configuring, to do migrations
on app startup 270-272
database migration, performing 274-277
installing, into project 269
SQL Scripts, embedding in
project 272, 273
used, for managing migrations 269
default keyword 47
dependency injection 285
document body
styling, with CSS 122, 123

E

Emotion
App component, styling 130-133
components, styling 129
Header component, styling 133, 134
installing 129, 130
nested elements, styling 134-137
pseudo-classes, styling 134-137
reusable styled component,
creating 138-141
endpoints
load testing, with WebSurge 326-329
protecting 373
protecting, with custom
authorization policy 376-384
protecting, with simple
authorization 373-376
end-to-end tests
about 446
implementing, with Cypress 471
ESLint 43
event listener 116
events
handling 116
export keyword 47

F

fetch
used, for interacting with authenticated
REST API endpoints 431
used, for interacting with
unauthenticated REST
API endpoints 396
fetch function 50

forms
　submitting 201
form styled components
　creating 188-190
form submission
　implementing, in answer form 207-210
　implementing, in ask form 203-206
　implementing, in search form 202, 203
form validation
　implementing 196
function-based components
　creating 83
function props 103-105

G

generic HTTP http function
　extracting out 400-405
generic types 107
GetQuestions action method
　extending, for searching 290-292
getUnansweredQuestions function
　modifying, so that it
　　asynchronous 106-108

H

Header component
　creating 84, 85
　elements, adding 86-88
　refactoring, to use React
　　Hook Form 186-188
　styling, with CSS 125, 126
　styling, with Emotion 133, 134
HomePage child components
　creating 93
HomePage component
　creating 88, 89

　testing 469, 470
home page styling
　completing 141

I

implicit return 84
import statements 46
input change event
　handling 117, 118
integration tests 447

J

JavaScript Object Notation (JSON) 524
Jest
　React tests, implementing with 461
　working with 461-464
JSON Web Token (JWT) 366
　URL 366
JSX 46, 78-81

L

lazy loading 173
Link component
　using 156, 157
links
　implementing 156
linting
　about 65
　adding, to React app 65
　adding, to TypeScript app 65
　rules, configuring 67-69
lint TypeScript code
　Visual Studio Code,
　　configuring to 65-67

M

map method 52
minification 45
mock data
　creating 89-92
model binding 290
model validation
　adding 306
multi-mapping 329
multi-results 332

N

N+1 problem
　about 323-326
　resolving, with Dapper
　　multi-mapping 329-332
nested elements
　styling, with Emotion 134-137
non-null assertion operator 209
npm 33

O

OpenID Connect (OIDC)
　about 42, 365-367
　authentication flow 365, 366

P

page
　navigating, programmatically 157, 158
Page component
　testing 464-466
paging 335
polyfill 51
presentational 115

Prettier
　adding 70, 71
promise 106
props
　about 93
　default 98-101
　optional 98-101
pseudo-classes
　styling, with Emotion 134-137
pure function 216

Q

Q&A app
　build pipeline, implementing 524-531
query parameters
　using 169-173
Question component
　creating 95, 96
　styling 143, 144
　testing 467, 468
QuestionList component
　creating 93-95
　styling 141, 142
question page
　implementing 161-166
question page route
　adding 158-160

R

React app
　code autoformat, adding 69
　creating 62
　creating, with Create React
　　App (CRA) 64, 65
　linting, adding 65

React components
  testing 464
React frontend
  about 33
  backend web API, consuming 48-52
  components, fitting 45-48
  configuring, for staging and
      production 505-507
  dependencies 41-43
  entry point 33, 34
  executing, in development mode 34-37
  publishing process 38-41
  publishing, to Azure 507
  publishing, to production 507-510
  publishing, to staging 510-512
  single page, serving 43-45
React Hook Form
  about 185
  boilerplate code, reducing with 185
  installing 186
  reference link 201
React Router
  installing 151
React templated app
  creating 22-24
React tests
  implementing, with Jest 461
reducers
  about 215-217
  creating 224-227
Redux
  about 214
  installing 218
  key concepts 215-218
  principles 215
render prop 105

repository class
  creating 253-256
repository method
  creating, to add answer 268
  creating, to add new question 265, 266
  creating, to change question 266, 267
  creating, to check whether
      question exists 263
  creating, to delete question 267
  creating, to get answer 264
  creating, to get questions 256-258
  creating, to get questions
      by search 259, 260
  creating, to get single question 261-263
  creating, to get unanswered
      questions 260
REpresentational State Transfer
    (REST) API
  about 494
  answer, posting to 434, 435
  question, obtaining from 405, 406
  question, posting to 431-434
  question, searching with 407
  unanswered questions,
      obtaining from 397-400
request/response pipeline 27
resource group 488
Return on Investment (ROI) 447
reusable styled component
  creating, with Emotion 138-41
route parameters
  using 158
routes
  declaring 151
  lazy loading 173-176
routes not found
  handling 154, 155

S

search form
  form submission,
    implementing 202, 203
  selector 231
semantic version
  reference link 34
sign-in and sign-out flows
  recapping 408, 409
sign-in and sign-out routes
  creating 409, 410
sign-in processes
  implementing 417
  testing 421-424
sign-out processes
  implementing 418, 419
  testing 421-424
single-page applications (SPAs)
  about 365, 471
  architecture 21
spread syntax 226
SQL Scripts
  embedding, in project 272, 273
SQL Server Management
    Studio (SSMS) 245
Startup class
  about 26
  Configure method 27, 28
  ConfigureServices method 26, 27
state
  about 106
  creating 219, 220
store
  about 215
  components, connecting to 229
  creating 228, 229

strict mode
  about 81-83
  enabling 81-83

T

tagged template literal 131
  reference link 140
template literals 99, 131
ternary operator 98
TypeScript app
  benefits 63
  code autoformat, adding 69
  creating 62
  creating, with Create React
    App (CRA) 64, 65
  linting, adding 65

U

unauthenticated REST API endpoints
  fetch, used for interacting with 396
Uniform Resource Locator
    (URL) 487, 518
union type
  reference link 161
unit tests 445, 446
unnecessary request fields
  removing 312
  removing, from posting answer 315-317
  removing, from posting
    question 313-315
useEffect
  using, to execute logic 108, 109
useState
  used, for implementing
    component state 110-115

V

validation
  adding, to post answer 310-312
  adding, to post question 307-309
  adding, to update question 309, 310
  implementing, on answer form 199-201
  implementing, on ask form 196-199
Visual Studio Code
  configuring, to lint TypeScript code 65-67

W

web API
  at runtime 32
Webpack 38
WebSurge
  using, to load test endpoint 326-329

X

xUnit
  about 447
  .NET tests, implementing with 447
  working with 448-452

Y

YAML Ain't Markup Language (YAML) 524

Made in United States
Orlando, FL
21 November 2021

10607752R10311